Kay Fisker

Copenhagen Housing Types (1936)
Row-house Types (1941)

Kay Fisker

Copenhagen Housing Types (1936)
Row-house Types (1941)

Edited by Luca Ortelli and Chiara Monterumisi

General Management: Lucas Giossi
Editorial and Sales Management: Sylvain Collette and May Yang
Production Manager: Christophe Borlat
Editorial: Alice Micheau-Thiébaud, Jean Rime, Janice Gaugenot
Graphic design: Kim Nanette
Communications Manager: Manon Reber
Accounting: Daniela Castan
Logistics: Emile Razafimanjaka
Translator: Andrew Swearingen

Cover illustration: Kay Fisker, sketch for the Borups Allé/
Stefansgade housing block, undated

EPFL PRESS
is an imprint owned by the Foundation Presses polytechniques
et universitaires romandes (PPUR), a Swiss academic publishing company
whose main purpose is to publish the teaching and research works of
the Ecole polytechnique fédérale de Lausanne (EPFL), of universities
and other institutionsof higher education.

PPUR, EPFL – Rolex Learning Center, Station 10, CH-1015 Lausanne,
info@epflpress.org

www.epflpress.org

First edition, 2024
ISBN 978-2-88915-441-8

Printed in Czech Republic

Table of contents

Martin Steinmann walking along the *Hornbækhus* façade [Photo by Bernard Zurbuchen, 2006]

Foreword

Luca Ortelli

Nowadays, Kay Fisker and his work are less known and appreciated than they should be. There are mainly two reasons for this condition: on the one hand, Denmark's relative "foreignness" to the Modern Movement, to its proclamations and debates, and on the other hand, the specific features of the architecture of Fisker and his fellow achitects in the first decades of the twentieth century. These two motives are inextricably linked together, to the point of one becoming the cause of the other and vice versa. Another argumentation, on a different level, is the scarcity of contributions in English about his work – a gap recently filled by Martin Søberg's monograph.[1]

It should be remembered, however, that international critics observed with attention and interest the emergence of Scandinavian cultures in the interwar period, making it clear early on that those experiences were profoundly different from what was being produced in Central Europe and particularly in Germany (see, in this regard, the text below by Chiara Monterumisi, which accurately illustrates Fisker's engagement and how he was perceived in the architectural debate, particularly about housing).

Scandinavian architecture of the early twentieth century had taken on quite particular characteristics, especially in comparison with orthodox modern architecture, due to the lucid continuity with the values and practices of tradition or, we could say, the search for *modernity without becoming avant-garde*.

The aspect that most profoundly divided the avant-garde from other contemporary experiences consisted precisely, for the latter, in the rejection of the *tabula rasa* and the desire to not interrupt the relationship with history. This rejection, was not accomplished as a reaction to the positions of the Modern Movement but presented itself as the "natural" continuation of architecture in its historical dimension. As such, it was often considered as an almost unconscious choice, as if there were no alternative. In reality, however, these considerations do not apply indiscriminately to all architects who did not militate in the ranks of the avant-garde. In fact, as Manfredo Tafuri pointed out when speaking of some Danish architects,[2] the history of modern architecture should also deal with the position of those who consciously chose to not be in accordance with the latest techniques, styles and standards – in other words, not in accordance with the idea that Modern Movement was the only possible form of actuality.

In this regard, there is no doubt that Kay Fisker's position was a conscious one, and from the beginning of his career. Thus, his is not an unconscious or opportunistic choice, but a lucid one consistent with the goals of his work, as Tobias Faber pointed out: "Throughout his long life, he consistently maintained the line of his architectural conception, while being informed on all contemporary trends and significant architectural personalities."[3]

Among the main publications on Fisker, several are particularly notable: Hans Erling Langkilde, *Arkitekten Kay Fisker*, 1960, Various authors, *Kay Fisker*, København, 1995; and the monographic issue of the Swiss architecture magazine "Archithese" No. 4, 1985, devoted to the Danish architect.

More recently, two publications show interest in him from a new point of view, that is, indicating the possibility of considering him not only from a historical point of view but also as a possible reference or source of inspiration in the field of contemporary design.[4] These publications are in fact edited by architects with both professional and academic engagements.

The architect

Kay Fisker was born in Frederiksberg District, in Copenhagen, in 1893 and was educated at the Royal Danish Academy of Fine Arts. In 1915 he won a competition, in collaboration with Aage Rafn (1890–1953), for designing and building a series of stations for the local railways Almindingen-Gudhjem, on the Island of Bornholm, Baltic Sea. The five stations constitute a brilliant interpretation of traditional rural buildings, enriched by the exquisite capacity of introducing small *disturbances* in the articulated composition of volumes. Four of them are in bricks-masonry and the fifth is in timber.

After this first project, Fisker worked in various architectural offices in Denmark and in Sweden, and successfully took part in the annual competitions launched by the newspaper Politiken, concerning the design for summer cottages. Fisker's propositions are small, simple volumes with pitched roofs and an unexpected disposition of windows and doors combined with large mural surfaces, giving the houses a strong presence despite their reduced dimensions.

After getting some commissions for private country-houses, Fisker adopted this same principle, introducing unforeseen solutions for giving each room good natural lighting, specific orientation and a particular view of the surrounding landscape. Friis' country house in Snekkersten, north of Copenhagen (1917–18), owes its discrete character to the massive brick-masonry interrupted by generous white-frame windows. From that moment on, Fisker remained faithful to brick-works for a large majority of his buildings.

In 1925 Fisker completed the *Danish Pavillon* at the *Exposition Internationale des Arts Décoratifs et Industriels Modernes* in Paris: a symmetrical and austere volume that enhances the blind brick surfaces favoured by the young architect. Even if the building was not so extraordinary, it has to be noted that in an exhibition dominated by eclectic historical exercises, Fisker's submission was in good company with Le Corbusier's, Melnikov's and Bergsten's.

At that time Fisker had already built the *Hornbækhus* in Copenhagen, his most famous, meaningful, iconic example in a long series of housing buildings.

Later, together with his associate Christian Frederik Møller, he won the 1931 competition for the university campus in Aarhus in collaboration with Povl Stegmann and landscape architect Carl Theodor Sørensen. The complex was developed over several years in different stages and the rules defined for the competition and its first developments are still followed today.

Beyond this and other extraordinary projects, Fisker's main interest is undoubtedly housing, his favourite theme as a designer and as an educator. For his entire career, Fisker always divided his commitment between professional practice and teaching at the Royal Academy in Copenhagen, where he held the chair of Housing (*Bolig klasse*) for many years.

Hornbækhus

The famous *Hornbækhus* block of flats (1920–22), as mentioned above, is particularly significant for both Fisker's work and all of housing architecture in Denmark. Located in *Nørrebro*, one of the ten districts of Copenhagen, north-west of the historic center, the large courtyard block follows the geometry of the streets that surround it, with the almost imperceptible bend on *Borups Allé*, a major artery whose construction began some twenty years before the conclusion of the building.

Hornbækhus adopts the urban form of the courtyard block (*karré* in Danish) typical of European early twentieth century reformist policies, which would be embraced as the main instrument of Copenhagen's urbanisation by many architects born around 1880 and by the younger Kay Fisker. In fact, some fifty such buildings were constructed in Copenhagen in less than twenty years, constituting truly recognisable and uniform "urban pieces" due to the systematic use of brick, strict facades based on the repetition and alignment of openings, sloping roofs covered with tiles. From this point of view, *Hornbækhus* confirms a direction of work already assumed in other buildings in Copenhagen, among which the *Struenseegade* complex (1918–20) by Povl Baumann (1878–1963) and the *Karré* in *Vilhelm Thomsens Allé* (1921) by Henning Hansen (1880–1945), should be noted. Steen Eiler Rasmussen observed that "*The blocks erected in Struenseegade in 1919 by architect Povl Baumann, display the new building style in all its purity and they have become the norm for all subsequent housing construction.*"[5]

Hornbækhus, façade giving onto Ågade [Photo by Bernard Zurbuchen, 2006]

The complex consists of two identically sized *karré* between which is a kind of square open to *Hans Tavsens Park*. On the opposite side, along *Struensee Street*, the blocks face two long buildings, also designed by Baumann, that complement the existing blocks, composed of different building units. As a whole, the project constitutes a proper urban fragment that, among other things, illustrates the transition from the nineteenth-century fragmented block to the new approach, which sees collective housing as the protagonist. The second example, by Henning Hansen, with its perfectly square footprint, corresponds almost didactically to the definition of the *karré* as an architectural and urban type. These two projects were chosen, among others, to illustrate the book *Modern Danish Architecture*[6] and it should be noted that the volume, for which Fisker was the main editor, does not include any of his own buildings.

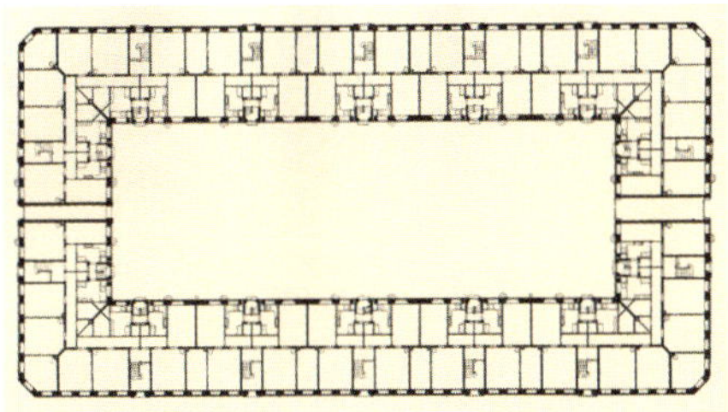

Povl Baumann, *Struenseegade* complex, plan of a karré [from Fisker, Yerbury, *Modern Danish Architecture*, 1927]

The main goals of the architects engaged in the development of Copenhagen in those years were responding to the dramatic housing shortage and achieving a concrete alternative to the architecture and urban planning of the previous century. Large unitary buildings, each corresponding to a block, resorting to the use of traditional brick-work, stripping the fronts of all historicist reminiscences, exalting simplicity and repetition as the canons of a new aesthetics – both popular and monumental, thanks to urban presence and massive bulk, – were the instruments adopted for the achievement of the above-mentioned goals.

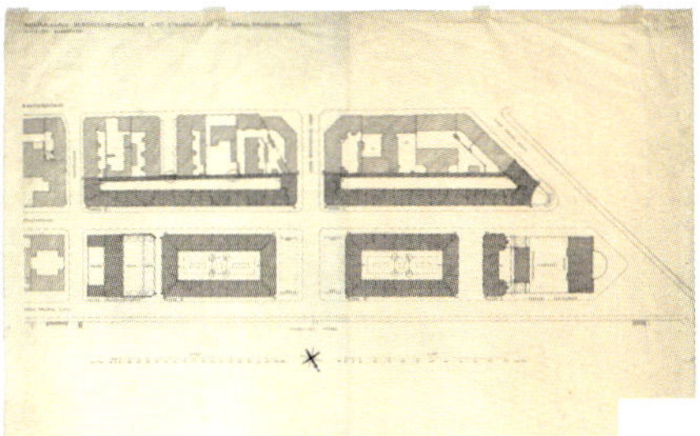

Povl Baumann, *Struenseegade* complex, general plan, 1918 [Danmarks Kunstbibliotek, Digital Collection, Inventory number 12317h]

In relation to the two aforementioned projects, *Hornbækhus* stands out first and foremost for its size: the courtyard/garden could in fact abundantly contain Baumann's two blocks.

The building consists of some 300 apartments spread over 5 floors. The uniform facades present more than 2,000 identical windows, perfectly aligned and at a constant distance from each other, the only difference being that those occupying the urban fronts, in red bricks, display plaster frames, while those facing the garden, in yellowish bricks, have none. The diagonal connection of the facades in the corners of the courtyard – the only concession to this *tour de force* that exalts the most banal elements of Danish architecture – allows the windows to unfold without the slightest rhythmic change. Beyond its solid and ponderous presence, the autonomy of the building is reinforced by the massive treatment of the exterior corners, in rendered stones.

A specific feature of the Danish experience is the collective character of the central open space – in *Hornbækhus* designed by landscape architect Gudmund Nyeland Brandt – reserved in principle for the building's inhabitants and not accessible to the public, similar to housing courtyard blocks in Hamburg and unlike the large residential courtyards of Vienna (*Wienerhöfe*). Another specific element is the fact that, due to building regulations and fire safety measures, each apartment is served by two staircases, the first accessible from the street, the other from the courtyard. In *Hornbækhus*, in the buildings cited above and in many other examples, the visibility of stairs "on the façade" is systematically denied so as not to constitute a disruptive element of the peremptory and obsessive windows layout. This solution, which some might consider "brutal," (practicable only because in many cases the windows in Denmark open outwards) is, as a matter of fact, in clear opposition to functionalistic precepts. It should be noted, however, that this choice is asserted without qualms or pretensions, to affirm unity and homogeneity and aim to celebrate an order fundamentally opposed to the typical composition of nineteenth-century bourgeois architecture and equally opposed to the mechanical articulation advocated by mere functionalism.

Due to this fact, the architecture of the *karré* during the interwar period presents an absolute clarity of purpose and goals. Typologically, the apartments are characterised by a very simple and efficient distribution that provides each unit with double exposure and cross ventilation, thanks to the limited depth of the volumes, always less than 11 meters. In most cases, toilets and kitchens, grouped around the secondary staircase, overlook the courtyard, while the main rooms face the street.

The exaltation of homogeneity and unity embodies a precise choice that would accompany Fisker throughout his career as an architect and intellectual: it is the problem of authorship with the consequent rejection of the individualism that had characterised nineteenth-century architecture. From this particular point of view, the Danish approach to functionalism assumed an uncommon character, as we will see below. Fisker stated that "… through conscious work on proportions and measurements, we have managed to introduce a concept of order again, after the individualistic chaos of Nyrop's time."[7] The question of order, as we shall see, is fundamental to Fisker and is the most effective antidote to the individualism characteristic of the National Romantic architecture

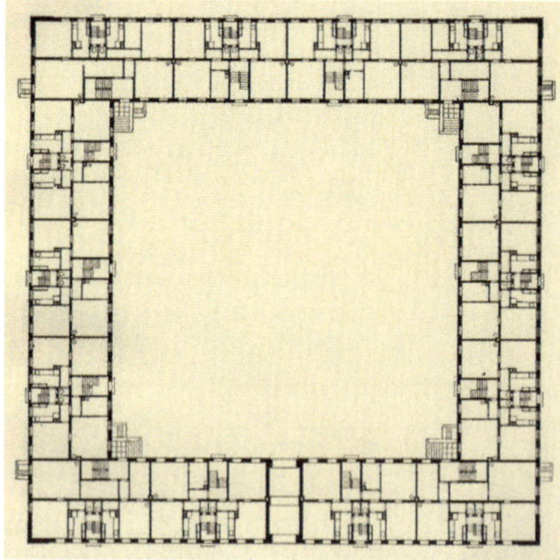

Henning Hansen, plan of the karré in *Vilhelm Thomsens Allé* [from Fisker, Yerbury, *Modern Danish Architecture*, 1927]

Hornbækhus, courtyard façade [Photo by Bernard Zurbuchen, 2006]

of the last decade of the nineteenth century, of which Martin Nyrop (1849–1921), architect of the Copenhagen City Hall, is the most famous representative.

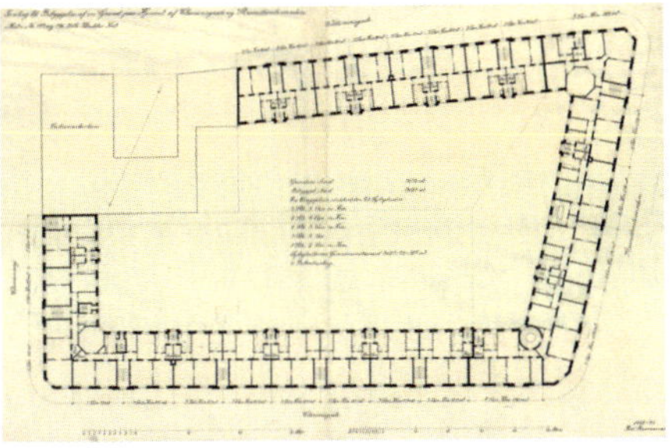

Povl Baumann, *Classens Have*, Typical Floor Plan, 1924 [Danmarks Kunstbibliotek, Digital Collection, Inventory number 13029b]

Copenhagen Housing Types

The great uniformity of the fronts, the distributional rationality and the use of non-rendered brick masonry are characteristic features of many municipal housing buildings. In addition to *Hornbækhus* and the already mentioned buildings by Baumann and by Hansen, other projects should be indicated as examples of the same qualities, among others the *Classens Have* building (1922–24), by Peter Nielsen, Ole Falkentorp and Baumann himself, which, unlike the previous examples, is configured as an open courtyard.

In the book reproduced in the following pages (*Københavnske boligtypers – Copenhagen Housing Types*), Kay Fisker laments the limitations of typological experimentation arising from the regulations on which the *State Housing Fund* (*Statsboligfond*) was based. As already seen, a characteristic aspect of Copenhagen housing – a crucial point and a real obsession for many planners – is in fact the requirement to design buildings in which each apartment is serviced by two staircases. Until the end of the second period of *State Housing Fund* in 1928, this rule, together with conventional control of dwellings' surface, produced buildings that, according to Fisker, inhibit or even prevent any typological progress. This point of view, while perfectly understandable, overshadows an important aspect, namely the rigor shown by architects engaged in social housing in Copenhagen in producing evidence of great skill in spite of regulatory restrictions. If we look at the way the corner problem is solved, for example, we cannot fail to recognise the quality of the results, in spite of those very restrictions. Beyond the shared means of expression, Fisker's solutions in *Hornbækhus* together with those adopted by Hansen and Baumann deserve our attention. And it is precisely the problem of the corner that determines, in a second phase, the adoption of open urban forms, characterised by the presence of large and sunny gardens, progressively freed from all the ancillary activities traditionally destined for interior courtyards.

J. C. Petersen, Povl Baumann, *Classens Have*, Arendalsgade 2 [Danmarks Kunstbibliotek, Digital Collection, Inventory number daf_0073_185]

Strictness and rigor in the design process can be perfectly seen in the way Fisker approaches the typological problems in the text *Copenhagen housing types from 1914 to 1936* that precedes the presentation of the chosen examples. In fact, the booklet is proposed as an authentic handbook. Inspired by similar German studies, such as those of Alexander Klein and Otto Haessler, it is based on a series of typological plans according to different criteria, from urban form to the number of staircases, including the nature of structural elements and distribution systems. The general observations are basic and insist on finding the balance between costs and benefits, systematically referring to economic and social conditions. The texts show, in the elementary nature of the arguments, all the difficulties characterising housing design, without delving into aesthetic issues but limiting itself to the technical aspects (see, in this regard, the explanation of the way projects are presented and the use of different graphic scales aimed at maximum comparability of the examples).

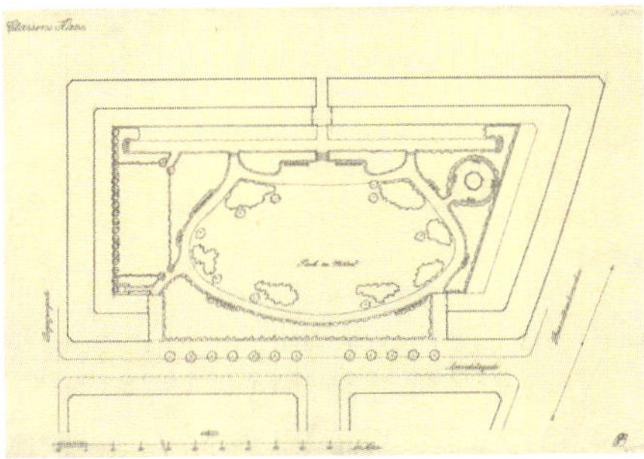

Povl Baumann, *Classens Have*, Site Plan, 1924 [Danmarks Kunstbibliotek, Digital Collection, Inventory number 13029a]

The severity of Fisker's look at the *Statsboligfund* experience is diluted when it takes a broader perspective, considering the trends that were emerging at the time the booklet was published. In the conclusion of his text, Fisker acknowledges that "*Statsboligfund* Period housing, despite its stereotypical formalism, often seems to exhibit more correct measurements, more comfortable dimensions in terms of detail, and more poise in the cityscape than the troubled flickering new houses with their compressed window heights, often unsightly balcony shapes and ugly colours."

From a typological point of view, the real and substantial difference, from which new solutions arise, is the modification of the building regulations and the consequent possibility of limiting the number of staircases to one, with the obligation, as a countermeasure, to equip apartments with balconies, supposed to be used as fire escapes. This opportunity opens a new era in which the architectural expression of buildings is characterised by the multiplication of balconies, often combined with bow-windows, to the point where they become decidedly "cumbersome" elements. Thus, the peremptory volumetric clarity that had characterised previous social housing is fragmented, transforming the facades into a congestion of protrusions overshadowing the qualities peculiar to the long, quiet and nevertheless powerful brick facades. This aspect is also visible in projects in which balconies are taken as a theme and repeated with regularity, as in the case of the 1935 project by Povl Baumann and Knud Hansen in Storgaarden, considered by Fisker to be "certainly the best multi-storey residential building of the 1930s"[8] (see *Københavnske boligtypers – Copenhagen Housing Types*, page 77 and IV_{41a}). In this particular case the collective character is in fact replaced by the affirmation of the individuality of each single apartment, emphasised by the screens protecting the balconies from the neighbours' sight.

While the new housing buildings represent progress in terms of habitability, there is, in parallel, an undeniable loss in urban terms, corresponding to the appearance of more or less abstract sequences of linear buildings. The most visible difference, apart from the distributional aspects, is in fact the weakening of the close link between buildings and open spaces (see, in this regard, the summary representation of the different urban forms: closed and semi-closed blocks, linear buildings, preceding the catalog of dwelling types in *Københavnske boligtypers – Copenhagen Housing Types*).

Then there is another issue that concerns housing in Copenhagen and Fisker's production as well, once again related to stairwells. As we have noted, in the *Hornbækhus* and the other examples we have referred to, the presence of stairwells is "denied" in the facades: the rhythm and position of the windows lighting the stairs does not contradict the alignments of the other windows, thanks to the expedient of opening them to the outside (even if this solution can be found in many Danish buildings of the nineteenth century, it must be acknowledged that it can be considered an extreme and "brutal" option). We thus witness, when observing Fisker's projects, a radical change that consists, precisely, in the "correct" positioning of windows at the stairwells, with the resulting misalignment towards the other openings. The *Gullfosshus* (1926–27) is the obvious demonstration of this, as Fisker himself shows on page 42 of the book reproduced here. The result is remarkable, certainly more reasonable, but it loses some of the force that *Hornbækhus*'s unbroken, homogeneous sequence of windows possesses. *Gullfosshus*'s fronts look different. When viewed frontally, the presence of the stairs is instantly striking, making the overall composition immediately legible, while when viewed foreshortened, they reveal unexpected geometries enhanced by diagonal lines.

Fisker's architecture

All of Kay Fisker's projects – developed alone or in collaboration with others – are carefully designed and show unquestionable positive qualities in terms of construction, volumetric definition, and also in terms of typology and distribution. Another evident characteristic is the general layout – the so-called *urban form* – which, despite its limited formal variety, always proves capable of capturing and enhancing the particular aspects of the part of the city involved in the project.

The elementary buildings designed by Kay Fisker and his fellows from the early 1920s onward define the face of the city with great precision and equal discretion. Taken as a whole, the brick facades that punctuate the urban areas affected by the most intense housing activity have something extremely familiar and unobtrusive about them, despite their large size and because of the calmness that results from the clarity of the street frontages, the silent presence of multitudes of ordinary windows, and the timidly decorated front doors.

An extremely important aspect of the *State Housing Fund* that began in the 1920s is the unity of purpose and the sharing of the same architectural, urban and social ideal by Kay Fisker and other architects who were his contemporaries or from the previous generation. Even the most unfocused observer, walking the streets of Copenhagen, will notice this extraordinary unity, to which Fisker remained faithful until the end of *State Housing Fund* experience. If we add up the community of purpose, the willingness to conform to it, and the restrained and repetitive character of that architecture, we realise how far that experience is from contemporary trends. Nevertheless, Kay Fisker rightfully attracts the attention of critics, architects, and students, perhaps not many but certainly more today than in past decades.

Within Fisker's production in the field of housing, beyond its great overall quality, there are projects that we now consider memorable. Memorable, among Fisker's buildings, are those in which the architecture configures and celebrates large unbuilt collective or public spaces in the form of gardens or squares.

As already pointed out, ***Hornbækhus***, compared to most of the later works, embodies the collective ideal by exalting its qualities thanks to the absolute homogeneity that makes us perceive it as a "large common house" rather than a summation of individual dwellings. The long fronts punctuated by the regular rhythm of openings, however, has none of the deliberate radicalism of Loos's peremptory facades in the almost contemporary *Otto-Haas-Hof* in Vienna.[9] Thanks to the use of brick, to which Fisker would always be faithful, the *Hornbækhus* turns out to be anything but abstract; rather, the material presence of brick interrupted by those 2,000 simple windows gives the building a somewhat austere but ultimately friendly domestic character, as far removed from the experimentalisms of the Berlin and Frankfurt avant-garde as it is from the sometime clumsy monumentalism of the *Wienerhöfe*.

Gullfosshus (1927) is certainly another remarkable project that could be considered a variant rather than an evolution of *Hornbækhus* – indeed, it would be reductive to consider Fisker's work from an evolutionary point of view, given the persistent fixity of many aspects of his architecture. What is remarkable and memorable about this project is first of all the refined brickwork in two different colours, in addition to the already mentioned treatment of the openings that bring light to the stairwell. The building presents a massive volume, seemingly more powerful and severe than *Hornbækhus*, despite the fact that it is dimensionally smaller, thanks to the fact that it can be observed from the wide perspective of *Artillerivej*. Situated to the south of the city centre, the building is contiguous with a series of elongated, well-structured blocks representative of the building style of the last decades of the nineteenth and early twentieth century.[10] In relation to this piece of the nineteenth century city, the building designed by Fisker constitutes a clear break and an equally evident paradigm shift. To the narrow courtyards punctuated by the protrusion of the secondary stairwells, Fisker opposes a vast, generously sunlit garden, without thereby changing the distributional arrangement of the main rooms facing the street and the secondary rooms facing the courtyard/garden. On both street and garden façades, the apartment windows are grouped around those of the staircase, thus renouncing the peremptory rhythm that characterises *Hornbækhus*.

Gullfosshus, façade giving onto Artillerivej [Photo by Bernard Zurbuchen, 2006]

Another noteworthy project is the ***Dronningegården*** complex (1942–58), designed and executed in collaboration with F. C. Lund, C. F. Møller and S. E. Kristensen. It defines a large theatrical rectangular space, originally intended as a garden and now crossed by two thoroughfares, the major axis of which is parallel to one of the axes of the nearby Rococo octagonal *Amalienborg* square.

The central space is punctuated by twelve 9-storey volumes with sloping roofs separated by lower ones, that face each other on the long sides.

The massive character of the whole is not contradicted by the numerous loggias, grouped together, in the case of the volumes with sloping roofs, or alternating with the generous square windows on the short sides of the large central space, or "excavated" in the façade with which it thus assumes, also thanks to the protruding staircases volumes, an almost archaeological aspect, as happens on the fronts facing Adelgade.

Fisker's writings

During his career, Fisker edited major books devoted to Danish architecture,[11] in addition to the two reprinted in the next pages. He also edited *Arkitekten* magazine from 1918 to 1926 and devoted himself to teaching for more than forty years (assistant lecturer at the Academy of Fine Arts School of Architecture 1920–24, then lecturer and finally professor at the same institution from 1936 to 1963). In addition, Fisker is also the author of a number of writings that deserve to be remembered for their extreme clarity, intellectual lucidity and their still valuable relevance.

The most remarkable, and probably the most original as well, was published in 1964, one year before his death, and it could be consequently considered his legacy, beginning with its title: *Cult of personality or anonymity*.[12]

Demonstrating an excellent knowledge of the architectural scene of his time, supported by the numerous trips he undertook beginning in the 1920s, Fisker, confirms in his last writing, his preference for an orderly and modest architecture and warns against the danger of falling into the cult of personality. The paper concludes with these words, which make Kay Fisker one of the least listened-to architects among those who, in different ways, marked twentieth-century architecture: "We must remember that architects who succeed in ordering the image of our cities and our landscape and who manage to create a human milieu through valid dwellings, like a frame around a good form of life, are of greater value to society than those who produce an individual, sensational work of art."

In many of his writings, Fisker focuses essentially on the quality of housing without taking too much consideration of other aspects. In fact, in the central part of *Copenhagen Housing Types*, the examples are treated simply: a typological catalog in which only the plans and a few explanatory captions appear, to ensure the highest degree of comparability, as had already been the case for the Frankfurt exhibition on the *Existenz Minimum*. The photographs on the pages following the typological catalog are, accompanied by sparse captions and illustrate the architectural results brought about by the adoption of specific typological solutions, giving the impression that they are intended to illustrate the stages of a natural evolution. The improvement of housing, considered the necessary framework for a good form of living, is presented with a certain coldness, sacrificing on the altar of a supposed evolution several other elements that nevertheless participate in the definition of architectural quality.

Such an attitude is certainly due to Fisker's substantial aversion to any kind of formalism, to anything that does not directly touch housing in its distributive aspects – quality in execution being taken for granted, given the high standard of construction in Scandinavian countries.

For Kay Fisker, one of the fundamental aspects of architecture is collectiveness – not limited to the way in which spaces are organised to facilitate, evoke, or enhance the possibility of sharing them by a community. The collectiveness that Kay Fisker speaks of is related both to the conception of architectural design and to the values it can and should convey. In this sense, he pursues a kind of erasure of any possible claim of the architect-designer as author, anticipating the current debate regarding the notion of authorship.

In *Cult of Personality or Anonymity*, after some remarks regarding the leading figures in the architecture of the 1960s, we read: "One would like to hope that there will continue to be great geniuses in architecture and hope that we will always be thrilled by their splendid work. These great architects may give us a strong individual experience, but admiration becomes a cult of personality. We cannot build architecture for everyone with such individualism. It is the neutral, anonymous architecture that should mark our environment, and that is what we must strive to improve. Such architecture cannot submit to fashion and cannot take inspiration from great individual performance. Common architecture must be anonymous and timeless."[13]

In another famous text,[14] this one from 1950, Fisker sets out his views on functionalist architecture. For the Danish architect, there is no contradiction between functionalist and traditional architecture, the latter being by its very nature functional to its purpose, to the local materials and techniques, and to the economic and social conditions in which it is realised. Such a view is perfectly in keeping with the position Danish architecture occupies, in the first decades of the twentieth century, in the European context: a position that recognises and brings to the foreground a form of objectivity that finds its own origin in tradition. Martin Steinmann highlighted this aspect in the monographic issue of the Swiss journal *Archithese*,[15] the first major publication devoted to Fisker outside his native country. Steinmann questions whether the buildings built in Denmark in the 1920s and 1930s "derive from classical architecture or from the architecture that Philip Webb, the great English protagonist of traditionalism [...], characterised as *commonplace*." In his text, Steinmann rightly points out that Danish architecture of the 1920s and 1930s embodies a realist conception of tradition. "Tradition does not refer here to an image that would be preserved and even less to the genius of a people reflected in that image; it refers to the material and intellectual conditions in which architects work."

Fisker's position towards tradition in its most realistic sense is expressed in the following considerations.

"As long as bricks are our cheapest building material and as long as the brick-making industry finances construction, brick will continue to dominate Copenhagen's buildings. We should certainly not regret this, but try again to gain an understanding of the character and properties of brick as it was a generation ago. During the *Statsboligfonds* Period, we polished up the brick houses to make them look neoclassical just as faithful modernists are now polishing them up to make them look like concrete houses. Instead, we should strive to develop a brick technique on the same level as the period of Plesner and Nyrop with excellent technical ability and which also produced equally beautiful material effects. We should also learn that brick houses, especially in these iron-deficient times, should not be built with concrete forms."[16]

City of bricks

Thanks to the work of Fisker and his fellow architects, Copenhagen began to emerge in the early 1920s as a city characterised by great unity of purpose and consequent architectural homogeneity. The absolute fidelity to brick as a building material is reiterated by Fisker in a 1939 article.[17] In this text, the usefulness and many merits of reinforced concrete are acknowledged, but in parallel the reasons for its inappropriateness to Danish architecture are stated. Fisker criticises the fact that brick buildings had been constructed in Denmark adopting forms made possible by reinforced concrete. Acknowledging the ubiquity of brick occasioned by the nature of the Danish soil, he asserts that "our buildings depend on brick," and as such they are all the more efficient and economical the more limited in size and regularly distributed the windows are. Those who see these statements as evidence of a regressive position or as a refusal to confront new materials and new building concepts are wrong. In reality it is an affirmation of the extreme need for clarity, an unreserved fidelity to what we call constructive truth. It should also be remembered that the use of brick, when in accordance with its nature, constitutes a guarantee for the achievement of that *order* which on several occasions Fisker declares to be the goal of all good architecture.

Good architecture, for Kay Fisker, must be simple, clear, unpretentious, anonymous and timeless. This assumption finds its roots in the work and thought of Heinrich Tessenow, deeply appreciated by Danish architects in the early twentieth century, and for more than one reason a kind of alter ego for Fisker. It is therefore no coincidence that in 1964, the Heinrich Tessenow Medal was awarded to Kay Fisker himself.

Fisker emphasises that Tessenow, unlike his English contemporaries such as C. F. Voysey, does not disdain classicism but uses it as a tool of order and dignity, never at odds with utility and technique.[18] The German architect's influence on Fisker is not evident at the formal or typological level. From this point of view, Tessenow's fundamental contribution takes the form of his numerous designs and production of terraced houses, a theme that Fisker addresses in the publication of the booklet *Rækkehustyper*,[19] analogous to the *Københavnske bolygtyper*. From a professional point of view, Fisker had few opportunities to deal with this type of dwelling, and as remarkable as the result is, one gets the impression that he was more at ease with the large housing blocks of his city of bricks.

While it is clear that for many reasons Kay Fisker was the leading personality among the architects active in Copenhagen in the first decades of the twentieth century, it must be said that for the public – and sometimes even for less shrewd architects – recognising his buildings among dozens of similar ones is not an easy task.

From an architectural and, above all, political point of view, the large collective spaces of Copenhagen's housing blocks represent a clear social conquest. Such a vision includes the recognition of uniformity as a carrier of important social meanings and shared values. In this respect, the large courtyards are a conscious and powerful reaction to the excesses of building speculation and the miserable living conditions characteristic of European cities until the outbreak of the First World War.

Walking through the neighbourhoods of the modern city, those in which Copenhagen has built a large part of its housing since the 1920s, one is struck by the quality of the whole rather than by any particular building. Here the ideal of a *simple, clear, unpretentious, anonymous and timeless architecture* has been attained thanks to the contribution and passionate work of Fisker and his fellows: more or less well-known architects who collectively designed remarkable buildings, comfortable dwellings and vast gardens, giving life to the *city of bricks* that makes some districts of the Danish capital memorable as a whole.

Notes

1 Martin Søberg, Kay Fisker. *Works and Ideas in Danish Modern Architecture*, Bloomsbury Publishing, London, 2021.

2 Manfredo Tafuri, *Letter to Renato De Fusco*, "Op. cit.", n. 51, 1981. In this paper Tafuri includes three Danish architects – Carl Petersen, Ivar Bentsen and Edvard Thomsen – in the list of those who consciously chose a different line from the official positions of the Modern Movement.

3 Tobias Faber, Kay Fisker, in Various authors, *Kay Fisker*, Arkitektens Forlag, København, 1995.

4 Stephen Bates, Bruno Krucker, Katharina Leuschner (editors), Hornbækhus Building Register, 2013 – Andrew Clancy, Colm Moore, *Kay Fisker: Danish Functionalism and Block-Based Housing*, Lund Humphries, London, 2022. See also my *Architecture ancrée dans le quotidien. Kay Fisker et ses compagnons de route*, "Matières", n. 12, 2015.

5 Quoted by Fisker in *Copenhagen Housing Types from 1914 to 1936*, reproduced here at page 35.

6 Kay Fisker and Frank Yerbury (edited by), *Modern Danish Architecture*, Ernest Benn, London, 1927; German edition: *Moderne Dänische Baukunst*, Verlag Ernst Wasmuth, Berlin, 1927.

7 Kay Fisker, *Mindeudstillingen af Aage Rafn arbejder (The memorial exhibition of Aage Rafn's works)*, "Arkitekten U", 44, 1954.

8 Kay Fisker, *Povl Baumann fylder 80 år (Povl Baumann turns 80)*, "Arkitekten", n. 23, 1958.

9 Built between 1924 and 1925, designed by Adolf Loos, Karl Dirnhuber, Margarethe Lihotzky and Franz Schuster, the building is part of the so-called *Red Vienna* housing program.

10 See *Københavnske boligtypers – Copenhagen Housing Types*, pages 24–27 and also Knud Millech, *Kay Fisker, Danske arkitekturstrømninger 1850–1950 (Trends in Danish Architecture)*, København, 1951.

11 Beyond the already cited *Modern Danish Architecture*, see Knud Millech, Kay Fisker, *Danske arkitekturstrømninger 1850–1950 (Trends in Danish Architecture)*, København, 1951.

12 Kay Fisker, *Persondyrkelse eller anonymitet*, "Arkitekten", n. 26, 1964.

13 Kay Fisker, *Persondyrkelse eller anonymitet*, "Arkitekten", n. 26, 1964.

14 Kay Fisker, *Den funktionelle tradition*, "Arkitekten Månedshæfte", n. 35, 1950.

15 Martin Steinmann, *Die Tradition der Sachlichkeit und die Sachlichkeit der Tradition. Zur Architektur von Kay Fisker*, "Archithese", n. 4, 1985, now in German and in French in Martin Steinmann, *Forme forte. Ecrits/Schriften 1972–2002*, Bikhäuser, 2003.

16 See page 43 of the booklet *Copenhagen housing types* reproduced here. Ulrik Adolph Plesner (1861–1933) built numerous villas, public buildings and housing in and around Copenhagen, making extensive use of brick construction. Martin Nyrop (1849–1921) was the greatest interpreter of Danish National Romanticism. Elsewhere, Fisker considers Nyrop the emblem of the 'individualistic chaos' of late nineteenth century architecture (see footnote 6).

17 Kay Fisker, *Arkitekturbetragtninger*, "Samleren", n. 4, 1939.

[18] Kay Fisker, *Heinrich Tessenow in memoriam*, "Arkitekten Ugehæfte", n. 36, 1951.

[19] Kay Fisker, *Rækkehustyper. En oversight udarbejdet paa Kunstakademiets Arkitekturskole, under ledense af professor Kay Fisker*, "Arkitekten, Akademisk Arkitekturforening", 1941.

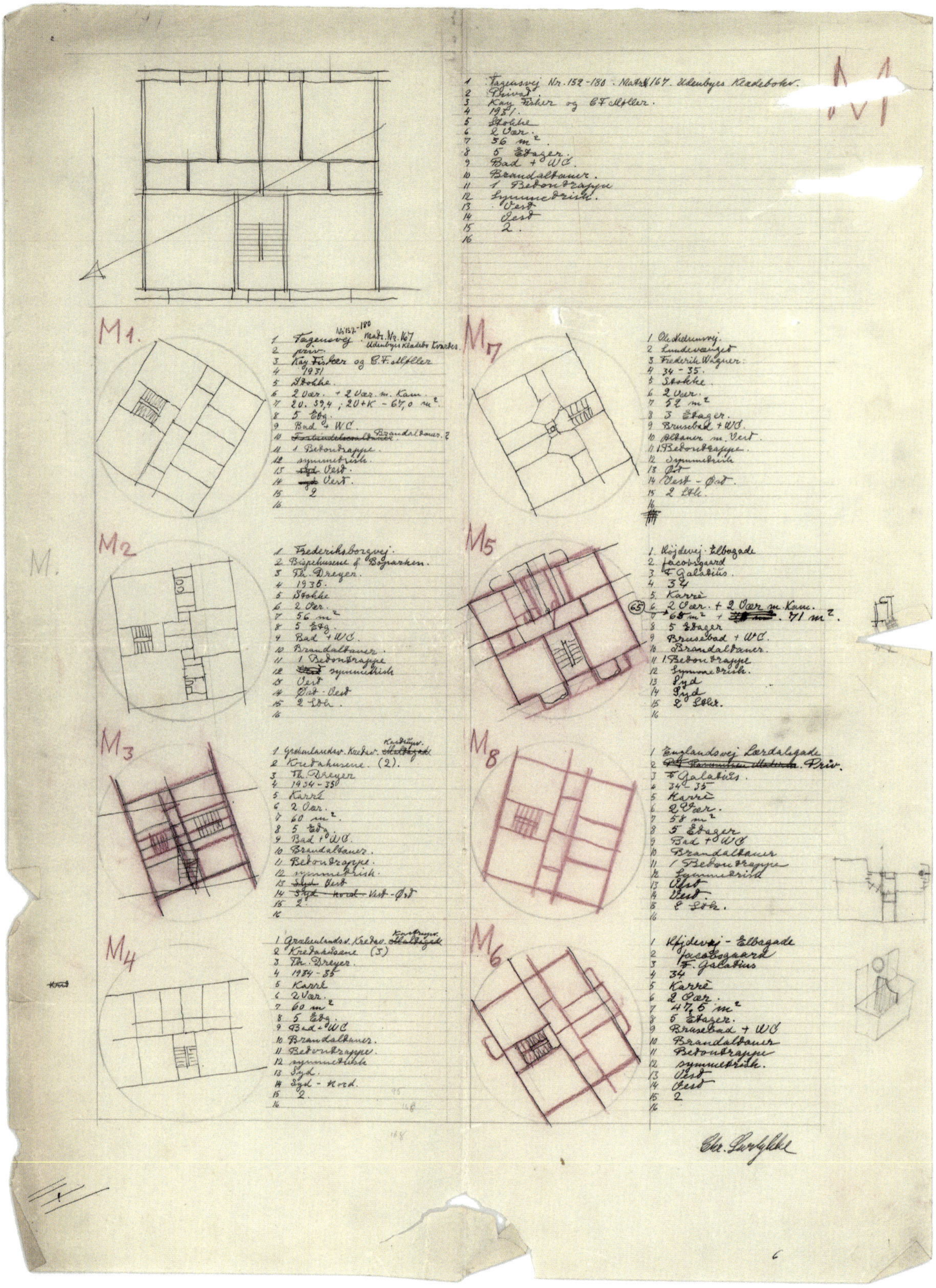

Sample of the preparatory plates (Plan Types) for the 1936 book pages layout [Danmarks Kunstbiblioteket, *Københavnske boligtyper*, 1192, mappe 2, 60977]

Delving into Kay Fisker's investigations on housing typologies

Chiara Monterumisi

In 1936, in two consecutive monthly issues[1] of the Danish journal *Arkitekten*,[2] architect Kay Otto Fisker (1893–1965) presented a thorough eighty-page account of Copenhagen housing types accompanied by an impressively rich set of comparative plates of various kinds, as well as photos and quantitative data in the form of charts. The magazine survey came out in two separate parts (namely *Københavnske Boligtyper from 1856 until 1914* and *Københavnske Boligtyper from 1914 to 1936*), covering two housing policy periods each with distinctive relevance to development of the Danish capital. The outcome of studies on residential building history, mainly examining the formation and transformation of "multi-storey residential buildings and small flats",[3] the survey was conducted under the guidance of Kaj Gottlob (Ist period: 1856–1914) and Fisker himself (IInd period: 1914–1936) during their last years at the School of Architecture of the Royal Danish Academy of Fine Arts.

Fisker's aim in collecting these works was to offer a multifaceted perspective, showing the heterogeneity of architecture as a conflation of historical research, research by design and technical knowledge. Together with the other people involved in the detailed survey, he "felt that by reworking and adding supplementary material these could be of interest also to circles outside the Academy".[4] The *supplementary material* consists of a set of photographic apparatus and drawings produced by study teams of five to ten students who analysed the theme of residential types over four periods (1856–1900, 1900–1914, 1914–1928 and 1928–1936) primarily in Copenhagen within the two main time frames in which the survey is arranged. As stressed by Fisker, "the present study is an attempt towards more systematic working methods in the study of architecture at the Academy and should not be considered an exhaustive account of the subject's architectural heritage. It may nonetheless contribute to shedding light on the development of the multi-storey residential buildings, especially during the major building periods around the turn of the century and in the post-war years which have so greatly influenced the city".[5] Despite the title of the investigation containing the geographical reference to the Danish capital, he offered "exceptional instances of foreign types and, in some cases, unbuilt types"[6] in order to widen understanding of type formation.

The date of publication is no banal coincidence, since 1936 marked his appointment as professor of architecture (*Bygningskunst*) at the Royal Academy in Copenhagen, an institution with which he had a long-standing relationship. He achieved this professorship after being Edward Thomsen's assistant (1919–1923) – one year before obtaining his diploma – in the course named Danish Class (*Dansk Klass*) with its particular focus on vernacular architecture where students "almost never designed more ordinary urban housing projects".[7] Around the time of his graduation in January 1920 Fisker received his first commission to design two nearby residential large perimeter blocks, the Borups

Plad (1919–1921) and Hornbækhus (1920–1923)[8] – the latter still widely hailed as one of his most iconic works.

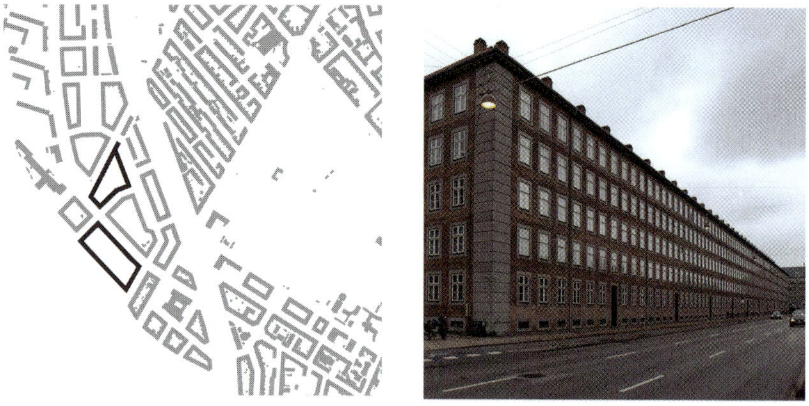

Urban fabric diagram depicting in black *Borups Plad* and *Hornbækhus* and urban façade of the latter [Author's drawing; Sandra Gonon, Arkitekturbilleder]

In 1924,[9] as an associate professor at the Royal Academy School of Architecture, he established the *Boligbyggeri* course (or *Bolig Klasse*) with its keen interest in housing, over which he presided until 1955.[10] Shaping this course absorbed all his energy over the years. It proved a delicate and demanding task "to gather students from the Academy's own preschool and graduates from the technical schools into a class unit and to introduce these students to the housing and architectural problems of the time".[11] One may safely call it the "Fisker class", in which generations of students benefited from his architectural know-how. The fact that many academic colleagues referred to that third-year course by his name does not reflect any personal narrowness of interest or individualism; it was simply a testimonial to the constant commitment with which he sought to put across an objective way of viewing and practising the discipline.

His interest in housing was increasingly a mixture of teaching experience and his practice as an architect ever since his days as a student and his internships at Copenhagen and Stockholm. In those early years while he forged ahead with his research, flanked by students, a range of commissions from different Copenhagen municipal housing cooperatives came his way as an independent architect:[12] for example, Glænøgaard (1923–1927), Gullfosshus (1924–1927), Amagerbo (1924–1926), Jagtgaarden (1924–1925), Brigadegaarden (1926–1928), Vodroffsvej (1928–1930). In support of these building ventures Fisker published very brief descriptions backed by an effective array of drawings and photographs in the pages of *Architekten*. Most of these projects are included in the 1936 volume, where they are classified either by building site or building type.[13]

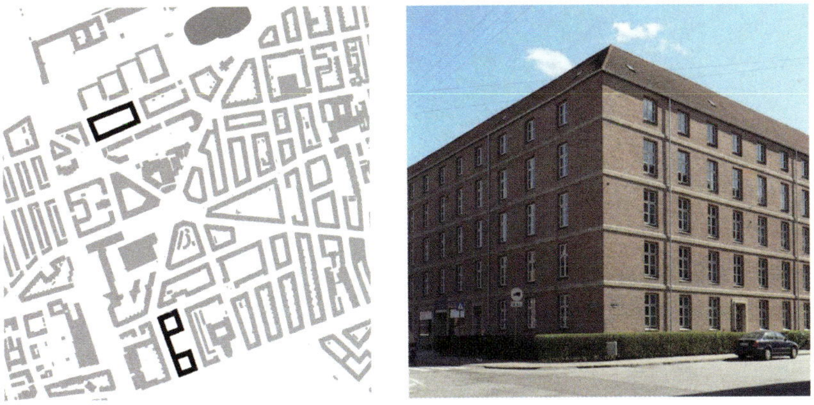

Urban fabric diagram depicting in black *Glænøgaard* and *Jagtgaarden* and urban façade of the former [Author's drawing; Marti Toft Buchardi Bendtsen, Arkitekturbilleder]

Urban fabric diagram depicting in black *Gullfosshus* and its courtyard [Author's drawing; Chiara Monterumisi photo]

Urban fabric diagram depicting in black *Brigadegaarden* and *Amagerbo*, and the green yard of the latter [Author's drawing; Sandra Gonon, Arkitekturbilleder]

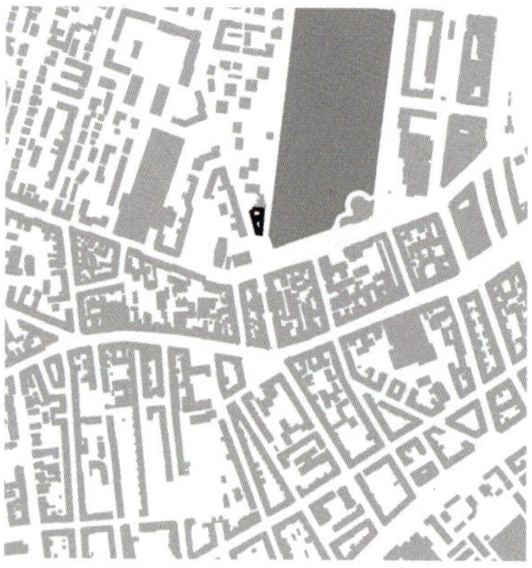

Urban fabric diagram depicting in black *Vodroffsvej* and its urban façade [Author's drawing; Sandra Gonon, Arkitekturbilleder]

The penchant for housing was not unique to Fisker, around whom there formed a circle of other teachers and architects. They grasped the public utility of those housing policies in the interwar period, key decades in hectic city modernisation but contained within an encompassing social project underpinning the inspiring welfare system of the years to come.[14] Such values, central to those involved in catering to the urgent demand for housing as a topical modern issue, clearly extend to the academic world responsible for training new generations of architects and urban planners. Clear evidence of this keen interest in the issue springs from the pages of the journal *Architekten*. From the late 1920s to 1940s onwards, more and more room would be devoted to presenting new projects for Danish towns, competitions, exhibitions, miscellaneous (local and international) thoughts on the topic and discussion of regulations, such as ground occupation and density, etc.. Related drawings, varying in scale, were central to the debate.

That a survey such as Fisker's could serve a wider spectrum both in the academic and the practising realms is also borne out by the publication of the 80-page analysis in the form of a separate special edition released the same year (1936), though in a limited run. The book was published under the title *Københavnske Boligtyper en oversight* (An overview of Copenhagen housing types) and for the cover he used part of the map illustrating the distribution of housing initiatives in the capital. Contents, visual apparatus and layout appeared just as conceived for the Danish journal, showing his close involvement in the editing, a talent he had honed during his time as an impressively young co-editor on the board of *Architekten* back in 1918.[15]

Fisker championed the idea that quality architecture should be made available outside its own sector: the housing issue affects us all and can only be solved by concerted collective action.

The 1936 text was not his last word on the housing issue. Indeed, as a "continuation of previous studies on residential buildings",[16] the thorough examination *Rækkehusetyper en oversight* (An overview of row house types) was published in 1941. It followed the previous formula: first, a forty-page article in *Arkitekten* historical and analytical text, entitled *Om rækkehuse, kamhuse, kædehuse og andere huse* – on row, comb, chained and other types of terraced house –, accompanied by photos and taxonomical plates) published in two consecutive monthly issues[17] and, then, the separate book released the same year. Here, the reference to Copenhagen was dropped from the title, and the analysis collected "both Danish and foreign buildings, both projected and completed, and includes a total of 120 types".[18] For both the 1936 and 1941 accounts, the *supplementary material* is a selection of a more extensive production of analytical documents produced within the *Bolig Klasse*.

The contents of the two texts are complementary and provide a multifaceted fresco spanning the ninetheenth and twentieth century on how to build the city, essentially by continuation of and variation on two major traditional models of building: the perimeter block (*karré bebyggelser*), and the terraced house (*rækkehuse bebyggelser*), though also including multiple variants and hybrid versions thereof. However, a third type, that is the ordinary detached single-family house, was investigated by his students too,[19] but was not taken into account in his set of publications. In 1933, predating Fisker's works, his colleague Povl Stegmann (1888–1944) took up the same typological approach (comparative and analytical drawings) for examining the third group.[20]

The 1936 survey went beyond the unique focus on first perimeter blocks crowding the inner space with wings or T-shape protrusions carried out in the two periods (1856–1900, 1900–1914), and indeed it covered the whole morphological development of multi-storey buildings. Particular attention was addressed to the 1920s experiments featuring large green meadows (*karré bebyggelser* and *halvlukkede karré*), which still retain a certain continuity with the benchmark type that traditionally connoted the city, down to the explosion of the block (*aabne bebyggelser*) in the 1930s housing estate comprised of rows of blocks (*stokbebyggelser*). "In the modern metropolis area, the majority of the population lives in houses with multi-story flats located along paved streets regardless of the sun. It is the tradition of the big city, and although we now find this form of housing a bit unfortunate and outdated, so that we preferred to build the new residential areas as open park buildings or as garden residential areas with terraced houses or completely detached single-family houses, it will take a long row before the city changes character".[21] Communal urban policies in the 1920s–1930s, but above all the estate market, preferred to promote multi-storey blocks, and hence new experiments on low-rise row houses got pushed into the background. The first valiant efforts at building new terraced-houses (e.g. Bakkehusene,[22] low-rise houses by Ivar Bentsen's and Thorkild Henningsen in 1922–1923 for the KAB - *Københavns Almindelige Boligselskab*[23]) were met with a lack of understanding from both public and authorities.[24] Although row houses had been a major topic "in the propaganda of modern architects around the world at large exhibitions with model cities that have been held around Europe for the last fifteen years", these types "have not been yet adapted and fine-tuned according to the demands of everyday reality".[25] However, the persisting acute housing crisis seemed to give this last group a "special second chance", including the Copenhagen context. On the one hand, the above-mentioned example "seems like the best vindication of the type, especially when compared to the five-storey blocks built during the same period from the beginning of the 1920s"[26] while, on the other hand, the newer ones developed a technically simplified layout.

Urban fabric diagram depicting in black *Brønsparken* and the façade series [Author's drawing; Hegnshusene 1-184 in Brønshøj, 2000. Photographer: KL/VISDA. Københavns Stadsarkiv]

In the course of those early decades, Fisker proposed a few terraced houses[27] publicised outside the Danish borders, although never realised. Indeed, the first built project was the Brønsparken arrangement (1937–1941, also known as Hegnshusene[28]) for the *Foreningen Socialt Boligbyggeri* (The Social Housing Association)[29] with assistance from C. F. Møller and Erik Jensen, as well as C. Th. Sørensen for his landscaping expertise.

At that time, Fisker's systematic and comparative investigation extended beyond the Nordic world of criticism, and its success was certainly due to the increasingly active cultural climate of those years with their conferences and debates among groups and associations springing up on a local and international scale (e.g. CIAM - Congrès Internationaux d'Architecture Moderne, IFHTP-International Federation for Housing and Town Planning, which somehow stood as an alternative to the so-called monolithic modernity embodied by CIAM, etc.), as well as journeys and meetings focusing on modern housing and town planning. Textbooks and works of history have tended to highlight certain architectural figures and critics and give more prominence to the architectural output of some countries rather than others; but some key events in the interwar period were attended by Danish scholars, including Fisker, though he never embraced modernist principles in any dogmatic sense. Evidence of this as yet under-examined activity of his has survived in the form of catalogues to exhibitions where he was an invited speaker or participant, the proceedings of meetings that he attended, articles in non-Nordic reviews too, archive material such as correspondence, lectures given outside Denmark, and so on. Fisker emerges as a key figure for those interested in the Nordic world of architecture, especially its residential side.[30] One significant example was the fruitful exchange with Catherine Bauer (1905–1964), an American educator and a leading member of affordable housing policies, over the preparation of the book *Modern housing* (1934), where she introduced the American audience to the latest developments in European modernist housing (including Danish cases).[31] Later on, she would pave the way for Fisker's trips, exchanges and visiting professorship in the USA.

Fisker's role as the spokesman for Danish architecture overseas progressively stepped up following the Second World War, and included two-way exchanges with figures from other countries. A major contribution in this came also from his colleague, Steen Eiler Rasmussen (1898–1990),[32] one of the main critics and town planning experts in Denmark at that time. Part of the connection between the two men was precisely Fisker's 1936 survey which we are highlighting here.

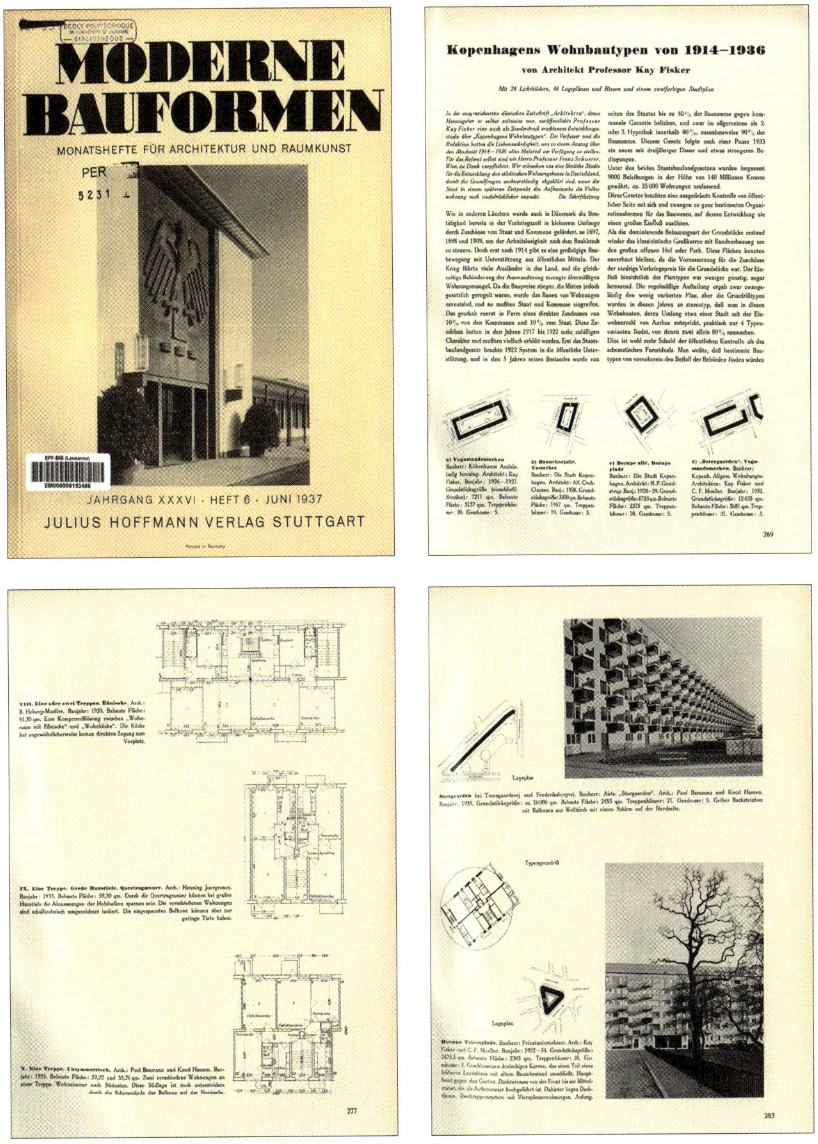

Cover of *Moderne Bauformen* (1937) and a selection of pages containing the German translation of a short extract of Fisker's survey.

Within this climate of collaboration, especially over the common problem of housing, the 1936 text caught the eye of Franz Schuster (1892–1972).[33] In 1937, as secretary to the association *Internationaler Verband för Wohnungswesen* (International Housing Association)[34] Schuster recommended that the magazine *Moderne Bauformen* publish a German translation[35] of a short extract from the Fisker survey in its June edition.

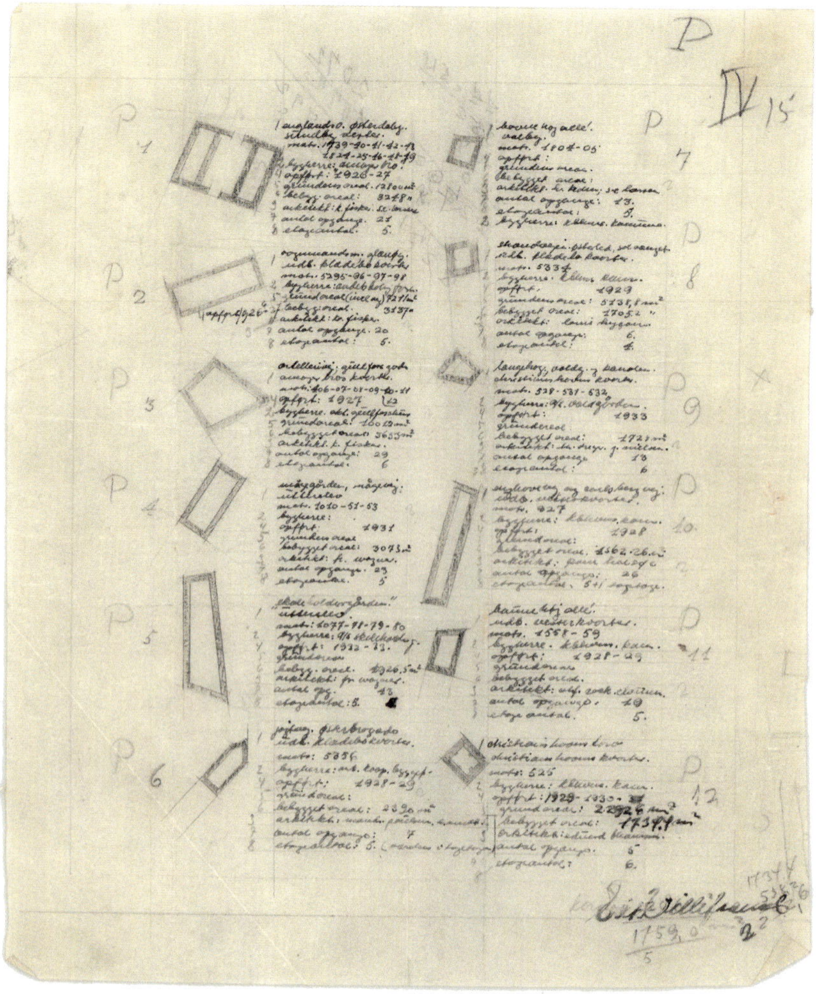

Sample of the preparatory plates (Building development plans) for the 1936 book pages layout [Danmarks Kunstbiblioteket, *Københavnske boligtyper*, 1192, mappe 2, 60977]

The editors were full of praise for the research on Copenhagen housing types and their development, and hoped that a similar type of survey based on morphological comparison might be adopted in Germany as well.[36] The translation focused on the second part of the *Arkitekten* survey, that covering the period 1914–1936,[37] precisely only on the Fisker's account. A notable amount of graphic material accompanied the text, though the new layout for the German journal disregarded what Fisker had intended as one complete book. In place of the thirty-five detailed taxonomic plates produced by the students, a selection of photographs was presented along with a plan of the respective building layout, and an assortment of housing types. In the conclusive section of the volume, the editors also provided a one-page short abstract of the extract in English without pictures.

To date, the partial Schuster translation is the only (lukewarm) attempt to circulate the text in anything but the original language with its restricted reading public, as well as the only recognition for its operative qualities of objective methodology, which were worthy to stand in line with the modern principles being promoted by the dominant German contribution to the international debate.

Today, more than eighty years after the release of the two analyses (1936 and 1941), it is time to shed light on this almost untrodden ground: providing the first-ever annotated English translation will widen the scope of investigations beyond the self-explanatory visual accompaniment to the texts.

Among Fisker's output as an editor of books, *Københavnske Boligtyper en oversight* (1936) and *Rækkehusetyper en oversight* (1941) are very little-known and merit broader contextualisation as befits an author who rose from local to international eminence. In justice to the importance and complementary nature of the two texts, the translations in question offer a facsimile of the size and page layout.[38] Looking at the plates elaborated by students under the Fisker guidance for both 1936 and 1941 texts, it is evident how the *typological approach* developed in modern culture allows establishing a particular interaction between the architecture of the past and the field of design. In a nutshell, "this implies subjecting the historical material to a radical process of abstraction, through which its most general, permanent aspects can be distilled".[39]

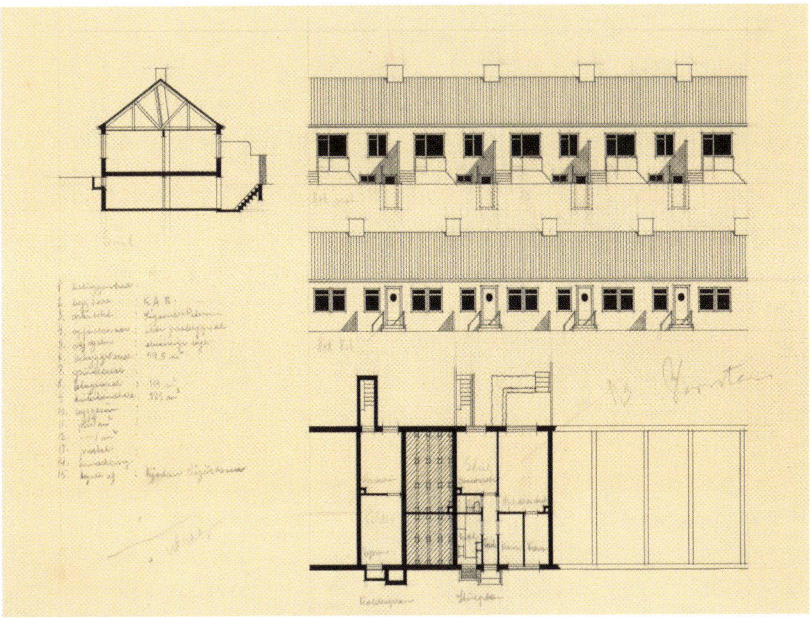

Sample of the preparatory plates for the 1941 book pages layout. The Danish case here portrayed was not included in the publication [Danmarks Kunstbiblioteket, *Rækkehuse samlet i en studiekreds på arkitektskolen*, 1190, mappe 2]

We feel the Danish architect's meticulously detailed contribution to this collective research conducted within his course; his guiding hand can be felt behind the overall contents' organisation and the selection of the students' plates (or parts of them) and consequently their adaptation for the purpose of the two publications. As the preparatory samples of the books' pages shown,[40] Fisker worked (in collaboration with few students)[41] at the preparation of the layout and graphical appearance of the drawings containing in the different sections. Though originally published as journal articles, in their separate book form they succeed in their attempt to divulge knowledge specific to the field as well as backing up his ideas on the topic via thorough critical texts and a specific language code, namely analytical drawings. As with many other modern architectural books, "production and reproduction were two sides of the same coin, and print was the medium of communication, both within the profession and with a wider audience. The industrial aesthetic became as intrinsic an aspect of the design of architectural books as it was for buildings. These two moments, [...] confront us with the rise of the industrialised book (and the editor) and the configuration of the book as a unique visual device (with the designer taking part in a complex chain of decision making)".[42]

The fresh knowledge contained in both books forms not only starting point, but also a point of arrival: first, they allow the Danish voice on the housing question (mainly Fisker's) heard within the international debate; second, Danish planning ventures and housing policies during the interwar-period are discussed and implemented by frontline operators; and third, we get a glimpse of the educational method adopted by Fisker within the broader Danish teaching reform. The blend of education and architectural practice has not been studied in detail, making publication both timely and much-needed.

There have of course been some valid monographic studies of the architect (largely in Danish), chiefly historical in orientation (1960),[43] and a fresh new thorough analysis of Fisker's ideas and thoughts (2021) in English.[44] From the Danish critical milieu there are also some relevant books of group papers (1965 and 1995)[45] on the occasion of exhibitions in Nordic towns, and also the catalogue of the exhibition *Kay Fisker. Københavnske boligtyper* (1993)[46] celebrating the centenary of the Danish architect through a display of the original drawings of 19 housing buildings dating between 1918 and 1945. There have been a handful of special issues including some from outside the home borders,[47] some papers by foreign critics in the 1960s and 1980s (mainly German, Italian, Swiss and American) who tended to praise his leading role in the transition and housing production, and in recent years a very few doctoral theses largely outside Denmark. Add to this some recent instances of articles proposing a new look at the literature on certain projects in light of the returning issue of densely compact cities[48] both in practice and in academic realms. Kay Fisker's output, and his approach to town planning, have here proved a source of instruction and interest to a number of design studios/ateliers which have found that the Copenhagen experience rewarded their "research by design" approach.[49] Nevertheless, to date there has been no in-depth study on these 1936 and 1941 analyses or on the activity of the Fisker *Bolig Klasse*.

Evidently, Fisker was an architect who monopolised attention much more at home than abroad, where other Danes figured more prominently. Yet he left his mark on many generations of Danish architects, and this surely merits attention and contextualisation such as he has not yet received. Today, we appreciate Fisker's determination in drawing up a major overview of the housing question, the enduring validity of which is one of the reasons behind the present publication of the English facsimile translation. 1924 was precisely the year when he embarked on the *Bolig Klasse* and, therefore this publication aims to celebrate the legacy of Fisker's commitment one hundred years later. He considered the multifaceted housing topic of "great value in terms of knowledge of the purpose and nature of the buildings".[50]

Dissemination of ideas

Københavnske Boligtyper, a detailed study supervised by Fisker, has its place in a research path blazed ten years earlier by Steen Eiler Rasmussen. Fisker himself said he initially intended to embed a re-print of the Rasmussen overview in its entirety[51] within his own 1936 analysis, so important did he believe its multidisciplinary perspective and its undeniable status as a starting point. He went on to say that he abandoned the idea after talking to his colleague about the new editorial projects stemming from years of research conducted during his course *Boligbyggeri*. Fisker's survey differs from its counterpart in illustrating four fully completed projects at the four moments indicated, and its in-depth analysis based on a wealth of newly available information and the tool of analytical design.

In 1926, the critical mouthpiece of *Architekten*[52] again accorded space to Rasmussen's report on the decade of construction after the war (1918–1928) – although that decade had not yet ended nor had actual building of what had been planned been completed, for which reason it is generally, but somewhat incorrectly, referred to as the *Statsboligfond* period (State Housing Fund). Helped by three academy students, A. C. Gravesen, Henri Garrigues and Helge Finsen, Rasmussen sought to give some preliminary order to a mass of miscellaneous quantitative and graphic information. He confessed to some difficulty in finding and presenting the data in a clear and readable way; data on constructional and economic aspects, distribution of apartments in the city and types of rent, density of blocks within the urban fabric, types of apartment and their layout. The material is supported by a number of building analysis schemas and an urban map marking the sites of enclosed residential blocks built as entire units (classified according to the number of storeys). When comparing Rasmussen's map with Fisker's (See p. 115, whereas p. 31 of the separate book), the increase in multi-apartment building constructions over the time-span of 10 years is evident.

One needs to know that this retrospective look at the period's building activity was not confined to publications, but included back-up material for the exhibition *Bygge– og Boligudstilling* (Building and Housing Exhibition) held at the Academic Architects' Association[53] on 19th–28th February 1926. More significant still, it marked the first time that thoughts on the housing question were expressed by the *Akademisk Architektforening*, unlike the past when "similar exhibitions were organised in a random way as consortia, whose only positive result was profit for the benefit of the organisers".[54] Coinciding with the days of the exhibition was an intense calendar of meetings attended by many association members, of which Rasmussen's lecture, *Byplaner og Boligvilkaar* (City Plans and Housing Conditions) was a noteworthy event.[55] The curators and members of the association sensed people's difficulty in responding to that unprecedentedly grave problem; the efforts of some colleagues in the sector were not yet backed by the convinced collective spirit needed to organise rapid measures geared towards a solution.

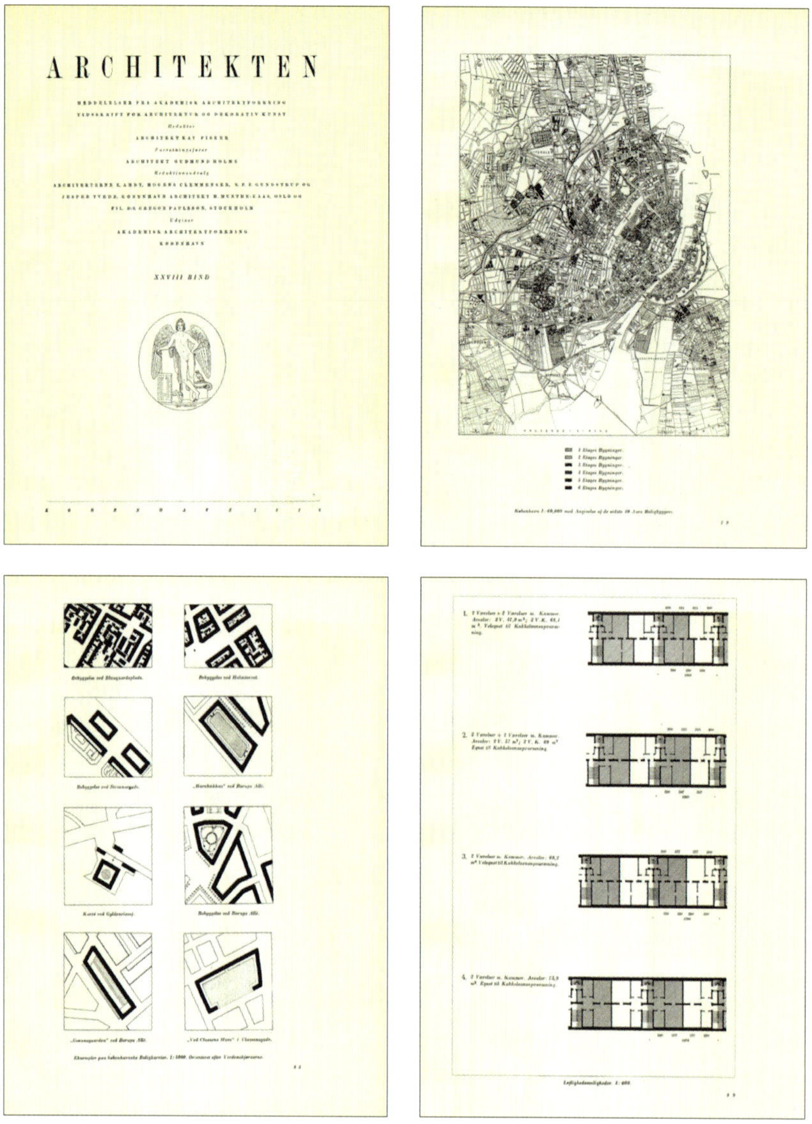

Cover of *Architekten Maanedshaefte* and samples of Rasmussen paper (1926), for example the Copenhagen map. The diagram bottom left displays: *Hornbækhus* by Fisker, *Vigerslev Allé* by H. Hansen, *Borups Plad* by Fisker, *Grønnegården-Borups Allé* by P. Baumann, *Ved Classens Have* by C. Petersen and P. Nielsen

The topic addressed by Rasmussen and other members of the association clearly intended to pave the way for the future, showing the public their sincere sense of responsibility towards the common weal. Such material sought to exert a "beneficial and stimulating effect on the mood within the construction world and thereby contribute to its various forces being set in motion".[56] Apart from the analytical and graphic material that Rasmussen and his students displayed, the *Building and Housing Exhibition* was an opportunity to show drawings, sketches, models and photos of projects completed or being planned by professors and architects of the institute, as well as items of furniture and equipment.[57]

The exhibition material was not confined to the Nordic milieu, but attracted German interest and especially that of the Ernst Wasmuth Publishing House. The latter invited the Danish organisers to attend at Berlin (11th September – 9th October 1926) as part of a far more widely divulgative framework[58] which had previously featured prominent examples of exhibition concept as proposed in 1924 by the German architect and professor Peter Behrens (1868–1940) along with the students of his course at the *Akademie der Bildende Künste* in Vienna.[59] "It gives a more richly faceted picture than an ordinary exhibition: one sees how the rays of the gifted artist's talent are refracted in the perception of the young students".[60] The exhibition was an integral part of the course in atelier form and became an ongoing event yearly enriched by new material (plans and models) rotating in venue (Berlin, London, Essen, Mannheim, Hamburg and New York) over the timespan 1924–1930. Following Behrens' lead, the Danish exhibition displayed works of prominent younger figures who were destined to become the leading architects of their country in years to come. Besides professors Ivar Bentsen, Kaj Gottlob, Edvard Thomsen, Vilhelm Wanscher, municipal landscape designer professor G. N. Brandt as well as the architects Kaare Klint, Kay Fisker and Steen Eiler Rasmussen, "the vast majority [...] are student workers, for the most part selected by last year's school exhibition".[61] German appraisals on critical journals referred to "a sober objectivity in the modern spirit", "an unaffected but self-confident simplicity", "houses which grow naturally out of the landscape"; they wrote about "the architects' lack of keenness to experiment", but also "an avoidance of architectural licentiousness", and ultimately "a strict and sure taste", which some of the experts found "cold right to the innermost heart" whilst others regarded it as "salutary like an old and timeless tradition".[62] Nevertheless, a few comments were somewhat disparaging: certain German critics pointed out the lack of experimentation showing how Scandinavia lagged behind the rest of Europe in architectural development.

The following year the debate on how to tackle the local housing shortage with architectural and planning tools took another step forward at the *Nordisk Byggnadsdag* (Nordic Building Days) in Stockholm – the first of a long series.[63] There, many architects, urban planners and engineers met to pool their answers to urban design and building, and learnt from each other's experience through lectures and an exhibition of already implemented housing projects in Nordic cities.[64] The *Nordisk Byggnadsdag* held in June 1927 was a platform for exclusively Nordic circles, unlike the exhibition that was to open at Stuttgart in July of the same year, the *Weissenhofsiedlung* Building Exhibition (visited by many Nordic architects) which gained huge international resonance. Nevertheless, the three-day event in Stockholm and many other local initiatives reflected a no waiting-on-the-side-line approach, although their geographical position often marginalised their impact on the awareness of the wider world. Theirs was far from the role of a backwater on the fringe of circles active in the European debate; Nordic delegations participated in foreign conferences and younger architects made many trips abroad from which they reported to the pages of critical Nordic journals on the state of the art, migration of ideas and project innovations.

Among the many conference accounts of the Nordic Building Days we should remember Fisker's paper, entitled *Københavnske boligtyper* (Copenhagen housing types).[65] There, the Danish architect outlined the downsides and improvements in the residential construction sector during the ten years of state control and went on to discuss seven examples from the 1919–1925 time-frame: three designed by him (Borups Plad, Hornbækhus and Jagtgaarden), two by Povl Baumann (Grønnegården-Borups Allé, 1923 and Struenseegade, 1918–1920), and one each by Johannes Strøm Tejesen (Prinsesses Charlottesgade, 1917–1918), Henning Hansen (Vigerslev Allé, 1918–1920), Carl Petersen and Peter Nielsen (Ved Classens Have, 1924–1925).[66] His account was supported by morphological diagrams of some building blocks within the urban fabric – this comparative plate derived from the above-mentioned 1926 Rasmussen article –, a whole typological assemblage of floor plans, some pictures and dwelling types.

Fisker had mixed feelings about the *Statsboligfond period* (1918–1928): "public supervision has enabled a number of improvements in housing and living conditions, which by private means would hardly have been implemented. On the other hand, such public intervention has functioned in many respects as a straitjacket, forcing a degree of uniformity on construction [...leading] to complete stagnation in the evolution of housing form. [...] Although the housing types themselves have thus generally remained at a proven and solid stage, if not entirely on a par with the other developments of the time, on the other hand, in many other areas such as the main forms of the buildings, a number of improvements have been obtained, just as the authorities' design requirements have also led to actual, qualified architects coming to work on this construction process, which was previously largely designed and built by craftsmen and contractors without the assistance of architects".[67]

His presentation at the first *Nordisk Byggnadsdag* gives some clue to the direction his research (and design) method was taking during the previous years. In reading that analysis, one is forcibly struck by the link with the rich book to be published in 1936, which was one of the points of arrival after many years' research at the Royal Academy. *Københavnske boligtyper* was, remember, the outcome of the fruitful debates with Rasmussen, whose interest in housing Fisker shared, and even more of the 1927 event held three years after Fisker's *Boligbyggeri* course began.

Again in 1927, in May to be precise, an exhibition arranged at the R.I.B.A. in London turned the spotlight on the production of the last couple of decades under the heading of *Modern Danish architecture*.
Intent on reforming the A.A. Architectural Association, British photographer F. R. Yerbury (1885–1970) and architectural historian Howard Robertson (1888–1963) documented a broad range of landmarks in modern architecture thanks to their field trips (1925–1930) around Europe and the USA. Such journeys also spawned collaborative ventures with architects and critics or universities in the countries they visited. One such was with Rasmussen who was a visiting lecturer at the A.A. Architectural Association for a few months in 1927.[68]

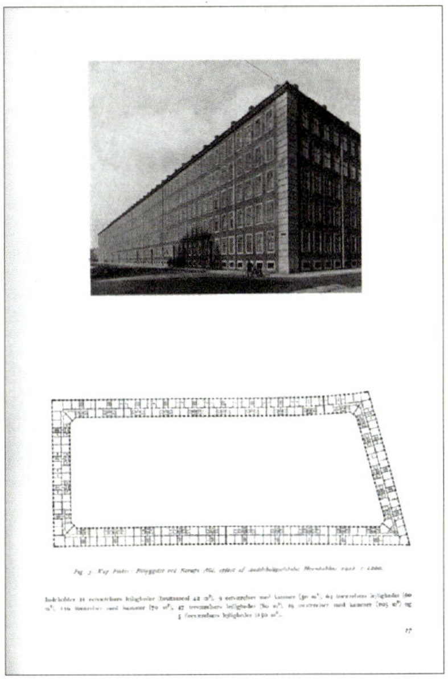

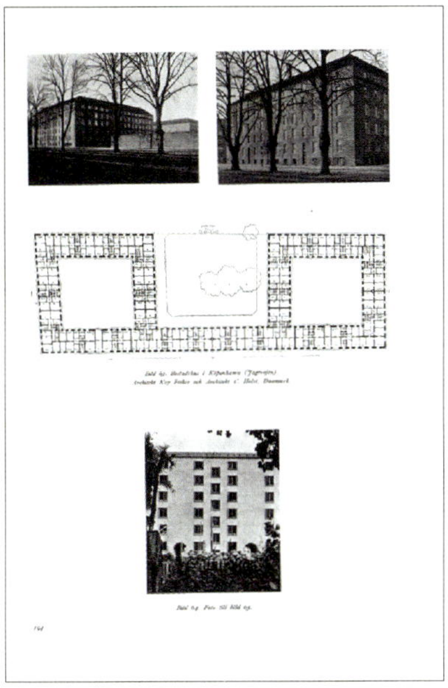

Nordiska Byggnadsdag proceeedings' book cover and some examples illustrated in Fisker's 1927 account. Clockwise order: *Prinsesses Charlottesgade* by Johannes Strøm Tejesen; *Jagtgaarden* and *Hornbækhus* by Fisker

While the 1926 exhibition in Berlin focused both on completed construction projects and on works from the Danish schools of architecture, the English one spotlighted only 179 finished buildings illustrated by drawings, photos and architectural models. The event[69] was accompanied by a catalogue, *Modern Danish architecture* (1927), curated by Kay Fisker and Aage Rafn (1890–1953). In the preface Yerbury praised their enviable excellence in domestic architecture as good design and taste are often their main concern.[70] Unlike the Swedish counterpart *Swedish Architecture of the Twentieth Century*,[71] here the visual apparatus also included three large housing perimeter blocks, respectively designed by Peder Vilhelm Jensen-Klint (På Bjerget low-rise complex around the Grundtvig church, 1924–1926), Povl Baumann (Struenseegade block, 1918–1920) and Henning Hansen (Vigerslev Allé block, 1918-1920). Pictures and ground floor plans of the entire blocks illustrated the projects also in the catalogue.[72]

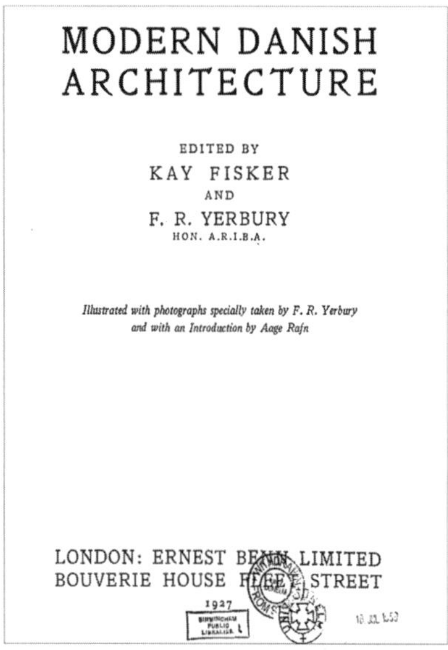
MODERN DANISH ARCHITECTURE

EDITED BY
KAY FISKER
AND
F. R. YERBURY
HON. A.R.I.B.A.

Illustrated with photographs specially taken by F. R. Yerbury and with an Introduction by Aage Rafn

LONDON: ERNEST BENN LIMITED
BOUVERIE HOUSE FLEET STREET
1927

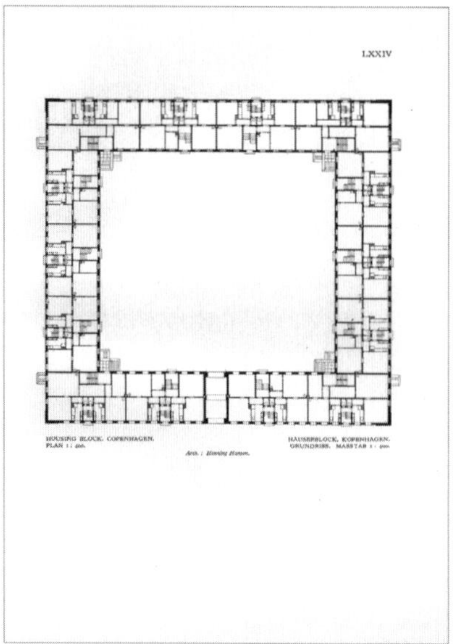

Covers of English version of the volume *Modern Danish architecture* (1927) and some sample pages. Clockwise order: photo and plans of Hansen housing block and a Baumann *Struenseegade* block

The broad resonance of that publication caused Werner Hegemann (1881–1936), city planner, critic and editor of the journal "Wasmuths Monatshefte für Baukunst und Städtebau" (1924–1933),[73] to bring out a German translation, *Moderne Dänische Architektur* in facsimile layout.

The friendship and critical exchange between the Danish spokesman Rasmussen and Hegemann "facilitated a liaison that resulted in numerous articles on Nordic topics in the German Wasmuth's periodicals"[74]

and also in other publications in subsequent years. We may here cite the article published by Rasmussen in 1928[75] in the German journal where he praises Fisker's ability to confer distinctive character on each of the residential buildings. "[…] the floor plan shows an almost military-style order: one and the same apartment is repeated in a simple sequence. The design of the exterior corresponds to this simple arrangement […]. Fisker was one of those pioneering leaders in Denmark who started building large blocks of flats without any protrusions and with the same windows in endless rows. His last work shows how far one can get with the simplest means: there is only an undivided block with window openings, which is effective through its building material and the relief of the facade".[76]

Out of the many residential buildings commissioned, Rasmussen chose three blocks that had been finished by that time: Glænøgaard (1923–1927), Amagerbo (1924–1926) and Gullfosshus (1924–1927), which are fully documented with drawings and photographs.
In 1929, Hegemann invited Kay Fisker to the *Nordische Architektur der Gegenwart* – held in Kiel's Thaulow-Museum (15th June–15th July) within the larger event named *Nordisch-Deutsche Woche für Kunst und Wissenschaft* – to curate the Danish section of the most representative architectures. Of course, room was also found for him to present some recent designs of his own, including the Vodroffsvej project produced in tandem with C.F. Møller.[77] Hegemann's familiarity and fascination with the Danish setting would lead him to include as many as seven residential projects, five of them by Fisker, in his richly photographic sketch-book of 500 examples entitled *Façades of Buildings. Fronts of Old and Modern Business and Dwelling Houses* (1929).[78] Other 1930s articles in the German magazine included a report on Royal Academy teaching courses written by Otto Brendel[79] and a brief account of two Fisker never-built residential projects in row arrangements (*siedlung*) penned by Hegemann himself.[80]

The local residential output was largely publicised through conferences and international debates on the topic of housing and town planning organised during the interwar period, where the Danish contingent (somewhat outnumbered) presented their latest projects and solutions. One example is the turnout for the conference held in Berlin in 1931[81] by the organisation IFHTP. This was a broad-ranging conference with many sessions, debates and exhibitions, the focus being on the *Internationaler Verband für Wohnungswesen* (International Housing Association) venture promoted by secretary Franz Schuster who had invited "architects and engineers of various countries that have been endeavouring with success not only to raise the standard of dwellings, but also to lower the building cost".[82]

Among the projects ancillary to the programme of seminars, Fisker's certainly stood out. What caught the eye especially were the two typological synoptic plates (1:100) showing the architectural type development: on the one hand, twelve plans of multi-storey blocks built mainly by the cooperative KAB spanning from an early example dated 1890 to eleven modern ones (1921–1935)[83] and, on the other hand, three plans of terraced houses from 1890, 1922 and 1932. On a more detailed scale (1:20) there followed an in-depth illustration of the Østergården block (1929–1932)[84] designed by Fisker in collaboration with C. F. Møller.

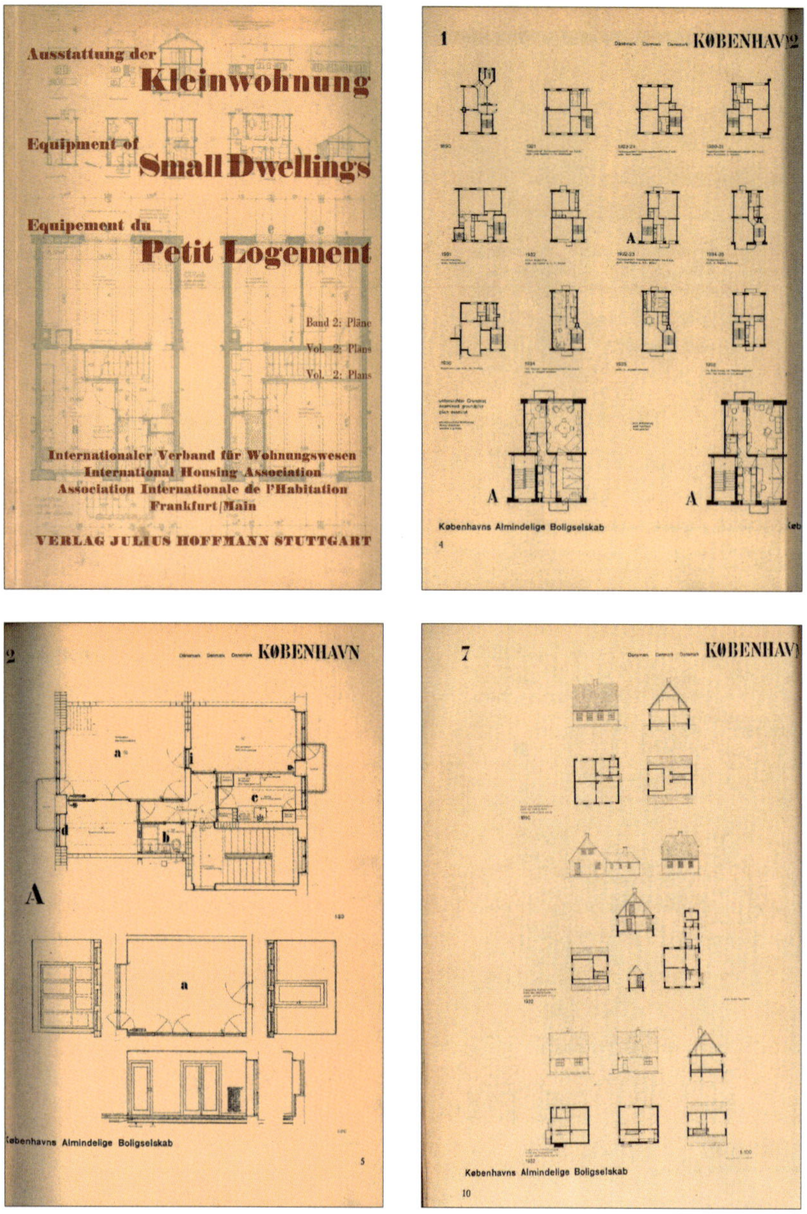

Cover of the catalogue *Ausstattung der Kleinwohnung / Equipment for small dwellings / Equipement du petit logement* and a selection of pages illustrating dwelling samples for multi-apartment blocks and row houses

This event led to a synergic exchange among the group concerned with housing within the IFHTP, and prompted Schuster a few years later to republish the above-mentioned German translation of an extract from *Københavnske Boligtyper en oversight* in 1937.

In the North, meanwhile, came the moment for the Second *Nordisk Byggnadsdag*, held in Helsinki in 1932. There, Fisker was not a speaker, but in the exhibition a very large space was given to many recent housing interventions by him and others, illustrated by detailed drawings on different scales and pictures.[85]

The Danish section within the conference exhibition showed eight examples of multi-storey buildings mainly in the form of large courtyard blocks, but also four terraced houses and three single-family/cottage houses.[86] Side by side with some completed buildings were a few tables drawn up by his *Bolig Klasse* – plainly showing that such material was a real tool of transference of architectural ideas on par with completed buildings themselves.

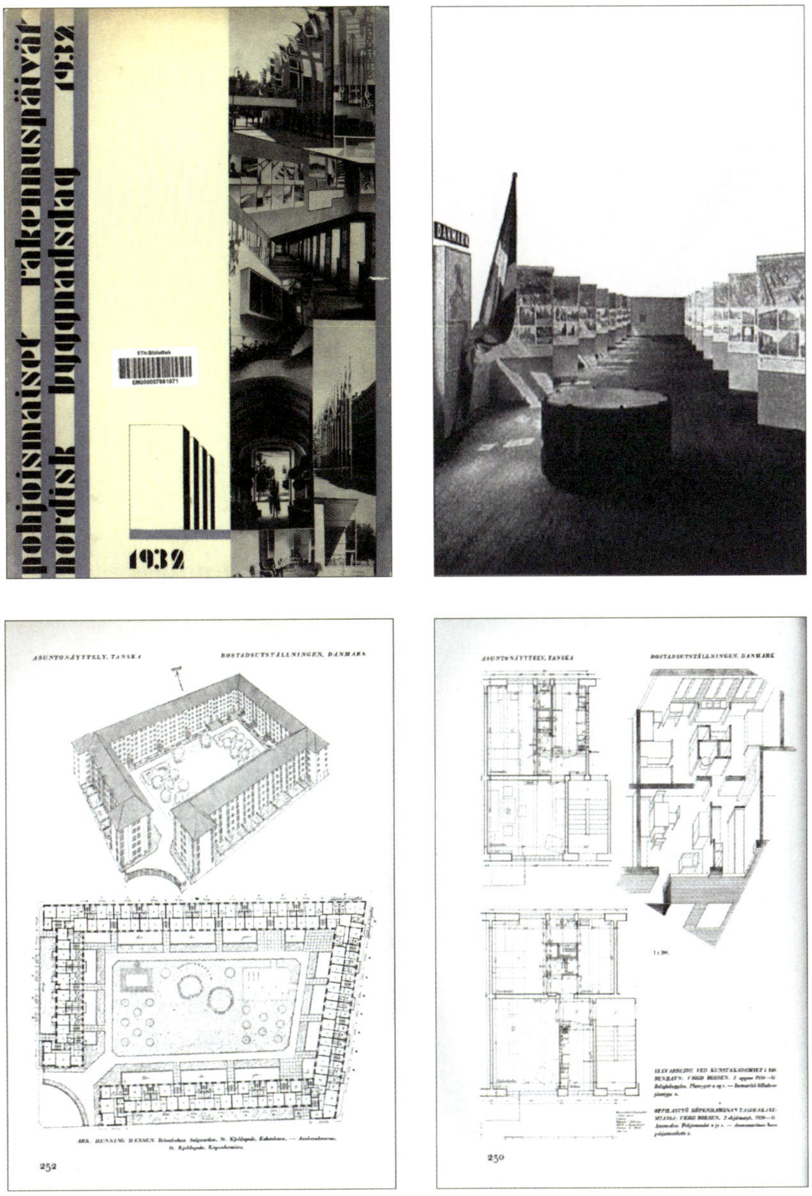

Proceedings book cover of the Second *Nordisk Byggnadsdag* (1932) and a selection of pages. Clockwise order: exhibition galleries, students' work from Fisker's class and the courtyard block *Solgaarden* (1929) by Henning Hansen and C. Th. Sørensen

At the conference exhibition, some Nordic architectural works were displayed with similar techniques emulating the standardised German presentation by means of plans and diagrams, such as the one that Ernst May used at the second CIAM *Die Wohnung für das Existenzminimum* exhibition in Frankfurt.[87]

A few years later we see Fisker again shining at the third *Nordisk Bygningsdag* held in Oslo in 1938. More than ten years after the first presentation of the series at Stockholm, he lost no opportunity to pursue a subject of which he was a profound connoisseur. Though his contribution limits the typological scope of the analysis – *etagehuset* –, it greatly increases the geographical coverage of works produced in those last two decades. In his paper *Etageboligens udvikling i de seneste aar* (Development of multi-storey buildings in recent years)[88] alongside three cases of different types (*Halvlukket karré*: semi-closed block; *Stokkebebyggelse*: parallel block buildings; *Blokbebyggelse*: rows of block buildings) from Copenhagen (i.e. Ved Classens Have by Carl Petersen and Peter Nielsen, 1924–1925; Boparken by Thorvald Dreyer, 1933; Storgaarden by Povl Baumann and Knud Hansen, 1936) we find examples from Stockholm (Kungsklippan by Sven Wallander and H.S.B. housing cooperative, 1935), London (Highgate by Berthold Lubetkin and Tecton, 1935), Rotterdam (Bergpolder by Johannes A. Brinkmann and Leendert C. van der Vlugt, 1930–1935), Paris (Cité de la Muette à Drancy by Eugène Beaudoin and Marcel Lods, 1932–1936) and New York (Sunlight Towers by Lawrence Kocher and Gerhard Ziegler, 1937).

Concise though it is, the paper covers architectural/planning aspects as well as technological/economic ones, providing an eloquent tribute to the lasting relevance of multi-storey buildings, including arguments concerning density, planning, construction costs and techniques, etc.. Stylistic considerations are deliberately played down, if not omitted. "Despite all the efforts, it will probably be a long time before the low-rise houses can economically compete with the tall buildings. For the time being, the multi-storey housing will still exist as an economic compromise solution and, [...] as urban formations are shaped, will continue to be a natural form of housing in the big city".[89]

Fisker does point out the positive features of various experimental variations on the multi-storey house format. Basically, changes to the stereotypically obsolete form typical of the congested block brought an enlargement of the courtyard (*lukkede karré* and *halvlukkede karré*) and real hygienic improvements to dwellings, as well as providing common spaces and facilities (central heating, machine laundry, vacuum cleaner room, vegetable gardens, etc.), though modern-minded architects tended to frown on the system and preferred the north-south settlement (*lamelbebyggelser*).

Later on, intermediate forms of experimentation that were less "schematic and monotonous [until] one is tired of this military march of uniform rows of bars"[90] were introduced in open-air areas, anticipating the trends of later decades for setting residential estates in peripheral areas of "heterogeneous and picturesque character".[91]

Experimentation would also extend to the basic unit of the estate: the same dwelling layout might efficiently form the typological floor of tall buildings around one or multiple staircases as in certain foreign building plans that Fisker studied and presented. One example is Le Corbusier's *Ville Radieuse*, "which is a lyrical and imaginative project, perhaps at the moment unreal, but which stands for me (Fisker) as one of the strongest expressions of the development that the multi-storey buildings will undergo in the time to come".[92]

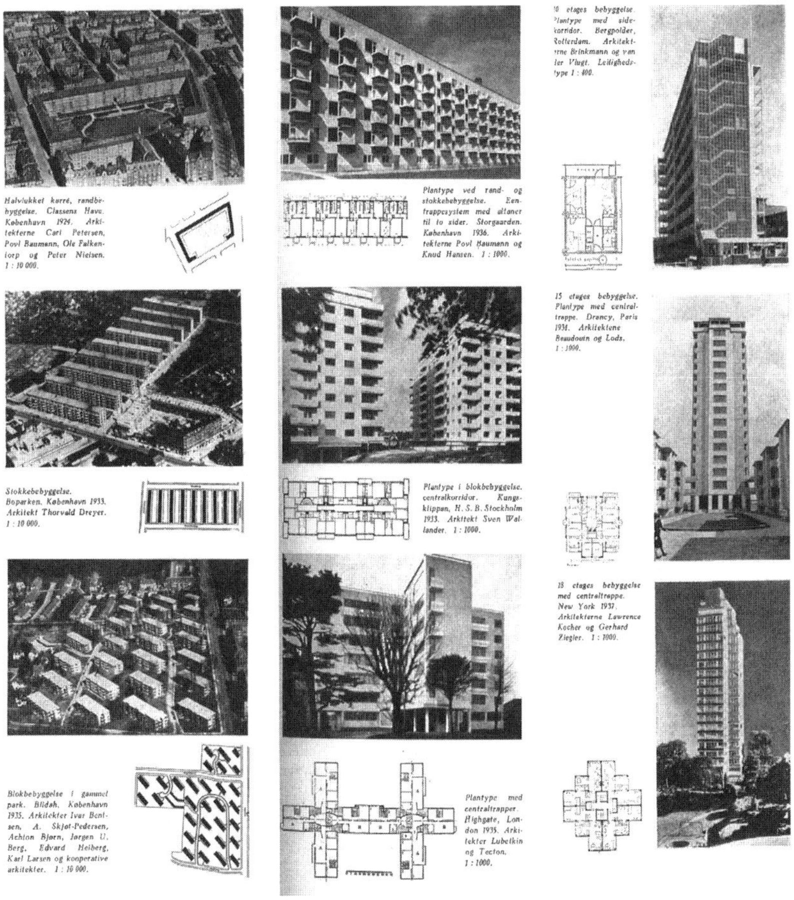

Selection of images from *Etageboligens udvikling i de seneste aar* (1938)

In 1938, the same year as the conference in Oslo, Denmark took another step forward, introducing a new town planning law (*Byplanloven*) and new reforms that brought rent reductions for families with many children. We are now close to the Second World War, but for Denmark (and all the Nordic countries) the most difficult years of the housing crisis were behind them. Though there was a lull in the conferences and travelling by which ideas and hands-on experience circulated, Denmark's status as German protectorate at first enabled the country to go ahead with building new residential areas. In the general climate of uncertainty with war looming, the number of housing units being created was lower than in previous years. Occupation, when it came, brought the building market to a standstill and caused a new and acute housing shortage in the post-war period. The rest of Europe was almost at a halt with experiments in planning and housing, though "Arkitektur" still featured new projects. However, the destruction of Danish towns was relatively limited, and when Marshall Plan aid arrived, things quickly resumed where they had left off. The Nordic countries emerged into the international limelight as inspiring models for social and architectural values, where new models of neighbourhoods developing in areas of suburban expansion embodied one of the central aspects of welfare state programmes. In such a framework, though other young Danish architects were present on the national and international scene – one thinks of two pupils, Arne Jacobsen (1902–1971) and Jørn Utzon (1918–2008)[93] –, Fisker was still seen as referential figure. His knowledge of the housing issue grew over the ensuing years, as did the awareness that housing history needed to be studied if one was to come up with valid new forms of accommodation suited to modern society.

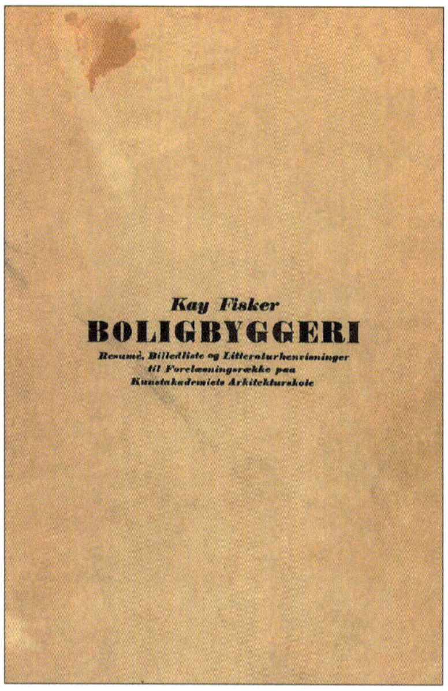

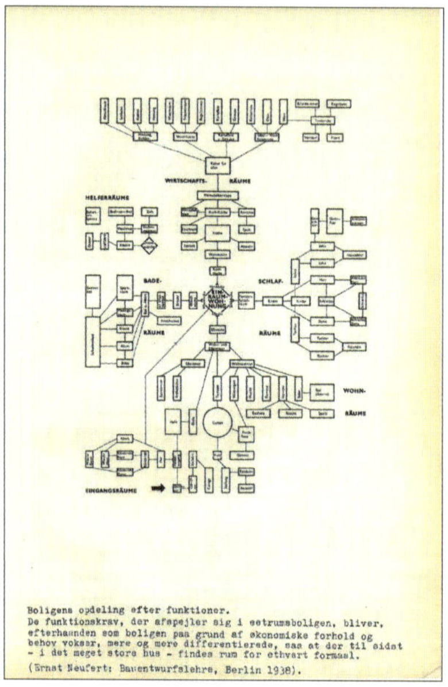

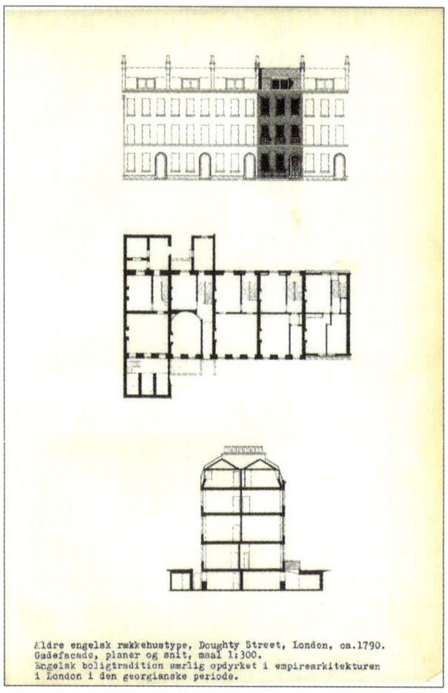

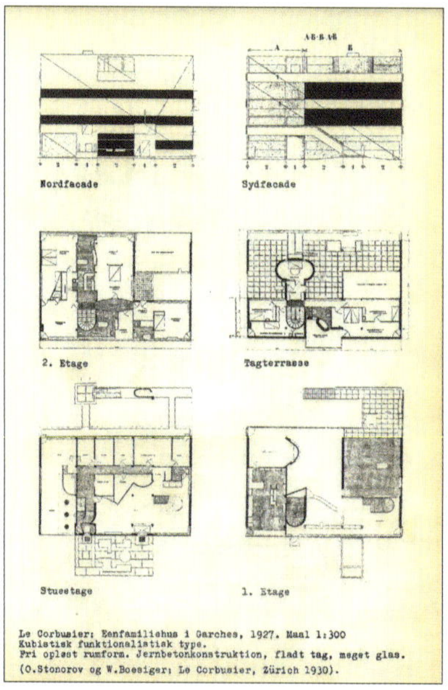

Cover and some plates from *Boligbyggeri* (1946–1947) lecture note book. Clockwise order: Neufert diagram published in *Bauentwurfslehre* (1936), plans and elevations of *Villa Stein* by Le Corbusier and of a typical English late-eighteenth-century terraced house

From the 1940s onwards he amassed collections of lectures notes of the *Bolig Klasse* covering many topics, and he printed copies of them in handout form (sadly not yet translated into English)[94] free of charges for the students. The collected editions still in existence show the rich content and fine editing organisation typical of Fisker. The principal objective is giving students a clear idea of architecture's role in the overall structure of society.[95] That mission, to hand on knowledge is also found in the more carefully composed publications we have mentioned, and is a central theme in this preface to the translation of the 1936 and 1941 surveys.

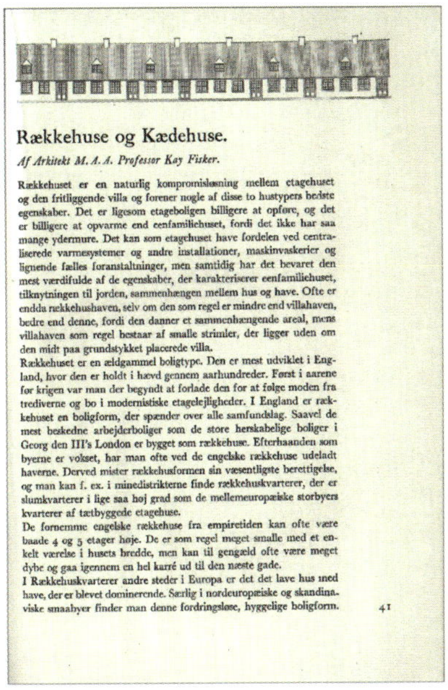
Rækkehuse og Kædehuse.

Af Arkitekt M. A. A. Professor Kay Fisker.

Rækkehuset er en naturlig kompromisløsning mellem etagehuset og den fritliggende villa og forener nogle af disse to hustypers bedste egenskaber. Det er ligesom etageboligen billigere at opføre, og det er billigere at opvarme end eenfamiliehuset, fordi det ikke har saa mange ydermure. Det kan som etagehuset have fordelen ved centraliserede varmesystemer og andre installationer, maskinvaskerier og lignende fælles foranstaltninger, men samtidig har det bevaret den mest værdifulde af de egenskaber, der karakteriserer eenfamiliehuset, tilknytningen til jorden, sammenhængen mellem hus og have. Ofte er endda rækkehushaven, selv om den som regel er mindre end villahaven, bedre end denne, fordi den danner et sammenhængende areal, mens villahaven som regel bestaar af smalle strimler, der ligger uden om den midt paa grundstykket placerede villa.
Rækkehuset er en ældgammel boligtype. Den er mest udviklet i England, hvor den er holdt i hævd gennem aarhundreder. Først i aarene før krigen var man der begyndt at forlade den for at følge moden fra trediverne og bo i modernistiske etagelejligheder. I England er rækkehuset en boligform, der spænder over alle samfundslag. Saavel de mest beskedne arbejderboliger som de store herskabelige boliger i Georg den III's London er bygget som rækkehuse. Efterhaanden som byerne er vokset, har man ofte ved de engelske rækkehuse udeladt haverne. Derved mister rækkehusformen sin væsentligste berettigelse, og man kan f. ex. i minedistrikterne finde rækkehuskvarterer, der er slumkvarterer i lige saa høj grad som de mellemeuropæiske storbyers kvarterer af tætbyggede etagehuse.
De fornemme engelske rækkehuse fra empiretiden kan ofte være baade 4 og 5 etager høje. De er som regel meget smalle med et enkelt værelse i husets bredde, men kan til gengæld ofte være meget dybe og gaa igennem en hel karré ud til den næste gade.
I Rækkehuskvarterer andre steder i Europa er det det lave hus med have, der er blevet dominerende. Særlig i nordeuropæiske og skandinaviske smaabyer finder man denne fordringsløse, hyggelige boligform.

41

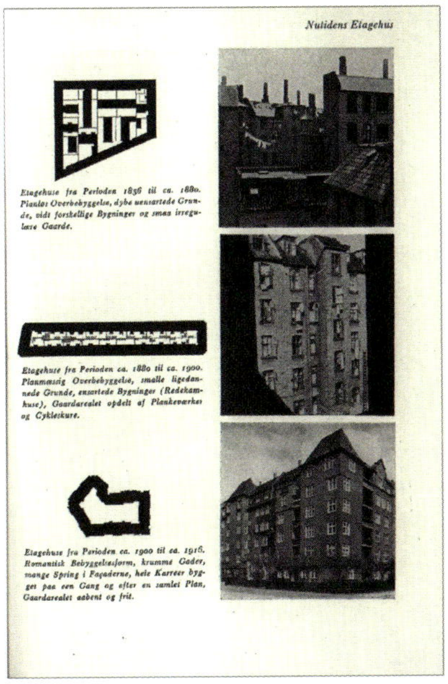

Cover book and a selection of pages from *Huset i Byen* (1945). Clockwise order: two pages from Fisker's account and one page from Rasmussen's text

Perhaps of all the lecture collections the one entitled *Boligbyggeri* (Housing, winter semester 1946–1947)[96] gives the best idea of the range of housing know-how he passed on, and his method of observing the issue and providing a valid series of toolkits for tackling the question. He supervised the copyright of the detailed lecture handouts, but unfortunately not the proofreading of the integration because he was in the USA., and the Academy office carried out the duplication and bookbinding work.[97]
The collection is divided by themes: techniques-materials-functions, forms of housing type and settlement. Each section is briefly summarised and then illustrated by a miscellaneous collage of images of the widest-ranging kind (taken from larger sets of slides he projected in the lecture hall).

The broad spectrum of knowledge (spanning centuries and continents) draws the students' attention to house designs that have never really changed over time or across cultures: designs that have stayed the course, sometimes hybridising with local traditions as well as socio-economic and climate patterns.[98] Each section ends with a selected bibliography of books, journals and manuals from Denmark and abroad. And at the end of the coursebook, there is an extensive bibliography arranged by country.

In a nutshell, the *Boligbyggeri* lecture handout encapsulates a twofold target: on the one hand, it sums up the learning guidelines and, on the other hand, it becomes an indispensable source on the students' desk during the elaboration of the two design assignments.

At the same time as he was putting together his lessons, Fisker took part in a popular radio programme promoted by the *Akademisk Arkitekforening*, joined by some long-standing colleagues and assistants.[99] This once again confirmed the "pedagogical thrust"[100] the Danish professors outside the academia circles and of the same architects' association, which sought to sensitise local people on the important issue of housing and the town. In 1945 that radio venture, accompanied by in-depth notes on the historical development of architectural types, was published as a catalogue to the exhibition the association mounted, under the title *Huset i byen. købstadsboligen Etagehuset Enfamiliehuset* (The house in the city. The city residence, the storey house, the single-family house). On that occasion Fisker focused on *Rækkehuse og kædehuse* (Row houses and Chain row houses), fresh from the detailed analysis he and his students had performed in 1941 survey,[101] while his colleague Rasmussen concentrated on *Nutidens Etagehus* (Today's block of flats). Times and residential building practice were changing in Denmark as elsewhere, and this change is reflected in Fisker's own wording, in line with the hints contained in *Om rækkehuse, kamhuse, kædehuse og andere huse*. "Inside modern urban building and construction technology, the development has given low buildings and tall multi-storey building of 10-12 floors the most opportunities. One must therefore expect that in the city of the future, the medium-rise buildings that now dominate will come to play a lesser role, and the very tall and the very low house types will dominate the cityscape".[102]

In 1946, after almost twenty years of research and courses at the Royal Academy, Fisker was invited to make his own critical contribution to the monumental comprehensive and photographic documentation of contemporary Danish domestic design including buildings, interiors, furniture, lamps and fabrics as well as glass, ceramic and silverware, etc.), entitled *Moderne dansk boligkunst* (Modern Danish Housing Art). In his essay *Boligens former* (Forms of housing)[103] he stressed that, although Danish architecture had gone in for a futuristic "liberated line", the legacy of Danish form and building tradition, responding to climatic and topographical conditions, would inevitably go on influencing the way the North built.

Moderne
DANSK
BOLIGKUNST

Redigeret af
SIGVARD BERNADOTTE
og
JOHS. LEHM-LAURSEN

SKANDINAVISK BOGFORLAG
ODENSE 1946

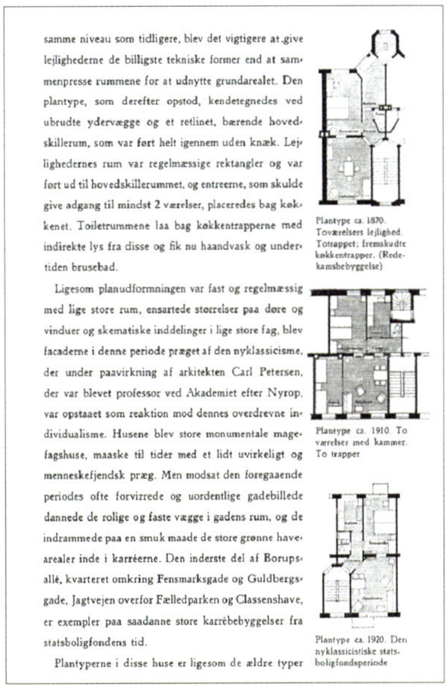

samme niveau som tidligere, blev det vigtigere at give lejlighederne de billigste tekniske former end at sammenpresse rummene for at udnytte grundarealet. Den plantype, som derefter opstod, kendetegnedes ved ubrudte ydervægge og et retlinet, bærende hovedskillerum, som var ført helt igennem uden knæk. Lejlighedernes rum var regelmæssige rektangler og var ført ud til hovedskillerummet, og entreerne, som skulde give adgang til mindst 2 værelser, placeredes bag køkkenet. Toiletrummene laa bag køkkentrapperne med indirekte lys fra disse og fik nu haandvask og undertiden brusebad.

Ligesom planudformningen var fast og regelmæssig med lige store rum, ensartede størrelser paa døre og vinduer og skematiske inddelinger i lige store fag, blev facaderne i denne periode præget af den nyklassicisme, der under paavirkning af arkitekten Carl Petersen, der var blevet professor ved Akademiet efter Nyrop, var opstaaet som reaktion mod dennes overdrevne individualisme. Husene blev store monumentale magefagshuse, maaske til tider med et lidt uvirkeligt og menneskefjendsk præg. Men modsat den foregaaende periodes ofte forvirrede og uordentlige gadebillede dannede de rolige og faste vægge i gadens rum, og de indrammede paa en smuk maade de store grønne havearealer inde i karréerne. Den inderste del af Borupsallé, kvarteret omkring Fensmarksgade og Guldbergsgade, Jagtvejen overfor Fælledparken og Classenshave, er exempler paa saadanne store karrébebyggelser fra statsboligfondens tid.

Plantyperne i disse huse er ligesom de ældre typer

Plantype ca. 1870. Toværelsers lejlighed. Totrappet; fremskudte køkkentrapper. (Redekamsbebyggelse)

Plantype ca. 1910. To værelser med kammer. To trapper

Plantype ca. 1920. Den nyklassicistiske statsboligfondsperiode

baseret paa 2-trappesystemet, men behovet for køkkentrapperne, hvis væsentligste berettigelse, udover brandsikringen, var transporten af brændsel til kakkelovnene og nedbæring af skarnkasseaffald, forsvandt i nogen grad med indførelsen af centralvarmeanlæg og nedfaldsskakte. I slutningen af tyverne blev der derfor i lighed med hvad der var almindeligt i vore nabolande opnaaet adgang til at opføre 5—6 etages huse med kun een trappe, naar husene forsynedes med brandaltaner. Denne ordning lovfæstedes i Københavns nye byggelov, der blev vedtaget i 1939 og revolutionerede i mange henseender boligbyggeriet. Der blev nu helt andre muligheder for en friere planudformning end tidligere, og de nye planer kom i ret høj grad til at afvige fra de traditionelle boligtyper. Altanerne, som oprindeligt var en brandsikring, blev efterhaanden en gevinst for lejlighederne. De blev værdifulde opholdspladser i det fri og blev saa populære, at man ogsaa anbragte dem paa huse, som ikke efter loven krævede dem. Samtidig med at altanerne paa en naturlig maade accentuerede facaderne, blev hele den ydre uformning præget af funktionalismens udtryksfuldhed, der ligesom Nyroptiden krævede ærlighed, det ydre skulde udtrykke det indre. Men medens Nyrop og hans skole arbejdede æstetisk med denne „ærlighed", kastede man nu i mange tilfælde — paavirket af Weimarrepublikkens Tyskland, særlig Gropius' Bauhausskole

Plantype 1930. Eentrappesystem, brandaltaner. Bad indføres. To værelser og to kamre

Plantype 1933. Projekt fra konkurrence afholdt af Socialt Boligbyggeri. Eentrappesystem. Accentuering af lejligheden med større opholdsstue med spiseplads og flere mindre værelser

Plantype 1935. Projekt fra konkurrence afholdt af Stockholms kommune. Større opholdsstue, flere kamre. Spiseplads i forstue

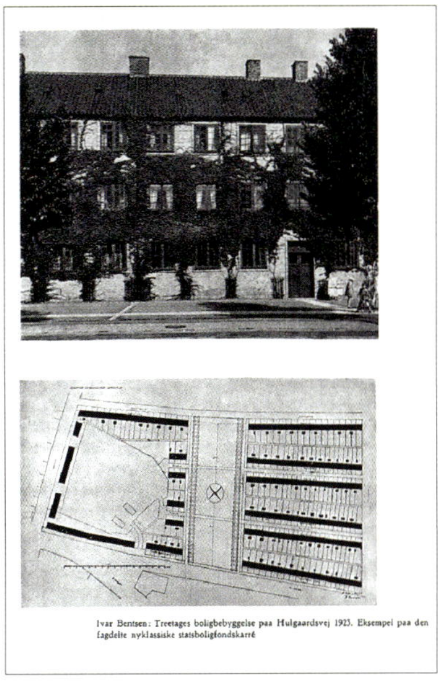

Ivar Bentsen: Treetages boligbebyggelse paa Hulgaardsvej 1923. Eksempel paa den fagdelte nyklassiske statsboligfondskarré

Selection of pages from *Boligens former* (1946) illustrating development of plan types for multi-apartment dwellings and realised projects of row houses *Hulgaardsvej* (1923) by Ivar Bentsen

"The strong development of all branches of society and the growth of social and democratic ideas must necessarily mean that the predominance which had hitherto been placed on the external aesthetic framework in construction has disappeared. The analysis of the housing requirements became the prerequisite for the design. Appropriateness, economy, understanding of social requirements, the new constructions and materials were the factors that determined the shape of the house. It is incredible what was sacrificed to serve the new views. Architects with a strong aesthetic sense threw everything overboard in the belief that when all the above factors were present, the form itself would become consequently good architecture".[104]

Such thoughts seem to anticipate his non-dogmatic approach to the modern movement encapsulated in the "functional tradition"[105] concept he would voice via "Arkitekten" in 1950. *Boligens former* traces the main evolution of housing in the city of Copenhagen from the eighteenth century down to contemporary times, casting a broad but succinct eye on the formal traditions of other countries over that period too. His sixty-eight-page account concentrates on three main forms, namely: the multi-storey block (*etageboligens*), the row/terraced house (*reækkehuse*), and single-family house (*enfamiliehus*). The graphic apparatus is impressive: site plans, typological assemblages, building type plans and photographs ably support his argument.

Work on all the previous publications already described would provide a solid basis for future articles outside the Nordic circles, such as *The history of domestic architecture in Denmark*, found in the special issue *The Architecture of Denmark* of "Architectural Review" in 1948.[106] The publication was thematically arranged in various articles penned by other Danish authors. The release of the special issue was purposefully timed to coincide with the *Danish Art Exhibition* held at the Victoria and Albert Museum in London. The editorial staff of the English magazine introduced Fisker as the "pioneer of the modern Copenhagen flat block". His account was richly illustrated[107] and it was divided in two thematic sections: "flats" and "houses" covering the realisations for the capital city from late eighteenth century to the 1940s.

The resonance of the special issue was so significant, that the following year the publishing house re-printed it as a booklet with drawings and texts.[108]

One further international example comes in the 1949 special issue of the French journal "L'Architecture d'Aujourd'hui" entirely dedicated to Danish architecture. The editorial staff-architect Marcel Jolivel curated the structure of the volume comprising thematic sections for each building type, but he was helped by Kay Fisker for the selection of the projects and the collection of all the visual apparatus.[109]

Fisker was invited to pen the introductory account entitled *Evolution de l'architecture danoise*. Some drawings of Danish architect Preben Hansen (1908–1989),[110] already published in the book *Huse i Danmark* (Houses in Denmark, 1942).[111] In the sections of the special issue dealing with "habitations collectives" and "habitations individuelles" there was not even one of Fisker's housing projects. Although, the presentation was focused mainly on well-known buildings – this is the case of those acting as inspiration to the rest of that war-ravaged world – a number of lesser-known examples of residential construction were also included.[112]

Covers and a few pages of the magazines *Architectural Review* (reprint edition, 1949) and *L'Architecture d'Aujourd'hui* (1949).

One last example, published in Denmark in 1951, is the fine volume *Danske arkitekturstrømninger 1850–1950: en arkitekturhistorisk undersøgelse* (Trends in Danish architecture 1850–1950: an architectural and historical study) co-authored with his colleague Knud Millech (1890–1980).[113] The role and development of housing in all its various types figure prominently in the majority of the ten chapters arranged by architectural periods,[114] Millech taking responsibility for the older ones due to his historical knowledge, while Fisker focused on recent periods.[115] As expected, the interest goes more to multi apartment complexes, single-family houses and semi-detached houses, while terraced houses are very little illustrated.

All his studies and presentations prove how housing would continue to play a central position among his interests as an architect, professor and populariser. The 1936 and 1941 overviews have tended to serve so far as a pretext for enlarging Fisker's wider areas of research and critical output.

Fisker and his educational programme

Anyone reading *Københavnske Boligtyper* and *Rækkehusetyper* even for the first time will clearly grasp the work that lay behind those pages, the lectures' systematic treatment of issues, the joint critiques discussed over the atelier tables, the collective assignments where drawing takes pride of place. This was a complete novelty for the Royal Academy of Copenhagen, a genuine new scheme of organisation and regulations within the overall reform of the education system that got underway in1924.

Since its foundation in 1754, the Royal Danish Academy of Portraiture, Sculpture and Construction (*Det Kongelige Danske Skil-dre-, Billedhugger- og Bygnings- Academie*) had sought to educate "a national body of artists from both free and applied arts to a notion of good taste; how this aim should be achieved and what the relationship should be between art and craftsmanship were the subjects of several reforms for the following two centuries".[116] Yet for a long time the education of architects had more to do with the artistic side; know-how of any technical branch was outsourced to workshops with old master builders, internships at draughtsmen's offices and building sites. Some attempts at "a reformative attitude towards pedagogy of drawing, focusing on technical knowledge"[117] were made well before 1924 by key figures within the Academy, like Gustav Friedrich Hetsch (1788–1864), and outside it such as P. V. Jensen-Klint (1853–1930) who left to embark on his independent crusade, the *Den Fri Architektforening* (Independent School of Architects) in 1909 along with a group of young architects. "As the years went by, however, dissatisfaction again arose, as the school naturally paid most attention to the needs of the artisans, and in 1908 a special department was established at the Academy itself for the technical branch of architecture".[118]

In 1909 against this general background, Fisker was accepted at the School of Architecture within the Royal Academy of Copenhagen. Klint's subversive gesture was by no means unique: other groups formed, sometimes without quitting Academy studies, rejecting the standard of teaching there, and the dogmatic adherence to the prevailing canons of style. For instance, Fisker himself joined the student league of the *Kanonarkitekterne* (The Canon Architects) that wanted Danish building culture to focus on popular architecture and local craftmanship rather than historical styles. The group included a few very close colleagues of Fisker's from the years to come, like Povl Stegmann, Aage Rafn, Mehrn Ludvigens, Otto Valentiner, Ejnar Dyggve, A. G. Jørgensen, Ingrid Møller, Volmer Drosted and Emil Kock. Similar episodes took place in other Nordic countries: one thinks of the 2-year independent *Klara Skola* (1910–1912)[119] in Stockholm, promoted by Erik Gunnar Asplund (1885–1940), Osvald Almqvist (1884–1950) and Josef Östlihn (1882–1941) among others, where the "fathers" of National Romanticism – Ragnar Östberg (1886–1945), Carl Westman

(1866–1936), Carl Bergsten (1879–1935) and Ivar Tengbom (1878–1968) – were invited to participate as teachers. The year Fisker entered the Royal Academy of Copenhagen coincided with the launching of a course that would fuel the subsequent radical change in teaching methods. "The intention with the creation of the class was to provide the school with a teaching of the domestic, more modest construction, as a counterweight to the Academy's hitherto rather unreal teaching of monumental architecture".[120] On Hanck Kampmann's (1856–1920) initiative and as a natural consequence of keen contemporary interest, reflected in widespread surveying of bourgeois and rural architecture, *Den Danske Klasse* (The Danish Class) was established. The course would last until 1924; for a year or so before graduating Fisker himself would be a teaching assistant to it, together with Thomsen (1884–1980).

Reverting to the 1924 reform: a Danish delegation – composed of teachers Ivar Bentsen, Edvard Thomsen, Carl Brummer (1864–1953) and Jesper Tvede (1879–1934) – would report on its proposed contents before the *International Congress on Architectural Education* organised in London from 28th July – 2nd August 1924[121] by the Board of Architectural Education within the Council of the Royal Institute of British Architects. The heavy attendance at the event showed how widespread interest was in the topic, the impact of which can be appreciated from the papers presented, round tables discussing education in the past, present and future, not to mention displays of students' works. That international-scale report on the ongoing education reform in Denmark proved a decisive spur to action and implementation. "At present [1924] the Royal Danish Academy is the only institution that provides complete training for architects in Denmark, though a Technical School of Building (*Den Bygningstekniske Skole*) and other general technical schools offer fairly comprehensive courses in architectural construction. The custom of students working as assistants in architects' offices whilst they are attending academy and school courses still persists. A programme of reform is, however, proposed by which students qualifying through the Academy will spend four whole years attending regular classes and two years at night classes".[122] The first effect of that reorganisation was to make sure students were fully and regularly occupied in daily lectures, thereby shortening the time needed to qualify as an architect – something that until 1924 had not been achievable till the age of twenty-six or thirty. Secondly, and perhaps most importantly, the reform demanded that professors revise the content of their programmes, broaden the range of subjects on offer, and especially rethink the process of disseminating knowledge.

Shortly after the Danish delegation's presentation at the London conference, British photographer Yerbury would bring out his book *Modern Danish architecture* in which he spoke glowingly of the link between that education reform and what he had seen and documented for himself on his visit to the country in 1925. Though the reform was then only one year old, he would say in the preface: "Undoubtedly the main credit for Denmark's present architectural achievements must be accorded to its system of training, for although Denmark, like other countries, has its due share of those who profess to practice architecture without any basis for their claim, nearly all those who have any recognition as architects have received a definite system of training under the auspices of the Academy at Copenhagen, or in the studios of the leading Architects. In any country the advent of a really great architect is a rare occurrence. When such a one does arrive he works in his own fashion, and is a law to himself, but the business of the Academies and Teachers is to train and develop the average architect on such lines as will ensure that his future work shall at any rate maintain the standards of logical construction and good taste universally agreed upon as the basic principles of building. That the Danish Architects have been successful in doing this will be obvious from the illustrations of this book".[123]

Fisker had himself witnessed the early decades ushering in a change in society and hence in the Academy. Right from the start of his involvement in the School of Architecture as a young assistant teacher he felt responsible to future generations for setting up "training courses instilling in architecture students that cultural sensibility and the skills needed if architects were to fulfil their role in society".[124] Since the beginning of the *Bolig Klasse*, the thrust of his efforts was not so much teaching architecture as educating the class in building a project. The various papers in which he specifically describes his working method reflect that important etymological and semantic distinction between "teaching" and "educating". Fisker's aim is not just "to imprint signs (in the mind), to give instruction, to train via examples", but rather implies "full involvement by teacher and learner, such that the didactic style of training courses in architecture, given the social role that the architect is called upon to fulfil, can but be one of educating".[125] Aptly enough, in the issue of "Arkitekten" celebrating Fisker's seventieth birthday (1963) his former student and studio co-worker Poul Kjærgaard recalled his gifts as a real *pædagogen* (educator).

His experience both as a pupil and as a teacher, together with various formative journeys, constitutes the living source on which he would draw in honing his daily educating and working method, pursuit of which needed to be as complete as possible, since "a significant part of the students finish or interrupt their education at least for a long period after their third year grade".[126] His own education, we should remember, was based on his student years (1909–1920) and his parallel internships as a not yet qualified architect, for instance in Copenhagen at the firms of Anton Rosen (1913), Povl Baumann (1915) and Hack Kampmann (1918) alongside his colleague and friend Povl Stegmann, as well as a period of apprenticeship (1916) to the studio of Erik Gunnar Asplund and Sigurd Lewerentz. "Due to isolation imposed by the First World War, the only opportunity which the Scandinavians enjoyed of getting out and seeing things was by visiting each other".[127] But, starting with the 1918 trip to London to do research on housing laws commissioned by the Danish Housing Committee, Fisker began to travel widely in Europe, the Far East and the USA[128] drawn by a personal thirst for knowledge, but also in order to attend conferences and exchanges with other universities. On top of such travelling, he went on trips with his class, organised from year to year, to learn about the architectural progress in neighbouring Nordic countries and the more dynamic set-ups elsewhere in Europe.[129]

In his *Bolig Klasse* course, Fisker sought a close and fruitful collaboration with other disciplines directly related to construction, and consequently with other colleagues;[130] young architects need to extend their field of intelligence and sensitivity in tackling complex and comprehensive questions like the housing question. Since the very beginning, the list of disciplines showed a great flexibility to integrations and modifications. For instance, the yearly educational programme in 1936 came to include the subjects: Architecture/Building Art (580 Hours per year / 18 per week), Painting (267 / 6), Surveying (267 /6), Construction Technology (60 /2), Perspective (148 / 7), Urban Building (67 /2), Garden Art (26 / 1), Engineering House Building (100 /5), Architectural History (24 /1), Danish Architectural History (24 /1), Art History (24 /1), Writing (23 / 1), Socio-economic studies (26 /2), Financing (26 / 1), Drawing Technique (110 /6), Engineering installations (18/1) in addition Lectures on Special Topics (30 /2).[131] The teaching hours per day covered the time span from nine a.m. to six p.m. The contribution of the various disciplines followed the students through all the activities of the course, both in the research phases and into the two design assignments.

A very multidisciplinary spirit emerges from the wide range of different topics comprising much more in the 1936 analysis than in the 1941 one.

The brand-new schedule as a permanent day school necessarily implies a transformation in the working method carried out in the atelier, which came to resemble in spirit the design offices outside the Royal Danish Academy. "In the current form, the teaching is a joint teaching, not as before an individual teaching with individual assignments for each student. The assignments can thereby be brought into a firmer form, treated methodically through lectures, examinations and demonstrations and can, by illuminating the non-uniform solutions, give the students an overview and orientation towards the assignment, which individual teaching does not make possible. As the education in draughtsmanship no longer takes place in parallel with the academy teaching but forms part of the school education, the aim is to replace it by making task-solving, both in content and in the manner of execution, as realistic as possible in a school setting".[132] For one thing, the students' capacity for historical research (inter alia) in relation to housing issues was developed through drawing: or more precisely, analytical re-drawing of case histories from Copenhagen and other European cities. As a preliminary exercise, students naturally took part in measuring and examining *on-site* the objects they were working on, whether houses, homes, furniture, or city plans. To a certain extent here the typological-based approach fulfilled the role of mechanism to elucidate architecture in an understandable way.

"Drawing is not a form of representation, but the art of measuring, the art of the number. It is, in other words, first a respectful act of what we can perceive with our eyes. Through drawing, we can transfer the appearance of things into the truth of the number."[133] Understanding the building tradition in all its proportions entailed plotting what one was studying. It was not just an exercise in style. Both the earlier *Dansk Klass* with its field trips organised by student associations (e.g. *Foreningen af 3 December 1892*) and P. V. Jensen-Klint's independent venture had trained his sights on the practice of drawing as the true instrument of knowledge. Both depicts a key aspect of Danish architectural culture.

Each of the two assignments[134] of the *Bolig Klasse* were part of a single project using the same site and programme of a very pragmatic nature, however the results might differ from student to student, and also entailed economic and town-planning considerations. Drawing proved to be the *fil rouge* between the stages of the research and the two assignments: from the instrument of analysis, it became the *instrument of the project*.[135] Both assignments the same uniform graphic convention and the same scale of representation. "The intention is first and foremost to provide students with an understanding of the importance of such a uniform mode of production and to counteract their possible artistic aspirations, to make them understand that working drawings are a means of communication that must speak a clear and distinct language that is understood by all who handle them, and not graphic works of art that are to express an individual talent".[136] This paved the way for multiple and comparative interpretation of the main features of the case study, beyond any mere considerations of architectural idiom.

The taxonomic plates incorporated in the 1936 and 1941 books stemmed from those first analytical exercises and clearly illustrate Fisker's systematic method. They were not a collection of *models*: that is, objects that should be repeated as they stood, but rather a collection of *types*: that is, objects from which everyone can conceive works of art that may have no resemblance to one another.[137] Rasmussen shared this view: in a 1926 article he warns the reader[138] about what the drawing of comparative plates entails. The overview of *existing housing types* amassed by Fisker and his students thus is made up of other architects' solutions to similar building and distribution problems (sometimes even those from previous centuries), which do not purport to be the only solutions possible, let alone stand as *theoretical ideal types*.[139] They reflect the background of their times, the social structure, conditions and way of life. Hence, alongside valid examples affording ideas still of relevance to project design, we find others that are dated and limited the design development. Fisker is fully aware that his survey on multi-storey buildings is not just a collection of interesting ideal plans, which was the purpose of certain published and influential German text-books on building typology of the time, like Alexander Klein's studies,[140] Otto Volcker's *Wohnbaufibel* (1932), Ernst Neufert's *Bauentwurfslehre* (1936)[141] and Otto Haesler's *Zum Probleme des Wohnbaues* (1930).[142]

But what makes the 1936 *Københavnske Boligtyper* and 1941 *Rækkehusetyper* so special is not the number of examples described but the precise, systematic analysis of important architectural themes. The approach thus owed something to that peculiar typological thinking reinterpreted by modernist architects as a conceptual basis for standardisation in the overall improvement of the housing realm a feature of the 1920s–1930s both in Denmark and on the international scene.[143]

One *Arkitekten Maanedshæfte* issue of 1932 gives us a detailed account of the *Bolig Klass*'s doings those first eight years.

Undervisningen i boligbyggeri ved Kunstakademiet (Education in housing construction at the Academy of Fine Arts) paints a vivid picture of how the course was organised but, most striking of all, the students' analysis and project design plates markedly differ from the exercises in style displayed at the London Meeting in 1924.[144]

Following an overall guideline, each project is now drawn to the most suitable scale: site plan, typological plan, principal elevation, dwelling types and sun-orientation analysis, main section displaying the technical and material choices, axonometric view of housing estate or dwelling, etc. By the end the students will possess not just their assigned case studies analysis and completed project, but a series of other inputs from the phase of project presentation before the whole class and the group's suggestions for revision.

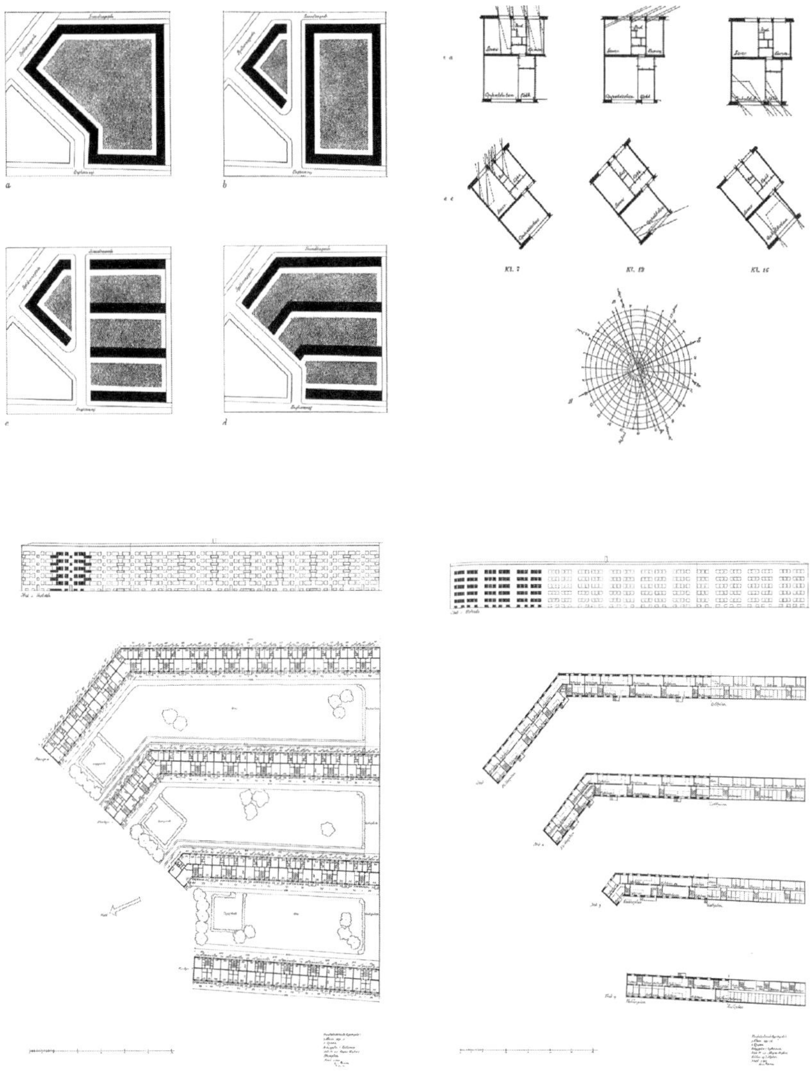

Samples of *Bolig Klass* assignments' plates from the 1932 issue of *Arkitekten Maanedshæfte*

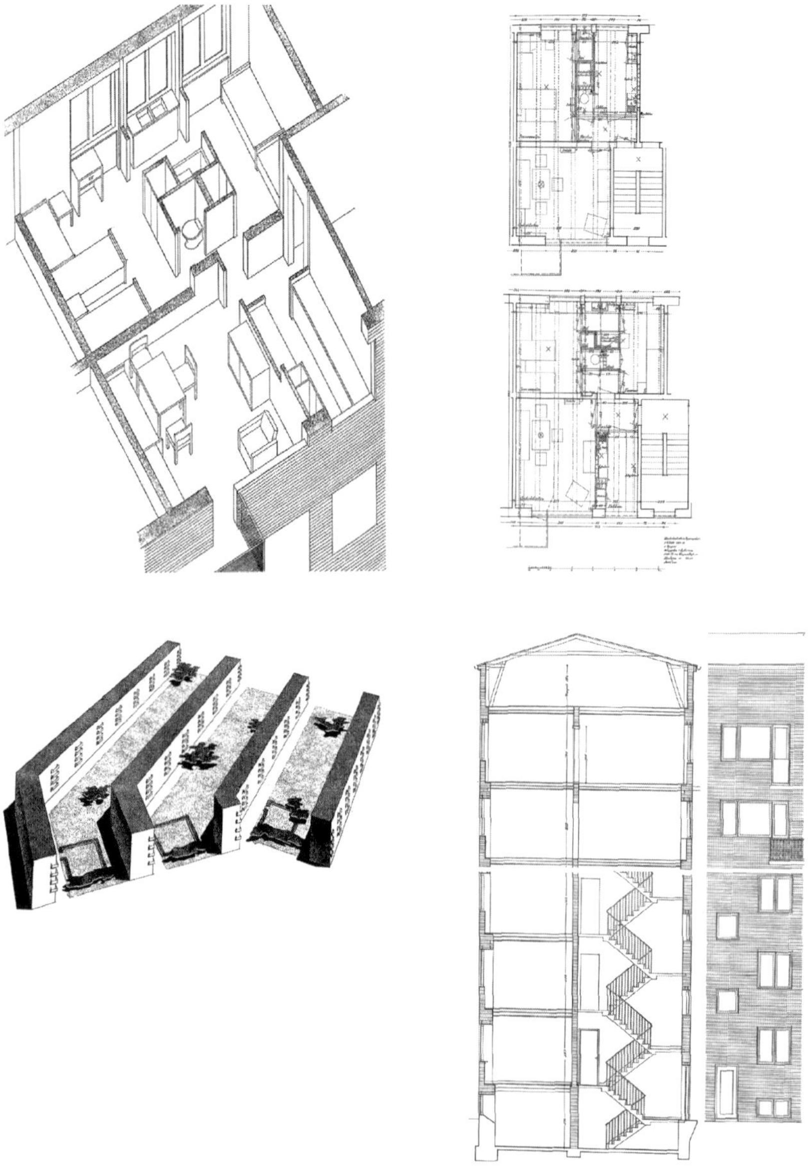

Samples of *Bolig Klass* assignments' plates from the 1932 issue of *Arkitekten Maanedshæfte*

The teaching programme of the *Bolig Klass* supervised by Fisker for over thirty years (1924–1955) steered many a generation of Danish architects through decades of deep change on many fronts, at home and abroad. "From the start Kay Fisker was one of those few who studied and thought how to achieve renewal in the passing generations; he was quick and ready to give his own role a special slant in the transition period between the two eras, while his first projects and implementation thereof showed him sailing above the anguish of the moment".[145]

Structure of the two books

1936 Københavnske Boligtyper en oversight

The book is a clear example of a collective effort carried out under the supervision of the *Bolig Klasse* professor.

The narration follows a timeline beginning in 1856 and provides an eighty-year multidisciplinary portrait of multi-storey housing construction and its development.

The layout design starts from the cover which, as mentioned, presents an excerpt of the Copenhagen map (1:3,000) on both front-cover and back, spine included. Inside the text, there is a larger-scale version (1:60,000) of the Copenhagen urban area (also known as "Greater Copenhagen") encompassing at that time the municipalities of Frederiksberg, Gentofte and the former Copenhagen County. There, the housing instances built in 1914–1936 are classified by three different light-red hatches according to the degree of building density: high-rise (five to six floors), mid-rise (three to three-and-a-half floors) and low-rise (one to two floors). The decision to use that map as the cover and backdrop for the title focuses the reader immediately on the main topic and city being addressed in the book. Fisker also designed the colour scheme: all cadastral contour lines nuanced in brownish like the engraving maps, while the hatches turn black corresponding to the black colour of the book title. In the study the map is an important aid to understanding; on the cover it becomes an eye-catching device thanks to neat graphics. All the names of the students who worked on the analytical drawings are listed on the book cover, together with Fisker's own at the top, the aim being to reflect the collective character of the survey.

A brief word on the cover design for some of the books Fisker edited. As we stated previously, the survey published in 1936 was closely linked in methodology and in publishing style to the *Rækkehusetyper* 1941. The two books differ a bit in the structure of the examination, however, but also in their cover layout.

On the 1941 cover, Fisker exploits his subject matter graphically: he plays up the serial nature of the terraced house, and consequently across the front cover run twelve diagonal lines of row house prospects repeated almost *ad infinitum*. Looking at this editorial project, one thinks at once of another venture of his, curated together with his colleague Knud Millech in 1951. The cover for *Danske arkitekturstrømninger 1850-1950: en arkitekturhistorisk undersøgelse* has a distinct graphic affinity with the 1941 book, though this time the multi-storey housing building prospects are arranged on horizontal lines. Though the 1936 and 1941 books make housing the main subject right from the outside cover (i.e. map of the town and rows of prospects), one curiously notes how the 1951 text focuses the cover design on housing series built in the course of the whole century rather than employing the many different of works of architectures and types detailed in the thorough book.

Københavnske Boligtyper is slightly a bit more than A4 format, the page layout keeping the text in a 2:3 proportion enabling small pictures with captions, graphs and tables to be inserted. The book opens directly with the critical examination, indeed there are neither table of contents nor frontispiece.

The structure of the eighty-page survey is the following: the first section (issue No. 5; 1856–1914) included three papers as well as sixteen full-page plates, while the second part (issue No. 6-7; 1914–1936) comprised two papers, a set of comparative plates (four full-page schemes as well as fifteen pages, and ten pages of photos). Of the five commentaries two were penned by Fisker, one by the architects and assistants of the Rasmussen course (namely Peter Bredsdorff and Ole Reimer), one by Fisker's own co-workers (first students and then architects-to-be) Poul Kjærgaard, Sven Dahlstrøm, Stig Svanholt and Niels Schou, while the last commentary was by the principal administrator of the City Directorate, architect Enrico Hansen. The five accounts evidently differ in the proposed visual apparatus: from drawings, passing via photos and statistical charts depicting data distribution.

A brief explanation of the layout and contents of the many taxonomic plates is needed, because for reasons to do with the objects displayed, these present differences.

At the end of the Kjærgaard, Dahlstrøm, Svanholt and Schou paper, there are full-page plates depicting thirty-two cases ($I_1 - I_{32}$), two case studies per page. The focus is here addressed exclusively to housing blocks built in Copenhagen during 1856–1914. The comparative plates include ground-floor assemblages, main cross-sections, small site plan schemes and pictures of the main façade.

Another substantial set of full-page plates follows the Fisker and Hansen accounts opening the second section. Fisker groups the 1914–1936 projects according to various subsystems of elements that converge to define the precise types.

Four full-page plates display a selection of solely Copenhagen "building development plans" (1:5,000) classified by morphological arrangement: enclosed blocks (*lukkede karréer*), semi-enclosed blocks (*halvlukkede karréer*) and open complexes (*aabne bebyggelser*). In some cases, the type is treated more deeply in subsequent plates.

Fifteen full-page plates of "plan types" (1:200 and 1:500), illustrating each with nine to five examples are categorised in fifteen groups ($III_{33} - III_{34}$ and $IV_{35} - IV_{47}$). The primary component of distribution, the staircase system, generates multiple variations when combined with different dwelling size and number. In addition, the building depth is a distinguishing factor between the different cases due to local regulations and technical aspects. Much like what Fisker does for the critical texts, these typological plates unveil examples designed in foreign countries as well. *Københavnske Boligtyper* ends with an expose of thirty photos depicting solely bird-eye views and built instances from Copenhagen. Of the ten pages, two illustrates the evolution of the plan development within the urban fabric via aerial pictures; then the focus moves on to nineteen projects.

One should note the great care taken to provide a detailed list of key information (e.g. geographical position, date of construction, client, multiple quantitative data, components of distribution, etc.) for each case study of all the analytical plates. The reader is also helped by alpha-numerical codes denoting each case study, which prove useful when it comes to linking the drawings to the text. For example, anyone approaching the Danish context for the first time should recognise that building block names refer to the site location (mainly crossroads), but also to the cooperative and/or institution that awarded the commission, e.g. the Hornbækhus Cooperative Housing Association.

Both for the comparative drawings of 1856–1914 and of 1914–1936 housing types, the block depth is always given – a basic design requirement for anyone working in housing. In fact, a such measure is a distinguishing factor between the different cases due to local regulations and technical aspects.

Managing and validating the consistency of all the impressive quantity of local and foreign data was not an easy task in an analogical world. Therefore, Fisker asked "for forbearance with regard to the errors and shortcomings that exist, and with an eye to continuing these studies, add[ed] that the Academy would be grateful to be made aware of any errors or misconceptions".[146]

Of the one hundred twenty-two examples mentioned in the text and visually shown in the book, twenty-three relate to foreign cases, where the majority regard Nordic cities. The non-Danish examples are coming from buildings seen during field trips with the students, but also from references presented at the *Bolig Klasse* and hence comprised in the lectures' dedicated literature. The attribution of some projects is not easy to grasp from the data and drawing provided. In very rare cases, the name of architect(s)/association(s) and the builders is stated as "unknown". To provide a comparative-overview of the topic, other cities are included:[147] Stockholm (eight buildings erected for private and housing cooperative clients and two displayed at two exhibitions),[148] Gothenburg (two parallel blocks, of which one for a housing cooperative),[149] Åbo/Turku (one built parallel block),[150] Oslo (two realized open blocks),[151] Breslau (one enclosed block),[152] Vienna (two buildings, of which one realised for the municipal housing program),[153] Frankfurt (three parallel blocks for the municipal estates),[154] Stuttgart (two buildings, surely one of them was built and for the purpose of an exhibition),[155] Karlsruhe (intervention with parallel blocks)[156] and Berlin (one parallel block).[157]

1941 Rækkehusetyper en oversight

Diverging from the choral character of the 1936 survey, here Fisker's is the lone voice of historical and architectural analysis alongside the students' work in performing re-drawings.

The 1941 examination uses the 2:3 page layout proportion of a roughly A4 format of the previous one. It starts directly with the critical account, indeed there is neither table of contents nor frontispiece.

The care in the editing arrangement is this time a bit more summary and less detailed in structure, especially for the release in form of two consecutive monthly issues of *Arkitekten*. The forty-page survey begins with thirteen pages of critical text, a six-page photographic report, a twenty-three synoptic plates, and then a section portraying in detail a selection of 15 Danish row houses complexes among those of the precedent plates. But the set of drawings was published halfway between the two issues.

Though less endowed with quantitative data referring to the Copenhagen examples and their evolution thorough the decades, *Om rækkehuse, kamhuse, kædehuse og andere huse* does outline the development of that housing form within a broad and solid historical and geographical setting, tracing the contaminant factors that bear on the way it was deployed and incorporated in housing estates. The most historically-grounded cases Fisker cites are the Fuggersiedlung complex (sixteenth century) in Augsburg and the Nyboder row houses (seventeenth century) in Copenhagen. Another "pioneering"[158] name mentioned in the book is M. H. Baillie Scott (1865–1945). His experiments, amply illustrated in multiple publications and in many issues of the journal "The Studio", transformed the English architecture and greatly influenced developments in the rest of Europe.[159]

In support of the disparate possibilities of "distribution system" of the housing types and green area layouts, the Danish architect supplied exhaustive and appropriate images and/or drawings of the cases. He added two pages illustrating sixteen possible forms of aggregation that the housing type in question institute with road layout and garden.

The set of photos portrays Danish projects in the first four pages, while the last two show some German, American, Swedish and Finnish examples. The majority of them are identified by page number and alpha code linking to the subsequent drawing plates.
Each page of the synoptic plates displays two cases (never-implemented designs, competition designs and built complexes) featuring a specific "form of aggregation" and "distribution system", where the access from the street to the house plays a central role. The analysis is always more or less the same in format, the same drawings being used to represent each project (1:250). As in the 1936 text, some further descriptive and quantitative data are provided. The latter include: road system, built-up area, plot area, floor area, volume and materials, etc.

Of the one hundred-twenty examples collected in the survey (shown in the text and in the photographic as well as taxonomical plates), ninety-eight are related to Copenhagen (although six were proposals for the *Construction crisis* competition held in 1940),[160] and the remaining were undertaken outside Denmark. As stated by Fisker, the "examples have been chosen due to their type being considered of particular interest and less because of their architectural value".[161]

Unlike the 1936 text, here, useful information integrated into the data caption helps the reader understand which project is referred to in the drawings as well as which architect(s)/association. In some cases, the literature reference (books and/or journals) from which the dwelling types were taken is pointed out in the caption too. The distribution of the cases is the following:[162] Stockholm (4),[163] Finland (one realised in Kotka and one student's proposal for Helsinki),[164] United Kingdom (2),[165] Munich (6),[166] Zurich (5),[167] Stuttgart (1), Augsburg (1), Barcelona (1),[168] Pessac (1),[169] and USA Florida (1).[170]

The time has come for the two books to speak themselves.

Notes

1 See No. 5 (pp. 85–112) and No.6–7 (pp. 113–164) of the volume XXXVIII.

2 When Steen Eiler Rasmussen replaced Kay Fisker as principal editor, the magazine of the *Akademisk Architektforening* was split into two issues of different character starting from 1927: a weekly booklet ("Architekten Ugehæfte") with current contents in brief form, and a monthly one ("Architekten Maanedshæfte") with wider thematic articles. For further details see the special issue (1938) marking forty years of the journal (*Særhæfte, udgivet i Anledning af Tidsskriftets 40 Aars Jubilæum*), pp. 1–25 , as well as the special issue "Arkitekten magasin" (No. 23, 1998) for the 100th anniversary focused on the transformation of the journal via the many directors' imprinting, and Olaf Lind, *Arkitekten Steen Eiler Rasmussen*, pp. 261–264.

3 Fisker, K., *De Københavnske Boligtypers udvikling*, in "Arkitekten Maanedshæfte", vol. XXXVIII, No. 5, 1936 p. 85 [separate book, p. 1].

4 *Ibidem.*

5 *Ibidem*, p. 87 [separate book, p. 3].

6 Fisker, K., *Københavnske Boligtyper from 1914 to 1936*, p. 121 [separate book, p. 37].

7 Søberg, M., "A Clearly Defined Form", in *Kay Fisker. Works and Ideas in the Danish Modern Architecture*, Bloomsbury Visual Arts, London, 2021, p. 13.

8 See Boldsen, F.C., *Boligselskaberne II*, in "Architekten", Vol. XXV, 1923, pp. 393–398.

9 Yet in 1924, it will be recalled, the French government invited Denmark to take part in the *Exposition internationale des arts décoratifs et industriels modernes* to be held in Paris the following year. The Danish Commission chose Fisker for designing the national pavilion.

10 After 1955 he went on teaching at the same institute; the posts he held were of growing importance, including that of Director. Around the end of his academic involvement, he was a visiting professor in the USA, both at the Cambridge MIT (1953 and 1957) and at the Harvard University School of Design (1953). He would retire from Royal Academy School of Architecture in 1963.

11 Kjærgaard, P., *Pædagogen Kay Fisker*, in "Arkitekten", Vol. 65, No. 3, 1963, p. 50.

12 Starting from 1929 and up to 1955, Fisker embarked on a joint practice with architect C. F. Møller (1898–1998). Their cooperation began with designing the University of Aarhus (1931–1946), together with architect Povl Stegmann (1888–1944) and landscape designer C. Th. Sørensen (1893–1968).

13 Reference to the 1936 text: Glænøgaard (development plan plate A_a), Amagerbo (development plan plate B_a), Brigadegaarden (development plans' plate B_b), Gullfosshus and Jagtgaarden (plan type plates III_{33C} and III_{33F}).

14 See Bro, H., *Housing: from night watchman state to welfare state*, in the "Scandinavian Journal of History", Vol. 34, No. 1, 2009, pp. 2–28.

15 The Danish Association of Architects invited him to serve as co-editor (1918–1920) and during these years he focused on reorganising the print and format drawing on the fine book production that went into the volume *Liselund* (1918). Later on Fisker became editor-in-chief of the journal (1920–1926). In the following years, he continued actively collaborating with the magazine.

16 Fisker, K., *Om rækkehuse, kamhuse, kædehuse og andere huse*, in "Arkitekten Maanedshæfte ", vol. XLIII, No. 2, 1941, p. 17 [separate book, p. 1].

17 See *Rækkehusetyper I* in No. 2 (pp. 17–40) and *Rækkehusetyper II* in No. 3 (pp. 41–56) of the volume XLIII.

18 Fisker, *Om rækkehuse, kamhuse, kædehuse og andere huse*, p. 18 [separate book, p. 2].

19 In the digital collection of the Danmarks Kunstbiblioteket there are plates illustrating Danish and foreign case studies of this housing type: see "Enfamiliehuse samlet i en studiekreds på arkitektskolen" ark_ 60117, 1190, mappe 3.

20 Stegmann, P., *En Boligtype og dens Forudsætninger*, in "Arkitekten Maanedshæfte ", Vol. XXXV, No. 9, 1933, p. 177–199.

21 Fisker, K., "Boligens former", in *Moderne dansk boligkunst*, Bernadotte, S. Paursen, J. L. (edited by) Skandinavisk Bogforlag, Odense, 1946–1947, vol. I, p. 47.

22 For a further outline of the project, see: Boldsen, F.C., *Boligselkaberne*, in "Architekten", vol. XXV, 1923, pp. 345– 364.

23 In 1920, the KAB – Copenhagen Housing Association was established under the support of the founder and lawyer Frederik Christian Boldsen (1877–1954), and it quickly became the country's largest construction company.

24 Fisker, *Om rækkehuse, kamhuse, kædehuse og andere huse*, p. 19 [separate book, p. 3].

25 *Ibidem*, p. 20 [separate book, p. 4].

26 *Ibidem*, p. 19 [separate book, p. 3].

27 See: Hegemann, W., *Zeilenbau-Siedlungen von Kay Fisker*, in "Wasmuths Monatshefte für Baukunst und Städtebau", Vol. 25, No. 4, 1930, pp. 95–96. The proposals presented in the account are: Vognmandsmarken comprising concentric half circles of multiple segmented housing bars, and a plan for Damhussøen area of ten parallel bars.

28 Reference to the 1941 text: Rækkehuse plate, p. 47 [separate book, p. 31].

29 It was founded by lawyer Rasmus Nielsen in 1933, aiming to alleviate the housing shortage in Copenhagen and in many provinces. For a better understanding of the association inception and the first buildings' initiatives, see Buhl, O. (edited by), *Socialt Boligbyggeri, Udsnit af 15 aars boligbyggeri 1933–1941*, Foreningen Socialt Boligbyggeri, København, 1941.

30 Of particular interest is the selection of correspondence among Fisker and international architects and critics in: Quagliotto, S., "Il dialogo coi moderni", in *Kay Otto Fisker. Architetto danese della monumentalità del quotidiano*, Campisano Editore, Rome, 2021, pp. 45–68.

31 Cf. Søberg, M., "The functional tradition", 2021, pp. 158–159. In the section "Denmark is an orderly country" of the Bauer's book, the Danish cases are: Fuglevænge (1927–1929) by Povl Baumann and the community housing around the Grundtvig Church (På Bjerget, 1924–1926) by Peder Vilhelm Jensen-Klint, Vilhelm Wittrup, Charles I. Schou, Georg Gøssel.

32 From 1924 onwards he became an associate professor of urban planning at the Royal Academy and, starting from 1928, actively collaborated with the *Dansk Byplanlaboratorium* (The Danish Town Planning Institute) through the long-drawn preparation of the new Copenhagen plan. As of 1938 he was appointed professor in *Bybygning* (City Planning), a post he held until 1968. It shows a different attitude to teaching from that of his colleague Fisker. For further details on him, see the monographic study: Lind, O., *Arkitekten Steen Eiler Rasmussen*, Gyldendal, Copenhgaen, 2008.

33 Pupil and coworker of Heinrich Tessenow, a prominent exponent of the housing policies of so-called Red Vienna, and lastly an architect involved in Frankfurt housing programs under the leadership of Ernst May. The Schuster project in Vienna dated from 1927 was comprised in the 1936 text (plan type plate IV_{461}).

34 For further information about internal controversies among planning and housing sections among the IFHTP, including the decision to step outside and establish the Verband in 1929 with its centre in Frankfurt and later the reconciliation between the two sides in 1936, see Geertse, M., *Defining the universal city. The International Federation for Housing and Town Planning and transnational planning dialogue 1913-1945*, Ph.D. Thesis, Vrije Universiteit Amsterdam, 2012, pp. 152-204.

35 See Fisker, K., *Kopenhagens Wohnbantypen von 1914–1936 von Architekt Professor Kay Fisker*, in ""Moderne Bauformen", Vol. 36, No. 6, June 1937, pp. 269–288.

36 *Ibidem*, p. 269.

37 See *Københavnske Boligtyper from 1914 to 1936*, in "Arkitekten Maanedshæfte", Vol. XXXVIII, No. 6–7, pp. 113–128 [separate book, pp. 29–44].

38 See the section "Editors' notes" at the beginning of the book.

39 Arís, C. M., "The notion of type in modern architecture", in Mion, C., Licitra, F. (eds.) *Variations of Identity. Type in architecture*, Éditions Cosa Mentale, Marseille, 2021, p. 218[orig. ed. *Las variaciones de la identidad. Ensayo sobre el tipo en arquitectura*, 1993].

40 See in the digital collection of the Danmarks Kunstbiblioteket : (1936) "Københavnske Boligtyper samlet i en studiekreds på arkitektskolen", ark_60977, 1192, mappe 2 and (1941) "Rækkehuse samlet i en studiekreds på arkitektskolen" ark_60118, 1190, mappe 2.

41 Fisker, *Om rækkehuse, kamhuse, kædehuse og andere huse*, p. 19 [separate book, p. 3].

42 Tavares, A., "Cross-Sections through an Endless Library", in *The Anatomy of the Architectural Book*, Canadian Centre for Architecture, Montreal; Lars Müller Publishers, Zurich, 2016, p. 15.

43 See Langkilde, H. E., *Arkitekten Kay Fisker*, Arkitektens Forlag, København, 1960; Faber, T., *Kay Fisker*, Arkitektens Forlag, København, 1995.

44 Søberg, M., *Kay Fisker. Works and Ideas in the Danish Modern Architecture*, Bloomsbury Visual Arts, London, 2021. The same book has been published in Danish too, but with an impressive visual apparatus, see: *Kay Fisker. Moderne arkitektur – levende tradition*, Strandberg, Copenhagen, 2023.

45 See Skriver, P. E., Fisker, S., Monies, F., Faber, T., Ahlberg, H., Hansen, H. H., *Arkitekten Kay Fisker 14.2.1893 - 21.6.1965*, Architekten [catalogue of the exhibition held at the Kunstindustrimuseet - Copenhagen]; Fisker, S., Fisker, J., Dirckinck-holmfeld, Kim (edited by). *Kay Fisker*, Arkitektens Forlag [catalogue of the exhibition held at the Kunstindustrimuseet – Copenhagen, 1995].

46 Mortensen, P.D., Fich, M., *Københavnske boligtyper en oversight*, Kunstakademiets Arkitektskole - Laboratoriet for Boligbyggeri og Galleriet, Copenhagen, 1993.

47 In this regard, see the special issue on collective effort: Jørgensen, E. B. (edited by), *Kay Fisker*, in "Archithese", vol. 4, No. 85, July.

48 For example, see: Steinmann, M., "Die Tradition der Sachlichkeit und die Sachlichkeit der Tradition. Zur Architektur von Kay Fisker", in "Archithese", Vol. 4, No. 85, July, pp. 2–8. Re-printed version accompanied by French translation in: "La tradition de l'objectivité et l'objectivité du traditionalisme. Considérations sur l'architecture de Kay Fisker" in *Forme forte. Escrits/Schriften 1972-2002*, Birkhäuser, Basel, 2003, pp. 49–58; Tornow, B., *Kopenhagen, Ydre Nørrebro. Wohnen im Grossblock einer privaten Genossenschfat*, in Harlander, T. (edited by), *Stadtwohnen : Geschichte, Städtebau, Perspektiven*, Deutsche Verlags-Anstalt, München, 2007, pp. 202–207; Sonne W., *Dwelling in the metropolis: Reformed urban blocks 1890–1940 as a model for the sustainable compact city*, in "Progress in Planning", No. 72, 2009,

pp. 53–149; Torricelli, C., "Complesso di appartamenti Hornbækhus, Copenhagen di Kay Fisker", in Biraghi, M., Ferlenga, A., *Architettura del Novecento. Opere, progetti, luoghi. A-K*, Einaudi, Torino, 2013, pp. 453–459; Floris, J., *Dronningegården and Kay Fisker's Continuum*, in "OASE", No. 92, 2014, pp. 30–35; Ortelli, L., *Architecture ancrée dans le quotidien. Kay Fisker et ses compagnons de route*, in "Matières", No. 12, 2015, pp. 116–133; Sonne, W., "Copenhagen and Scandinavia", in *Urbanity and density in 20th century design*, Dom Publisher, Berlin, 2017, pp. 85–87; Baratelli, G., "Towards the Modern Block: Evolution of an Urban Type in Kay Fisker's Prewar Architecture", in Calatrava Escobar, J. (edited by), *La casa. Espacio domésticos, Modos de habitar (II Congreso Internacional Cultura y Ciudad, Granada)*, Abada Editores, 2019, pp. 554–565.

49 These include: "Master Project: Territorial density Collective living in Copenhagen" (2013) at Studio Krucker Bates (TUM -Technical University of Munich), "Housing Copenhagen"(2015–2016) at Atelier Ortelli Bachelor BA5-BA6 (EPFL - École Polytechnique Fédérale de Lausanne), "March Economy Housing studio unit" (2016) at Clancy and Moore Studio unit (Queen's University, Belfast), etc. Starting from the drawing materials produced during these experiences, some publications have appeared, for example: Krucker, B., Bates, S., *Hornbækhus: building register*, Schiermeier, Munich, 2013; see also the study integrated with analytical text by: Clancy, A., Moore, C., *Kay Fisker. Block terrace square*, Lund Humphries Publishers, London, 2022.

50 Fisker, *De Københavnske Boligtypers udvikling*, p. 86 [separate book, p. 2].

51 The link with Ramussen is a deep one, thus some excerpts are reprinted in certain sections: "Building development plans. Enclosed blocks", "The plan types" and "The types with more than two flats per staircase".

52 Cf. Rasmussen, *Ti års boligbyggeri i København*, in "Arkitekten", Vol. XXVIII, No. 9–10 February, 1926, pp. 78–96.

53 The association, founded in 1879 and still existing today, represents all architects who have undergone their training and received a graduation certificate. Their purpose is to bring together Danish architects, who according to its statute can be members, to work together for architecture and for the reputation and interests of the architectural profession. However, it ranges beyond tasks of a purely professional nature, and targets more than a professional audience. Thus it promotes a monthly and weekly journal, a permanent exhibition of building construction for a wide audience as well as special thematic exhibitions held in the headquarters, Bredgade 66, and at the Building Information Centre with its complete archive for technical building investigations. For further info, see: Akademisk Arkitekforening, "Hvad er Akademisk Arkitektforening?", in *Huset i byen. købstadsboligen Etagehuset Enfamiliehuset*, Copenhagen, 1945, pp. 95–99.

54 Rasmussen, E., *Dansk Bygge- og Boligudstilling*, in "Arkitekten", Vol. XXVIII, No. 9-10 February, 1926, p. 77.

55 See the catalogue of the event: Akademisk Arkitektforening, *Dansk Bygge- og Boligudstilling afholdt af…*, Akademisk Architektforening, København; and *Bygge- og boligdstillingens møder og foredrag*, in "Architekten", Vol. XXVIII, No. 9-10 Febraury, 1926, pp. 122–124.

56 Rasmussen, *Dansk Bygge- og Boligudstilling*, p. 77.

57 See *Dansk Bygge- og Boligudstilling*, in "Arkitekten", Vol. XXVIII, No. 12, Febraury, 1926, pp. 117–121.

58 The Danish exhibition was likewise rotating: the Technical College of Charlottenburg, Munich, Stuttgart, Kiel and several other German cities.

59 From 1921 on, Beherens took over from Otto Wagner and conducted his own course until 1937. For a detailed description of his teaching method

see the catalogue of the exhibition stopover in New York: Behrens, P., "Zur Erziehung des Baukünstlerischen Nachwuchses", in Grimme, K.M. (edited by), *Peter Behrens und seine Wiener akademische Meisterschule / Peter Behrens and his academic master-school*, A. Luser, Vienna, 1930, pp. 9–12. And about the exhibitions see: Calandra di Roccolino, G., *Peter Behrens e l'America*, in "La Rivista di Engramma", vol. 150, No.1, 2017.

60 *Dansk Udstilling i Berlin*, in "Arkitekten", Vol. XXVIII, 1926, p. 400. See also *Chronic. Dänische Architekturausstellung in Berlin*, in "Wasmuths Monatshefte für Baukunst und Städtebau", Vol. 10, No. 9, 1926, p. 396.

61 *Ibidem.*

62 Cf. Faber, T., *Nuova Architettura Danese/ New Danish Architecture*, Edizione di Comunità, Milan, 1968, p. 6.

63 See the proceedings book containing all the papers as well as all the drawings and pictures shown extract of the exhibition panels: Eriksson, A. (edited by), *Nordisk byggnadsdag 1927: förhandlingar och utställning*, Stockholm.

64 Cf. Asgaard Andersen, M., *Swedish Architecture in Nordic Contexts 1930–1950*, in "Konsthistorisk tidskrift/Journal of Art History", Vol. 85, No. 1, 2016, p. 67. For a more detailed understanding of the Danish and Swedish participations to the event, see: Monterumisi, C., Søberg, M., *Reformistic approach to housing masses in the metropolis: 1920s Copenhagen and Stockholm perimeter blocks*, in "Planning Perspectives", 2024 (in publishing).

65 See Fisker, K., *Københavnske boligtyper*, in Eriksson, A. (edited by), *Nordisk byggnadsdag 1927: förhandlingar och utställning*, Stockholm, 1927, pp. 10–19.

66 With reference to the 1936 text, only some of these were represented in the synoptic tables: Grønnegården-Borups Allé and Struenseegade (plan type plate III_{33H} and III_{33A}), Ved Classens Have (photographic collection at the end of the text).

67 Fisker, *Københavnske boligtyper*, 1927, p. 10.

68 Cf. Rasmussen, S. E., Saint, A. (edited by), *First Impressions Of London: Or, Sir Edwin In Wonderland*, in "AA Files", No. 20, Autumn, 1990, p. 16.

69 See Robertson, H., *Exhibition of modern Danish architecture*, in "Architect and building news", Vol. 117, No. 27 May, 1927, pp. 887–898.

70 Yerbury, F. R., *Preface*, in *Modern Danish architecture*, Ernst Benn, London, 1927, p. 6.

71 The Swedish exhibition was held in 1924 and the catalogue was published the following year with the assistance of the local architect Hakon Ahlberg. See *The exhibition of Swedish architecture at the R.I.B.A*, in the "Architects' Journal", Vol. 59, May 1924, pp. 835–843.

72 The review of the catalogue penned by Rasmussen shows a certain intolerance of banal errors of attribution, as well as his disappointment in learning that his colleague Fisker, who prepared the graphic material with loving care, had not been consulted over the galley proofs. The version that came out did in fact skip certain pictures and drawings, and one notes that some of Fisker's layout instructions were not followed. Nonetheless the Danish critics were fairly satisfied, all in all, with that richly documented overview. See Rasmussen, S.E., *Bøger og blade - Modern Danish architecture*, in "Architekten Ugehæfte", vol. XXIX, No. 42, 1927, p. 171.

73 Working alongside him, the curator of the journal was architect and theorist Leo Adler (1891–1962), whose interests focused mainly on housing programs and efficiency, as demonstrated by his publications and studies, e.g. *Neuzeitliche miethäuser und siedlungen* (Modern rental houses and settlements, 1931) where few cases of Kay Fisker were presented. Hegemann came in contact with Nordic countries during his field trips throughout Europe and the USA in 1909. Later on, he was in charge of foreign delegates at the Gothenburg Tercentennial Jubilee Exposition in 1923, arranged in the framework of the first of the post-WWI IFHTP conference.

74 Crasemann Collins, C., *Werner Hegemann and the search for universal urbanism*, W.W. Norton, New York NY, 2005, p. 342.

75 See Rasmussen, S. E., *Drei Wohnhausblöcke in Kopenhagen*, in "Wasmuths Monatshefte für Baukunst und Städtebau", vol. 12, No. 5, 1928, pp. 194–202.

76 *Ibidem*, p. 194.

77 Hegeman, W., *Die Nordische Woche*, in "Wasmuths Monatshefte für Baukunst und Städtebau", vol. 13, No. 11, 1929, pp. 454–455.

78 The Fisker housing blocks illustrated are: Hornbækhus, Jagtgaarden, Vognmandsmarken, Gullfosshus.

79 See Brendel, O., *Stil und Sachlichkeit: Zu den Schülerarbeiten der Akademie in Kopenhagen*, in "Wasmuths Monatshefte für Baukunst", vol. 11, No. 1, pp. 39–47.

80 See the reference in footnote 27.

81 See the catalogue published after overcoming some obstacles in 1935: Schwan, B,. *Städtebau und Wohnungswesen der Welt / Town planning and housing throughout the world / L'urbanisme et l'habitation dans tous les pays*, Verlag Ernst Wasmuth, Berlin. Of the Danish delegations, there were published two contributions were published by Kai Hendriksen, chair of the Danish Laboratory for Town Planning and F.C. Boldsen, director of the Copenhagen General Housing Company (KAB).

82 Schuster, F., *Der Bau von Kleinwohnungen mit tragbaren Mieten / The Building of small dwellings with reasonable rents / La Construction de petits logements à loyers abordables*, Verlag des Internationalen Verbandes für Wohnungswesen, Frankfurt am Main, 1935, p. 3. As stated by the same editor, this publication was a supplementary collection of many plans from various countries accompanied with explanatory texts. Fisker included an extract of the Danish delegation text in the survey of 1936, see *De Københavnske Boligtypers udvikling*, pp. 126–127 [separate book, pp. 42–43].

83 Hillerofhus by Ivar Bentsten and Th. Henningsen (1921), Vestergaarden by Wittmaack and Hvalsoe (1930–1931), Stadtverwaltung by Helweg-Møller (1931), Privat Consortium by K. Fisker and C.F. Møller (1932), Østergården by K. Fisker and C.F. Møller (1932–1933), Bryggervangen by Søgaard Petersen (1934–1935), Project by Ib. Lending (1935), Dominis by Søgaard Petersen (1934) and (1935), Erweiterung von Nurnberggaarden by K. Fisker and C.F. Møller (1935).

84 See the Internationaler Verband för Wohnungswesen, *Ausstattung der Kleinwohnung / Equipment for small dwellings / Equipment du petit lodgement,* Julius Hoffman Verlag, Stuttgart, Vol. I (texts) and vol. II (plates), 1935.

85 See the Danish section of the exhibition presented in the book-catalogue: *Nordisk Byggnadsdag 1932 - Pohjoismaiset rakennuspäivät 1932: Helsingfors, 4-6 Juli*, Akademiska bokhandeln, Helsingfors, 1932, pp. 245–265.

86 Some of them are also contained in the 1936 text: Enghavevej – Ny Carlsbergvej by Emanuel Monberg and John Strøm Tejsen, 1923 (aerial picture "Residential neighbourhood circa 1923", p. 155 [separate book, p. 71]); Solgården by Henning Hansen, 1929 (plan type plate IV_{43A}); J.H. Mundts Stiftelse Stormgade by Tyge Hvass 1933 (plan type plate IV_{46G}); Borups Allé by Niels Peter Pedersen Gundstrup, 1928 (development plan plate A_f);"Treleddet" Finsensvej in Frederiksberg by Palle Suenson and Thorvald Dreyer, 1930–1931, p. 159 [separate book, p. 75]; Bavnehøj Allé by Helge Holm and S.C. Larsen 1930; Vodroffsvej by Kay Fisker and C.F. Møller, 1928–1929; "Lille Tuborg" Gammel Vartov Vej by Charles Jacob Schou, 1933 (development plan plate Bg + p. 164 [separate book, p. 80]); Reækkehusene Godthaabsvej by Ivar Bentzen and Thorkild Henningsen, 1921; Reækkehuse Sundvænget by Thorkild Henningsen, 1925; Reækkehuse Bernstoffsvej by Thorkild Henningsen, 1927–1928.

87 Cf. Lending, M., *The Permanent Collection of 1925: Oslo Modernism in Paper and Models*, in "Architectural Histories", vol. 2, No. 1, 2014.

88 Fisker, K., "Etageboligens udvikling i de seneste aar", in Harald, H., Orvin J. E. (edited by), *Nordisk Bygningsdag III Beretning*, 16th–18th June, 1938, pp. 33–43.

89 *Ibidem*, p. 40.

90 *Ibidem*, p. 41.

91 *Ibidem*.

92 *Ibidem*, p. 43.

93 In 1924, Jacobsen attended the *Bolig Klasse* of Fisker and Kaj Gottlob. His project Bellavista (1934) was included among the case studies of the 1936 Fisker book (development plan plate Bm, plan type plate IV_{41H}). In 1937, Utzon moved to Copenhagen, where he followed the Fisker and Rasmussen courses.

94 *Boligbyggeri* (Housing, 1946–1947, integrated version of the 1942–1943 lectures' compendium), *Præfunktionalismen* (Pre-functionalism, 1950), *Formprincipper* (Principle of Form, 1956; re-published in 1999 by Tobias Faber), *Strejftog i den nyere arkitekturhistorie* (Incursion into the History of Modern Architecture, 1959). For a first-time impression of these publications see two paragraphs in Søberg's (2021) monographic book: "Beyond conventions", pp. 117–119 and "Fisker, the historian", pp. 148–151.

95 Monies, Finn, "Kay Fisker 1893–1965", in Hegner Christiansen, J., Zahle, K., Monies, F. (edited by), *De gamle mestre, Carl Petersen, Ivar Bentsen, Kaj Gottlob, Kaare Klint, Kay Fisker*, København, Arkitektens, 2000, p. 110.

96 The copies were supplied to students with a delay of approximately half a year due to shortage of paper for the duplication. This time, as for the 1936 and 1941 texts, Fisker expressed his apologies for there being no systematic appearance of the lectures' handout, no uniform layout across the sections, spelling mistakes and errors in projects' attribution.

97 Cf. Fisker, K., "Efterskrift", in *Boligbyggeri. Resumé, billedliste og litteraturhenvisninger til forelæsningsrække på Kunstakademiets Arkitektskole*, 1947, Copenhagen, p. 49.

98 Cf. Rossi, A., *The Architecture of the City*, MIT Press, Cambridge, Mass., 1982, p. 41.

99 With Fisker there were: P. Bredsdorff, C. Elling, S. E. Rasmussen, A. G. Jørgesen, H. E. Langkilde, H. Stephensen.

100 Akademisk Arkitekforening, "Hvad er Akademisk Arkitektforening?", in Bredsdorff, P. (edited by), *Huset i byen. købstadsboligen Etagehuset Enfamiliehuset*, Akademisk Arkitektforenings Byggeudstilling, København, 1945, p. 97.

101 Fisker, K., "Rækkehuse og kædehuse", in *Huset i byen. købstadsboligen Etagehuset Enfamiliehuset*, pp. 41–50.

102 *Ibidem*, p. 50.

103 See Fisker, K., "Boligens former", in Bernadotte, S., Lehm-Laursen, J. W. (edited by), *Moderne dansk boligkunst, Skandinavisk bogforlag*, Odense, 1946, pp. 47–114.

104 *Ibidem*, p. 70.

105 Fisker, K., *Den funktionelle tradition: Spredte indtryk af amerikansk arkitektur*, in "Arkitekten Maanedshæfte", vol. 52, No. 5–6, 1950, pp. 69–100.

106 See Fisker, K., *The history of domestic architecture in Denmark by Kay Fisker*, in "Architectural Review", Vol. 104, No. 623, November 1948, pp. 219–226. The same year, Fisker became member of the Royal Institute of British Architect (R.I.B.A. - London).

107 This time he included one housing block of his own production, namely the Hornbækhus.

[108] The Danish press lamented of not being involved in the editing of the texts and figures' layout. See Busck, A., *The Architecture of Denmark, Udsendt af The Architectural Press*, "Architekten Ugehæfte", Vol. LI, No. 24, p. 96.

[109] See Jolivel, M., *Un français au Denmark*, in "L'Architecture d'Aujourd'hui", No. 24 June, 1949, p. 1.

[110] He was press secretary for the *Akademisk Arkitektforening* since 1937, prehaps the reason his illustrations grabbed the attention of foreign journals.

[111] See Lassen, Erik, *Huse i Danmark*, Andr. Fred. Høst & søn, København, 1942.

[112] See *Noter og anmeldelser. L'architecture d'aujourd'hui — Danemark*, "Architekten Ugehæfte", Vol. LI, No. 34, p. 140.

[113] Millech was the originator of the architectural design collection now known as the Danish Art Library.

[114] The multiple housing references range from the third to the last chapter, namely: *Post Classicism, 1850–1855; Liberal Historicism, 1855–1870; International Historicism, 1870–1890; National Romanticism, 1890–1902; Neo-Baroque, 1902–1915; Neo-Classicism, 1925–1930; Functionalism, After 1930.*

[115] Cf. Jørgensen, A. G., *Levende arkitekturhistorie Boganmeldelse af Danske arkitekturstrømninger 1850-1950*, "Arkitekten Ugahefte", Vol. LIV, No. 29, 1952, p. 225.

[116] Gigliotti, A., Gigone, F., "A return ticket to academia", in *Drawings*, Calderoni A., Gandolfi C., Leveratto J., (edited by) "STOÀ: Strumenti per l'insegnamento della progettazione architettonica", No. 1, Vol. 2, Thymos Books, Napoli, 2021, p. 76.

[117] *Ibidem*, p. 79.

[118] Danish Delegation, "Architectural Education in Denmark", in R.I.B.A. (edited by), *International congress on architectural education- Proceedings 28 July-2 August 1924*, The Royal institute of British architects, London, 1925, p. 95.

[119] For the description of a design assignment developed by two groups of students of the Klara Skola, see Bergsten, C., *Ett bidrag till belysning af bostdsfrågan i Stad*, in "Arkitektur", Vol. 42, No. 9, 1912, pp. 105–111.

[120] Fisker, K., *Undervisningen i boligbyggeri ved Kunstakademiet*, in "Arkitekten Maanedshæfte", Vol. XXXIV, No.1–3, 1932, p. 49.

[121] In addition to the Danish delegation, there were also groups from Austria, Belgium, Denmark, Holland, Hungary, Italy, Norway, Spain, Sweden, America, England, France, Japan, Mexico, Australia, Canada, South Africa.

[122] Budden, L.B., "Review of the Congress", in R.I.B.A (edited by), *International congress on architectural education- Proceedings 28 July-2 August 1924*, The Royal institute of British architects, London, p. XV.

[123] Yerbury, F.R., *Preface*, 1927, pp. 6–7.

[124] Campioli, E. "Teaching architecture, educating to design", in Faroldi, E., Vettori, M., P, (edited by), *Teaching architecture. Two schools in dialogue*, LetteraVentidue, Siracusa, 2021, pp. 140–141.

[125] *Ibidem*, p. 142.

[126] Fisker, *Undervisningen i boligbyggeri ved Kunstakademiet*, p. 50.

[127] Jørgensen, L. B., "Erik Gunnar Asplund and Denmark", in Engfors, C. (edited by), *Asplund 1885-1940 : lectures and briefings from the International Symposium on the Architecture of Erik Gunnar Asplund 14th-17th October 1985*, Arkitekturmuseet, Stockholm, 1986, p. 25.

[128] For the complete list of his study trips alone or alongside colleagues and/ or students, see: *Kay Fisker 1983-1965*, in "Archithese", Vol. 4, 1985, pp. 53–56; and Søberg, M., *Kay Fisker. Works and Ideas in the Danish Modern Architecture*, 2021, pp. XIV–XVI. For a rich overview of archival items coming from study trips, see Dus, M., *Atemporalità di un'architettura anonima.*

Kay Fisker e l'Università Di Aarhus, Phd Thesis, IUAV Venezia, 2014, pp. 72–105.

129 On the many university exchanges and class trips, see the detailed report of the one scheduled for 27th January – 6th February 1935 to Stockholm and Gothenburg, upon Professor Asplund's invitation; see P.B., P.K.., *Kunstakademiets Studiereise til Sverrig*, in "Arkiketen Ugehæfte", n. XXXVII, No. 8, 1935, pp. 46–48.

130 In this regard, see for example the report of Rasmussen as professor of Urban Planning about the synergic collaboration with other colleagues, Fisker included: *Undervisningen i byplanljegning ved Akademiet Kopenhavn*, in "Byggmästaren", No. 11, 186–188.

131 Cf. Fisker, K., "Hovedskolens I. Klasse", in *Det Kongelige Akademi For De Skønne Kunster* (edited by), *Beretning 1937-1940*, København, 1940, p. 56.

132 Fisker, *Undervisningen i boligbyggeri ved Kunstakademiet*, p. 51.

133 Dal Co, F., *De moderne en de eigentijdse architectuurtekening*, in "OASE", n. 36, 1993, p. 4.

134 The first one dealth with ordinary single-family houses, while the second one a various housing types differing per building density to be accommodated in a large plot.

135 Cf. Gregotti, V., *Il disegno come strumento del progetto*, Marinotti, Milan, 2014.

136 Fisker, *Undervisningen i boligbyggeri ved Kunstakademiet*, p. 63.

137 Quatrèmere de Quincy, A., *Dictionnaire historique de l'architecture*, Librairie d'Adrien Le Clere, Paris, 1832, p. 629.

138 Rasmussen, S.E., *Ti års boligbyggeri i København*, 1926, p. 86.

139 Cf. Fisker, *Københavnske Boligtyper from 1914 to 1936*, p. 121 [separate book, p. 37].

140 Rasmussen was the first to introduce Klein's examinations in Denmark, at first by publishing extracts and then larger portions. See: Rasmussen, S. E., *Boligproblemer Teoretiske unders gelser af smaalejligheders anvendelighed*, in "Architekten Ugehæfte", Vol. XXIX, No. 32, 1927, pp. 25–127; Klein, A., *Om boligens rationelle udformning af baurat Alexander Klein*, Berlin, in "Architekten Ugehæfte", Vol. XXXI, No. 01, 1929, pp. 1–7.

141 In the first edition of the handbook, one project of Fisker in collaboration with C.F. Møller was included, precisely Herman Triers Plads (1930), in the category "Mietshäuser Zweispänner".

142 *Ibidem*, p. 122. Up until the release of Fisker's text in 1936, "Arkitekten" showed several times (directly and indirectly) the interest in Klein's typological analysis based on plans drawings and diagrams, mainly thanks to Rasmussen.

143 See Søberg, M. "The typological pursuit", 2021, pp. 75–80. Dus, M., "Progettista e professore", 2014, pp. 55–70.

144 *The Exhibitions of Students' Works*, in R.I.B.A. (edited by), *International congress on architectural education- Proceedings 28 July-2 August 1924*, The Royal institute of British architects, London, 1925, p. 158.

145 Rubino, L., "Kay Fisker (1893-1965): Per intrecciare utopia e tradizione nel modo più semplice", in Arne Jacobsen. *Opera completa 1909 / 1971*, Edizioni Kappa, Rome, 1980, p. 16.

146 Fisker, K., *De Københavnske Boligtypers udvikling*, p. 87 [separate book, p. 3].

147 In the following footnotes, only the recognised projects are presented.

148 (Text) Artur von Schmalensee, "Stockholmsutställningen" Plan Type No. 6, 1930; (IV_{42G}) Holger Blom, Traneberg barnrikehus - kv. Kolmården 2, 1936–1940; (IV_{42H}) Hakon Ahlberg (and Leif Reinius), Hjorthagen of smalhus, 1934–1937; (IV_{44B}) Helge Zimdahl and Niels Ahrbom, Plan Type "Standard för Bostad och Bohag" exhibition, 1934; (IV_{42F} and IV_{44E}) Eskil Sundahl - KF Arkitektkontor, Kvarnholmen - kv. Sicklaön 38:3, 1929–1931; (IV_{47B}) Niels Einar Eriksson, Eriksdal - Kv.

Gräset 3, 1931–1932; (IV_{47C}) Sven Markelius, Eriksdal - Ringvägen (Kv. Gräset 3), 1930–1931; (IV_{47D}) Ture Rydberg, Norrmälarstrand (kv. Mullbärsträdet 2), 1935–1936.

149 (IV_{42I}) H.S.B. Arkitektkontor, Project for a Landshövdingehus, 1931.

150 (IV_{44F}) Aino and Alvar Aalto, Standard Apartment House (Standardivuokratalo), 1927;

151 (IV_{37F}) Sverre Poulsen, Folkvang, 1932–1933; (IV_{45G}) Multiple architect(s); Harald Aar's plan, Søndre Åsen, 1925–1928.

152 (IV_{45E}) Plan Type presented at the *Die Wohnung für das Existenzminimum* in Frankfurt (1929), catalogue p. 120.

153 (IV_{46I}) Franz Schuster, Karl-Volkert-Hof, 1926–1927.

154 (IV_{37H}) Ernst May et al., Hellerof Siedlung, 1929; (IV_{42E}) Ernst May, Praunheim Siedlung, 1926–1929.

155 (IV_{40G}) Mies van der Rohe, Weissenhofsiedlung plan type, 1927.

156 (Text) Walter Gropius, Otto Haesler, Dammerstocksiedlung, 1928–1929.

157 (Text) Hans Scharoun, Gross Siedlung Siemenstadt, 1928–1931; (Text) Bruno Taut and Martin Wagner Berlin-Britz Siedelung, Neukölln, 1925–1931; (Text) Walter Gropius and Stephan Fischer Berlin-Haselhorst Siedlung, 1930–1935.

158 Fisker, K., *Tre Pionerer frå aarhundredskiftetet*, in "Byggmästaren", 1947, Vol. 15, pp. 221–232. In his account, he selected as key and forerunner figures, although yet underrated and not enough examined in details due to proximity of time, two English architects (C.F. A. Voysey and M. H. Baillie Scott) and one German (H. Tessenow).

159 Cf. Fisker, K., *Om rækkehuse, kamhuse, kædehuse og andere huse*, p. 20 [separate book, p. 4].

160 The open competition was organised by the Association of Architects in collaboration with the Danish Engineering Association. Representatives for both Associations were appointed as jury committee. The architectural programme consists in "affordable houses realised by Danish materials with the unique focus on low-rise typologies, i.e. single-family houses and terraced houses". All the 226 proposals were displayed in the exhibition rooms at Charlottenborg. See Fisker, K., Konkurrence om krisebyggeri, in "Arkitekten Ugehæfte", Vol. XLII, No. 37, 1940, pp. 173–174. A selection of the 226 competition entries can be found in: *Billige Boliger af Danske materialer. Resultaterne af en Konkurrence, udskrevet af Akademisk Arkitekforening i Samarbejde med Dansk Ingeniørforening*, in "Arkitekten Maanedshæfte ", Vol. XLII, No. 12, 1940, pp. 157–176.

161 Fisker, K., *Om rækkehuse, kamhuse, kædehuse og andere huse*, p. 18 [separate book, p. 2].

162 In the following footnotes, only the recognised projects are presented.

163 (Text) Erik Lallersted, Residential and office building (kv. Näktergalen 31), 1922–1923; (Text) Paul Hedquist Ålstensgatans radhus, 1929–1933 (Text, p. 36, separate book, p. 20) Eskil Sundahl – KF Arkitektkontor Kvarnholmen - kv. Sicklaön 38, 1929–1931.

164 (Text) Aino and Alvar Aalto, Sunilla cellulose factory housing estate; (p. 52, separate book p. 36) Hilding Ekelund, Plan type presented at the *Nordisk Byggnadsdag 1932*.

165 (Text; p. 51, separate book p. 35) M. H. Baillie Scott, Project in Hamstead, 1902.

166 (Text) Guido Harbers, Siedlung Ramersdof, 1934; (pp. 39–40; separate book pp. 23–24) Otto Völckers, Plans types published in *Wohnbaufibel* ; (p. 45, separate book p. 29) Emil Freymuth, Siedlung Ramersdof, 1934.

167 (p. 45, separate book p. 29) Max Haefeli, Rudolf Steiger, Werner Moser, Paul Artaria and Hans Schimdt, Wekbundsiedlung Neubühl, 1930–1932;

(p. 53, separate book p. 37) Paul Artaria, Model house presented at the *Schweizerische Landesausstellung*, 1939.

168 (p. 48, separate book p. 32) Le Corbusier and Pierre Janneret, Plan Type, 1933.

169 (p. 48, separate book p. 32) Le Corbusier and Pierre Janneret, Plan Type, 1925.

170 (p. 55, separate book p. 39) Howard Major, Model house, 1927–1929.

Editors' notes

Knowing that Fisker was aware of potential typos and errors in the text and plates, during the process of translation to English, we took care to ensure the consistency of the information and corrected errors where the available information made it possible.

During the reproduction of Fisker's pieces, the editors chose to use an A4 paper format, since the minimal reduction of the original book page measures (21x 31 cm) does not alter the layout prepared by the Danish architect, his colleagues and students.

The two reproductions follow the pages' numbering of the separate books, rather than the numbering used in the issues of the journal "Arkitekten", where the 1936 and 1941 accounts where firstly published. Regarding the English translation, the spelling of street names and similar elements follow the Danish spelling reform of 1948 with the exception of proper names, the names of companies and societies and certain municipalities.

Glossary
(in alphabetical order)

This section is meant to provide additional information that is useful for a complete understanding of the text as well as the photographic and drawing plates of both books.

Adresseavisen: Denmark's oldest classified advertising newspaper.

Alen : Old Danish unit of measurement for length. One alen corresponds to 0.627 m^2.

Akademisk Arkitekforening's Konkurrence om krisebyggeri: Academic Architectural Association Competition on construction crisis. In 1940, it was announced as an open competition to which 226 proposals of affordable low-rise housing typologies were submitted.

Arbejdernes Andels-Boligforening (AAB): Workers' Cooperative Housing Association.
Still active today, the AAB was established in 1912 as the first public housing organisation. It was founded by the chairman of the Building Carpenters' Union, Jens Christian Jensen. The association tackled the challenge of providing cheap and modern apartments for the working class and was closely linked to the labour movement and the Social Democratic Party. Many leading architects of the time worked for the association, i.e. Ivar Bentsen, Dan Fink, Bent Helweg-Møller, Louis Hygom, Christian Mandrup-Poulsen, Johannes Strøm Tejsen and Kooperative Arkitekter, etc.

Arbejdernes Kooperative Byggeforening (AKB): Workers' Cooperative Building Association.
As a non-profit and co-operative housing association in Copenhagen, it was founded in 1913 by a number of co-operative companies in the building and craft trades. The aim of AKB was, on the one hand, to build healthy and modern workers' housing where the working class could afford to live as an alternative to rental barracks and, on the other hand, to provide work for the member companies that made up the company. In 2007, AKB was merged with KAB with the continuing name KAB.

Ausstattung der Kleinwohnung: "Equipment of Small dwelling" catalogue (published after some obstacles in 1935) illustrating the outputs produced by many cities in Europe and the USA. These works were presented among the many activities, exhibitions and debates at the 1931 congress held in Berlin by the *International Federation for Housing and Planning*. There the delegations of the four continents (with a predominance of European countries) met to pool new initiatives for the cities and its inhabitants: in other words to raise the standard of city planning, dwelling and to lower the building costs.

A/S (Aktieselskab): stock-based corporation with public limited liability, which may be either publicly or privately traded. Many examples comprised in the text and plates were created with the support of real estate and rent corporations.

Baumadæk: Bauma type. According to the Danish Building code this type of slab consists of brick blocks with intended-shape in which reinforcement has been inserted, and which is subsequently poured with concrete.

Byggnadsfirman Lundberg&Blom: Lundberg&Blom Construction Company.

Corkoligno: commercial name of coupled panel of cork and Portland cement.

Der Internationale Verband für Wohnungswesen, Städtebau und Raumordnung: International Federation for Housing and Planning.

Eternit: commercial name of the manufacturing company dealing with construction systems in asbestos fibre cement.

Expanko: commercial name of vinyl cork flooring.

(Foreningen) Bedre Byggeskik : Literally "Better Building Practice", it was a Danish society established in 1915 and active until 1965. The aim was to improve architecture and building methods in the construction industry via a service of free assistance. A board of architects was available to revise drawings submitted voluntarily by craftsmen and builders.

(Foreningen) Socialt Boligbyggeri (FSB) : The Social Housing Organisation. It was founded by lawyer Rasmus Nielsen in 1933 aiming to alleviate the housing shortage in Copenhagen and in many provinces.

Frederiksberg Boligselskab: Frederiksberg Cooperative Housing Association.

Gasbeton: commercial name of one of the many manufacturing companies dealing with autoclaved aerated concrete.

Hyresgästernas sparkasse - och byggnadsförening (HSB): The Savings and Construction Association of the Tenants. It was established in 1923 by the architect Sven Wallander and today is the biggest federation of cooperative housing in Sweden. Pioneeringly HSB combined savings with construction in a single organisation. HSB expanded rapidly as an enterprise covering all the aspects stretching from design to production.

Icopal: commercial name of the manufacturing company dealing with pitched-roof waterproofing membranes and flat roof membranes systems.

Journalistforbunde: Danish Union of Journalists. It is the nationwide trade union for journalists, photographers, illustrators and other creative employees in the media and communications industry. It was founded in 1961 by a merger of the Journalistforening (founded in 1900 as Provinsjournalistforeningen), Socialdemokratisk Presseforening (founded in 1899) and Københavns Journalistforbund (founded in 1904).

KH-blocks: Danish patented product of concrete block (outside: raw and untreated; inside: fitted with thin cork sheets and then coated with a plaster layer), pioneeringly introduced by the engineer Kristian Hindhede in 1931–1932.

Københavns Almindelige Boligselskab (KAB): Copenhagen General Building Association.
Still active today, it was established in 1920 by lawyer Frederik Christian Boldsen, who held the position of director till 1945. The association quickly became the country's largest construction company in collaboration with a number of leading architects of the time. In 2007, KAB merged with AKB under the continuing name KAB.

Kooperative Arkitekter (KA): Cooperative Architects. It was a Danish collective architectural practice (1934–1946) based on cultural radical and socialist milieu of the 1920–1930s. Edvard Heiberg and Ivar Bentsen were the main figures of a larger group of members.

Kooperativa Förbundet (KF): Co-operative Union. Under the initiative of the two politicians Gerhard Halfred von Koch and Axel Rylander, it was founded in 1899 as Swedish federation of consumer cooperatives and retail groups. In the 1930s, it expanded rapidly, setting up various industries including the building sector for housing purposes. Nevertheless, in the 1990s, it returned to focus only on retail trade.

Kooperativa Förbundets Arkitektkontor / Kooperativa Förbundets Arkitekt-och Ingenjörsbyrå (KFAI): Architectural and Engineering Office of the Co-operative Union. The Swedish office was opened in 1925 – headed by architect Eskil Sundahl – to meet the cooperative (KF) needs for well-planned and functional buildings for commercial purposes and then comprising many other uses.

Kvadratalen: Old Danish square area unit of measurement. One kvadratalen = 0.39 m^2.

Landshøvdingshus: Governor's House. This housing type is commonly found in Gothenburg, but also in other Swedish cities. Three storey apartment blocks are characterised by the first floor being made of stone, while the second and third floors are made of wood.

Læææægeforeningens: Danish Medical Association. Formerly *Den Almindelige Danske Lægeforening* (DADL). Since its creation in 1857, it has been a professional interest organisation for doctors in Denmark.

Moler: natural clay from the Danish islands of Fur and Mors consisting of diatomaceous silica used to make fire-proof bricks.

Neubühl Werkbundsiedlung (1931): housing estate in the neighbourhoods of Zurich, based on the Stuttgart model. The site location on a green hill above the lake corresponds to the modern demand of light, air and sun. Thanks to an extensive standardisation and types' variations, the housing estate of row houses included 195 apartments in 10 different floor plan types. A construction office under the management of Alfred Roth and Max Ernst Häfeli had been set up beforehand, although the project was developed on a collective basis (e.g. Werner Moser, Rudolf Steiger, Paul Artaria, Carlo Hubacher, Ernst Roth, Hans Schmidt, etc.).

Nordisk Bygningsdag (1932): Nordic Building Days. The event in Helsinki was the second of a long series that commenced in Stockholm (1927) aiming to promote the debate and exchange between Nordic countries in the building sector.

Parkkvarterets Boligforening: Parkkvarteret's Housing Society.

Politiken: Danish daily broadsheet newspaper founded in 1884 as an organ for the so-called European wing of the Left Party. Still active today, it is a pioneer in the development of thematic sections and a general leader in the cultivation of modern subject areas and genre development.

Sound Dues: The Sound Dues (Øresundstolden) were a toll on the passage of ships through the Sound which constituted an overwhelming share of the Danish State's income in the sixteenth and seventeenth centuries.

Sperledæk: Sperle type. According to the Danish Building Code, this type of slab consists of clinker concrete blocks.

Standard (för bostad och bohag) 1934: Standard for Housing and Furnishings exhibition in Stockholm held at the Liljevalchs Konsthall organised by the Swedish Crafts Association and the Swedish Architects' Association. It was a follow-up to the development from the Stockholm exhibition four years earlier.

Statsboligfund: State Housing Fund. As a consequence of a law passed in 1917, the housing sector received a lot of financial support between 1917 and 1927, but in actual fact the first initiatives were produced in 1922. The municipality of Copenhagen frequently functioned as a commissioner of housing projects in that decade.

Stadsarkitektens Direktoratorat: Directorate of the City Architect.

Schweizerische Landesausstellung (1939): Swiss National Exhibition held in Zurich. Paul Artaria used the exhibition covering many topics as a prominent showcase for his simple wooden houses, combining the ideals of modernism with a down-to-earth theme in his model house.

Wiener Werkbundsiedlung (1932): housing estate in Vienna, based on the Stuttgart model, comprised 30 prototypes of 1:1 dwellings of different typologies. The complex was completed by many architects under the direction of Josef Frank.

MØRKHØJ
GYNGEMOSE
GRØNNEMOSE
UTTERSLEV MOSE
EMDRUP
LERSØPARKEN
IDRÆTS PARK
DAMHUSSØEN
VALBY
VIGERSLEV

Københavnske boligtyper

En oversigt udarbejdet under ledelse af
arkitekt, professor Kay Fisker af

Peter Bredsdorff
Ole Reimer
Poul Kjærgaard
Sven Dahlstrøm
Stig Svanholt
Niels Schou
Erik Stengade
Einar Graae
Poul Taubroe Petersen
Eigil Sørensen
C. J. Amnitzbøll
Knud Bartholdy
Ole Buhl
Erik Dahl
Aage Madsen
Bent Waagepetersen
Helge Lindahl
Ejvind Dietz
Oscar Hansen
H. S. Hansen Johnsen
Reinhold Jensen
Esben Klint
Poul Møller
Erling Paludan
Erik Remark
Gudm. Rafn
Peter Sandholt
Hans Schack
Chr. Suhrlykke Petersen
Hugo Sørensen
Erik Villefrance
Henning Agesen

med et oversigtskort udført af
Stadsarkitektens Direktorat
og en statistisk oversigt af
cand. polit. Enrico Hansen

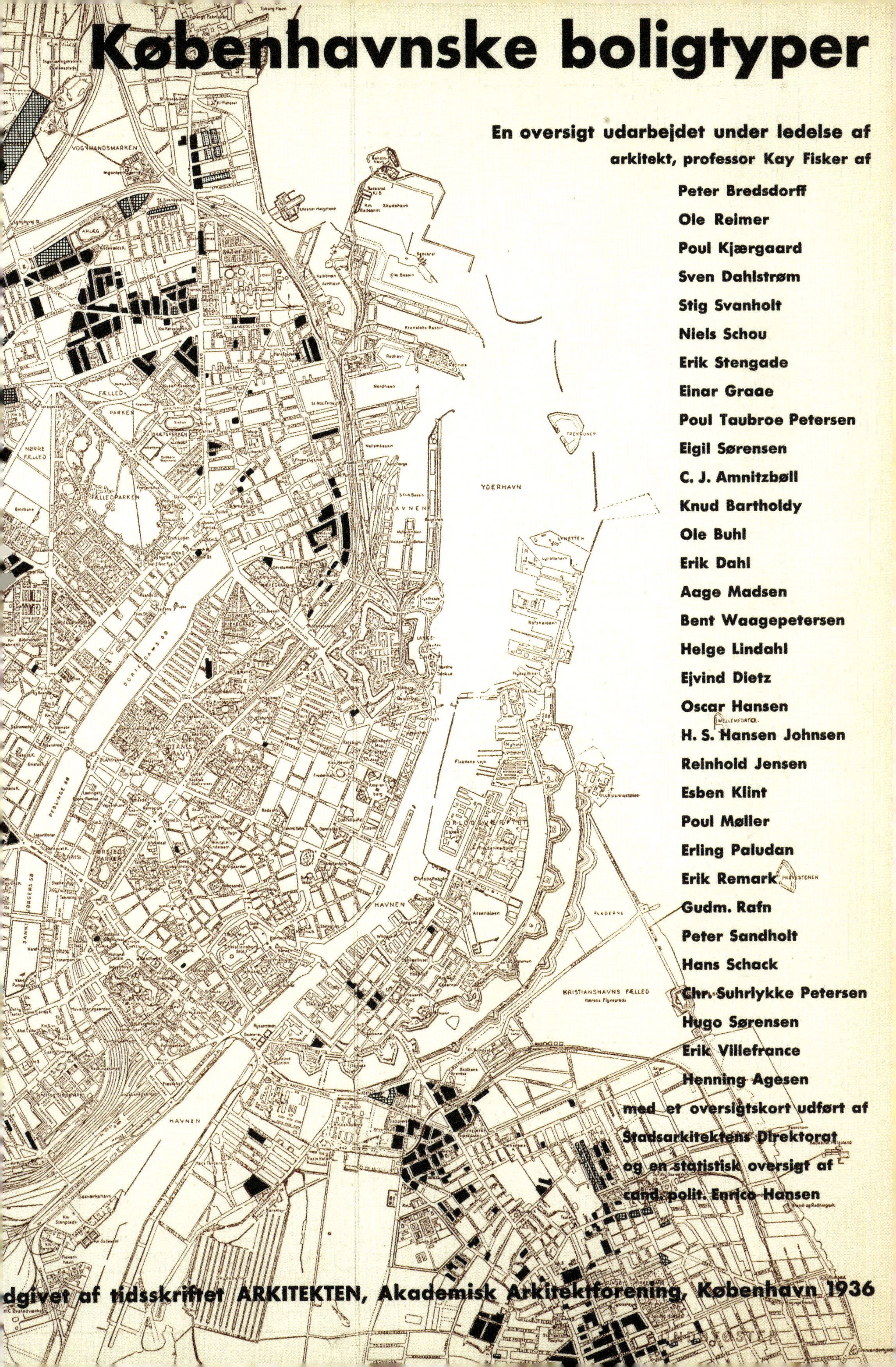

dgivet af tidsskriftet ARKITEKTEN, Akademisk Arkitektforening, København 1936

The evolution of Copenhagen housing types

by Professor Kay Fisker, architect

In the last few years, a number of studies have been carried out at the School of Architecture of the Royal Danish Academy of Fine Arts on the formation of residential housing typologies. With regard to older periods, these studies were part of a survey under the guidance of Professor *K. Gottlob*. In the case of newer building activity, as part of the study of housing construction and under my direction, these studies were assisted by the lecturers in home building from the School of Architecture's third year, *Palle Suenson* and *Eske Kristensen.*

As some of these studies were originally only conducted as independent research, we felt that by reworking and adding supplementary material they could be of interest to academic circles outside the Academy. I went on to collect four studies, each one conducted by study teams of five to ten students, and considered the periods from 1856 to 1900, 1900 to 1914, 1914 to 1928 and 1928 to 1936, each of which forms a complete set in the history of Copenhagen's residential buildings. Each period reveals a distinctive character, being very different from one another.

The year 1856 was chosen as the starting point for the four main groups because it was in that year that Copenhagen saw its first true building regulation. With regard to the chronological divisions, it may be objected that the first period actually ended with the building crash of 1908, and that the next period, in fact, extended all the way to 1916. Nevertheless, we consider that maintaining the above divisions is the most natural course of action.

The studies include only multi-storey residential buildings and small flats. The limit has been set at three large rooms with one small room and only exceptionally are flats larger than two rooms with one small room included.

In the case of older residential buildings, only those that were actually built and only in Copenhagen itself, are included. For the *Statsboligfund* Period and the most recent buildings, a very small number of international types are included for illustrative purposes, and, for the same reason, a few unbuilt types as well. In the case of the studies for the older periods, and following an account of the city's topography and economic history, the procedure has been to locate different housing types from different time periods in specific neighbourhoods and then, on the basis of the municipality's block layouts in these neighbourhoods, select building forms that are considered typical. However, in the course of such a selection, corner residential buildings, with their frequently irregular and atypical forms, have been omitted.

The residential buildings in question were then surveyed or copied in the local housing committee's archive or the Academy's study archives. On-site inspection examined whether the completed buildings corresponded to the copied designs. The buildings were also photographed and notes were taken of special features.

A basis for comparison was established by recording information at the same scale and drawing up schematic overviews of the types which could be considered the most characteristic.

All the older types are drawn in 1:100 and reproduced in 1:500. In the case of the oldest period and due to the form of development, the *entire* residential building, including plot boundaries, is recorded. As for the other three periods, only a double plan element, generally a stairwell, is recorded.
For the last two sections, the plan material is sorted into groups with a basic type as the point of reference. This is drawn in 1:20 as a detailed plan with installations and reproduced in 1:200. The attached type plans are, like the older types, drawn in 1:100 and reproduced in 1:500. The building floor plans are reproduced in 1:5,000, and both floor plans and type plans are reproduced with north facing up. Each of the four sections is denoted by Roman numerals, the types by Arabic numerals and the associated type variants by letters.
To illustrate the four main groups, a brief historical overview of typological backgrounds is included. This overview was prepared by architects *Peter Bredsdorff* and *Ole Reimer.*
The first of the four periods was examined in 1935 and examples were drawn by architects *Poul Kjærgaard, Sven Dahlstrøm, Stig Svanholt* and *Niels Schou.* This material was supplemented in the winter with material illustrating the pre-war period from 1900 to 1914 and was drawn by *Erik Stengade* and *Einar Graae,* later with the assistance of *Paul Taubroe Pedersen* and *Eigild Sørensen.* Illustrative material for newer constructions, in part the State Housing Fund Period 1914–1928, previously studied in 1925 by architect and associate professor *Steen Eiler Rasmussen* with the assistance of *A. C. Gravesen, Henri Garrigues* and *Helge Finsen,* whose study is published in *Arkitekten,* Vol. XXVIII, 1926, p. 77, and in part current constructions from 1928 to1936, has been collected and recorded this winter by *C. J. Amnitzbøll, Knud Bartholdy, Ole Buhl, Erik Dahl, Ejvind Dietz, Reinhold Jensen, Esben Klint, Helge Lindahl, Aage Madsen, Poul Møller, Erling Paludan, Erik Remark, Peter Sandholt, Chr. Suhrlykke Petersen, Bent Waagepetersen, Gudm. Rafn, Hans Schack, Oscar Hansen, Erik Villefrance, Hugo Aaby Sørensen, H. S. Hansen Johnsen og Henning Agesen.*
Oddly, neither the Danish Ministry of Internal Affairs, Copenhagen Municipality nor the Statistical Office possessed any map material showing the extent and distribution in the urban plan of these periods' very large and most important publicly organised building activities. At the time, in connection with Steen Eiler Rasmussen's aforementioned study from the Academy, the preparation of such an overview map had begun, but the work had not been completed beyond 1924. Since I considered such a map to be of great value in terms of knowledge of the scope and nature of the buildings, the *Stadsarkitektens Direktorat* has, at my request, permitted architect *Flemming Teisen* to compile the municipality's rather extensive material and prepare the reproduced map, which, however, has only been able to include buildings from 1924 to 1936 since the material for the older periods is too incomplete to provide an overview. The map is reproduced in 1:60,000 and the excerpt on the cover in 1:3,000. Also included in the excerpt is an account of the fitting out and equipping of a typical two-and-a-half-room flat from 1934, drafted by architect *Gunnar Holm* at the behest of *Københavns almindelige Boligselskab* (*KAB*) and published in *Ausstattung der Kleinwohnung,* published by *Internationaler Verband fur Wohnungswesen,* Stuttgart 1935.

At the end of the overview, the principal administrator, political candidate *Enrico Hansen*, prepared an overview of the extent of the four construction periods, price conditions, population growth, flat sizes and type numbers. Our original intention was to publish a complete record of the period's construction in its entirety with this publication in mind, but the material turned out to be too extensive.

The present study is an attempt towards more methodical working methods in the study of architecture at the Academy and should not be considered an exhaustive account of the subject's architectural heritage. It may nonetheless contribute to shedding light on the development of the smallest flats in multi-storey residential buildings, especially during the major building periods around the turn of the century and in the post-war years, which have so greatly influenced the city. When assessing this study, however, one must take into account that the selection of types has necessarily been rather arbitrary; that the studies were produced on the basis of quite dissimilar material and sometimes from very incomplete information, by students with very different views and abilities, and furthermore in a relatively short period of time. I therefore ask for forbearance with regard to the errors and shortcomings that exist, and with an eye to continuing these studies, add that the Academy would be grateful to be made aware of any errors or misconceptions.

Development until 1856

an historical overview by Peter Bredsdorff and Ole Reimer

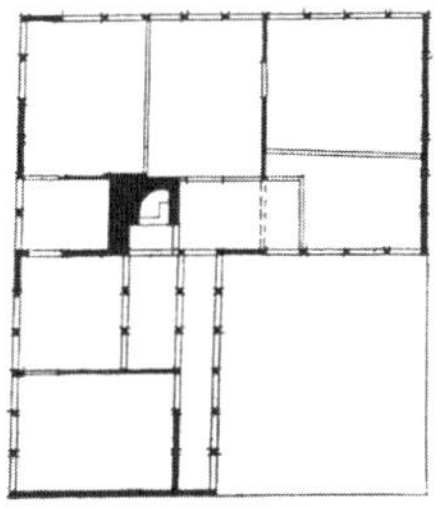

Nikolay Boye Bartskær's house. Circa 1680. The plan is the only known example of a half-timbered house in Copenhagen from this time. Regardless of the fact that it is a corner house, one can easily grasp the significance of the wooden partitions, the external gallery and the central fireplace.

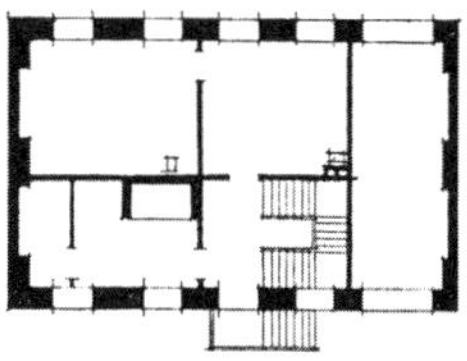

Master builder Krieger's model plan. 1729. From "Berechmungen und Dessins auf 3 differente grundgemauerte Gebaude", published in support of the city's reconstruction after the fire in 1728.

In medieval Copenhagen, practically every family lived in its own house, consisting of generally small and humble abodes. The city developed and grew without any regulatory dictates or any regard for the common good, and the town plan became erratic and often random. Over the course of the sixteenth century, Copenhagen's distinctive position as the country's capital became more strongly cemented: both financially, with independent city traders beginning to assert themselves abroad; and politically, given that the character of the city as the seat of the reigning monarch and central administration had become more prominent. Just after the dawn of the seventeenth century and following the best examples from international capitals and royal courts, modern fortifications and *new urban planning designs in the spirit of the Renaissance* were drawn up with clear and practical rectangular street grids in Christianshavn and "New Copenhagen", the neighbourhood between Gothersgade and the citadel.
Little is known about individual houses.
It must be considered fairly certain that the original house type was one in which the long side faced the street. However, gabled houses, which were common in northern German and Dutch trading cities with which Copenhagen was connected, seem to have played a large,

and perhaps dominant, role. This type was certainly natural for very narrow plots, and there were, after all, entire streets that had originally emerged as *market streets* with more or less itinerant stalls on small plots of land.
The design and fitting out of ordinary houses was entirely determined by the timber structure, and plan types were dominated by the taut bay divisions of the timber framework. A series of continuous partitions from one exterior wall to the other were a constructive necessity with the rooms arranged *en suite*. Upper floors were connected by an external corridor upon which the staircases were also built. Efforts were made to economise as much as possible on very expensive chimney structures and only a limited number of rooms were habitable in the winter.
At the end of the seventeenth century, a new residential building type emerged, one based on the construction of masonry foundations. Since the building's stability no longer depended on the *rigidity* of the timber-frame structure, but on the *weight and mass* of the brickwork, the continuous cross partitions were no longer a constructive necessity, and a very cost-effective plan type was developed in which a number of street-facing rooms were separated from those facing the yard by a *main partition*. Despite the ordinance of 1683, which required the use of foundation walls in large parts of the city as security against the fairly frequent fires, the new building type gained ground very slowly and only made a decisive breakthrough after the great fire of 1728.

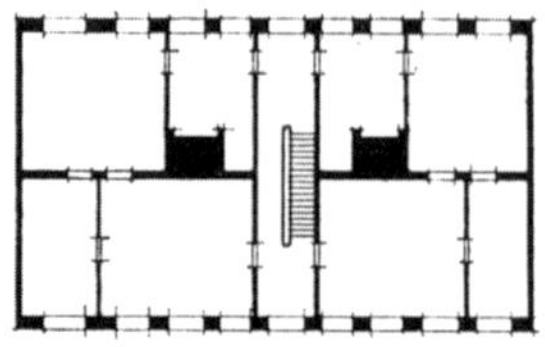

Studiestræde 16. Late eighteenth century. Plan of ordinary ground floor flat, clearly related to the Krieger house. Before 1800 the stairwells in these plan types were almost always continuous to allow the flats to have an entrance to living room and the kitchen.

The coup d'état and introduction of absolute monarchy in 1660 completed Copenhagen's development as an administrative city and seat of the royal court. The country's administration was completely centralised in Copenhagen while the city's self-government was effectively abolished. Now it only lacked an appearance that corresponded to the power concentrated in it. Initially, there was simply an attempt to surround Slotsholmen with monumental or at least uniform buildings. Later, interest focused on the building of "Frederiksstaden", the Amalienborg quarter. But even before construction began here, there had been scattered attempts to bring the existing neighbourhoods more into line with the contemporary demands for orderly and "uniform" cityscapes. Thus, already in 1693, oriel windows were banned and in 1737 the city clerk of works was ordered to ensure that the windows of new houses were of equal height with those of their neighbours.
The great fire of 1728 marked a new era for ordinary homes of the burgher class. Of the 1,450 properties destroyed by fire, only 40 were entirely, and 179 partially, built with masonry foundations. During reconstruction, however, houses with masonry foundations became the general rule, although it was difficult to enforce an effective ban on timber-frame constructions. Immediately after the fire, the new flat type with continuous *longitudinal partitions* received a kind of official stamp in a booklet of pattern drawings by master builder I. C. Krieger. The plan was very clear: Through a corridor, one entered a staircase facing the yard. From here there was an entrance to the kitchen and a parlour. As a rule, the kitchen and a smaller room faced the yard, while three, two, or sometimes just one room faced the street.

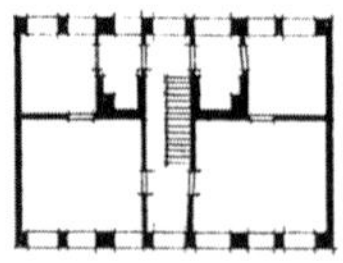

Wildersplads 15. Late eighteenth century. Significantly reduced version of the same plan system. Corresponding staircase and chimney placement.

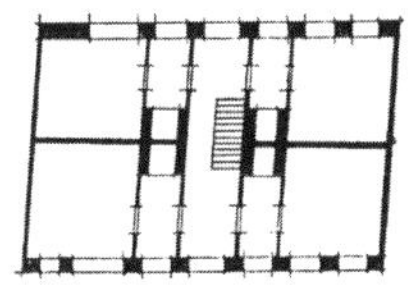

Studiestræde 8. Back building. Late 18th century. The plan type here is reduced to the absolute minimum: four flats per landing. A single living room is accessed through a single kitchen.

This plan was varied in countless ways, from grand single-family burgher townhouses to small multi-storey flats that could be built both on very wide as well as very narrow plots. Common to all the variants was that they almost always lacked entry halls, as well as a certain rigidity in the plan as a result of the flats usually being heated from a single fireplace. For the smallest flat types, this meant that all passage from the stairs to living rooms was through the kitchen.
For a long time, these somewhat impractical and slightly differentiated flat types were sufficient for Copenhagen's regular middle classes and only over a hundred years after the plan type had had its breakthrough did it lose its leading position in housing construction.

The last part of the eighteenth century saw the significant rise of the bourgeoisie. After the state-subsidised, tariff-dependant industrial enterprises from the age of mercantilism wound down, spontaneous industrialisation began to take hold. The old masters' small workshops were replaced by larger workshops, home industries and manufacturing, and a proper urban working class began to form.
Growing demand for the simplest and cheapest housing was a significant factor in this development. Families that owned their own homes outright became increasingly rare. Already around 1730, an average of eighteen people lived in each dwelling. Even for relatively modest-sized flats, there was a trend towards making them more comfortable and separating rooms with different uses more clearly from one another. But just as at the start of the century, it took a great fire for the new trend to make a serious breakthrough. As a direct result of this fire, in which 343 properties burnt down, a number of new building regulations came into force, e.g. the by-law of 1795. In addition to a strongly expressed desire for flats to have access to two staircases, it was decided that all exterior walls should be erected as masonry foundation walls, gables should be equipped with firewall parapets, wooden cornices were prohibited, and building heights and minimum wall thicknesses were established.
It had become common to build residential buildings with the staircases more centrally placed and the kitchen positioned so as not to make it difficult to connect with the other rooms. In the medium-sized flats, the entry hall became more common.
During reconstruction after the fire, a new, slightly larger house type took the leading position. In this type, the kitchen, a secondary staircase (according to regulations) and gradually additional rooms were pushed out into a side wing. The natural consequence of this plan, e.g. the type with a bedroom in a side wing, dining room in the outward corner and a communicating corridor to the kitchen, only appeared in the latter part of the nineteenth century.

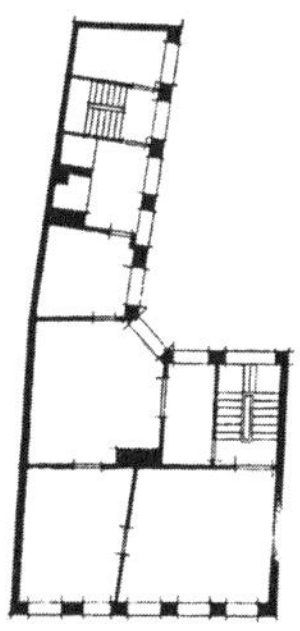

Skoubogade 4. Circa 1800. Typical flat with two staircases and a side wing. Particularly in plans where more than a single living room was located in the side wing, the lack of a separate connection to the kitchen was inconvenient.

Copenhagen housing types from 1856 to 1914

a study by Poul Kjærgaard, Sven Dahlstrøm, Stig Svanholt and Niels Schou

In the early nineteenth century, after a glorious boom period, the city had run into difficulties.

The great fire of 1795 and the bombardment of 1807 had left many houses in ashes. Money lost its value with the state bankruptcy in 1813 and upon Norway's secession, Copenhagen lost a large trade area. The Sound Dues drew trade away from the city, and it was cheaper to import goods via Hamburg, where a significant part of the middlemen's profits remained.

Under these difficult conditions, the city was forced into a prolonged period of stagnation, and it was not until the 1830s that its effects began to wane. Copenhagen now became a warehousing and shipping point for agricultural products strengthened by agricultural reforms, and after the Three Years' War over Schleswig-Holstein, the country almost completely shut down imports from Hamburg. Trade in Copenhagen gathered momentum again, and the level of trade, which was particularly low during the difficult years, faced a new boom period.

This increase in trade was followed by a similar upswing in industry. A wide range of technical advances had set progress in motion, the most important of which was the use of the steam engine as a motive force.

The growth of industry was due in large part to the enterprising trade associations established in the 1840s, which, to the protest of artisans, encouraged the bourgeoisie to engage in industrial entrepreneurship. These efforts were encouraged by favourable financing opportunities, with the limited company system becoming commonplace at that time and the rapidly expanding rail network multiplying its market access opportunities. Already existing industrial enterprises were rationalised and many new companies were formed, several of which became of lasting importance, e.g. Burmeister & Wain's engineering and shipbuilding and the Carlsberg breweries.

The self-conscious and enterprising bourgeoisie now saw as its task to acquire a political position corresponding to its considerable economic power and eventually it succeeded in vanquishing absolutism.

A municipal law from 1840 granted the bourgeoisie a measure of influence in the city's government. In the constitution of 1849 a commitment to complete autonomy was granted and finally in 1857 this promise was fulfilled by a new municipal law. In the same year, the Sound Dues were abolished and the old market and guild monopolies were replaced by the law on freedom of trade to the great benefit of growing trade and industry.

With all these advances, the preconditions were created for the city's transformation from a royal government and garrison town to a civilian-governed commercial and industrial city.

The numerous newly-formed enterprises drew significant manpower to the city and the population grew rapidly. However, the city was very

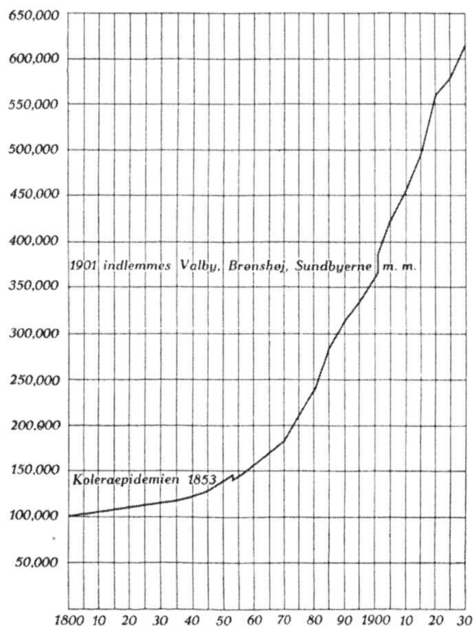

Copenhagen's population in the period 1800–1930

Gable end visible after demolitions in Vognmagergade. A clear testimony to the difficult years before the walls were pulled down, this shows construction occurred here in at least three different stages.

poorly equipped to receive this sizeable invasion, as accommodation conditions left much to be desired. In 1850, the city maintained the same boundaries that Christian IV had established 200 years earlier.

Copenhagen was a fortress city and the military authorities ordered that a large area, the so-called demarcation grounds, should not be urbanised. Within the demarcation line, which was located along on present day Falkonér Allé-Jagtvejen, only small one-storey wooden and half-timbered houses were allowed which could be quickly demolished in the event of a war, so that the enemy could not find cover, but which could also be directly shelled from the rampart's bastions. The distance to the areas on the other side of the demarcation line was far too great (about 3 km) for the means of transport of the time to consider expanding the city on the other side. Therefore, there was nothing else to do but huddle together behind the ramparts. During the period of stagnation between 1800–1830, the city made do with the available space, only in 1831 it did reach the same number of houses as in 1807. However, as early as 1840 the paucity of land within the ramparts began to make itself felt. It now became common to build new floors on top of the old buildings, and back and side buildings were built in abundance, and a large number of basements and ceilings were used for habitation. The Borgergade-Adelgade neighbourhood is typical of this period, which in its layout and initial settlement made perfect sense, but due to this massive urbanisation, was quickly transformed into a slum.

The situation gradually became entirely untenable, and it was clear that the city had to expand. Finally, in 1852 the military succumbed to public opinion, and it was decided to move the demarcation line to the inner banks of the lakes. The cholera epidemic in 1853 showed that this expansion had come too late. The emergence and vast extent of the disease was due solely to the poor hygiene associated with reckless overpopulation.

Building on the released land immediately took off and to a great extent the decisive factor for this construction was the gradual change that took hold in the nature of the housing supply. Previously, building activity had been largely based on self-financing, limited to only a few wealthy families. They rarely built in excess of their own needs, and consequently the poor had to lodge in the lower and upper floors of these row houses or in back and side buildings when these later became common, while the wealthy faced the street.

In the meantime, in 1851 the first general building society was established. This created the opportunity for the construction of larger-scale rental housing. The new neighbourhoods were also chiefly dominated by multi-storey buildings of small flats, determined by the new social class of wage labourers created by industrialisation. Initial construction outside the fortifications occurred where links to the city were best, namely along the roads leading out of the city centre through Nørreport and Vesterport, i.e., Nørrebrogade and Vesterbrogade, and later on newly paved streets in the Nørrebro neighbourhood such as Murergade, Tømrergade and Smedegade, and on Viktoriagade and Absalonsgade in the Vesterbro neighbourhood.

1856–1889

The layout of these streets initially occurred without any plan whatsoever. It was not until 1856 that a building act for Copenhagen was passed. This act established a set of hygienic, fire and building requirements for new constructions against the background of experience with fires and the cholera epidemic.

Before that time, certain provisions had existed, among others, the bye-law of 1795, which contained provisions for wall thicknesses, building heights, truncated corners, chimney construction, etc., and the *preference* of two staircases for each flat. Furthermore, the guild regulations contained a number of instructions on craftsmanship, but these various provisions, which had no legal force, were difficult to enforce and eventually were practically forgotten.

The law of 1856 contained all these requirements, in some cases in stricter form. For example, henceforth it was *compulsory* that every flat in new buildings should have access to two staircases. This law left its mark on neighbourhoods built in the immediately following years, foremost in the Vesterbro, Nørrebro and Gammelholm neighbourhoods.

Fifteen years after the first building act came the second in 1871, which only contained insignificant changes. The most important provision was the requirement for greenfield sites to be increased from ¼ to ⅓ outside the city walls.

Not even four years later, it had to be supplemented with the law of 1875, which prescribed the minimum distance between buildings which is still in effect to this day. Prior to that, there had been no provisions in this area at all, which has greatly influenced the neighbourhoods that had been built previously. Such neighbourhoods include the areas around Saxogade in Vesterbro and Fredensgade-Ryesgade and Skyttegade-Jægergade in Nørrebro.

By 1867, the military had definitively abandoned the city as a fortress. The last strip of the demarcation area between the lakes and the ramparts was handed over for development, and this was where the Frederiksborggade-Nansensgade neighbourhood originated in the 1870s.

The building act's requirement that each flat have access to two staircases has been a very decisive factor in construction since 1856, making buildings fundamentally distinct from those of the previous period. The oldest of the types examined, I_1, is only equipped with a single staircase (built in 1856, it was only the following year that the building act came into force outside the ramparts). The type corresponds closely to older plans such as the residential building shown from Fiolstræde 27. The only difference is a small entry hall with access to all rooms.

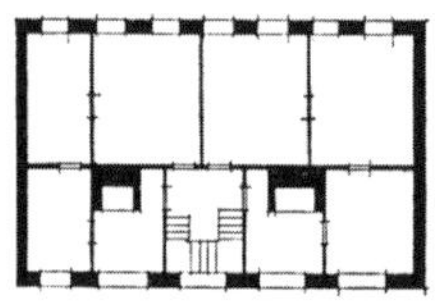

Fiolstræde 27: Typical example of a small multi-storey residential building after the fire in 1795. The large chimney structure had to serve all rooms, so there is no space for an entry hall.

After 1857, there is no way around the two staircases. However, it is obvious that, for economic reasons, every effort continued to be made to get by with as few staircases as possible in each property.

An expression of a building's staircase ratio is obtained by dividing the number of stairs in the building in question by the number of flats per floor. This figure, which in the study is designated the *staircase quotient*, does not necessarily provide a conception of the staircase conditions in a fire, but will always show the economics of the staircase arrangement, since a high quotient indicates an expensive installation and a low quotient a correspondingly cheap one (cf. I_{18}, quotient 1.25, with example I_{10}, quotient 0.17).

In some of the oldest types under study, namely larger flats, one immediately finds the later common system of main and kitchen staircases (e.g. I_3 and I_7).

In other cases, the law is fully enforced by providing the flats with access to the second staircase through a connecting corridor. This approach is particularly economically advantageous in small flats. For larger types (e.g. I_2), one would have thought that the equally inexpensive system of main and kitchen staircases would have been preferable.
The type with a connecting corridor between two-room flats, thereby economising on two staircases, was extremely common (e.g. I_4, I_5 and I_6). However, in terms of utility, it has major flaws when you consider that a flat has spaces on both sides of the corridor that serves as a connecting passage. In many cases, the passage between the two flats has been blocked up and the door to the stairs locked, so that, in fact, an ordinary 2-room flat has access to only one staircase, and hence is in violation of the law. Interestingly, an 1897 petition to the local housing committee regarding such an offence discovered by the police, reads as follows:
"Ever since a night shelter for the homeless was established by the Salvation Army in Saxogade, the occupants of the adjoining properties are regularly exposed to vagabonds lying and sleeping in the corridor between the stairs at night, which is a great nuisance. However, if the doors were allowed to be closed, this nuisance would be prevented."
It is a minor leap from a short connecting corridor to a regular corridor system, as shown in types I_8, I_9 and I_{10}. In these types, the rooms of the flat are situated side by side along the long corridor. In terms of usefulness, this type is better than the previous one, as the rooms of the flat are connected to each other without having to pass through the corridor. On the other hand, the flats are very small and frequently without an entry hall, and the often over thirty-metre-long and barely 1 m wide corridors are neither directly illuminated nor ventilated. A more humane and fairly common staircase system consists of two opposite-facing staircases with no separation between them and a presumably statutory spacing of just nine Danish *alen* (e.g. I_6, I_{12} and I_{16}).
Alongside the rapid development of typologies for individual flats, there is a general change in the building method for properties, too.
The oldest residential buildings outside the ramparts traditionally had a wing parallel to the street that was the width of the plot with a gate leading to the courtyard, where a low stable or workshop building was often erected (e.g. I_1).
At a later stage, when the streets were laid down at a greater distance from each other (no doubt for economic reasons) and as a result the plots gained considerable depth, they could not be exploited with sufficient advantage with such simple street buildings.
Thereafter new building forms become commonplace. The most natural type involves numerous parallel houses situated one behind the other. While earlier middle and back houses were usually built long after the front building (Adelgade-Borgergade), now the buildings were built all at once. A glaring example is I_5, with three identical row houses with a distance of 6.5 m and a distance to the neighbouring property line of just under 2 m.
Early on, another development enters the picture, involving the protrusion of a wing into the courtyard that is perpendicular to the

street. This wing may have an ordinary staircase with an entry from the courtyard (e.g. I_7, I_{13}, I_{14} and I_{16}) or it can contain a passage system; true corridor buildings are of this type (e.g. I_8, I_9, I_{10} and I_{12}). Initially, the T-shaped building occurs individually, but later appears under improved conditions among joint blocks with a common lightwell (e.g. I_{14}).

A rare form of residential dwelling made of small flats is the L-shaped building that is so common for larger flats. The rarity of this form is undoubtedly due to the fact that it requires a disproportionately large and expensive staircase (e.g. I_{17}, the staircase quotient).

The whole period is characterised by the unplanned way the plots were built on. The construction projects were small, rarely more than a single residential building with one main staircase, and this was built quite arbitrarily, without regard for the surrounding buildings. Interesting in this respect are three consecutive properties (e.g. I_{15}, I_{16} and I_{17}). From the street they look quite similar, but the shapes of the buildings are very different.

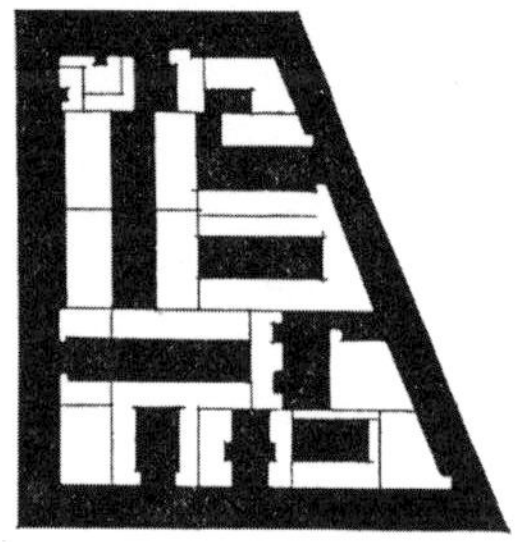

Period from 1856 to circa 1880

Disorganised overbuilding, highly variable plot sizes, vastly different buildings, small irregular courtyards.

The major building periods in the 1870s and 1880s are among the most lamentable in the city's history. During these years, thousands of small, wretched flats with narrow, dark rooms and miserable staircases were erected. For the speculative builder, it was all about ensuring maximum exploitation by keeping the standard of the flats to the absolute minimum of legal requirements. Although the city had gone through the tragic experiences of what overcrowding can lead to (the cholera epidemic), during these years, vast new slums were built. No one considered taking action or managed to slow down the wild, exploitative building spree. Tenants were aplenty, as ever-growing industry beckoned thousands of people to the city. The poor traffic conditions made it necessary to shorten the distance between home and the workplace as much as possible and the workers' low wages did not allow them to make any sort of demand regarding the quality of the housing. The only choice for these people was the cramped flats in these new districts just outside the inner city. While the flats in the first residential buildings outside the ramparts were quite large, the construction of small flats took off in earnest in the 1870s. This was greatly accelerated by the land tax act of 1802, which stipulated that all flats less than 69 *kvadratalen* (approx. 27 m^2) were exempted from this tax. In 1873, the provision was extended to all flats under 80 *kvadratalen* (approx. 31.5 m^2), which resulted in an effort to keep flats below this insufficient minimum. Thus, from this period it is not uncommon to find kitchens under 3 m^2 and often the flat's largest space is not even 10 m^2.

1889–1900

The building acts of 1871 and 1875 soon proved to be insufficient. In 1878 therefore, an audit committee was set up, but it was only eleven years later in 1889, that a new law was passed that is still in force. Its most significant amendments were the requirement that street width measure 30 *alen* (18.83 m) instead of the previously required 20 (12.55 m), as well as the requirement that living spaces contain a floor area of at least 15 *kvadratalen* (5.91 m^2) and a window facing the open air. The only requirement made by the Acts of 1856 and 1871 for such spaces was a minimum height of four *alen* (2.51 m).

Accordingly, the development of very small flats stops abruptly and the average area of the flats increases significantly, as the law's requirement

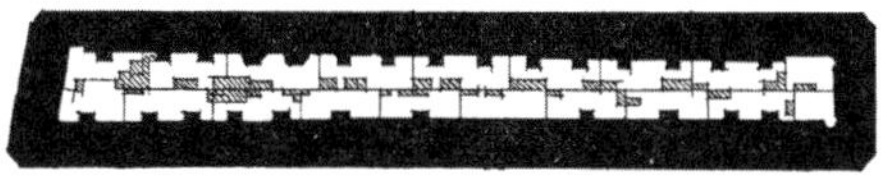

Period from circa 1880 to 1900

Plan-based overbuilding, narrow, identical plots, uniform buildings (comb houses), courtyards divided by fences and bicycle sheds.

of an increase in size of the smallest rooms, kitchen and maid's room is automatically extended to the other rooms.
As the law of 1889 prohibited long common corridors and required three doors between the two staircases, the prevalence of overcrowded buildings was significantly reduced. The only possible location of the staircases for many years remained the ubiquitous main and kitchen stairs.
At the same time, building styles clearly undergo change. The newly laid streets become wider and are placed closer together, thus reducing the depth of the plots, meaning there is no room for back and side buildings. Nevertheless, maximum plot utilisation is ensured by reducing the costly façade length as much as possible. To achieve this, kitchens and kitchen staircases must be pushed out into the courtyard. Here a number of inward-facing corners are found where it is often difficult to comply with the building distance rules. A particularly clear example of efforts to solve this problem is example I_{18}.
The protruding staircase towers are characteristic of buildings from this period. They are often assembled in long narrow blocks, the so-called comb houses with row development with the sparse courtyard area divided by fences and sheds. Also characteristic of the period are the flat slate roofs allowing builders to push the height stipulations to the limits of the law and, at the same time, constituting a dignified consummation of the Italian palace façade, which even the cheapest residential buildings were adorned with at the expense of real merit.

1900–1914

In the early 1890s, construction had decreased considerably, but around the turn of the century, a new recovery was in full swing. Extensive neighbourhoods were built, such as the Sønder Boulevard quarter, outer Nørrebro, Islands Brygge, the Aladdin quarter and some of the areas incorporated in 1901 (with their incorporation, the city's area had grown threefold from about 2,300 ha to approx. 7,000 ha, while the population increased by only 5½ per cent).
In the meantime, unfettered construction soon led to overproduction, and the number of vacant flats rose alarmingly. The banking crisis of 1908 brought an end to all construction, and in the following years very few flats were built: in 1911 only 650 compared with 6,500 in 1903.
This halt in new construction led to housing shortages in the space of a few years, as the large reserve of vacant flats was gradually exhausted, and by 1916 the situation had become so serious that the state and the municipality had to intervene.
In the plans for small flats in the period 1900–1914, there were few variations from the standard type established by the act of 1889 with the main and kitchen staircases. The most important change in the plan itself is the introduction of new service installations.The water closet became common shortly after 1900. For small flats, it was often located on the kitchen staircase for use by several families (e.g. II_{21}; only later did each flat have its own WC (e.g. II_{24} and subsequent types). Prior to the introduction of the water closet, in some cases, barrel toilets could be found on each floor (e.g. I_7 and I_{14}), but by far the most common were courtyard privies.
Cooking gas also becomes common around the turn of the century and as a consequence, the chimney structure is greatly simplified. Mid-eighteenth century types (Ex. I_1) still had open hearths that required a chimney of immense proportions. In the 1870s, cast iron stoves could be fed

to a normal 9" chimney (e.g. I_4 and several types up to II_{27}). With the introduction of gas, the chimney finally disappears completely from the kitchen (e.g. II_{28}, II_{31} and II_{32}).
The main difference between the 1900–1914 period and the immediately preceding one lies in the design.
The building style represents a reaction to the bleak, rectilinear street layout of the 1880s and 1890s. The aim now was a more romantic street image with curved streets and major offsets in the façades.
Construction materials also break with the previous period. External rendering and stucco are replaced by clean brick surfaces, and the flat slate roofs are replaced by steep tile roofs from which high gabled sections protrude that, together with oriel windows and balconies, break up the smooth street façades.
Construction projects increase in scale and, characteristic of this period, the building of even small flats is handed over to professional architects, who previously had usually only been called in for the design of the façades. Among the architects themselves is a growing interest in housing construction and urban planning, and this interest results in new, attractive residential neighbourhoods, built according to an overall plan under the leadership of the most important people of the time.

Period from circa 1900 to 1916
Romantic-style building, curved streets, numerous projections in the façades, the whole block built at once and according to an overall plan. Courtyard area open and free.

References list

J. P. Trap: København og Frederiksberg, 1929 (extensive bibliography).

Salmonsens Konversationsleksikon: Afsnittet om København

Københavns Kommunalkalender, 1934.

Kraks Tidstavler, 1930.

Villads Christensen: København 1848–1857, 1912.

Henrich Hansen: Bygningskommissionens Historie

Henrich Hansen: Historiske Meddelelser om Københavns Bygningsvæsen, 1931.

Carl Bruun: København.

O. C. Nielsen: Københavns Historie og Beskrivelse.

Stadsingeniørens Direktorat: Københavns byplanmæssige Forhold, 1932.

Jens Warming: Danmarks Erhvervs- og Samfundsliv.

Jens Walrming: Boliglovgivning (extensive bibliography).

Thalbitzer: Krediktkassen for Husejere i København 1797–1922.

V. Schou: Byggevirksomheden i Danmark i de sidste 75 Aar, 1911.

"Arkitektforeningens" journal I, 1908.

"Før og Nu" journal.

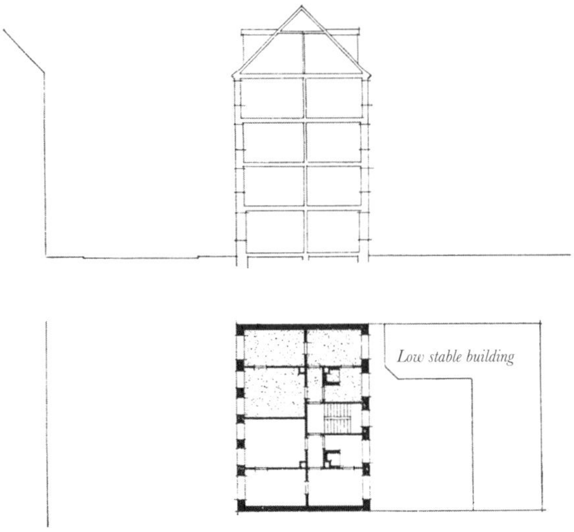

1 *Location: Eskildsgade 5*
2 *Year built: 1856*
3 *Number of residential floors: 5*
4 *Flat type: 3 rooms*
5 *Gross floor area: 51.5 m²*
6 *Room dimensions: kitchen 4.4 m², largest room 12 m²*
7 *Number of flats per floor: 2*
8 *Plot area: 240 m²*
9 *Built-up area: 103 m² and 73 m² stables, total 176 m²*
10 *Staircase quotient: 0.50*

I_1

Typical example of the very first buildings outside the walls. A direct descendant of the small Empire townhouse both in design and façade.

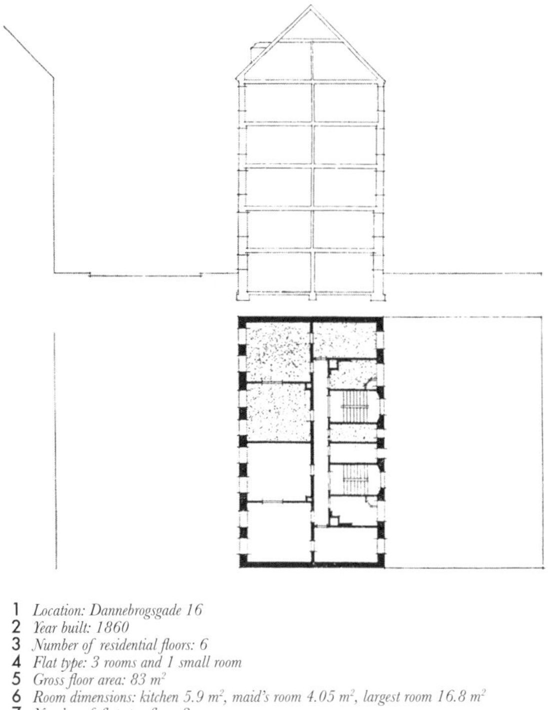

1 *Location: Dannebrogsgade 16*
2 *Year built: 1860*
3 *Number of residential floors: 6*
4 *Flat type: 3 rooms and 1 small room*
5 *Gross floor area: 83 m²*
6 *Room dimensions: kitchen 5.9 m², maid's room 4.05 m², largest room 16.8 m²*
7 *Number of flats per floor: 2*
8 *Plot area: 342 m²*
9 *Built-up area: 166 m² and 63 m² stables, total 229 m²*
10 *Staircase quotient: 1.00*

I_2

Unusual staircase placement for larger flats. Both staircases serve as main stairs for a single flat on each floor and the passage between them is only used in case of fire.

I_3

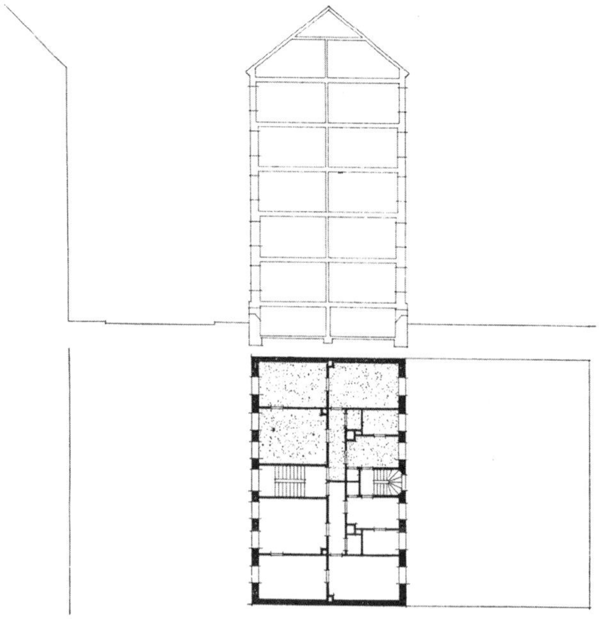

1 *Location: Viktoriagade 21*
2 *Year built: 1869*
3 *Number of residential floors: 6*
4 *Flat type: 3 rooms and 1 small room*
5 *Gross floor area: 89 m²*
6 *Room dimensions: kitchen 7 m², maid's room 3.85 m², largest room 16.5 m²*
7 *Number of flats per floor: 2*
8 *Plot area: 377 m²*
9 *Built-up area: 178 m²*
10 *Staircase quotient: 1.00*

The two staircases have different functions. The representational staircase to the street and the smaller kitchen staircase to the courtyard. Each flat has direct access to both staircases.

I_4

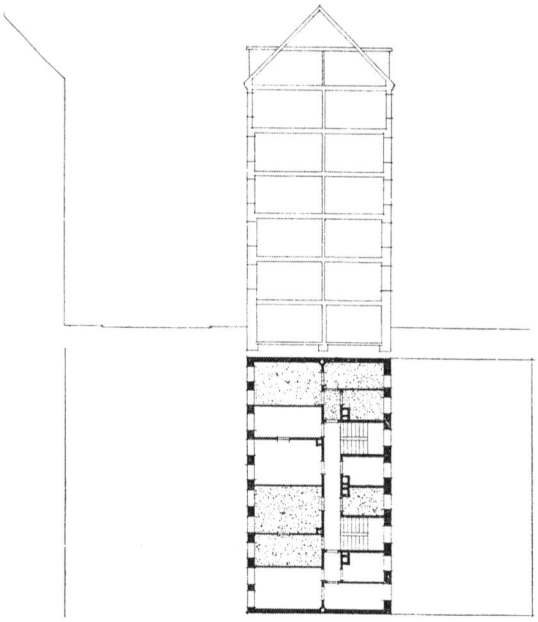

1 *Location: Slotsgade 21*
2 *Year built: 1873*
3 *Number of residential floors: 6*
4 *Flat type: 2 rooms*
5 *Gross floor area: 42.1 m²*
6 *Room dimensions: kitchen 5.2 m², largest room 14.2 m²*
7 *Number of flats per floor: 4*
8 *Plot area: 330 m²*
9 *Built-up area: 167 m²*
10 *Staircase quotient: 0.50*

The connecting passage between small flats is particularly economical, as it saves having two staircases. When the corridor is blocked up, as has probably often been the case, the result is ordinary two-room flats with staircase systems just like I_1.

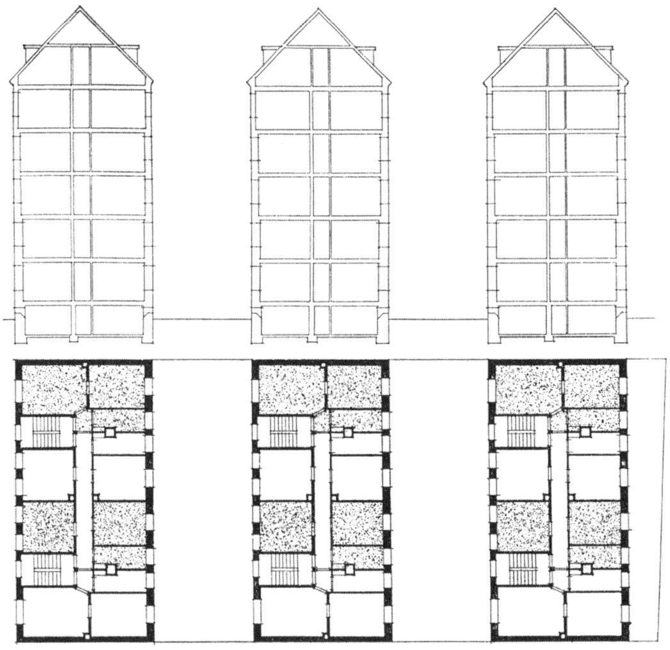

1 *Location: Saxogade 19*
2 *Year built: 1874*
3 *Number of residential floors: 6*
4 *Flat type: 2 rooms*
5 *Gross floor area: 44.5 m²*
6 *Room dimensions: kitchen 4.7 m², largest room 14.4 m²*
7 *Number of flats per floor: 4 per building, total 12*
8 *Plot area: 840 m²*
9 *Built-up area: 530 m²*
10 *Staircase quotient: 0.50*

I_5

Three relatively uniform contemporary residential buildings with connecting corridor. 172 people live on the entire grounds, which is the size of a common detached house plot.

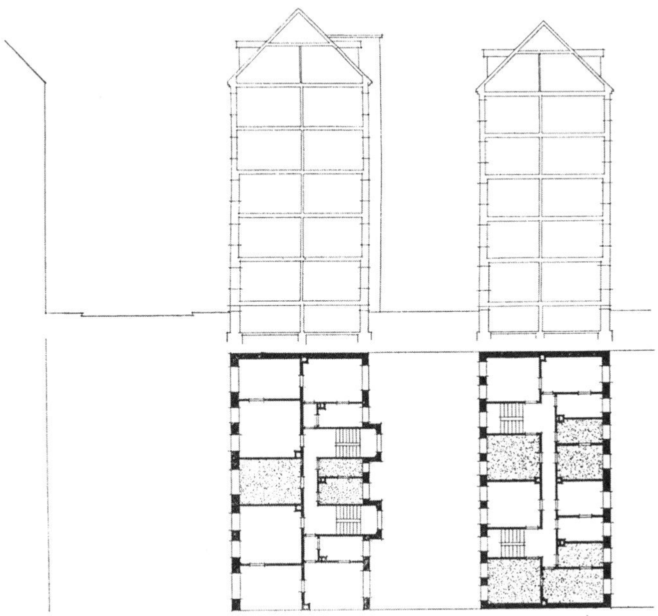

1 *Location: Absalonsgade 36*
2 *Year built: 1874*
3 *Number of residential floors: 6*
4 *Flat type: front bldg.: 3 rooms and 1 room, back bldg.: 2 rooms*
5 *Gross floor area: 3-room type 66.6 m², 1 room type 31.3 m², 2 room-type 37.5 m²*
6 *Room dimensions: kitchen 5.2 m², largest room in front bldg. 15.5 m², in back bldg. 10 m²*
7 *Number of flats per floor: front bldg. 2 flats w. 3 rooms and 1 flat w. 1 rooms + small room, back block 4 flats w. 2 rooms*
8 *Plot area: 770 m²*
9 *Built-up area: 454.5 m²*
10 *Staircase quotient: front bldg. 0.66, back bldg. 0.50*

I_6

This building, also with a connecting corridor, continues the old tradition of the better flats facing the street in contrast to I_5.

I₇

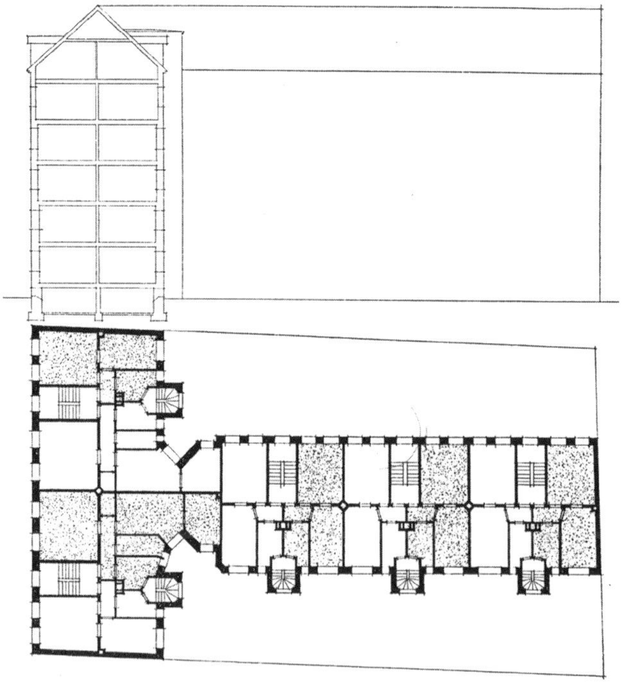

T-shaped building with ordinary main and kitchen staircase system. The staircase placement requires two gates through the front building.

1 *Location: Wesselsgade 22*
2 *Year built: 1868*
3 *Number of residential floors: 6*
4 *Flat type: 2 rooms and 2 rooms + smaller room*
5 *Gross floor area: 42.1 m²*
6 *Room dimensions: kitchen 4.5 m², maid's room 3.24 m², largest room 18.4 m²*
7 *Number of flats per floor: 8 flats w. 2 rooms and 2 flats w. 2 rooms + 2 smaller rooms*
8 *Plot area: 1285 m²*
9 *Built-up area: 482 m² and front bldg. 208 m², total 690 m²*
10 *Staircase quotient: 1.00*

I₈

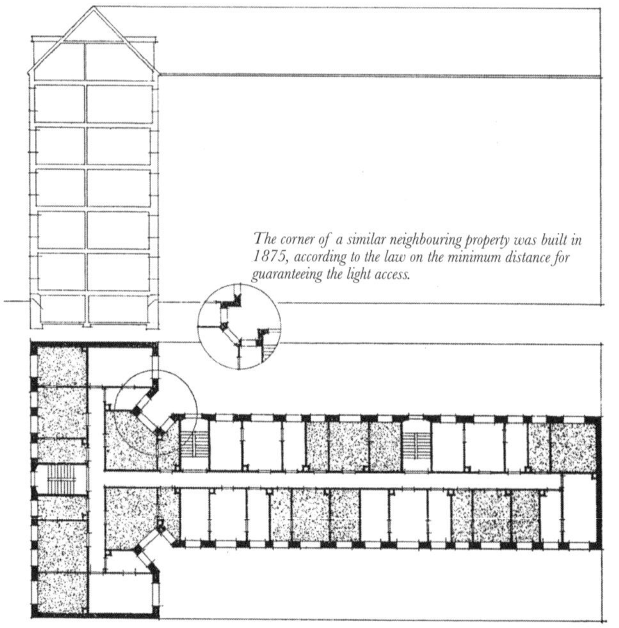

T-shaped building with corridor system. The corridor is 33 m wide and without direct light. The flats have no entry halls.

1 *Location: Fredensgade 14*
2 *Year built: 1874*
3 *Number of residential floors: 6*
4 *Flat type: 2 rooms and 1 room*
5 *Gross floor area: 2 rooms 40 and 30 m², 1 room 30 and 24 m²*
6 *Room dimensions: kitchen 3.9 m², largest room 11 m² and 9.1 m²*
7 *Number of flats per floor: 9 flats w. 2 rooms and 6 flats w. 1 room*
8 *Plot area: 760 m²*
9 *Built-up area: 446 m²*
10 *Staircase quotient: 0.20*

I9

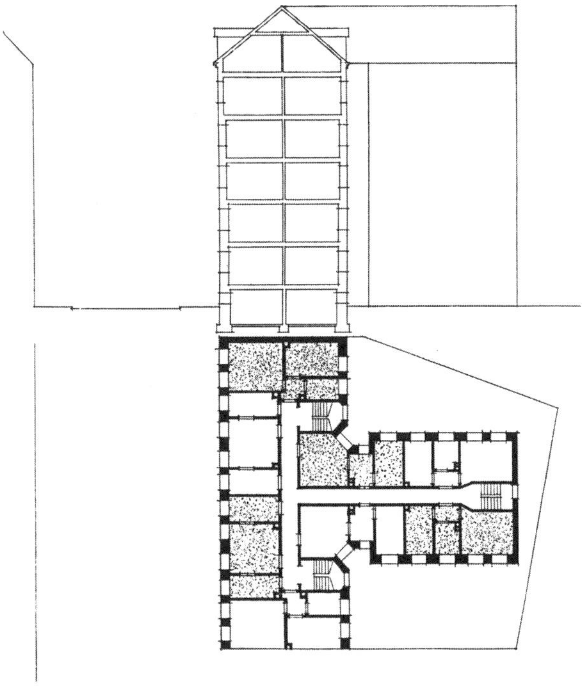

Smaller corridor building with decent staircase conditions (large staircase quotient).

1 *Location: Fiskergade 5 and 7*
2 *Year built: 1875*
3 *Number of residential floors: 6*
4 *Flat type: 2 rooms*
5 *Gross floor area: 40.4 and 34.8 m²*
6 *Room dimensions: kitchen 3 m², largest room 11 m²*
7 *Number of flats per floor: 8*
8 *Plot area: 426 m²*
9 *Built-up area: 281 m²*
10 *Staircase quotient: 0.38*

I10

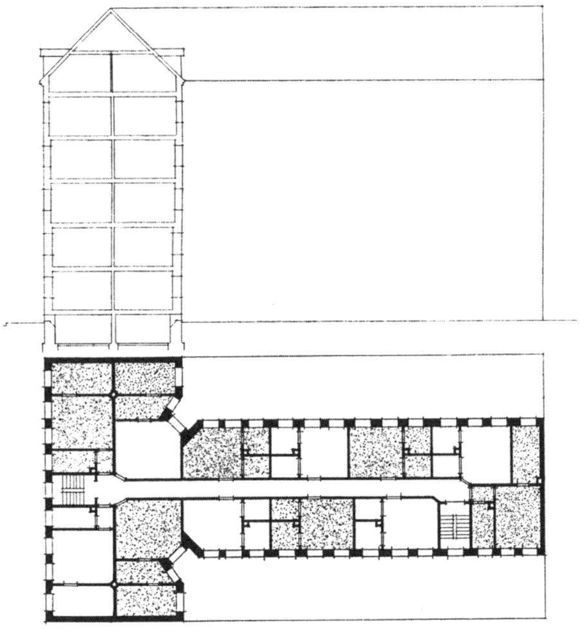

Corridor buildings with very small staircase quotient. One-room flats are the smallest found in the study.

1 *Location: Skyttegade 26 and 28*
2 *Year built: 1874*
3 *Number of residential floors: 6*
4 *Flat type: 2 rooms, 1 room with alcove*
5 *Gross floor area: 41.4 m², 1 room with alcove 26.7 m²*
6 *Room dimensions: kitchen 3.1 m², largest room 14.4 m²*
7 *Number of flats per floor: 5 flats w. 2 rooms and 7 flats w. 1 room with alcove*
8 *Plot area: 590 m²*
9 *Built-up area: 383 m²*
10 *Staircase quotient: 0.17*

I₁₁

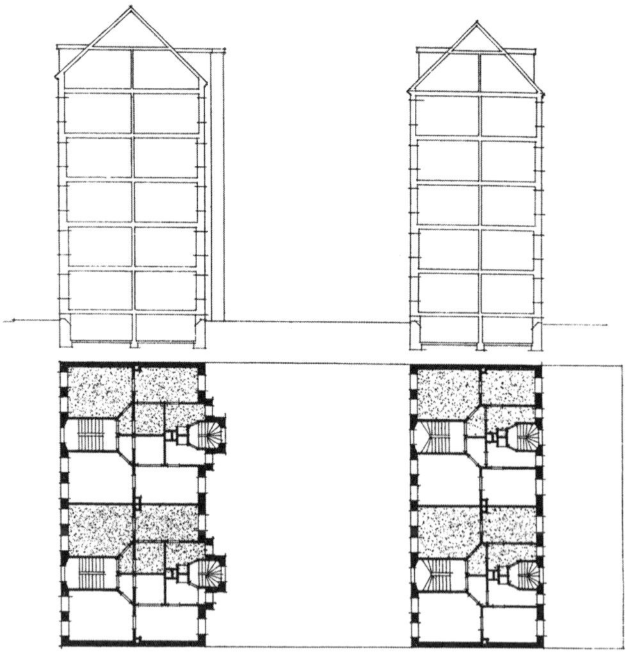

1 *Location: Saxogade 39, 41 and 43*
2 *Year built: 1879*
3 *Number of residential floors: 6*
4 *Flat type: front bldg., 2 rooms with alcove, back bldg. 2 rooms*
5 *Gross floor area: 2 rooms with alcove 47.5 m², 2 rooms 43.5 m²*
6 *Room dimensions: kitchen 4.3 m², largest room 12.8 m²*
7 *Number of flats per floor: 4 in front bldg., 4 in back bldg.*
8 *Plot area: 740 m²*
9 *Built-up area: front bldg. 190 m², back bldg. 173.5 m², total 363.5 m²*
10 *Staircase quotient: 1.00*

In the front building, by moving the kitchen staircase into the courtyard, the entry hall has acquired an alcove. The houses are quite similar.

I₁₂

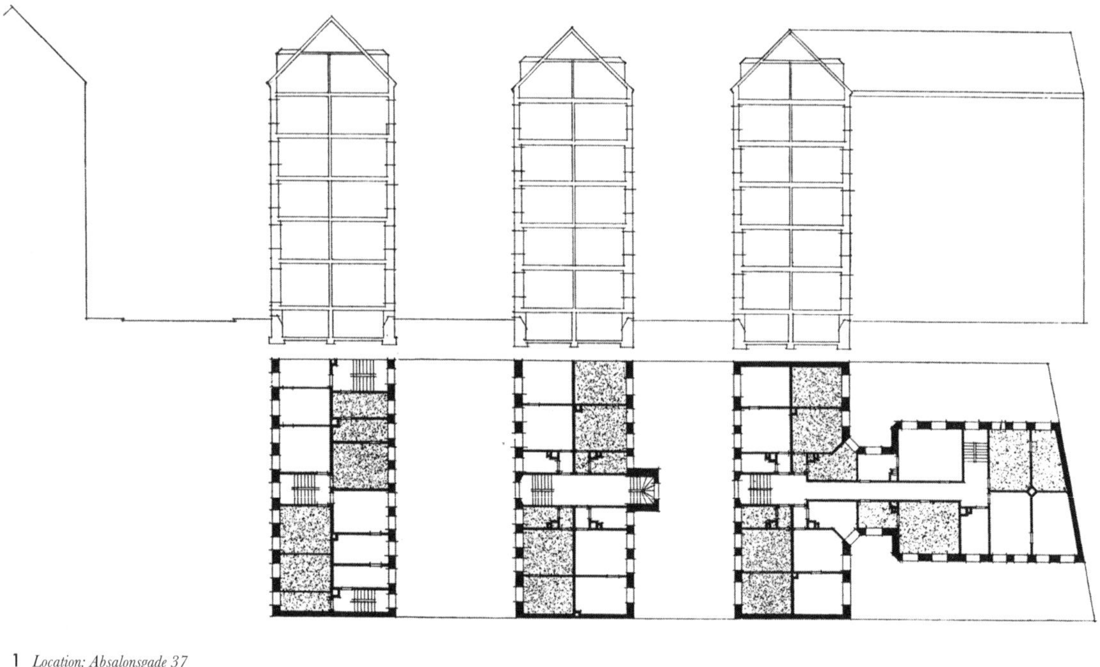

1 *Location: Absalonsgade 37*
2 *Year built: 1875*
3 *Number of residential floors: 6*
4 *Flat type: front bldg. 2 rooms, middle bldg. 2 rooms, back bldg. 2 rooms and 1 room*
5 *Gross floor area: 2 rooms 36 m², 1 room 32 m²*
6 *Room dimensions: kitchen 2.7 m², largest room 10 and 14 m²*
7 *Number of flats per floor: 4 in front bldg., 4 in middle bldg., 8 in back bldg.*
8 *Plot area: 920 m²*
9 *Built-up area: 546 m²*
10 *Staircase quotient: front bldg. 0.75, middle bldg. 0.50, back bldg. 0.25*

Photograph omitted for lack of space. However, the building's exterior is very similar to I_{15}. Interesting building form representing three different staircase systems: separate main and kitchen staircases, two staircases with an open connection, and a corridor system. Single-side flats (cf. building on Studiestræde 8, page 89).

I 13

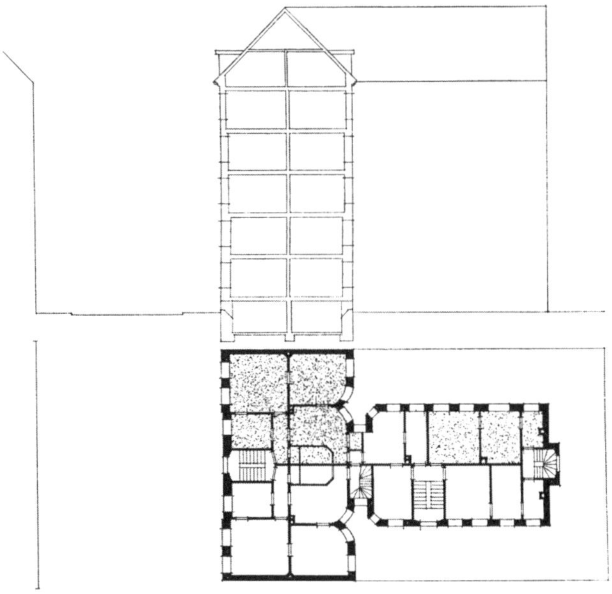

1 *Location: Vævergade 8*
2 *Year built: 1875*
3 *Number of residential floors: 6*
4 *Flat type: 2 rooms + 2 small rooms, 2 rooms*
5 *Gross floor area: 2 rooms + 2 small rooms 69 m², 2 rooms 31.5 and 39 m²*
6 *Room dimensions: kitchen 3.6 m², small maid's room 2.65 m², largest room 14.4 m²*
7 *Number of flats per floor: 2 flats w. 2 rooms + 2 small rooms, 2 flats w. 2 rooms*
8 *Plot area: 400 m²*
9 *Built-up area: 245 m²*
10 *Staircase quotient: 0.80*

Typical plan for a smaller T-shaped building. Large flats face the street. The kitchen contains a very small unlit room, originally a maid's room, later used for WC installation.

I 14

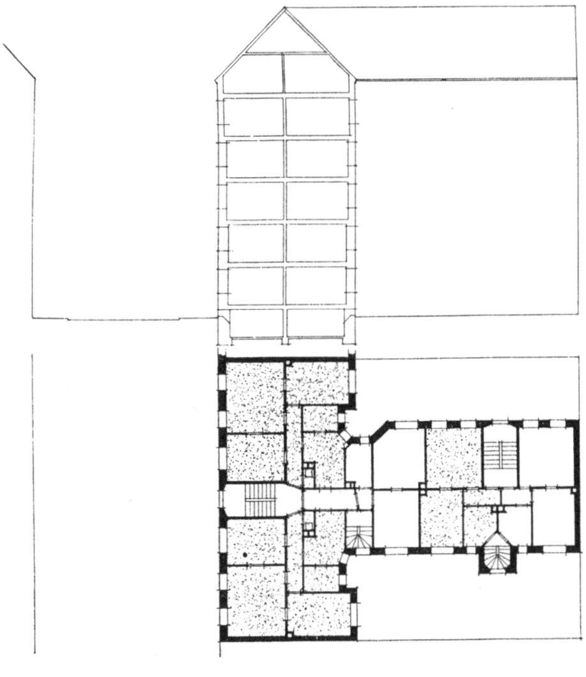

1 *Location: Oehlenschlægersgade 69*
2 *Year built: 1885*
3 *Number of residential floors: 6*
4 *Flat type: 3 rooms + small room, 2 rooms*
5 *Gross floor area: 3 rooms + small room 84 m², 2 rooms 49.4 and 45 m²*
6 *Room dimensions: kitchen 4.6 m², maid's room 4.1 m², largest room 18.4 m²*
7 *Number of flats per floor: 2 flats w. 3 rooms + small room, 3 flats w. 2 rooms*
8 *Plot area: 456 m²*
9 *Built-up area: 307 m²*
10 *Staircase quotient: 0.80*

Similar plan. The corridor between the street-facing staircase and the kitchen staircase is the kitchen corridor for the large flats and the main corridor to the small flat. Floor toilets in the street-facing flats. The property is part of a single development with communal light wells.

I_{15}

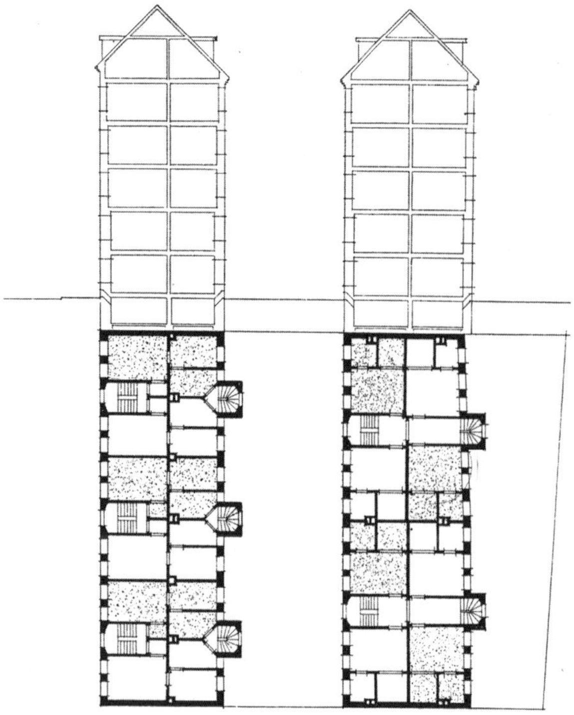

1 *Location: Saxogade 42*
2 *Year built: 1877*
3 *Number of residential floors: 6*
4 *Flat type: front block 2 rooms, back bldg. 1 room with alcove*
5 *Gross floor area: 2 rooms 36.3 m², 1 room with alcove 27 m²*
6 *Room dimensions: kitchen in front bldg. 5 m² and in back bldg. 3.4 m², largest room in front bldg. 11.2 m² and in back bldg. 10.6 m²*
7 *Number of flats per floor: 6 in front bldg., 8 in back bldg.*
8 *Plot area: 770 m²*
9 *Built-up area: 433 m²*
10 *Staircase quotient: front bldg. 1.00, back bldg. 0.50*

In the front building, normal two-room flats with main and kitchen staircases. The back building has small, single-side, one-room flats.

I_{16}

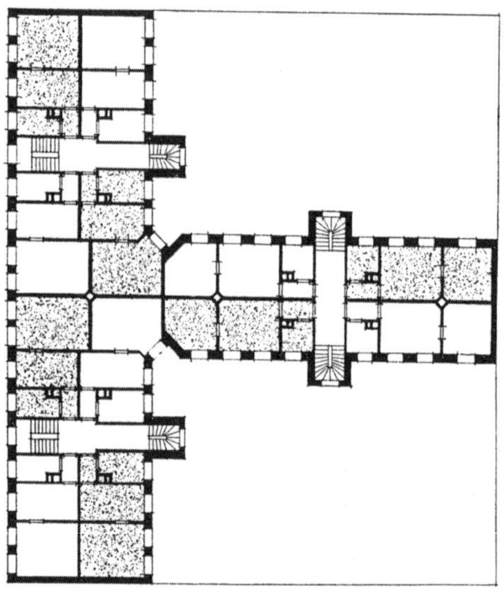

1 *Location: Saxogade 38–40*
2 *Year built: 1878*
3 *Number of residential floors: 6*
4 *Flat type: 2 rooms*
5 *Gross floor area: 39.6 m²*
6 *Room dimensions: kitchen 3.6 m², largest room 13.5 m²*
7 *Number of flats per floor: 12*
8 *Plot area: 900 m²*
9 *Built-up area: 437.7 m²*
10 *Staircase quotient: 0.50*

Single-side flats with open staircase passage measuring nine alen. The section closely corresponds to the neighbouring buildings I_{15} and I_{17}. All three buildings resemble each other from the street, but have very different development forms.

I$_{17}$

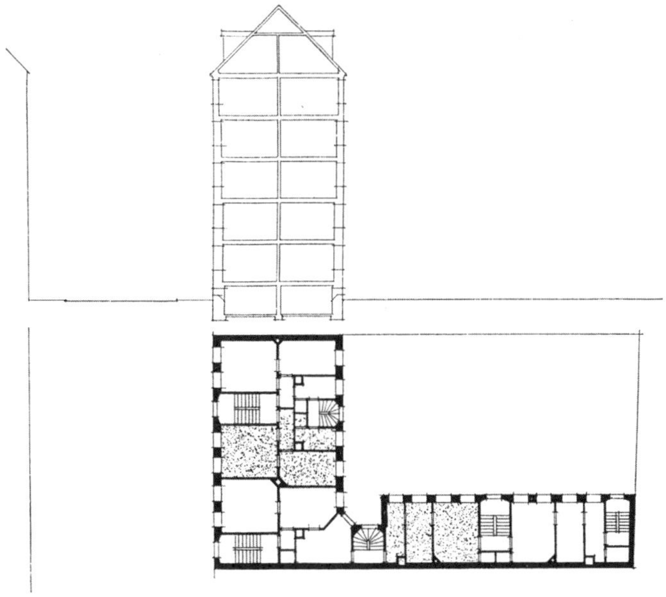

1 *Location: Saxogade 32, 34 and 36*
2 *Year built: 1879*
3 *Number of residential floors: 6*
4 *Flat type: 2 rooms*
5 *Gross floor area: 46.5 m², 49 m², 57 m², 45 m²*
6 *Room dimensions: kitchen 3.9 m², largest room 11.3 m² and 13.6 m²*
7 *Number of flats per floor: 5*
8 *Plot area: 450 m²*
9 *Built-up area: 214.4 m²*
10 *Staircase quotient: 1.20*

L-shaped building, rare for small flats due to the expensive stairwell (large staircase quotient).

I$_{18}$

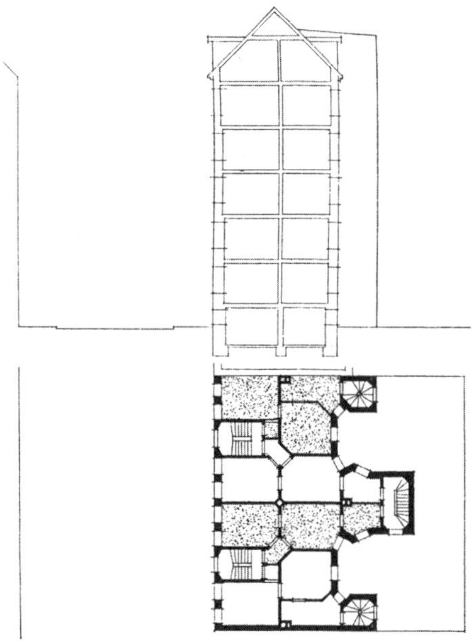

1 *Location: Jægergade 17 and 19*
2 *Year built: 1882*
3 *Number of residential floors: 6*
4 *Flat type: 2 rooms*
5 *Gross floor area: 40 m²*
6 *Room dimensions: kitchen 4.25 m², largest room 10.3 m²*
7 *Number of flats per floor: 4*
8 *Plot area: 255 m²*
9 *Built-up area: 160 m²*
10 *Staircase quotient: 1.25*

Typical building on narrow lot. The quite disorganised courtyard façade is due to efforts to comply with the statutory distancing between buildings while at the same time maximising the highest possible number of flats.

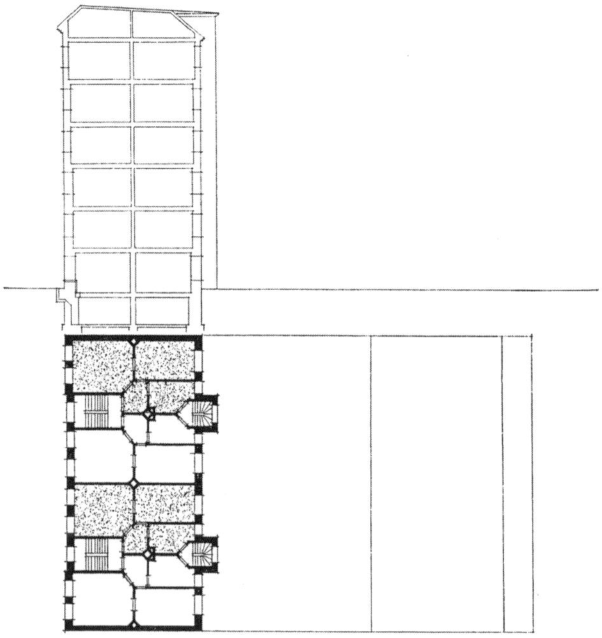

1 *Location: Olufsvej 6 and 6 A*
2 *Year built: 1886*
3 *Number of residential floors: 6*
4 *Flat type: 2 rooms*
5 *Gross floor area: 45 m²*
6 *Room dimensions: kitchen 5.3 m², largest room 13 m²*
7 *Number of flats per floor: 4*
8 *Plot area: 624 m²*
9 *Built-up area: 187 m² + back bldg. 176 m²*
10 *Staircase quotient: 1.00*

I19

The flat slate roof is characteristic of the 1880s. The building's height is the maximum legal limit. In this way, a spacious storeroom floor has been gained while simultaneously avoiding attic flats.

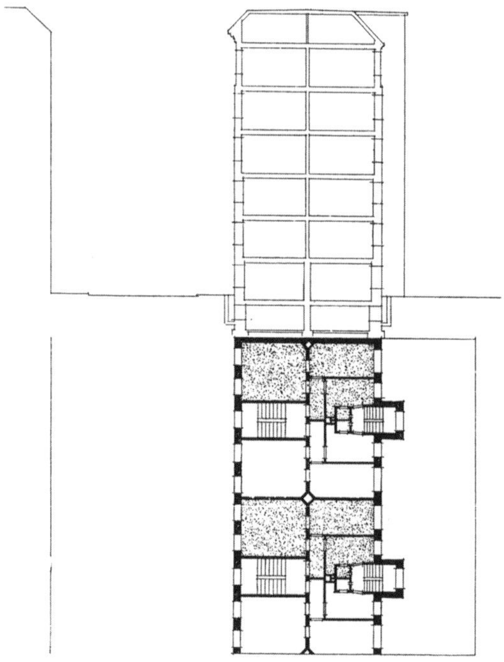

1 *Location: Ålborggade 16 and 18*
2 *Year built: 1892*
3 *Number of residential floors: 6*
4 *Flat type: 2 rooms*
5 *Gross floor area: 54 m²*
6 *Room dimensions: kitchen 5.94 m², largest room 16 m²*
7 *Number of flats per floor: 4*
8 *Plot area: 344 m²*
9 *Built-up area: 217.5 m²*
10 *Staircase quotient: 1.00*

I20

The system of main and kitchen staircases became universal after the law of 1889, which prohibited corridors and required three doors between staircases.

II 21

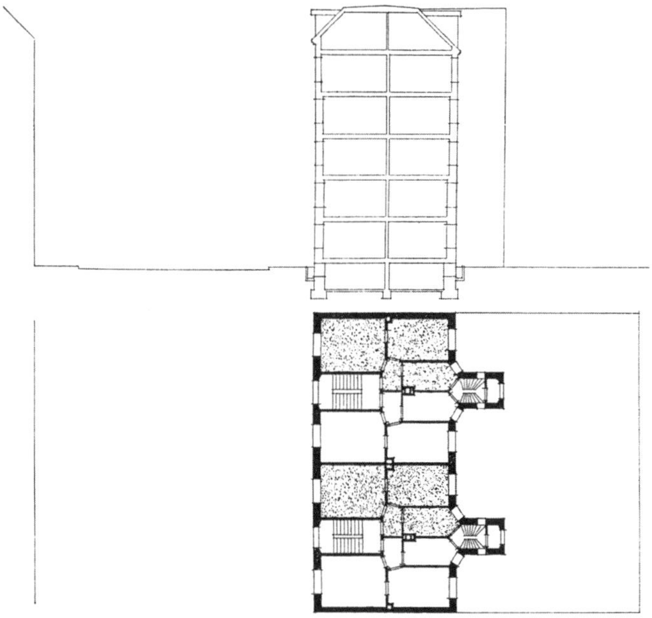

1 *Location: Flensborggade 49–51*
2 *Year built: 1902*
3 *Number of residential floors: 6*
4 *Flat type: 2 rooms*
5 *Gross floor area: 52 m²*
6 *Room dimensions: kitchen 5.4 m², largest room 15 m²*
7 *Number of flats per floor: 4*
8 *Plot area: 440 m²*
9 *Built-up area: 208 m²*
10 *Staircase quotient: 1.00*

Water closets placed on the landings for use by several families.

II 22

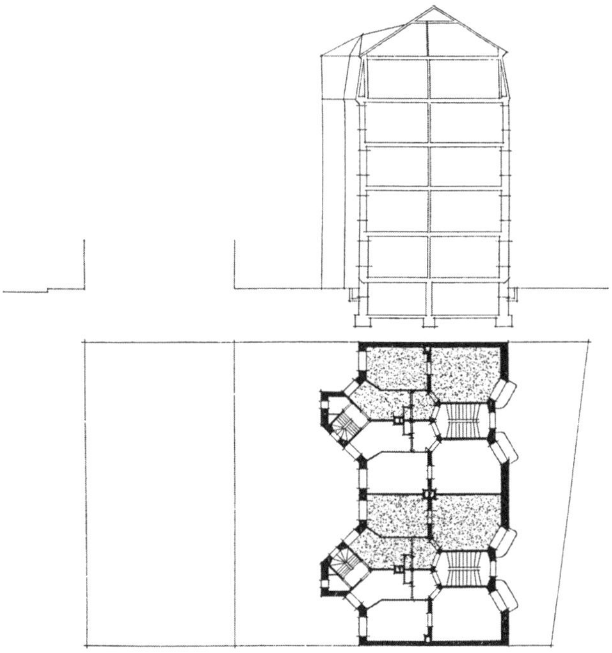

1 *Location: Absalonsgade 28*
2 *Year built: 1903*
3 *Number of residential floors: 5*
4 *Flat type: 2 rooms*
5 *Gross floor area: 53.2 m²*
6 *Room dimensions: kitchen 6.50 m², largest room 15.4 m²*
7 *Number of flats per floor: 4*
8 *Plot area: 654 m²*
9 *Built-up area: 213 m² + front bldg. 200 m², total 413 m²*
10 *Staircase quotient: 1.00*

Back building with balconies erected behind an old front building. The façades are clearly dictated by the rules for right-to-light distances between buildings.

II₂₃

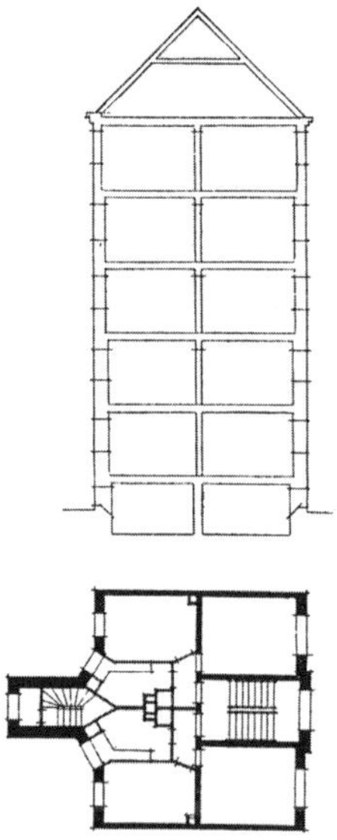

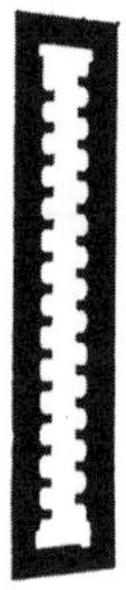

1 *Location: Gammel Kalkbrænderivej 40–48*
2 *Year built: 1903*
3 *Architect: Julies Bagger*
4 *Number of residential floors: 5*
5 *Flat type: 2 rooms*
6 *Gross floor area: 51 m²*
7 *Room dimensions: kitchen 6.6 m², largest room 14 m²*
8 *Built-up area: 3610 m²*
9 *Staircase quotient: 1.00*

Examined and drawn by Einar Graae

The water closet is still located behind the kitchen stairs. Extensions into the courtyard are thus very predominant.

II₂₄

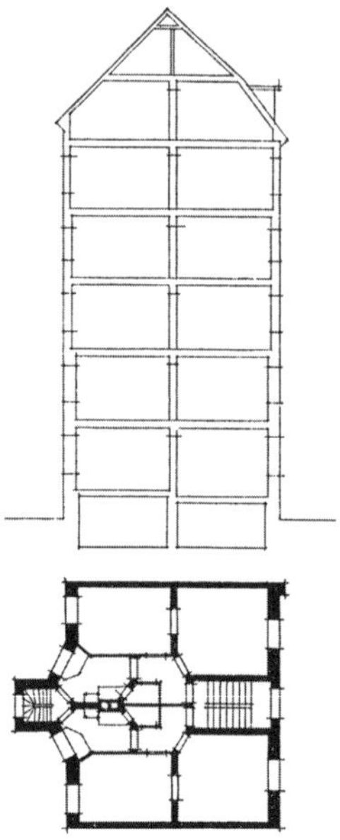

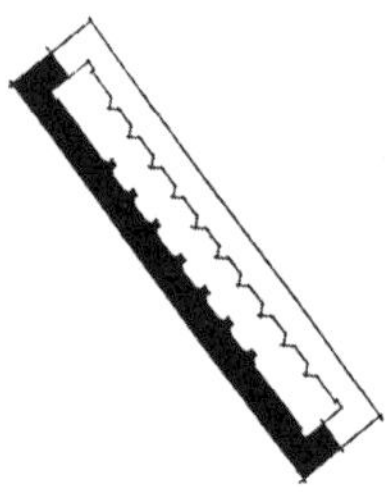

1 *Location: Njalsgade 8*
2 *Year built: 1909*
3 *Architect: Th. Gunderstrup*
4 *Number of residential floors: 6*
5 *Flat type: 2 rooms*
6 *Gross floor area: 61 m²*
7 *Room dimensions: kitchen 6 m², largest room 16.8 m²*
8 *Built-up area: 1700 m²*
9 *Staircase quotient: 1.00*

Examined and drawn by Einar Graae

Similar plan. The WC has now been moved into the flat, necessitating the oblique corridor.

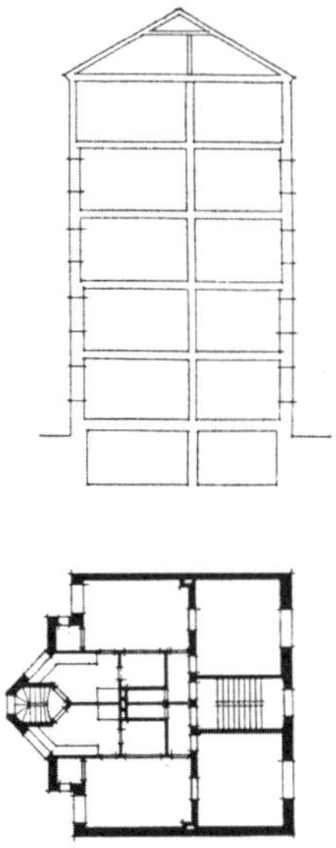

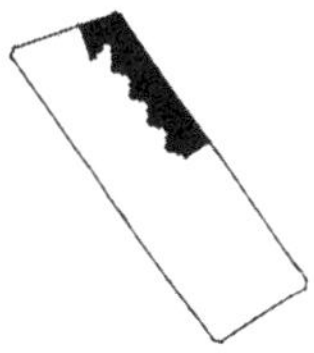

II25

1 *Location: Vardegade 7–13*
2 *Year built: 1904*
3 *Architect: Unknown*
4 *Number of residential floors: 5*
5 *Flat type: 2 rooms with alcove*
6 *Gross floor area: 61 m²*
7 *Room dimensions: kitchen 6.6 m², largest room 15.2 m²*
8 *Built-up area: 650 m²*
9 *Staircase quotient: 1.00*

Examined and drawn by Erik Stengade

Here the WC faces the outside with access from the bedroom.

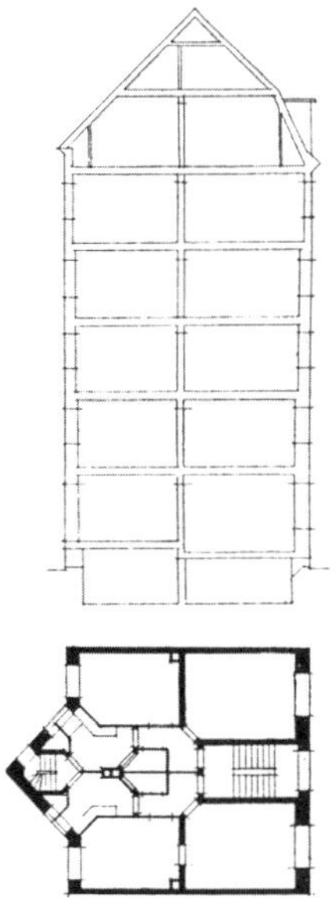

II26

1 *Location: Egilsgade 9*
2 *Year built: 1909*
3 *Architect: Th. Gundestrup*
4 *Number of residential floors: 6*
5 *Flat type: 2 rooms*
6 *Gross floor area: 57 m²*
7 *Room dimensions: kitchen 6.0 m², largest room 16.1 m²*
8 *Built-up area: 1800 m²*
9 *Staircase quotient: 1.00*

Examined and drawn by Einar Graae

An effort is made to make the courtyard projections more regular. Here everything is put within a right-angled corner.

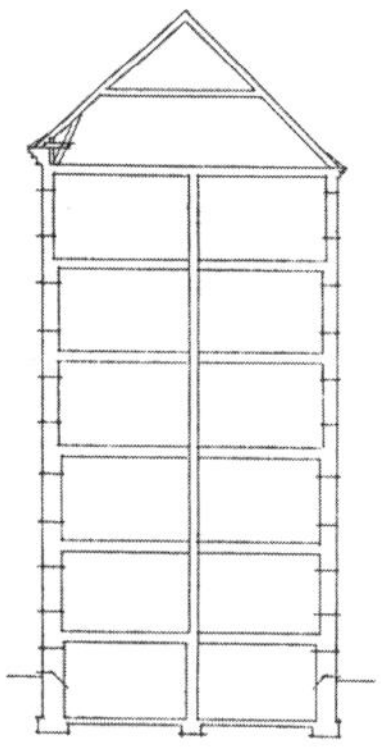

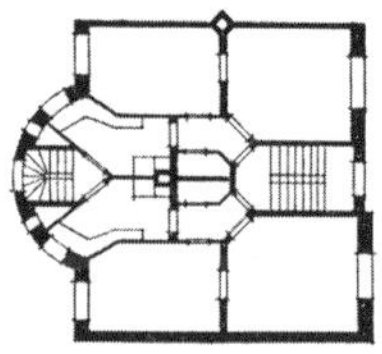

II₂₇

1 *Location: Henrik Rungsgade 4–6*
2 *Year built: 1907*
3 *Architect: Johs. Strøm Tejsen*
4 *Number of residential floors: 5*
5 *Flat type: 2 rooms*
6 *Gross floor area: 57.2 m²*
7 *Room dimensions: kitchen 6 m², largest room 16 m²*
8 *Built-up area: 229 m²*
9 *Staircase quotient: 1.00*

Examined and drawn by Poul Taubroe Pedersen

Here the projection takes a semi-circular form. The kitchen still has a chimney.

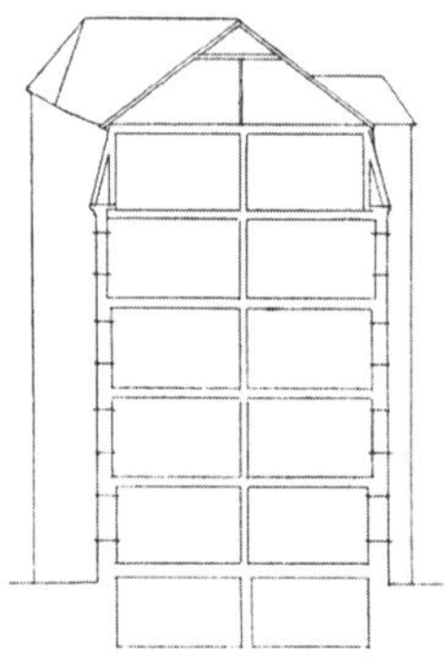

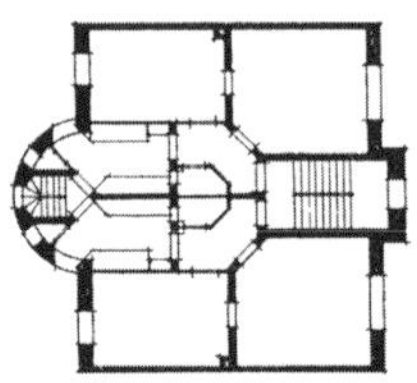

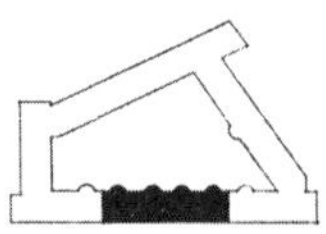

II28

1 *Location: Jagtvej 84-86*
2 *Year built: 1915*
3 *Architect: Mandrup-Poulsen*
4 *Number of residential floors: 5*
5 *Flat type: 2 rooms*
6 *Gross floor area: 70.2 m²*
7 *Room dimensions: kitchen 6.9 m², largest room 16.2 m²*
8 *Built-up area: 2534 m²*
9 *Staircase quotient: 1.00*

Examined and drawn by Eigil Sørensen

Similar plan. The introduction of cooking gas has rendered the chimney superfluous in the kitchen.

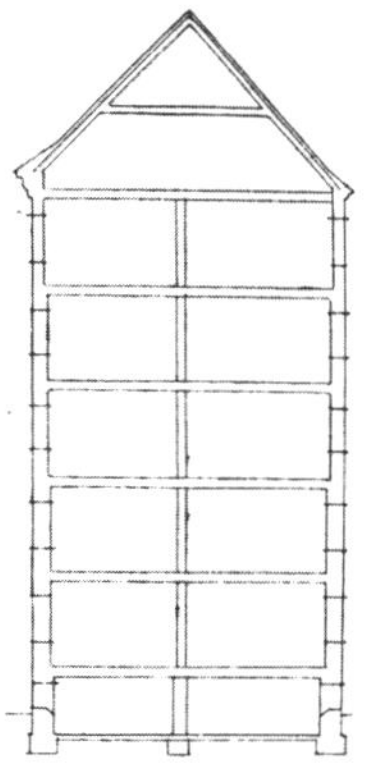

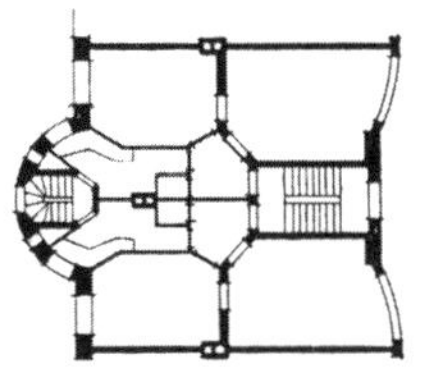

1 *Location: Njalsgade 38–50, Egilsgade 37–49*
2 *Year built: 1910*
3 *Architect: Kristen Gording*
4 *Number of residential floors: 6*
5 *Flat type: 2 rooms*
6 *Gross floor area: 61.2 m²*
7 *Room dimensions: kitchen 6 m², largest room 20 m²*
8 *Built-up area: 1320 m²*
9 *Staircase quotient: 1.00*

Examined and drawn by Erik Stengade

II29

The wide oriel window serves the living rooms of two flats.

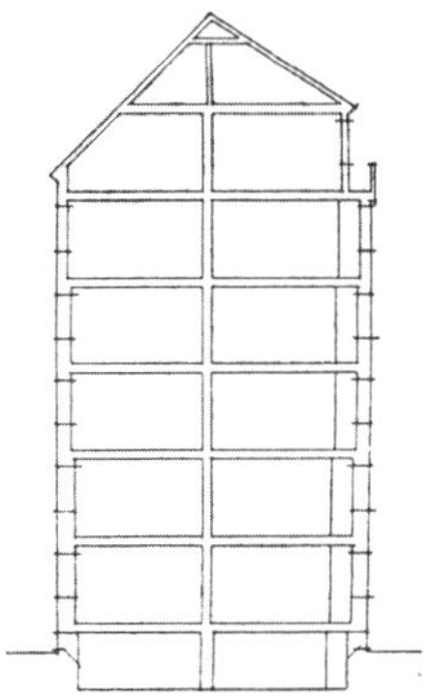

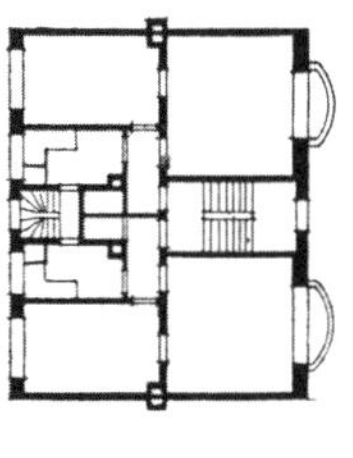

1 *Location: Gunløgsgade 2–18*
2 *Year built: 1912*
3 *Number of residential floors: 6*
4 *Flat type: 2 rooms*
5 *Gross floor area: 61.2 m²*
6 *Room dimensions: kitchen 6 m², largest room 20 m²*
7 *Built-up area: 2709 m²*
8 *Staircase quotient: 1.00*

Examined and drawn by Erik Stengade

II30

The façade length for each flat is larger than usual here, so all rooms can be kept within parallel walls. The façade avoids the symmetry of the plan diagram. In the first flat, the living room has a regular window, in the second, a bay window and in the third, the customary projecting oriel window.

II 31

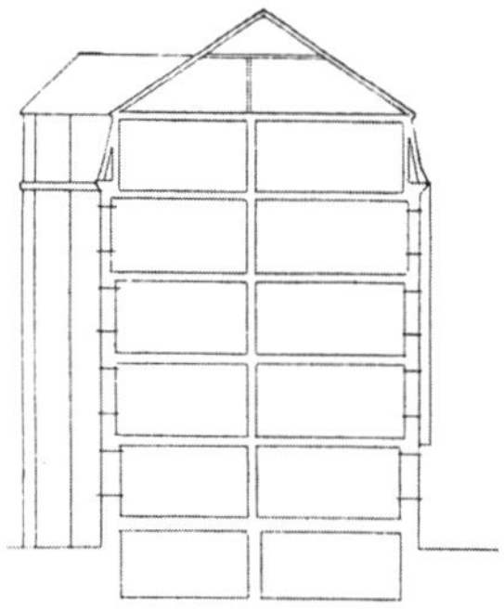

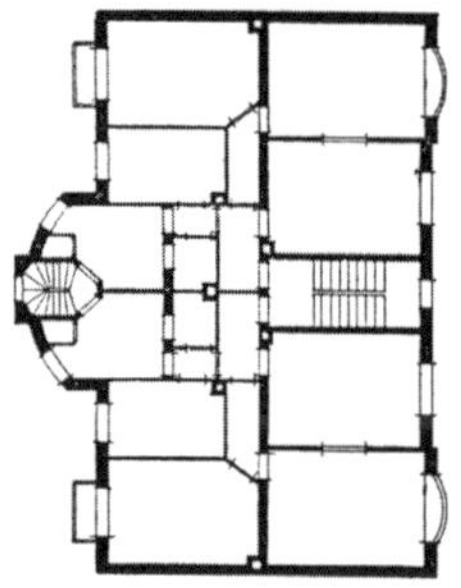

1 *Location: Henrik Steffensvej 3–7*
2 *Year built: 1907*
3 *Architect: Vilhelm Fischer*
4 *Number of residential floors: 5*
5 *Flat type: 3 rooms + small room*
6 *Gross floor area: 118 m²*
7 *Room dimensions: kitchen 12.3 m², largest room 20.2 m²*
8 *Built-up area: 1500 m²*
9 *Staircase quotient: 1.00*

Examined and drawn by Einar Graae

Example of larger flat from this period.

II 32

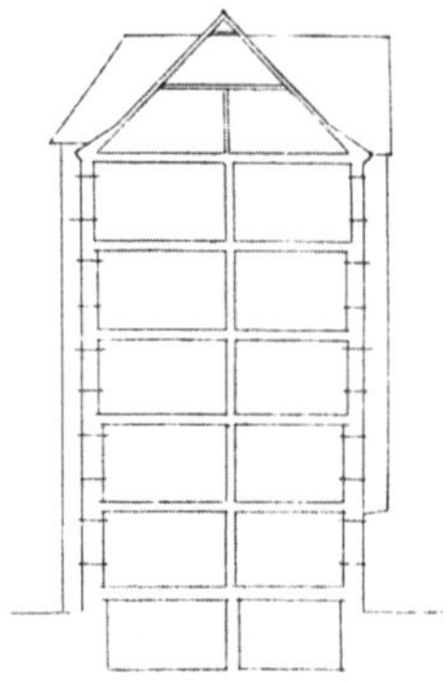

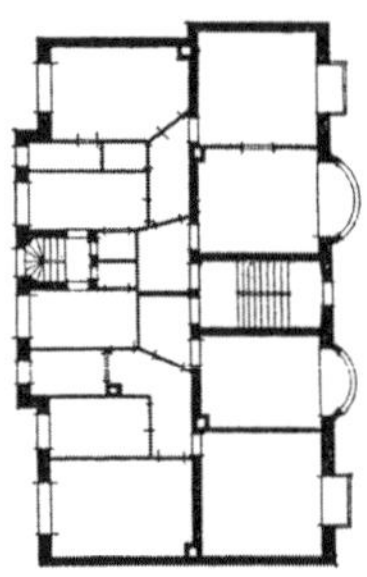

1 *Location: Sundholmsvej 51–55*
2 *Year built: 1913*
3 *Architect: Jens Landbo-Berthelsen*
4 *Number of residential floors: 5*
5 *Flat type: 3 rooms + small room*
6 *Gross floor area: 106 m²*
7 *Room dimensions: kitchen 7.2 m², largest room 16 m²*
8 *Built-up area: 1900 m²*
9 *Staircase quotient: 1.00*

Examined and drawn by Erik Stengade

Larger flat with split-level stairs.

Copenhagen housing types from 1914 to 1936

by architect, professor Kay Fisker

The decade of construction after the war (1918–1928), the one we generally, but somewhat incorrectly, sum up under the term *Statsboligfond* Period, is described by *Steen Eiler Rasmussen* in this journal in 1926 (Vol. XXVIII, p. 77), thus before the period could be said to have already ended.
Initially, my intention with this survey was to reprint this study in its entirety with the accompanying and quite comprehensive plan material. Nevertheless, after discussions with Steen Eiler Rasmussen, this idea was abandoned for several reasons, including the fact that, in many respects, the text is very much a product of its time, but even more importantly, because most of the plan types are theoretical in nature and therefore out of step with the system used in the study of the other three periods in this survey, which only comprises *completed* buildings.
Steen Eiler Rasmussen's plan overview appeared at a time when neoclassical, multi-bay housing was flourishing more than ever before within the context of Copenhagen residential construction, and although it was explicitly emphasised in his article that the plans were not suitable as models, their methodical analysis of plan options for a given basis nevertheless helped to clarify plan forms in the following years. Therefore, with an overview of the kind we intend to provide here, it will be more interesting to attempt to discover which traces of these plans can be found in the completed buildings rather than reprint the old theoretical plans.
The following examines a number of completed building types within the two main groups which were typical of this period (III_{33} and III_{34}). Furthermore, excerpts from Steen Eiler Rasmussen's text are reproduced which characterise these types in particular.

The *Statsboligfond* Period acquired its distinctive character through state support, which especially from 1918 to 1928, was the lot of housing construction. Admittedly, the state and municipalities previously also had to support housing construction, but in comparison to the State Housing Fund Period, the grants were very small. Thus, state aid was granted as early as 1887 and 1898. In 1909, municipal aid had to be provided to ease unemployment after the 1908 crash.
However, it was only after 1914 that the public sector had to attend to building activity on a larger scale. The war brought a large number of foreigners to the country at the same time as emigration was halted and thus there was unusual growth in the demand for housing. At the same time, construction costs rose and although they did not rise above the price index until 1918, they nevertheless frightened people off from starting building projects, especially in connection with the existing rent legislation. The risk was too great and, even in the most favourable cases, building was a questionable business as the regulation stipulated that rents could not be increased in proportion to construction costs. The state and municipalities therefore had to keep the building sector afloat. As is known, it came first in the form of direct subsidies: 10 per cent from the municipalities and 10 per cent from the state, but in many

cases these grants had to be increased by up to 40 per cent. In the years 1917–1922, this support was of a very random nature, with small and short-term grants, but in 1922 the State Housing Fund Act systematised state aid. During the five years of the first state housing law, loans were granted by the state for up to 40 per cent of municipal guarantees, investing up to 85 per cent, and exceptionally 90 per cent, of capital outlay. The law expired in 1928, but after an interval a new three-year law followed in 1933 with slightly stricter conditions.
Under the two *Statsboligfond* laws, approximately 9,000 loans totalling DKK 140 million were granted, corresponding to building societies with a total of around 35,000 flats.
This legislative system led to widespread regulation and control by the state and forced specific forms of organisation upon the building sector, which in turn had significant influence on building design, first and foremost on the *size* of the buildings that were constructed. The large neoclassical housing block emerged as the most dominant phenomenon in the building history of these years: a ribbon development block around a large open courtyard or park, which could be left undeveloped because, as a prerequisite for a state loan, the municipality's land price was kept at pre-war levels.
The open building complexes were the biggest and perhaps also the only good thing that the state injected into building *designs* in these years. Regarding the plan types themselves, state scrutiny certainly had an inhibitory effect. Admittedly, the neoclassical ideal of the time required a plan that was methodically organised and rather uniform. In regard to these housing complexes which were on a scale corresponding to the population of Aarhus, type development had become stereotypical during these years, indeed so stereotypical that one finds practically only *four* types of variants, two of which represent 80 per cent of all types. However, this was probably due more to state supervision than the schematic ideal form, which, after all, offers several plan options, as Steen Eiler Rasmussen's plan's collection also shows. It was known in advance that certain plan types were applauded by the authorities, and therefore experiments were embarked upon reluctantly which could lead to delays and make it difficult, perhaps completely impossible, to complete the building project. This is not a critique of the people who administered these areas, but rather of the system which inevitably leads to such conditions. In any case, the building method and development form are the greatest merits the State Housing Fund Period has conferred on us. About this, Steen Eiler Rasmussen writes:

Building development plans

Closed blocks

By far the majority of built housing is in the form of entirely enclosed blocks.
One of the first, and perhaps clearest, examples of this building style are the blocks on Struenseegade designed for the city by architect Povl Baumann in 1918, which has previously been extensively discussed in Arkitekten (Vol. XXIV, p. 41). Each building is a single block of flats that, as in older Copenhagen residential buildings, has the living rooms facing the street and kitchens, stairs and bedrooms facing the courtyard which contains the requisite bicycle sheds, carpet beating areas, dustbins and the like. The courtyard is typically "the ugly side". This is quite natural in situations where the courtyard is darker than the street, but when it occurs in a block where the courtyard is much wider than the street, it is not convincing. As an example of how a housing block can be designed with a more beautiful use of the courtyard, I mention a housing block by Dutch architect J. J. P. Oud, where the building with all its individual flats surrounds the courtyard garden, which is the building's most distinguished space. All of the flats' verandas face the courtyard, just as they all turn their backs to the street. This beautifully expresses the idea of shared ownership, which is the foundation of building society housing: all of the small homes come together to form one large whole for mutual benefit and enjoyment. There are a number of Copenhagen housing

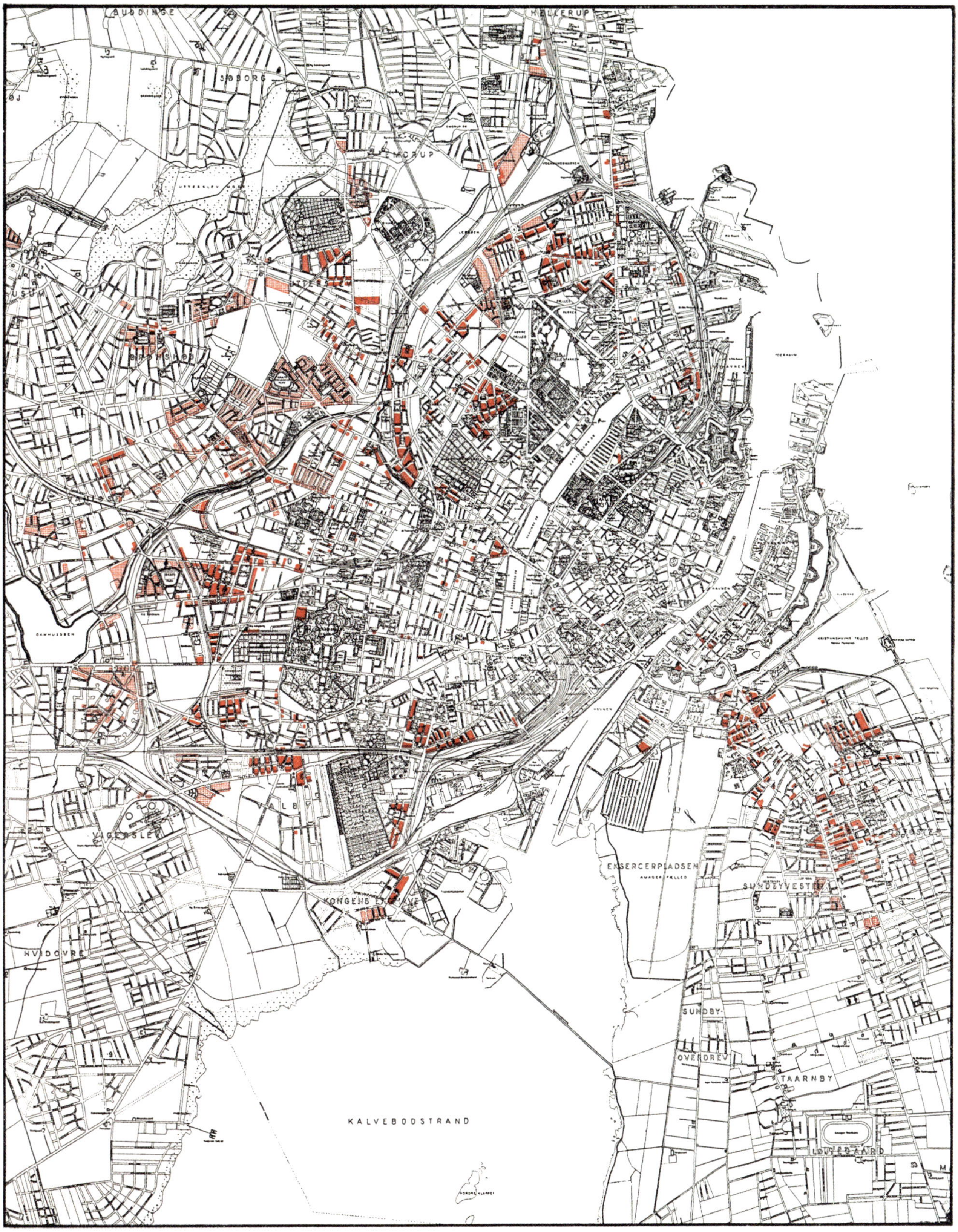

Copenhagen. *Plan 1: 60,000 showing extent and location of housing built during 1914–1936.*

- *high-rise buildings (5–6 floors)*
- *mid-rise building (3–3 ½ floors)*
- *low-rise buildings (1–2 floors)*

blocks that also surround a garden, but the living rooms still face the street, which can be quite sterile, and the courtyard side is furnished with a cheaper façade and places for drying clothes, storing dustbins, etc. This is the case of the very large housing block Hornbækhus, which indeed has a beautiful garden. In the largest of the Ved Classens Have housing blocks, the building has been opened towards the south and a very large municipal garden has been laid out in the interior. Here staircases, kitchens and outdoor spaces have been consistently placed to the north towards Classensgade and all rooms towards the garden. But between the building and the garden is the courtyard area that creates a barrier with its large wall. It would be appropriate if the blocks had been built in such a way that they were almost completely turned inside out, so to say: the outside became the "ugly side" and the inside the elegant one. This has been done in a single beautiful residential block on Gyldenrisvej, designed by architect Henning Hansen (Arkitekten, Vol. XXIV, p. 161). I often think it could be carried out successfully with ordinary block plans. In order for the flats to receive sufficient light, in most cases the street must have a much wider width than traffic requires. The surplus area is then generally used to lay out the front garden. The result is rarely good. The areas are too small for landscaping and it does not suit the streets and the large brick complexes. If the required tiny service area was located on the exterior side, then the entire interior of the block could face the garden – a real garden – attractively located and protected. The exterior courtyard would have to be surrounded by walls; a few small trees could be planted whose branches would extend out over the street.

But the question is whether the enclosed block is the best form for high-rise housing. While the neighbourhoods that were built just outside the ramparts until 1900 usually had very orderly rectangular blocks, this is not the case for the newer street plans drawn up after the turn of the century. There are two trends that have created the irregular and oblique block forms here: firstly, with regard to traffic, emphasis has been placed on diagonal connections and secondly, irregularity was the downright goal (this is not typical of Copenhagen; the trends can be found throughout contemporary European urban construction, cf. Austrian Sitte's agitation). As far as traffic considerations are concerned, there is a gradual realisation that there should be good main road arteries with quiet residential neighbourhoods between them completely free from through traffic, as well as an understanding that directing traffic through them is always very unfortunate. At the same time, the demand for irregularity has suffered a pitiful defeat. On the triangular oblique plots, regular façades have been built straight as a ruler, lined with windows in linear ranks. This kind of architecture might be good in an architecturally fixed street plan where the series of buildings' neutral walls frame the clear spaces of the streets. But in irregular neighbourhoods that have been thoughtfully designed with picturesque projections and recesses and little Sitte-style pleasantries, it all simply ends in failure. And from the streets one enters the no less dreary concrete courtyards, whose large spaces afford a playground for the children, who can jump about among clothes drying racks and bin stores. The Grønnegården plan at Borups Allé shows an attempt to better utilise the courtyard. Here, the section with the best light has been laid out with small gardens that belong to the ground floor flats, just as there are front gardens facing Borups Allé. But the building's complete closure into a block is unconvincing. As is known, corners are unprofitable to build on, especially when there is no need to economise on lot size. I think one would often end up with better structures if, instead of constructing square blocks, the buildings were laid out as parallel blocks, with gardens facing the sun and quite narrow residential streets in the shade.

In addition to the irregularities of the street plans, there are additional conditions that favour open, parallel blocks of flats rather than rectangular ones: namely the desirability of being able to divide the complexes into not too large land registry title numbers, and the irregularities of the terrain. For example, while the municipal housing blocks at Struenseegade are each listed as an indivisible property, there is now always a requirement that the residential properties be divided by fire walls into smaller parts, each with only five to six main staircases. These divisions, which externally appear as firewall parapets which characterise the building as being composed of individual parts, work against the density and unity of the block form, and this effect is further reinforced if the terrain's forms require space between the individual parts. In parallel blocks, on the other hand, divisions and spaces are entirely obvious, which articulate the buildings in a good way.

In the case of the *enclosed blocks*, however, Steen Eiler Rasmussen's plan to turn the block "inside out", with the main front facing the large open courtyard and the service area against the street, only rarely came to fruition. The only housing blocks I am familiar with showing this solution are those previously mentioned on Gyldenrisvej by Henning Hansen. In those years, despite all the propaganda in favour of more sensible building styles, the tradition from the period of the side and back buildings continued to dominate.

Parallel blocks only started to play a role much later – in the years after 1930. In the 1920s, the enclosed block is dominant. Even in the newest buildings, the enclosed block still plays a role, though no longer as an ideal form, but rather as a solution conditioned by special circumstances such as parcelling methods, street plans, etc.

Semi-enclosed block

Instead of the parallel block, the *semi-enclosed block*, as a variant of the enclosed block, gained in importance in the last years of the State Housing Fund Period. It was probably introduced by Henning Hansen's Solgården and for a number of years was very popular, especially with *Københavns almindelige Boligselskab* (*KAB*), which has used it for a large number of its later buildings, such as Vibehusene, Østergården, Roskildegården, Enghaven, Typographers' Foundation and many other places. Properly positioned in relation to the four points of the compass and the street plan, this type of building offers many advantages over the completely enclosed block. It allows the low-pitched evening sun to enter the courtyard, creating a link between the courtyard and the street, thereby providing a better opportunity for placing the staircases in the direction of the courtyard and possibly allowing better sunlight into the living areas. This form makes sense especially in cases where the courtyard area cannot be very large.

With this semi-enclosed block form, the idea of main entrances and living rooms facing the courtyard where the sun's direction makes such a move natural, has been implemented by and large. The courtyard area is generally laid out in such buildings in the form of gardens and playgrounds. Service areas have now been completely eliminated or at least reduced to a couple of carpet beating areas, as bicycle sheds and bin stores, which used to dominate the courtyards, can now be placed in the basements, because the coal cellars, which previously had occupied almost the entire basement, can be reduced thanks to central heating. The clothes drying spaces also disappear, as modern drying rooms with artificial drying, which are connected to machine washing systems, replace the drying spaces both in the open air and in the attics. Additionally, the carpet beating areas are replaced in some newer buildings by a common vacuum cleaner room in the basement.

The outdoor areas can therefore be laid out quite differently and more freely than before, and the design of these areas has also changed the character of the buildings in very crucial ways.

Parallel blocks

Parallel blocks have never been an important component of building activity in Copenhagen compared to abroad, especially in Germany. For a number of years immediately preceding Hitler, free-standing parallel blocks in Germany became a plan form that was firmly implemented – and sometimes very harshly – in relation to older surrounding buildings and roads. For example, the large Dammerstock settlement in Karlsruhe and Haselhorst, Siemenstadt and parts of Neukölln near Berlin are characteristic in this respect.

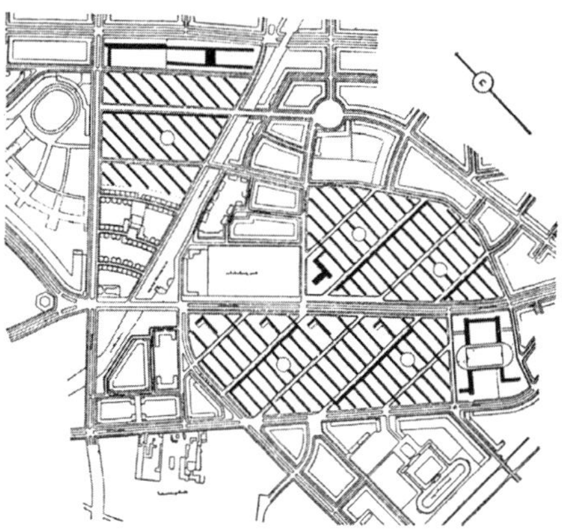

Berlin-Neukölln. Parallel blocks 1928. 1:15,000

The accuracy of this development method in relation to the requirement of proper sun orientation, distances between buildings, narrow access roads independent of traffic streets and in relation to a rational solution of plan types, is no doubt undeniable. When the type can no longer be said to be successful, it is probably because it is too schematic and monotonous. One tires of this military march of uniform parallel blocks, and has learnt that the windblown, unprotected outdoor spaces between the blocks are not ideal places to spend time as initially thought. Here at home, we are familiar with larger estates of this kind, especially Boparken on Frederiksborgvej, (D_g), Gartnervænget in Søborg, (C_j), and Nurnberggården on Holmbladsgade, (D_d), all five-storey buildings. Particularly noteworthy mid-rise buildings that are in accordance with this principle include Ringparken on Tesdorpfsvej, (D_c), the municipal buildings on Rentemestervej, (D_f), and the garden city along Grøndals Parkvej in Vanløse (D_e).

Building blocks

Parallel blocks in their original schematic form are disappearing for the aforementioned reasons. Instead, a number of intermediate forms have emerged: Truncated parallel blocks of approximately fifty to seventy metres m in length in the form of detached blocks, such as in Ryparken, (D_b), or even shorter as in Blidahpark, (C_h), although all still in a uniform, monotonous arrangement without regard for the surrounding buildings and former vegetation or consideration for outdoor use just like proper parallel blocks. In this regard, housing complexes with angular placements of the buildings such as Bellavista in Klampenborg, (B_m), Lille Tuborg on Strandvejen, (B_g), and the whimsical Store Taffelbay, provide greater value, especially when this design is combined, as in these cases, with older park vegetation that is preserved and utilised. Less fortunate angular building styles have been used for Tagensbo, (C_e), near Bispebjerg Hospital, where the rapidly rising terrain and the length of the buildings are disproportionate to the plan form.

L-shape building

At Traneberg and Stadshagen in Stockholm, very beautiful development plans have been executed with heterogeneous, *L-shaped buildings* in connection with parallel and detached blocks, all situated according to the conditions of the terrain, in close alignment with the contour lines. These residential buildings contain lovely sheltered outdoor areas and, as a whole, this blend of parallel and L-shaped blocks provides beautiful cityscapes. A similar example can be found here at home with Godthåbsvænget on Godthåbsvej, (C_d). There is no doubt that in the future we will increasingly work with such building methods that, in a natural way and without overly theoretical working principles, adapt to the conditions of the terrain and compass points and create usable open spaces.
Pages 52–55 depict a series of building development plans for completed Copenhagen residential buildings from 1914 until now, showing the development from the enclosed block to the semi-enclosed block and the parallel blocks to the fully open park blocks. The plans are all in the same scale, 1:5,000, with north facing up.

The plan types

As concerns flat typologies themselves, development has been very slow. Excluding the last few years, development has essentially been confined to improved service installations, especially with regard to heating systems and sanitary installations. Until 1930, the floor plan of the flat itself only slightly changed from the types from the 1880s. The lavatory moved from the courtyard up to the kitchen staircase landing and finally from there into the flat. Central heating and hot water became standard, finally in the bathroom as well.

Over time the plan underwent changing ideals of form: regular and schematic or romantic and irregular, in the direction of the current trends. But the content, size, number and location of the rooms still remained practically the same. The State Housing Fund Period began with a violent reaction to the pre-war picturesque and individualistic design that required irregular street scenes and varying shapes. Nonetheless, if larger housing complexes were built, each main entrance would be marked as an independent housing block. This Plesner-like tradition is most beautifully expressed in Plesner's own housing estates Åhusene and Vodroffsplads, and in his interesting project for the development of Islands Brygge (*Arkitekten*, Vol. IX, p. 218). It also dominates large neighbourhoods of the city such as Islands Brygge, Strandboulevarden, Henrik Steffensvej and Sønder Boulevard, the most characteristic perhaps being the large La Cour-like Amagerbro quarter, which, with its red buildings with oriel windows and overgrown Virginia Creeper vines, creates a beautiful cityscape.

With regard to the development from pre-war to State Housing Fund Period plan types, Steen Eiler Rasmussen writes:

Two-staircase system

In pre-war Copenhagen, construction focused on developing the plots as extensively as possible with the least possible façade length. For larger flats, this led to the familiar three-wing type: the living rooms in the wing facing the street with the dining rooms in the side wings. For smaller flats, it resulted in types with kitchens and kitchen staircases that protruded into the courtyard area as extensions from the building's mass of flat floor plans, where the spaces were squeezed together with skewed corners and triangular exterior spaces, to make the most of the façade length. In the newer building period, the task was different; as already mentioned, construction costs rose while basic prices were kept at the same level. The focus then was on providing flats with the simplest possible technical form, while the compression of rooms became less significant. We still find the older forms in the first of the properties which the municipality had erected to alleviate the housing shortage (in spring 1917), located on Princesse Charlottes Gade and designed by architect Strøm Tejsen. Later, the kitchen projections disappear, as in Mandrup Poulsen's building on Stevnsgade (1918–1919) and in Plesner and Mathiesen's building on Sønder Boulevard (1919–1920).

The blocks erected in Struenseegade in 1919 by architect Povl Baumann, (III_{33a}), display the new building style in all its purity and they have become the norm for all subsequent housing construction. In this case, the building is divided by a load-bearing, continuous partition, so that all of the flat's rooms are regular rectangles. The rooms lead to the main partition, the entrance is behind the kitchen, and the lavatories with indirect exposure are behind the kitchen staircase. The rooms are 6° and 5° wide, respectively. Staircases, kitchens and lavatories have minimum dimensions.

The flat type itself has been repeated many times since and the principle of the plan's structure has been followed in almost all subsequent housing blocks.

It is theoretically possible to investigate the different options for flat floor plans when setting requirements similar to the above types: outer walls must be straight; projections are permitted only for main staircases. In the middle of the building is one stone's width main partition – which is also continuous. The other walled partitions are 16 cm for heavy ones while light partitions are set at 8 cm. According to the Building Act, staircase width is set at 220 cm and 166 cm, respectively. All rooms must extend from the outer wall to the middle partition. Their width must be at least 315 cm (5°) and not more than 440 cm (7°), and each flat must have at least one room measuring 377 cm (6°). From the entrance there must be direct access to at least two rooms. The width of the small rooms must be at least 220 cm (3°) and not more than 250 cm (4°). The width of the kitchens must be between 200 and 220 cm. Corridors (hall or kitchen) can be inserted between the main partition and the small rooms and kitchens, respectively. The lavatories are placed behind the kitchen staircases.

There follows an account of the plan collection containing 33 theoretical plan types that I also refer to. From this account we have selected the types that have gained importance in completed projects which are reproduced in III_{33} and III_{34}.

The types are all based on the previously stated requirements and furthermore have a *two-staircase system*, which was a prerequisite in the Building Act. They can be divided into two main groups: *1.* types with continuous main partitions, interrupted only by doors, and *2.* types with the main partition space interrupted by the entry hall. They can further be divided according to the location of the staircases, namely as *a.* main and kitchen staircases facing each other at each end, "opposite", *b.* offset from each other on either side of the flat, "staggered", and *d.* located on the same side of the plan, "single-side".

Among the constellation of plans resulting from these typologies, four groups have become dominant, namely: *A* continuous partitions,

opposite-facing staircases, *B* interrupted main partition, opposite-facing staircases and *C* continuous main partition, staggered staircases and *D* continuous main partition, single-side staircases.
Of the completed types, type *A* represents approximately 60 per cent, at least.

In practical terms, these were the only types used until 1928. The housing commission set up in 1916 gave rise to the organisation of state-supported construction which was of great importance. However, it was not able to ease the Building Act straitjacket we had been squeezed into or otherwise improve the types in another way. On the contrary, as previously mentioned, the organisational form had an inhibiting effect on the development potential of the plan types. Many attempts have been made by architects to improve the types, both from a technical and functional standpoint. Alexander Klein emerged during those years with his interesting studies on housing types in Berlin and his analysis of requirements for modern housing. This work also left its mark here at home. Henning Hansen appeared at the Danish Association of Architect's exhibition in 1925 with a plan type with many small rooms, which was later executed in a slightly modified form in Solgården (IV_{43}). For the later exhibition in Forum, Monberg also executed a type that expressed Klein's principles.
The architects' efforts resulted in the possibility of obtaining dispensation from the two-staircase system according to the circular of 22.1.1929. This circular permitted a single fireproof staircase for five to six storey residential buildings if the flat is provided with connecting balconies on one side or independent balconies on two sides. This established a basis for the creation of entirely new plan types and in the following years single-staircase buildings with balconies were designed at a very rapid pace. They have become a prominent feature in the cityscape and have completely revolutionised Copenhagen's traditional type of residential building.

Single staircase system

As we were exempted from only one type of staircase system, the possibility of a more spontaneous floor plan was created. The plans were, of course, initially smaller and cheaper, but of even greater value was the fact that the interrelationship between the individual rooms became more varied and more advantageous in terms of use. And the balconies, which were a fire safety measure, became an asset for the flat. The architects were thus wise to make a virtue of necessity and design these balconies so that they became valuable places to spend time. Houses with balconies also became popular, so popular in fact, that now one dares not build a house without balconies, even though they are not required by law. In recent construction, the four floor plan systems of the State Housing Fund Period have been replaced by a large number of plan constellations, but which, as before, still contain the same core constructive requirements, including, by and large, those for the residential building's function and use. Yet, in the very last couple of years, there have been calls for a stronger accentuation of the rooms towards a single larger living room, several small rooms and omission of a dining room.
It is interesting, though not very well known, that in 1902 the test houses built by Ulrik Plesner at Duevej and Mariendalsvej on the initiative of

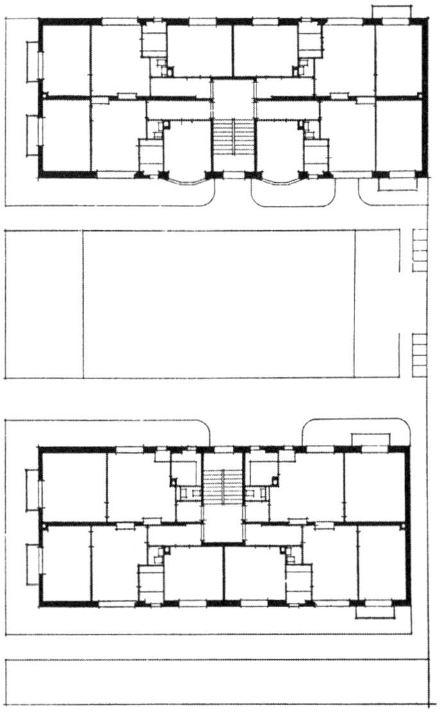

Ulrik Plesner: Experimental house on Mariendalsvej. Built in 1902. Single staircase system with balconies. Four flats per staircase. 1: 500

headmaster Fichs used types that perfectly correspond to the types we have arrived at now, 34 years later. The building style is the same: detached parallel blocks, floor plans with four single-side flats per staircase, the *single staircase system* with flights of stone steps and even fire escape balconies. The building was completed with an exemption from the municipality, which probably was mainly due to the telephone director at that time, city councillor Ms. Johansen. The plan type is correct and natural. The strangest thing is that it has not left a mark on the buildings that came after it.

The flat types consist of two rooms, one of which was originally intended as an open plan kitchen and is equipped with a cooking stove, a kind of central kitchen range that heats the whole flat. Next to this room is a small scullery with sink, larder and crockery cupboard. The ceiling here is lowered, and above it, a light shaft from a high-seated window allows light into the WC at the back.

The fire escape balconies are staggered from each other in such a way that one can jump vertically from one to the other. The staircase is made of granite with terrazzo landings with walls in bare red brick. The flat was originally provided with permanent furniture, wall cabinets and benches, but most of this has been removed.

The following plan overview contains a number of types that seem to me to be particularly characteristic of these new buildings. The selected types are characteristic from widely differing points of view: for constructive reasons, with respect to the position of rooms relative to each other, reciprocal room sizes, the position of the living room in relation to the staircase, the location of the bathroom, utilised floor depth, etc.

All of the reproduced types are grouped around a basic type. Where a basic type occurs in several buildings, the oldest example is given. The basic type is reproduced in 1:200 with indications of dimensions, installations and the north point. The type variants conforming to the basic type are reproduced in 1:500 and oriented with north facing up, giving the best basis for comparison. As some of the newest types work with asymmetric staircase systems, an entire staircase group is usually reproduced with at least two plan elements. All types are supplied with uniform information and a characteristic of the type's properties is attached to the basic type. As mentioned, the types only include completed buildings from Copenhagen, but in order to gain an understanding of type formation, exceptional instances of foreign types and, in some cases, unbuilt types, have been included. The task, moreover, has been only to provide an overview of *existing* housing types, not to treat theoretical ideal types, which, in recent years Swedish and Norwegian competitions and exhibitions and our own competition for concrete houses last year have provided interesting examples of. Also in this regard, I refer to Alexander Klein's studies, Otto Volcker's *Wohnbaufibel*, Ernst Neufert's *Bauentwurfslehre* and Otto Haessler's *Zum Probleme des Wohnbaues*, which contain interesting ideal plans, especially with regard to types with reduced floor depths that have had a great influence on recent German housing construction.

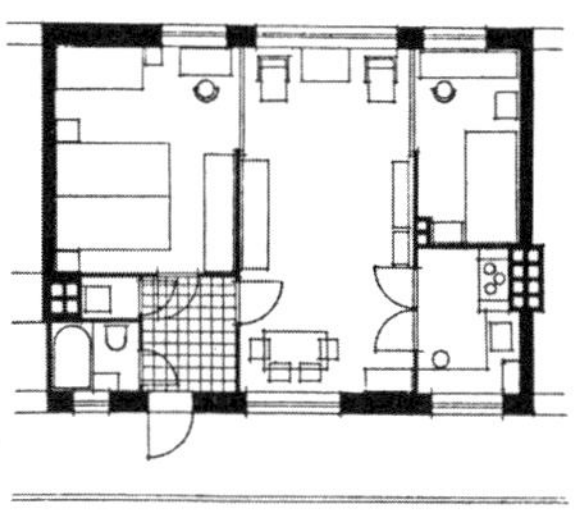

Alexander Klein: plan type with 6.5 m building depth and external corridor. Area 52 m², 1:250

As a characteristic is attached to each of the basic types, one is omitted here, as only a few of the types may require special attention. This applies, for example, to the types with many small rooms, types with a dining area, "variable" types, types with reduced floor depths and types with load-bearing cross partitions.

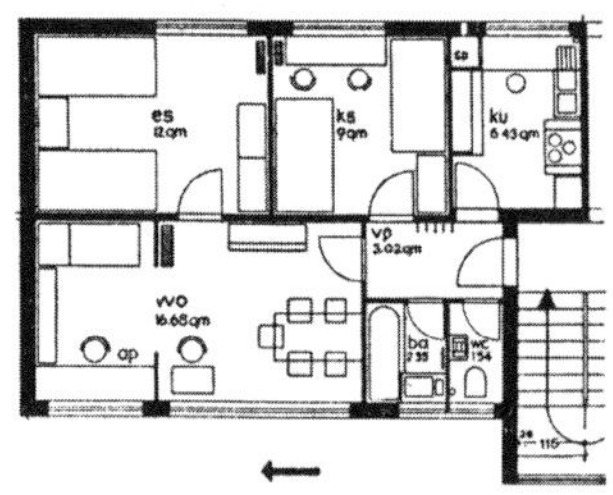

Otto Völckers: plan type with 6.5 m building depth with many small rooms. Area 65 m². 1:250

Types with narrow floor depth

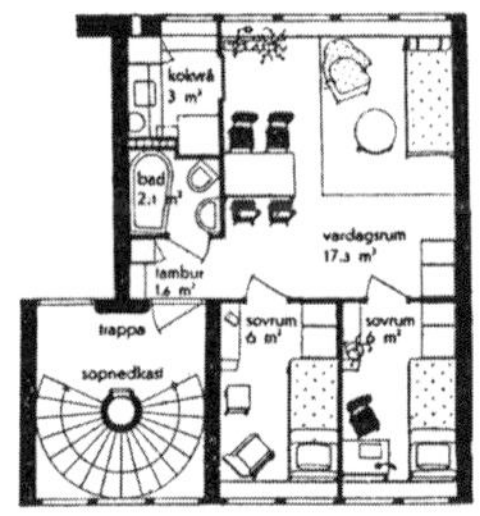

Helge Zimdal, Niels Ahrbom and Stig Ödeen: plan type with 8 m building depth. Area 45 m². Stockholm

In recent years, there has been much focus on *narrow floor depth,* particularly in Sweden and Germany. Especially the Swedes, who have so far worked with types up to a depth of 15 m, generally with two longitudinal main partitions, are currently and eagerly experimenting with housing depths as small as 6.5 m. From an operational standpoint, these types allow for very nice plans with windows along the long walls of the living rooms. Especially if one abandons the usual and rather pointless Danish housing requirements that the entry hall should provide access to all rooms and instead, as the Germans do, let the secondary rooms be accessed from a larger living room, then advantageous plans can be created on this basis. When this front room requirement is abandoned, the flat's area can be reduced to very small sizes, which can offset the somewhat more expensive construction method that requires a large exterior wall area, although this is somewhat offset by the small free-standing spans of the floor division. In any case, from an economic point of view, the Swedes have reached the conclusion that these types are competitive with housing of greater depth. In 1934, at the Standard for Housing and Furnishings exhibition in Stockholm, Helge Zimdahl and Niels Ahrbom had a type that stands out for me as one of the most beautiful housing types of recent years.

Types with load-bearing cross partitions

Load-bearing cross partitions begin to gain momentum after creating a legal basis for them, despite great opposition. They are advantageous from a construction point of view, with the flat's two cross walls creating a much more stable core than the intersecting longitudinal main partition. Furthermore, the solid cross partitions provide better insulation between the flat and a freer plan design. Finally, this type is advantageous for residential buildings with greater depths, which is of economic importance.

Types with a dining area

The types with a *dining area* and the types with *many small rooms* are among those that will undoubtedly gain significant ground in the coming years. At long last, they correspond to the view that people have reached after being subjected to persistent propaganda over many years: the utilitarian flat rather than one for show. But it has been hard slog to reach this point, and yet a large swathe of the population still demands the latter.

Types with many rooms

The modern flat requires many small spaces. The most important requirement for a home must be that each family member has his or her own space. Therefore, that two-room flats should not continue to dominate as much as they currently do in the production of housing. Approximately 70 per cent of total housing production consists of dwellings of fewer than three rooms, of which two thirds are two-room flats. And this type is now only suitable for families of two to three people. Families with several children require dwellings with one living room and several small rooms, which can be provided within the same area as two-room flats. The small rooms are, in fact, more important than the living room and the consequence of this must be that the smallest flats will only consist of small rooms. But the public is conservative on this point. Two-room flats and, when it can be afforded, two-room flats and a small room are preferred. Typically, the small room is often used as a "study", which is why housing societies generally require a double door between the study room and the living room. Of course, young married couples can use the two-room flat when they arrange things in such a way that each has a room for shared living and sleeping areas, but for large families, especially those lower down the social ladder, there must be a separation between bedrooms and living areas. Henning Hansen's first type of this kind in Solgården was a significant effort towards this. It did not become a type because the time was not yet ripe for it. But now these types are undoubtedly making an appearance.

"Variable" types

Possibly in connection with the aforementioned type with many small rooms, another type which undoubtedly will gain prominence in the future is the *variable types* with a constructive core with service installations and, in addition, light, changeable partitions. I am not referring to collapsible walls or other intricate mechanics, types that have been experimented with in Germany and America in particular, but rather on a level where the load-bearing structural joints are shaped so that the area can be easily divided into larger or smaller divisions according to the user's need.

Eskil Sundahl has built such types at Hästholmen near Stockholm (IV_{44e}), and several of our own buildings reflect such a design more or less strongly, for example in Godthåbsvænge, (IV_{44a}) and Damtoften, (IV_{44d}). The culmination of this principle is expressed in the aforementioned beautiful plan by Zimdahl and Ahrbom, (IV_{44b}), where there are six possible variations. Of these, the last is a division into neat small rooms, according to the logic of modern housing requirements as already stated, yet the least appealing of the variants.

Types with multiple flats per staircase

The types with *more than two flats per staircase* ought to be employed more often. In many foreign locations, such as in Stockholm and Vienna, they are quite predominant, but in Denmark, building laws have limited their use. They are so economically advantageous that the fact that they can be difficult to ventilate must be considered secondary. Incidentally, they can be ventilated by artificial means. The types are generally, and erroneously, used for expensive flats and "bachelor flats". Only in Bentsen and Gording's and in Monberg's municipal buildings, (IV_{35h}, IV_{45a}) on Rentemestervej are they used for very cheap flats.

In the first year after the introduction of the single staircase system, four flats per flight of stairs were built for each staircase in connection with fire escape balconies, as the circular only requires balconies facing both the courtyard and street sides, while nothing is said about whether these two balconies belong to the same flat.

This plan form was halted after being implemented in two cases, which is quite meaningless, and since then two-staircase systems are required for these types, hampering the plan arrangement to such an extent that the types are no longer cost effective and become useless. Incidentally, these types carry on naturally in *central staircase systems,* which are developed extensively in Sweden. The widely used skylit staircases in the middle of the block (cf. Sven Markelius's type, IV_{47c}) are not very appealing and the use of such staircases with skylights, which has begun here at home, should only continue under special conditions requiring such a solution. Better types are those in which, as in Hygom's house on Harsdorffsvej, (IV_{47a}), the central staircase system is linked to a light well. In the example mentioned, the type forms a plan element which could still be envisioned for a larger contiguous development. A dozen

Central staircase systems

years ago, Poul Henningsen and Jens Nielsen designed projects according to this principle, and later Hilda Rømer and Nyboe Petersen (IV_{47e}) have taken up the idea. In general, this plan principle requires split-level floor heights.

To me this plan principle seems to be resolved most beautifully in Niels Einar Eriksson's house on Sodra Ringvågen in Stockholm, (IV_{47b}), where the light well only lights up the stairs and is therefore of the same width as the latter, while its length corresponds to street width, which is why the staircase is illuminated to the same degree as if it were external.

Types with central gangway

In the case of the Swedish plans where as many as twelve to sixteen flats are arranged around this kind of central staircase, these types lead directly to *central gangway types,* which I nevertheless felt should be omitted from the overview.

Types with two-storey flats

Types with an external corridor

Unfortunately, other interesting but atypical plan forms have had to be omitted, such as types with *two-storey flats* in high-rise blocks; Anton Brenner has designed remarkable examples of these systems in Frankfurt and Schmalensee in Stockholm. The same applies to types with *an external corridor,* which provide excellent planning possibilities and which flourish extensively in Germany, but whose introduction has not been successful here at home. These central staircase types also correspond to those types in which, due to special conditions – as opposed to the conditions during the State Housing Fund Period – the lot size must be maximally utilised. In addition to the regular types with significant depth, these buildings do not form the basis for any true typology, although some of them do contain interesting floor plan solutions and for this reason I reproduce a few of them here: Gottlob's residential building in Baldersgade, which has six flats per staircase with very large depths; Skjøt-Pedersen's residential building on Hardorffsvej, where strong projections, both into the courtyard and into the street, create a very concentrated plan and *Kooperative Arkitekter*'s very ingenious Klampenborghus, where the consistent plan design is more confidently executed than its construction.

Types with large house depth

As a natural precondition for the floor plan, the question of furnishings should have been researched. The modern housing plan, especially the heavily accentuated plans divided into groups, can only be properly designed when a certain standard of furnishings is used as the basis for the design. For example, one would be able to design the plans much more advantageously and economically if the furnishings belonged to the flat rather than in the present situation where, even though a certain standard of furnishings can gradually be established, some elasticity in the use of the flat must be expected according to different needs. However, including the entire field of furnishings would be to veer too far off course. We had plans to incorporate furnishings into the designs, which is now always done in the Academy's project designs, but for existing plan types, one would either have to sketch actually existing furnishings in the types which in nine out of ten cases would be of no interest, or to design theoretically ideal furnishings that would be quite unrealistic. Therefore, we preferred to let this whole aspect of home design wait for another time.

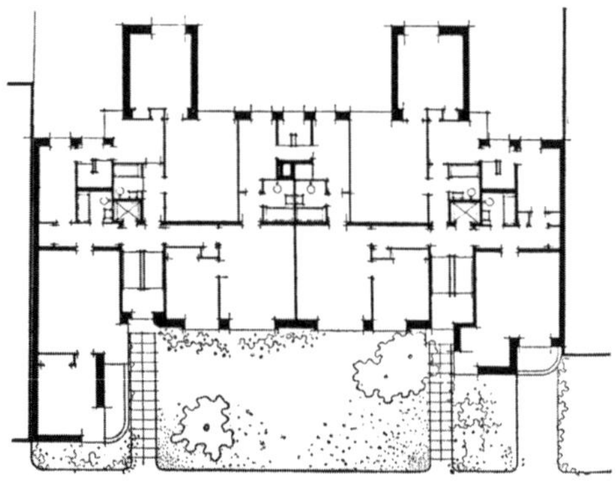

A. Skjøt-Pedersen: residential building, Harsdorffsvej. Extensive plot utilisation. Plan 1:500

Service installations

As stated, it is the *service installations* rather than the plan types that demonstrate progress.

In terms of content, the State Housing Fund Period flat corresponded on the whole to the pre-war types, but service installations and facilities

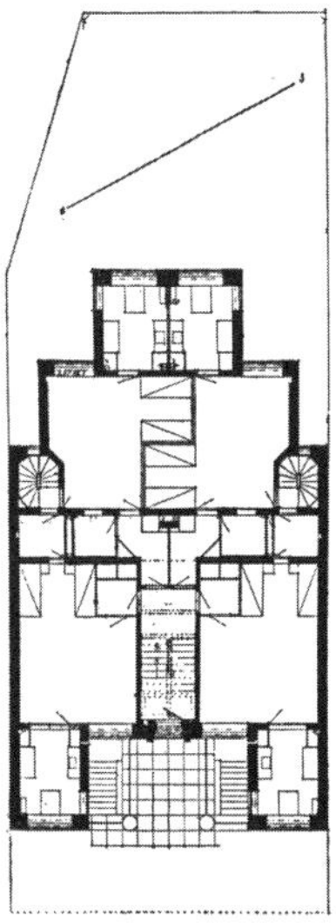

K. Gottlob: residential building in Baldersgade. Extensive plot utilisation. Plan 1:500

had been improved by including a WC in each flat, while electrical installations came with a lamp socket in the middle of the ceiling in each room and a single outlet in the living room. The best flats have central heating with a radiator in the living rooms, rarer in the bedroom and almost never in small rooms and kitchens, and for economic reasons they are placed by the main partition.

Where there is central heating there is usually also hot water in the kitchen, sometimes also in the lavatory. There is usually a basin in this lavatory, which is sometimes also equipped with a shower and thereafter referred to as a bathroom, but is rather remote from what we now understand to be a bathroom.

These types have no wardrobes, and generally, there are rarely any closets and there is a lack of space for many indispensable things, such as vacuum cleaners and ironing boards.

The kitchen furniture consists of a fixed table with pine wood and cast-iron sink, gas cooker with a terrazzo plate or tile, a plate rack, cupboards for kitchenware, crockery and brooms, as well as a larder that is not a small room but a food cupboard. In residential housing of recent years, this equipment has improved significantly. Central heating, hot water and bathrooms with baths are now natural components of even the smallest flat. In addition, refuse chutes, refrigerators, electric washing machines and ironing facilities have been installed in many buildings. Higher buildings frequently contain a lift.

In the kitchen, equipment consists of a sink, either of fireclay, enamelled cast iron or stainless steel, and it is often a double sink with a drain plug that can be used for washing up. The drain board is also often made of steel, the preparation table for cutting is sometimes made of hardwood, Oregon pine or teak. The unhygienic plate rack has been replaced by cabinets and both the bath and kitchen have tile walls. Additionally, one finds a wardrobe, meter box and sometimes another closet in the bedroom.

The flat has thus undergone considerable improvement in terms of equipment and technology, but much is still missing, something that has incidentally been stated many times before, such as sound insulation, efficient ventilation systems, pipe insulation, better flooring, jointless floors, etc.

As an example of how an inexpensive standard flat in the year 1935 is equipped, I include here an excerpt of a statement prepared by *Københavns almindelige Boligselskab* (KAB) together with architect Gunnar Holm and published in a conference paper from the International Federation for Housing and Planning: *Austattung der Kleinwohnung*. Stuttgart, 1935.

The flat in question (IV_{35a}) has a gross area of 52 m^2. Construction costs per flat stands at DKK 6,800 while the monthly rent is DKK 56.83. Monthly heating and hot water costs DKK 10.20.

The living room faces south towards the street with the staircase on the north side towards the courtyard. The flat itself is located in an east-west facing wing of a ribbon development around a large open garden-like courtyard.

The window is four frames wide to allow as much light as possible into the living room so that the light functions in a consolidating manner, providing the room with greater unity than in the older housing types where the corresponding two narrow windows divide the outer wall too much and where the light from the windows on each side of the dark centre column creates a high degree of glare. The window is moved to one side of the outer wall based on the desire to have a well-protected sofa space by the long wall. The door to the balcony is placed in such a way that it can be held open by the railing and hence forms a kind of windscreen for the balcony.

The door between the living room and the small room is designed as a double door so that these two rooms, if desired, can be as connected as possible, but this is a rare occurrence for KAB flats, as a single door is otherwise considered sufficient for the sake of already reduced wall space. In cases where residents want the small room used exclusively as a children's room, the double door can be blocked up to great advantage for both rooms. The door between the living room and the small room is mostly omitted in ordinary construction projects, but KAB attaches great importance to this door not only for the possibility of turning both rooms into living rooms, but especially so that the flat can be ventilated effectively. However, it cannot be denied that this reduces the options for living room furnishings which would otherwise be very good now that the fireplace no longer occupies the corner.

The bedroom is very small compared to the bedroom of old, but even though it is down to minimum size, it can be fully utilised as the former washstand and stove are no longer needed now with the aid of a bathroom and central heating. Thus, a fairly large area can be freed up.

The small room is so little that if more than one child sleeps in it, bunk beds must be used.

The bathroom, with indirect lighting, has no radiator, which is banned by the Building Act. It is equipped with a bath that tenants greatly appreciate. To make the room as narrow as possible, the so-called foot and sit baths, which have become very popular, have been used, and this type of bath is well suited for bathing children. A health congress held here recently strongly expressed the view that the shower did precious little to promote cleanliness, since the water and washing only come from above. The bath's water content of 168 L against the volume capacity of the normal bath of between 250 and 300 L saves water consumption. Baths, washbasins and WCs are placed as close to each other as possible for the sake of the pipe installation and to minimise the length of the room. However strong the desire to isolate the WC in a special room, the flat's small area does not allow this increase in size, just as the expense would presumably also increase, especially since the separate toilet room ought to be provided with a special washbasin.

Flush valves have been used for toilet flushing instead of the commonly used cisterns.

This has improved the room's appearance and avoided the disadvantage of dripping condensed water from the cistern and thus having to paint it regularly to prevent rusting. On the other hand, unfortunately, the installation of flush valves only leads to a slight reduction in the normal noise generated by the bathroom. Usually 11 to 13 rows of large white tiles are installed on the bathroom walls. In this case, only one row of tiles has been placed above the bath for reasons of economy. The kitchen floor area is 5.91 m² which is the minimum legal size when gas is used, as is the case here. Fittings are comprised of worktops with lower cupboards and crockery as well as broom and larder cupboards. The gas cooker consists of a built-in terrazzo plate. The kitchen sink is an enamel cast-iron sink with a receding edge at the top for spraying purposes. The worktop extends all the way to the edge of the sink. Both the sink's material as well as its traditional placement leaves much to be desired. Recently, therefore, stainless-steel sinks have been used, whose material has proved to be extremely suitable and where the sink's horizontal top edge can be placed over the kitchen worktop, which is a far better design, especially when the entire kitchen worktop is covered in linoleum or steel plate. There is worktop space on both sides of the sink for dirty and clean crockery just as there is a separate lamp over the sink and gas cooker. There are bottoms in all of the cupboards, and the skirting board is retracted so that the foot can fit under the cupboard and the doors are completely smooth on both sides. There are ventilation ducts 10 × 15 cm from each gas kitchen with an additional small pivoting pane installed in the kitchen window. It is common to lay three or four rows of white tiles over the worktop and gas cooker. The top is finished with a moulding which is grooved over the tile edge. Where there is no refuse chute, a shelf is often installed on the cupboard door under the sink for the refuse bin. The taps, both for the washbasin and the kitchen sink, are connected to a single outlet spout, which means an increase in the purchase price compared to the commonly used individual taps, but is due to the fact that the authorities do not charge for water consumption per m³ of water, but per draw-off point. There is no radiator installed in the kitchen, which is also an advantage for food storage. The larder is ventilated by means of two small openings to the outside.

An electrical outlet is installed in the kitchen for ironing. In larger flats, the kitchen has a built-in ironing board. The entry hall is built in the smallest possible size. The width of its narrow section is 82 cm and this must be considered the absolute minimum. Each hall has access to a wardrobe cabinet. In this case, the cabinet is built into the kitchen area. It is divided into a smaller upper cupboard and a tall lower wardrobe with a hat shelf, under which an oak or brass bar is installed for clothing hangers. A small niche is built into the wall between the living room and the kitchen's broom cupboard which yields space for the electricity meter. Generally, a hanging rack is placed around the entire entry hall with metal hooks for hats and coats. In this case, the racks are replaced with circular wooden boards. The single staircase system leads to the nuisance of residents putting their empty milk bottles outside their entrance door in the evening, when previously they placed them on the kitchen staircase. To mitigate this and to limit the theft of bottles left by the door in the morning, small iron plate cupboards were inserted on the inside of the front door with a hatch in the door itself. The cupboard has hatches facing both the staircase and the entry hall. Where feasible, however, it is preferable to incorporate these milk cupboards into the staircase wall. Balconies are constructed with a concrete base plate between the projecting iron. The balustrade consists of open wrought iron railing, but lately it has become common to have a closed parapet for the benefit of the balcony's shielding effect and the resulting reduced wind effect on the balcony door.

1921

1926

1931

With regard to residential housing *design* of the State Housing Fund Period, Steen Eiler Rasmussen wrote in 1926:

When we consider at length the buildings' exterior design, in the vast majority of cases we find the dimensions and forms of small houses being applied to large complexes. With a simple addition, the two and three-storey empire-style residential buildings have been transformed into kilometre-long façades with uniform, small windows. For a number of years, Bedre Byggeskik has been working to introduce small windows in small homes. It has not been entirely successful. But the architects have been successful with getting them into Copenhagen's huge housing complexes. They have not tried to show the building's divisions with its many entrances, but rather just papered them over with the same window pattern. The jerry-builder housing from around the turn of the century seem more real in all their tastelessness than the new blocks with their old-fashioned details. They seem more authentic in their goals, more naturally engaged in the task and are also more favoured by the common man. The correct design of multi-storey blocks has problems that are not yet solved.

Whether these problems will eventually be solved, I do not know. I do not think so. On some points we may have managed to address the problems more naturally, but on the whole, we have only gone from one period's formalism to the next.

Structures and materials are basically the same as they were twenty-five years ago. As long as bricks are our cheapest building material and as long as the brick-making industry finances construction, brick will continue to dominate Copenhagen's buildings. We should certainly not regret this, but try again to gain an understanding of the character and properties of brick as it was a generation ago. During the State Housing Fund Period, we polished up the brick houses to make them look neoclassical just as faithful modernists are now polishing them up to make them look like concrete houses. Instead, we should strive to develop a brick technique on the same level as the period of Plesner and Nyrop with excellent technical ability and which also produced equally beautiful material effects. We should also learn that brick houses, especially in these iron-deficient times, should not be built with concrete forms.

We have come so far that we have freed ourselves from neoclassicism's façade form. For example, we have placed the staircase window at the correct height relative to the staircase. We have also gradually learnt to provide living rooms with a large window and smaller rooms with a smaller one. We position balconies so that they do not cast shadows on the flat below and we have also realised that it is more comfortable to look out of a large pane than through windows divided by glazing bars. But we work with sizes that are far too cramped and the measurements of the details are too small. Windows have become wider, but in most cases too low and compressed. In almost all newer residential buildings, I find these units of measurement too small.

1936

There has also been an unfortunate tendency for garish colour effects: windows, doors and polished wall surfaces are painted a range of greens, reds or yellows which often do not suit the bricks and natural colours of the surrounding environment.

On the other hand, it has to be said that there have been lovely outcomes with regard to the integration of the buildings into the terrain, especially in old landscaped parks, especially in buildings such as Blidah, Bellavista, Lille Tuborg, Likkensgave and Jørgenshave.

Sometimes while abroad, I have had the opportunity to view slides of these houses surrounded by old trees and aided by excellent photography, and have noticed the admiration of foreigners for them.

Although those of us who know them inside and out may be a little less impressed, we must acknowledge that recent years in this field have infused us with new values in the interaction between architecture and nature.
We have added new aesthetic values to buildings, but lost some of the old ones which there was no reason to give up.
Just as Steen Eiler Rasmussen did in 1926, I will conclude by highlighting the previous period and claim that State Housing Fund Period housing, despite its stereotypical formalism, often seems to exhibit better measurements, more comfortable dimensions in terms of detail, and more poise in the cityscape than the troubled flickering new houses with their compressed window heights, often unsightly balcony shapes and ugly colours.
Problems still remain in the correct design of multi-storey blocks which have not yet been solved.

Housing construction conditions after 1856

by polit. cand. Enrico Hansen

1856–1900

In the middle of the nineteenth century, Copenhagen was a city of craftsmen and traders. There was no real industry, no uniform industrial working class and therefore no labour issues, but there was considerable disparity between rich and poor – about a tenth of the population lived below the poverty line.
The prevailing economic view was of "free competition". The idea was that when the individual managed his or her private finances based on narrow financial interests, he or she thereby also benefited society as a whole. From society's point of view, there should therefore be as little intervention as possible in the citizen's personal handling of his or her financial interests; all artificial interventions should be kept out, and economic forces should have free reign.
The years from 1850 to 1875 are noteworthy in the capital's building sector as the period in which construction began on the other side of the lakes, which was the beginning of the third major expansion of the capital. Seen with our eyes, however, it is striking how little care and foresight the authorities showed in leading this building phase. However, it must be borne in mind that not only did this fall completely in line with the prevailing spirit of "free competition" to intervene as little as possible in relation to the building industry, but there was also a significant lack of understanding that this was the beginning of a *trend* of the city's rise towards a new period of growth. The mid-1870s divide the period between 1855 and 1900. Before 1875, approximately 80,000 m^2 of floor space was built annually. After 1875, construction reaches an annual average of 180,000 m^2 of floor space.
The years before 1875 were difficult ones. The cost of living increased by between 5 and 10 per cent, rents by 30 to 40 per cent, while wages had difficulty keeping up, which is why during this period there was hardly any increase in "real wages".

After 1875, the picture is reversed. The cost of living starts to fall. However, rents show a further increase (about 50 per cent in relation to 1855) while wages increase by 75 per cent. When wages rise so sharply while the cost of living falls, it means a worker's income allows for the purchase of significantly more goods – better clothes, better housing and more food and leisure items.

The increase in rents must be explained by the fact that the statistics are compiled on the basis of the average rent for flats advertised to let in *Adresseavisen*. As it is undoubtedly new flats that are being advertised, it must be assumed that they are of a steadily increasing standard. This is the source of the rent increases, and when this period sees a residential building spree that is practically at full throttle for the entire period from 1877 to 1900, it is due to the *sharp increase in real wages* that provided the basis for building better and better flats and to continue letting them out.

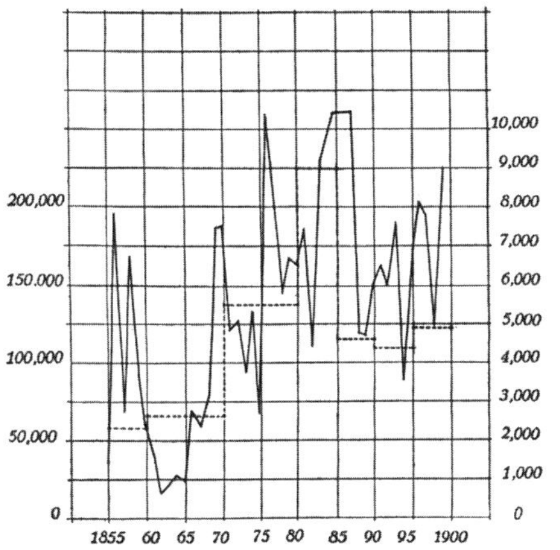

The strong fluctuations in the annual volume of construction are clearly indicated by the curve. At the same time, it should be noted that it was in the 1870s that the decisive shift in the scale of housing construction and population growth occurred.

The improvements that the building trade had to offer before 1875 were private kitchens with waste water drains for small flats and "water pipes inside the houses". Annual water consumption increased from 175 hl per inhabitant in 1860 to 240 hl per inhabitant in 1900. The provision of gas came after 1875. In 1880, ¼ of households had gas and in 190 1 it reached 97 per cent.

But improvements in housing conditions were also seen in many other fields. Subsequent tables for Copenhagen municipality will demonstrate this.

Location of the flats:

	1880	1885	1890	1895	1901
In the front building	76.4	76.6	78.6	79.3	82.2
In middle, side, and back buildings	23.6	23.4	21.4	20.7	17.8
In the basement	4.6	4.5	4.3	3.9	3.1

Distribution of flats by number of rooms as a percentage:

	1880	1885	1890	1895	1901
1 room	16.8	15.0	13.9	13.3	13.1
2 rooms	32.9	36.3	39.9	40.2	41.2
3 rooms	31.3	16.8	16.7	16.7	17.00
4 rooms		12.8	13.5	13.9	14.4
5 rooms		7.0	6.3	6.5	5.9
6 rooms	14.3	4.6	4.0	4.0	3.5
7 rooms		2.8	2.5	2.4	2.1
8 rooms and above	4.7	4.7	3.2	3.0	2.8
Total...	100.00	100.00	100.00	100.00	100.00

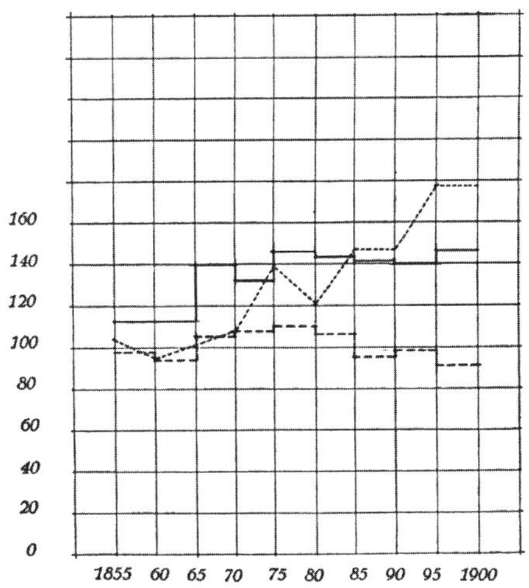

Index figure for rents 1855 = 100

Index figure for wages 1855 = 100

Index figure for retail prices 1855 = 100

The curves show the shift in economic conditions that began in the 1870s and which emerged most clearly since 1885. Strong increase in real wages, high rents and low cost of living.

The first table clearly shows the extent to which new construction in the 1880s and 1890s turned away from flats in side, middle and back buildings and in basements.

The second part of the table shows that the trend towards flats with two and three rooms and away from one-room and many-room flats also prevailed in these years. Population growth and housing construction went hand in hand during this period; the degree of parallel movement

between these two values can easily be seen from the curve at the top of page 45. However, high population growth should not be perceived as the cause behind the fervent construction or vice versa. It is the high increase in real wages that is the cause behind immigration to the city and housing construction. If we ask again why real wages had risen – that it was possible to provide the general population with a much larger share of consumer goods than before – it is presumably due to the breakthrough of industrialisation, great technical advances and the continuous development of economic organisation. It must be emphasised that the development of greater economic organisation in itself implies that free competition is limited. This tendency towards regulating the economy began ever so slowly in the 1870s and grew steadily stronger.
However, the significant progress that took place in the period up to 1900 had a dark side for the vast majority of the population. For the poorest section of the population, conditions seem to have worsened. Observing the following small table illustrating the poorest housing conditions, one will see that 1895 seems to be the high point with regard to poor housing conditions for the poorest section of Copenhagen's population.

Flats with 8 occupants and above:

	Number of one-room flats	Number of two-room flats	Total number of occupants	Per cent of population
1880	55	540	5,337	2.28
1885	57	738	7,131	2.67
1890	68	1,087	9,783	3.28
1895	54	1,244	11,040	3.44
1901	66	1,287	11,642	3.36

1900–1916

The years before 1907 are marked by the build-up to the building crisis of 1907–08, and the years from 1909 to 1916 by the effects of the building crisis. However, the use of the term "building crisis" is somewhat misleading.
If the banks in the years following the turn of the century and up to 1907 had ushered in a period of reckless lending to one industry sector or another, such as the cement industry, hardly anyone would have called the crisis that occurred in 1907 the "cement crisis". But now that anyone and everyone could see that there was too much construction, they chose to call the crisis in 1907–08 a "building crisis". The crisis had nothing to do with the building industry except that the *banks* had excessively financed it and on an unhealthy basis. It was the banks that had erred, and the crisis was a *banking crisis.* The reason for stressing this point is because the mentality from these years is still prevalent. If there is somewhat of an abundance of building one year, there is an immediate cry of "building crisis" so emphatically that one almost thinks that building activity is evil. It is forgotten that the question is whether credit extended to building activity has been granted on a sound basis.

Year	Danmarks Nationalbank's Base Rate	Increase in m² to floor area Cph. and Frbg.	Available flats as per cent of total
1900	5.87	439,676	0.9
1901	5.33	476,011	2.2
1902	4.05	370,267	3.3
1903	4.37	627,503	5.1
1904	4.50	608,718	6.8
1905	4.30	479,088	7.6
1906	5.22	592,381	7.5
1907	6.18	376,810	7.3
1908	6.13	488,056	6.4
1909	4.94	105,430	5.9
1910	5.00	116,182	4.0
1911	4.62	78,872	2.5
1912	5.06	183,651	1.4
1913	5.75	321,374	1.1
1914	5.52	325,298	1.4
1915	5.27	248,884	1.3
1916	5.00	223,284	—

By observing the curve of the extent of construction in these years, one will notice that the height of building activity peaked around the years 1903–04 rather than immediately before the crisis in 1907–08. It is also noteworthy that the rising vacancy rate for flats does not appear to have affected the extent of building activity. Perhaps it was the old flats that were vacant and the new ones that were available to let. The statistics provide no information on this question. On the contrary, the high base rate seems to have had a decisive influence, partly in the sense that the very high interest rates in 1907–08 halted building activity, but also in the sense that the relatively high interest rate which was still in force inhibited building activity.

The prevailing conventional wisdom is that after the various bank collapses in 1907–08 the "banks" had amassed so much interest in new buildings that, in order to increase rents, they refused to grant new building loans, so that newly built flats would not force down rents in the acquired properties. That this negative view should also be the only correct one is hardly acceptable. The high interest rates that prevailed in the years right up to 1916 had undoubtedly managed to suppress building activity in the absence of any increase in real wages, despite the fact that there was fairly strong population growth in these years. Another way to put it is that building activity was stopped too late in relation to the base rate increase in 1907. That was the banks' first mistake. The next mistake was in keeping building activity to a minimum for far too long. When they finally wanted to breathe new life into the building sector again, it was too late. Because of the price increases, no one dared to build. The improvement in housing conditions that began so strongly after 1875 continued during these years. The tables and curves showing the location of the flats in the properties, the distribution of flats by number of rooms (pages 45 and 46), and the overpopulation of the flats (page 51) illustrate this. The movement towards better installations also continued. Thus, in 1901 only 3 per cent of flats had electric light and a water closet, while in 1916 this figure had reached 60 per cent. However, central heating and hot water for domestic use was practically inexistant in 1916. Likewise, the table below gives an interesting indication of the extent to which the flats had attached baths.

Number of flats with bath access:

	1906	1911
Copenhagen	3.8	6.8
Frederiksberg	8.3	12.5
Gentofte	16.2	19.6

If conditions had developed favourably after 1916 to the degree that the population had the requisite purchasing power (rising real wages) and stable building costs, there would have undoubtedly been an interest in generalising further improvements to the flats. If conditions had been normal, the installations, etc., that we get after 1928 – i.e. 12 years later – we should have had in the years after 1916. But that is not how things went. Instead, one had to struggle against the housing shortage with all one's might. If building activity was not under way *before* 1916, to the extent that housing production did not meet demand, it became even more difficult to get housing production up and running *after* 1916, despite continued strong population growth.

The relationship between housing construction and population growth for the years from 1900 to 1930 is as follows:

	Number of newly built flats-annual average	Population growth-annual average	Number of new flats per 1,000 individuals-population growth
1901–06	5,562	13,181	442
1906–11	2,143	9,849	218
1911–16	2,441	10,673	225
1916–21	3,621	12,631	286
1921–25	4,916	5,662	867
1925–30	4,882	6,904	698
1930–35	9,670	13,640	709

As can be seen from the figures, flat access from 1906 to 1921 was unreasonably low in relation to population growth. The difficulty of kick-starting building activity after 1916 was due to strong price increases for materials and labour, as well as to relatively high interest rates, which led to significant losses due to depreciation and difficult loan conditions. The curve demonstrates how strong the price index increase had been for building labour costs. Yet, high building costs do not in and of themselves mean that building activity grinds to a halt. But when one is uncertain about future construction cost levels, especially if there is an expectation that they will be lower, it is unfeasible to build on the basis of private enterprise. After all, capital is invested over many years. If construction costs fall, then one has been unable to take advantage of the price drop, since it is not possible to recoup significantly any of the capital invested, even within a time range of ten to twenty years. This halted private building activity and the strong population growth led directly to the housing shortage, and at the same time to the regulations in which housing rents became legally fixed. There were no available flats. Those of limited means who lost their housing had to be accommodated as homeless,

and existing housing had to be utilised more intensely. This is demonstrated by the two tables showing the increase in the number of persons per household (flat) and number of persons per room until 1921. Flat overpopulation, which reached its height in 1921, also shows how difficult things were.
Of course, when building activity could no longer be avoided, more for reasons of employment than housing, legislation was passed on state and local authority aid for the building sector. The aid granted was partly in the form of an exemption from municipal property taxes and partly in the form of grants – up to 20 per cent from the state and equally as much from the municipality – and finally as a loan or loan guarantee. From 1922 until 1 October 1928, the loans were granted as State Housing Fund loans paid out as bonds, so that losses due to depreciation fell to the borrower. The loans could be granted up to 40 per cent of the cost price with collateral that was within 80 (exceptionally 90) per cent of the total cost price.
On the basis of the state aid legislation, a very significant upswing in building activity took place in the capital. The extent of the state's support has been shown by the fact that of the 66,000 flats built in the capital in the years 1916 to 1931, just over 12,000 were built directly by the municipalities, while 29,000 were built by private builders or building societies with state aid. Two-thirds of all constructed flats were thus supported, and one must include in the reckoning that in these years, the municipality and the state contributed between DKK 250 to 300 million to building activity in the capital.
When there is a shortage of accommodation it is a matter of course that the main emphasis of subsidised construction must be on producing housing space. The question of improvements and service installations – besides the generally accepted ones – had to be put aside. While in previous periods it was water and gas installations that had become standard, in these years all flats were only supplied with electricity. In 1916, 60 per cent of flats had electricity, while in 1921 it was approximately 90 per cent. WC installation also increased by 66 per cent in 1925 and 75 per cent in 1930. The reason for not attaining 90 per cent is because the oldest and humblest flats were unsuitable for such installations. It was only after 1925 that the building industry seriously became interested in central heating, hot domestic water and baths. In 1925 only about 4 per cent of all existing flats had central heating and hot water; in 1930 it had increased to 10 per cent.

About bathroom, the percentages are as follows:

1916	7.8	percentages of apartments
1921	12.2	percentages of apartments
1925	16.4	percentages of apartments
1930	21.1	percentages of apartments

One of the most significant improvements attained during these years of construction – both as a result of state support for the building sector as well as a result of the municipality's land policy – is that significantly larger areas for courtyards (courtyard gardens), front gardens, roads and open green spaces, etc., are laid out than those required by existing road

After 1928

and building legislation. These efforts have been so well-received by the population that it now pays off for a private builder not to exploit a plot's maximum possible building space.

The conditions of the building sector during this period must be seen in opposition to the preceding years. The level of interest rates has remained relatively *low.* Building costs have remained fairly *constant*, and, finally, it must be pointed out that real income has shown a clear tendency towards an *increase.* On this basis, private construction of rental flats has started again, parallel with building activities supported by the state and municipality.

The increase in revenue has created purchasing power for service installations in the newly built flats. As many flats have been built in the last five years, a large percentage of them now have a bath, central heating and hot water as standard facilities.

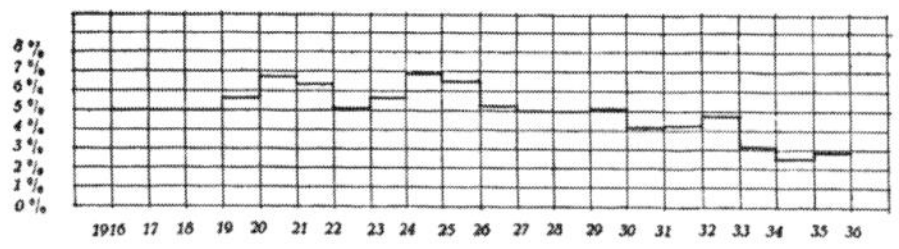

Danmarks Nationalbank's base rate shows which high interest rates were actually in force from 1916 to 1930. Only after 1928, and especially after 1930, did interest rates reach a fairly favourable level.

Percentages of service installations in all flats:

	Bath	Central heating	Hot water
1916	7.8	7.8	7.8
1921	12.2	12.2	12.2
1925	16.4	4.7	4.3
1930	21.1	10.7	10.2
1935 (estimated)	33.0	25.0	25.0

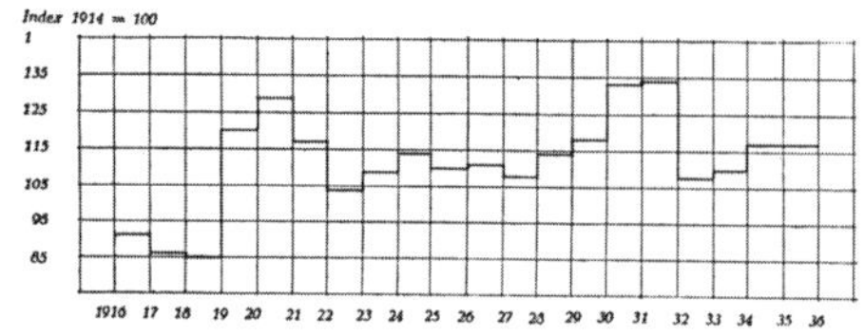

Building labour costs reached their height in 1920 and then fell. Only in 1928 did they seem to have reached a fairly constant level.

It is important to emphasise that these technical installations have not alone characterised residential building activity. Efforts to create properly located residential areas with sufficient free space in connection with having flats and living rooms face the light and sun have also played a part. Changing housing ideals is a natural consequence of changing housing needs. Simply in terms of the number of people in a single household, there has been a noticeable decline in the last 15 to 20 years because there is less domestic help, not so many children, fewer lodgers, and more single people living in their own flats.

When flats calculated by room number simultaneously show a tendency towards the average type – two to four rooms – there is more room space for each person so that Greater Copenhagen as a whole now has one room for each inhabitant.

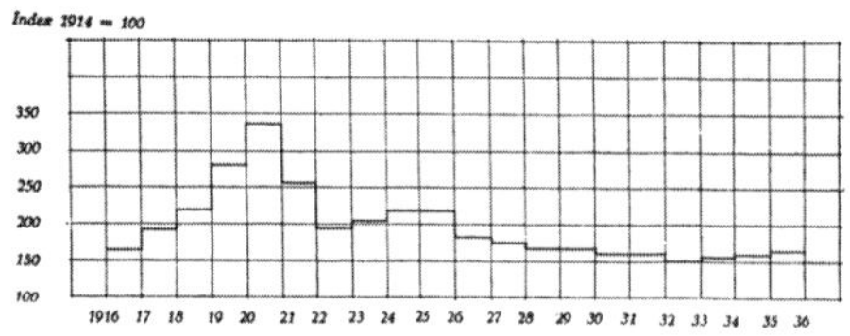

Real income was at a level of 110 from 1923 to 1927. In 1928, there was an increase that nevertheless could not be fully maintained.

Average Number of Persons per Household:

	Copenhagen	Frederiksberg	Gentofte	Greater Copenhagen
1901	3.82	4.00	4.39	3.86
1906	3.65	3.85	4.27	3.78
1911	3.52	3.71	4.09	3.57
1916	3.45	3.56	3.99	3.49
1921	3.49	3.58	4.06	3.53
1925	3.32	3.36	3.86	3.25
1930	3.13	3.16	3.70	3.16

Average Number of Persons per Room:

	Copenhagen	Frederiksberg	Gentofte	Greater Copenhagen
1901	1.29	1.09	1.05	1.19
1906	1.24	1.06	0.95	1.18
1911	1.19	1.00	0.89	1.15
1916	1.18	0.97	0.84	1.13
1921	1.21	0.98	0.86	1.17
1925	1.14	0.91	0.83	1.08
1930	1.08	0.87	0.82	1.02

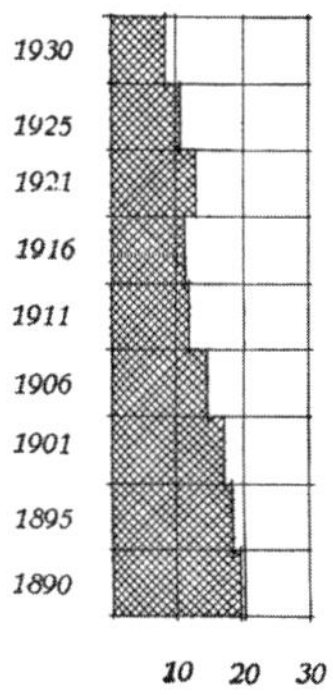

Overcrowded flats as percentage of total. Note the decreasing line's interruption during the housing shortage (1921).

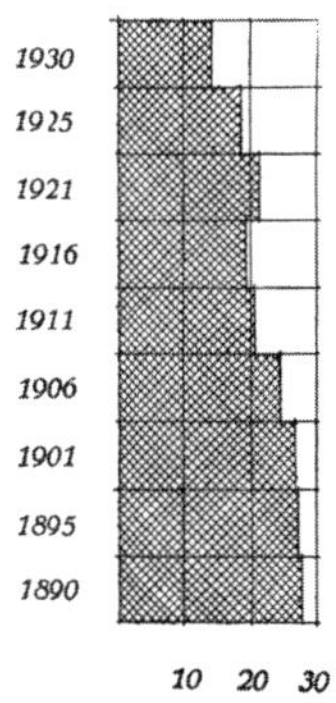

Residents in overcrowded flats as a percentage of all residents (Copenhagen Municipality). Although the decrease has been maintained – except during the housing shortage – 14 per cent of inhabitants still live under such poor living conditions.

The strong improvement in housing conditions of the last three generations with regard to service installations, flat location and actual use of space per resident has required a conscious effort on the part of housing engineers. Nonetheless this the housing problem itself has not been eliminated. There are still a number of issues that need to be resolved. Firstly, there are *the overcrowded flats*, i.e. those with an average of more than two people per room. Overcrowded flats can be found to the greatest extent in those neighbourhoods in which the buildings are outdated, unsanitary and essentially run-down. Herein lies *the problem of urban redevelopment.* Ordinary utilitarian buildings should be demolished when they reach an appropriate age. The overcrowded flats are also inhabited by people with children, often with many children. The diminishing birth rate is presented to us as a doomsday scenario. So then why do we give the children we have the worst possible conditions from the start? There is a *special housing issue for people with children.* At present, they are most often given the poorest housing when they should arguably have the best.

The builder usually has at his disposal only the last 10 to 20 per cent of the cost. The rest of the money – 80 to 90 per cent – is secured by the builder from society's general savings, which is readily made available to him. Furthermore, as a rule, buildings have a lifetime of 100 to 150 years – i.e. from three to five generations. *The builder builds to a much greater extent for others than for himself.* Nevertheless, this individual is allowed to do as he pleases provided his plans do not stray too far from tradition. Factories and housing are being built in the east and west. From a societal point of view, there must be losses in that all this is not based on *a fixed plan.* The question, then, is whether preparatory and planning work, which establishes a restrictive framework for where and how to build, would not pay for itself many times over. These are large sums, in fact entire annual savings, which range from DKK 200 to 400 million per year.

Building development plans

Enclosed blocks, *1:5000. North is up*

A

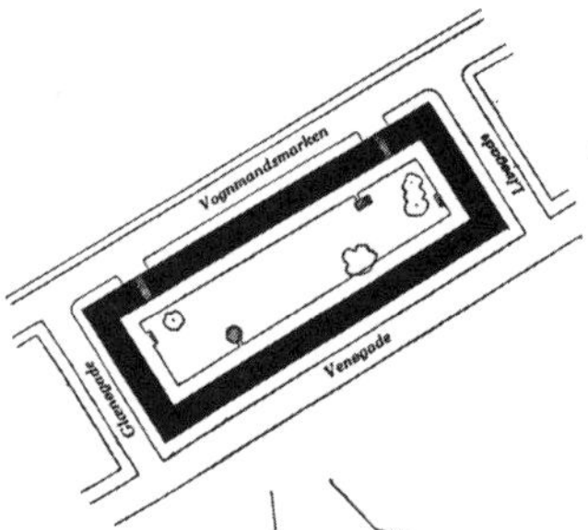

a
1 *Location: Vognmandsmarken, Glænøgade*
2 *Client: Københavns almindelige Boligselskab (KAB) Boligselskab (KAB)*
3 *Architect: Kay Fisker*
4 *Year built: 1926–27*
5 *Plot area: (incl. street) 7211 m²*
6 *Built-up area: 3137 m²*
7 *Number of main staircases: 20*
8 *Number of floors: 5*

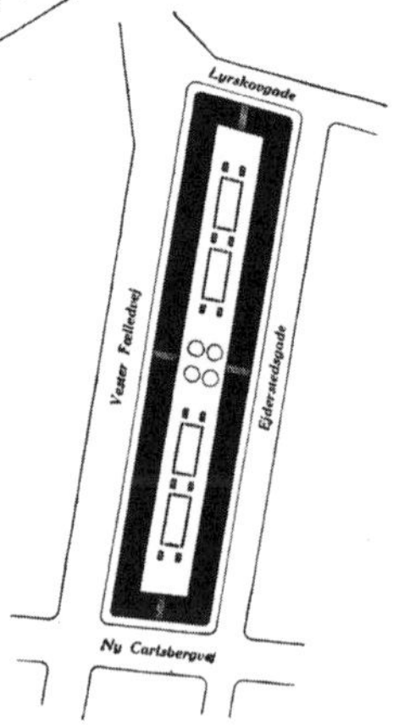

b
1 *Location: Enghavevej and Carlsbergvej*
2 *Client: Municipality of Copenhagen*
3 *Architect: City architect Paul Holsøe*
4 *Year built: 1928*
5 *Plot area: 8353.5 m²*
6 *Built-up area: 4562.26 m²*
7 *Number of main staircases: 26*
8 *Number of floors: 5 and 1 attic*

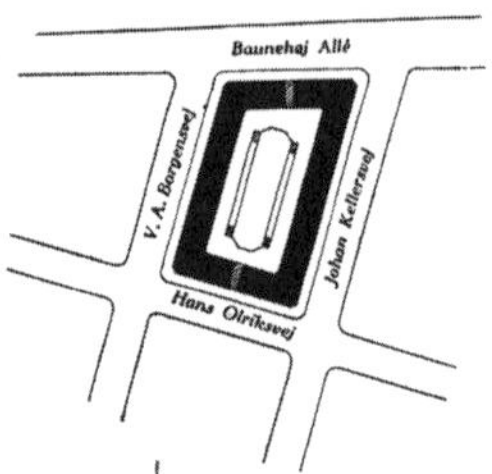

c
1 *Location: Baunehøj Allé, Vesterbro*
2 *Client: Municipality of Copenhagen*
3 *Architect: Alf. Cock-Clausen*
4 *Year built: 1928*
5 *Plot area: 3300 m²*
6 *Built-up area: 1957 m²*
7 *Number of main staircases: 19*
8 *Number of floors: 5*

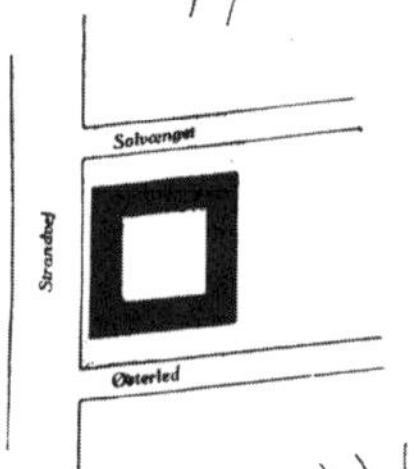

d
1 *Location: Strandvejen, Østerbro*
2 *Client: Municipality of Copenhagen*
3 *Architect: Louis Hygom*
4 *Year built: 1929*
5 *Plot area: 5138.8 m²*
6 *Built-up area: 1705.2 m²*
7 *Number of main staircases: 6*
8 *Number of floors: 4*

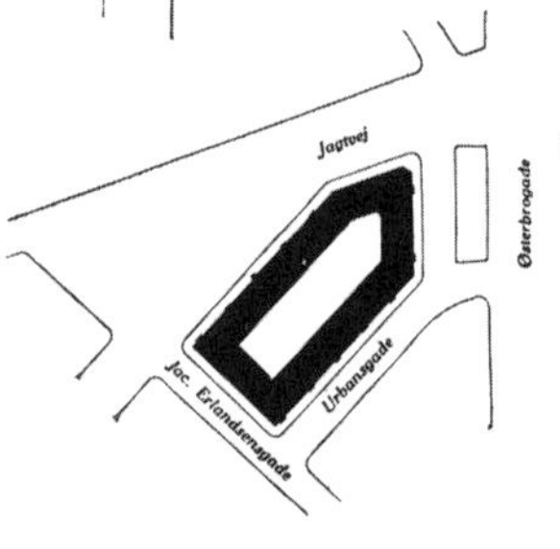

e
1 *Location: Jagtvej, Østerbrogade*
2 *Client: Arbejdernes Kooperative Byggeforening*
3 *Architect: Mandrup Poulsen, E. Ambt*
4 *Year built: 1928–29*
5 *Plot area: 3627.9 m²*
6 *Built-up area: 2390 m²*
7 *Number of main staircases: 7*
8 *Number of floors: 5 (rooms in attic)*

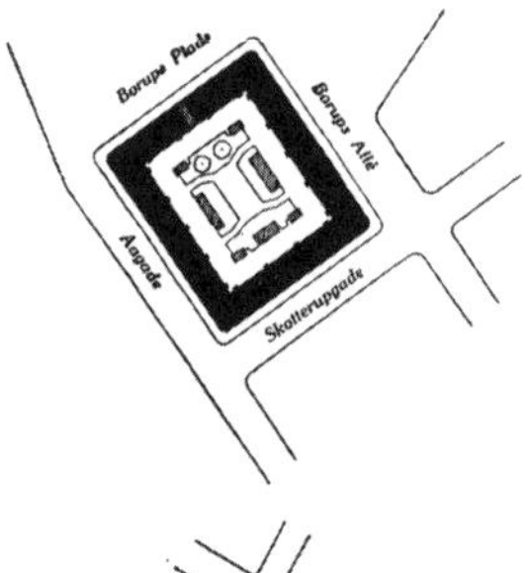

f
1 *Location: Borups Allé, Borups Plads*
2 *Client: Municipality of Copenhagen*
3 *Architect:, n. P. Gundstrup*
4 *Year built: 1928–29*
5 *Plot area: 4753 m²*
6 *Built-up area: 2375 m²*
7 *Number of main staircases: 18*
8 *Number of floors: 5*

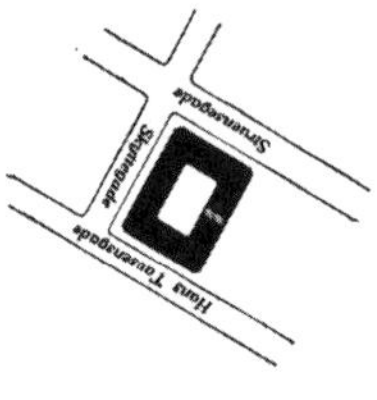

g
1 *Location: Hans Tavsens Gade*
2 *Client: Hans Tavsens Gaard A/S*
3 *Architect: C. F. Møller, C. Neye*
4 *Year built: 1929*
5 *Plot area: 1547 m²*
6 *Built-up area: 985 m²*
7 *Number of main staircases: 5*
8 *Number of floors: 5*

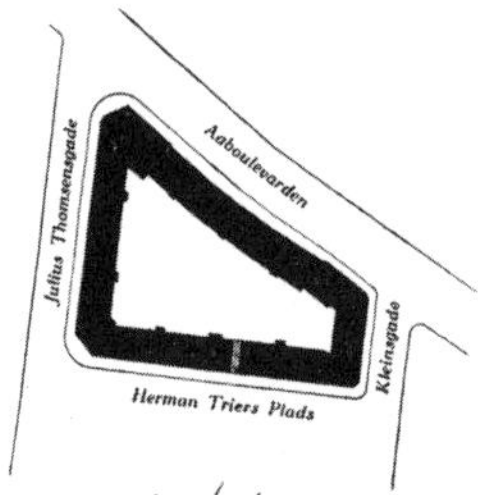

h
1 *Location: Åboulevarden, Kleinsgade*
2 *Client: private*
3 *Architect: Wittmaack and Hvalsøe*
4 *Year built: 1930–31*
5 *Plot area: 5971.9 m²*
6 *Built-up area: 3257 m²*
7 *Number of main staircases: 6*
8 *Number of floors: 5*

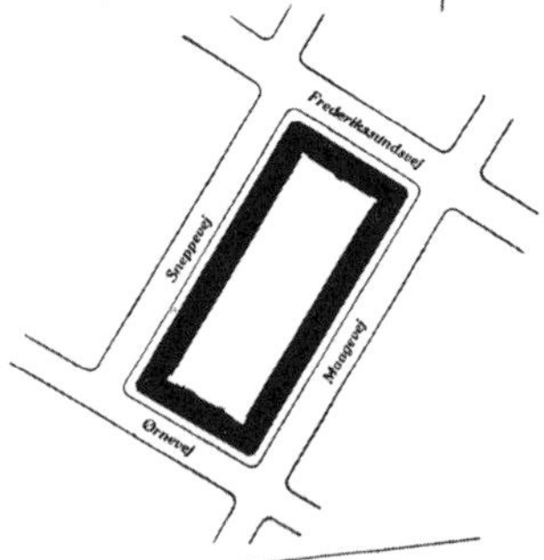

i
1 *Location: Mågvej, Utterslev*
2 *Client: Maagegaarden A/S*
3 *Architect: Fr. Wagner*
4 *Year built: 1931*
5 *Plot area: 3073 m²*
6 *Built-up area: 3073 m²*
7 *Number of main staircases: 23*
8 *Number of floors: 6*

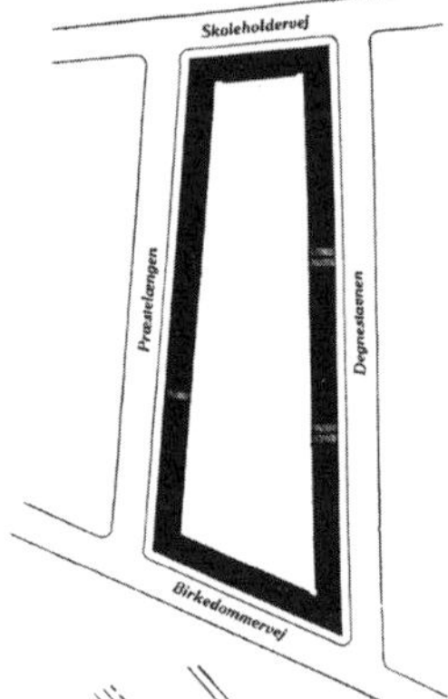

j
1 *Location: Tomsgårdsvej, Utterslev*
2 *Client: Skoleholdergaarden A/S*
3 *Architect: Fr. Wagner*
4 *Year built: 1932–33*
5 *Plot area: 12964 m²*
6 *Built-up area: 4926.5 m²*
7 *Number of main staircases: 43*
8 *Number of floors: 5*

k
1 *Location: Åboulevarden, Rosenørns Allé*
2 *Client: private*
3 *Architect: Kay Fisker, C. F. Møller*
4 *Year built: 1932*
5 *Plot area: 3475.5 m²*
6 *Built-up area: 2305 m²*
7 *Number of main staircases: 9*
8 *Number of floors: 6*

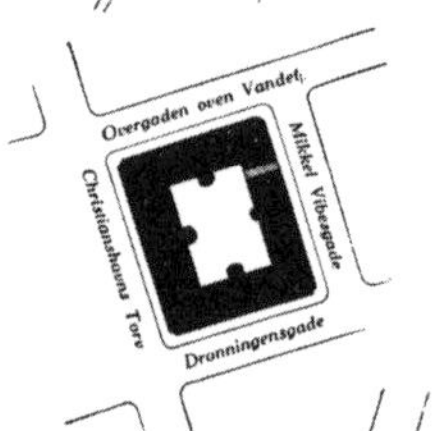

l
1 *Location: Christianshavns Torv*
2 *Client: Municipality of Copenhagen*
3 *Architect: Edvard Thomsen*
4 *Year built: 1930*
5 *Plot area: 22926 m²*
6 *Built-up area: 1734.4 m²*
7 *Number of main staircases: 5*
8 *Number of floors: 6*

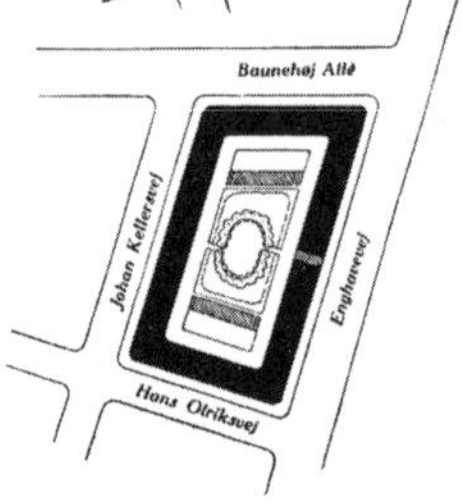

m
1 *Location: Enghavevej, Baunehøj Allé*
2 *Client: Municipality of Copenhagen*
3 *Architect: Povl Baumann*
4 *Year built: 1928–29*
5 *Plot area: 5295 m²*
6 *Built-up area: 2551 m²*
7 *Number of main staircases: 21*
8 *Number of floors: 5*

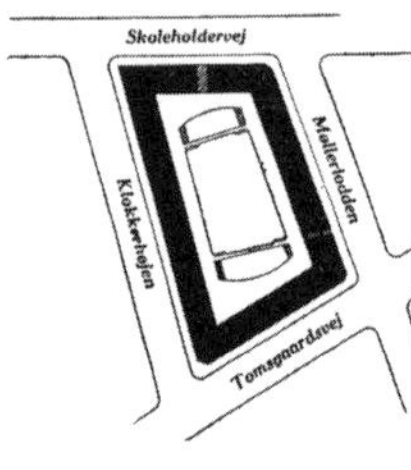

n
1 *Location: Tomsgårdsvej, Utterslev*
2 *Client: Municipality of Copenhagen*
3 *Architect: Ivar Bentsen*
4 *Year built: 1934*
5 *Plot area: 5025 m²*
6 *Built-up area: 2416 m²*
7 *Number of main staircases: 16*
8 *Number of floors: 5*

Elaborated by Erik Villefrance and Hugo Åaby Sørensen

Semi-enclosed blocks, *1:5,000. North is up*

B

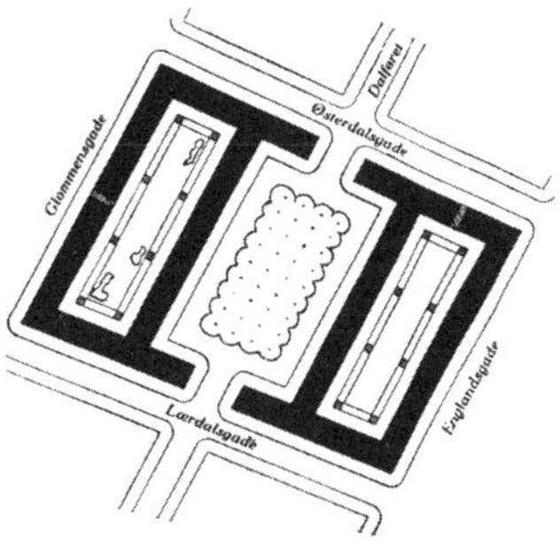

a 1 *Location: Englandsvej, Østerdalsgade*
2 *Client: "Amagerbo" Co-operative Housing Association*
3 *Architect: Kay Fisker and S. C. Larsen; southernmost block: F. Galatius*
4 *Year built: 1926 and 1935*
5 *Plot area: 12800 m²*
6 *Built-up area: 3248 m²*
7 *Number of main staircases: 42*
8 *Number of floors: 5*

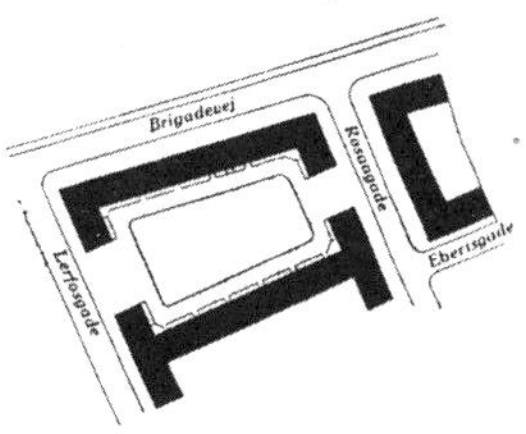

b 1 *Location: Brigadevej*
2 *Client: Brigadegaarden A/S*
3 *Architect: Kay Fisker and S. C. Larsen*
4 *Year built: 1928*
5 *Plot area: ca. 10670 m²*
6 *Built-up area: 3340 m²*
7 *Number of main staircases: 24*
8 *Number of floors: 5*

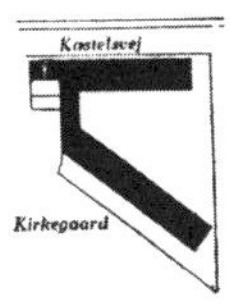

c 1 *Location: "Kastelshaven", Kastelsvej*
2 *Client: Københavns almindelige Boligselskab (KAB)*
3 *Architect: Ivar Bentsen and Peter Nielsen*
4 *Year built: 1928*
5 *Plot area: 26546 m²*
6 *Built-up area: 1291 m²*
7 *Number of main staircases: 5*
8 *Number of floors: 6*

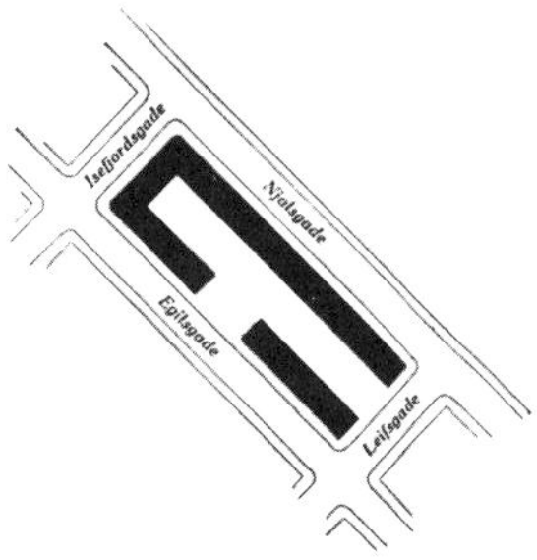

d 1 *Location: Isafjordsgade and Egilsgade*
2 *Client: "Isafjord" Co-operative Housing Association*
3 *Architect: Louis Hygom*
4 *Year built: 1929*
5 *Plot area: 4146 m²*
6 *Built-up area: 2291 m²*
7 *Number of main staircases: 15*
8 *Number of floors: 6*

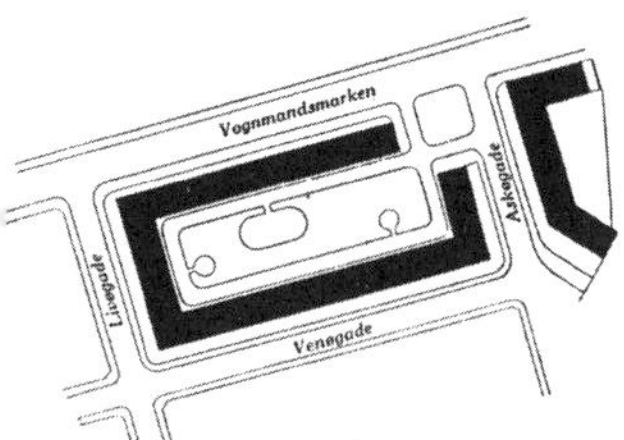

e 1 *Location: "Østergården", Vognmandsmarken*
2 *Client: KAB*
3 *Architect: Kay Fisker and C. F. Møller*
4 *Year built: 1932*
5 *Plot area: 12435 m²*
6 *Built-up area: 3681 m²*
7 *Number of main staircases: 31*
8 *Number of floors: 5*

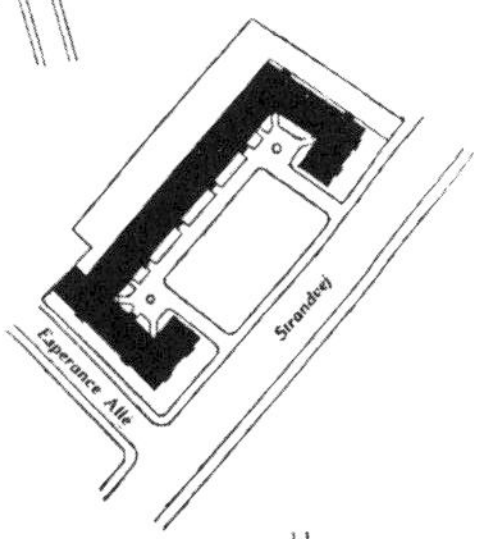

f 1 *Location: "Constantia", Strandvejen*
2 *Client: private*
3 *Architect: H. Dahlerup Bertelsen*
4 *Year built: 1932*
5 *Plot area: 8084 m²*
6 *Built-up area: 2464 m²*
7 *Number of main staircases: 9*
8 *Number of floors: 3*

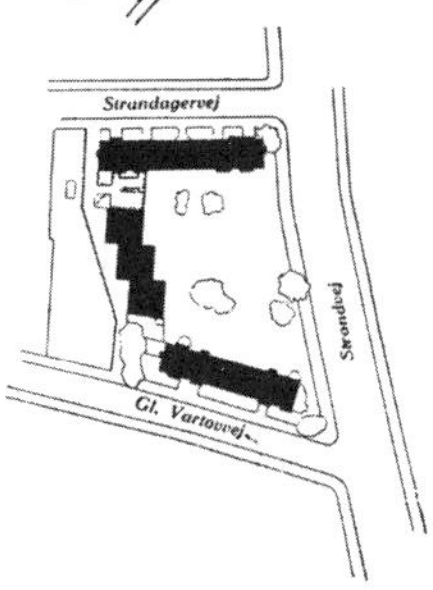

g 1 *Location: "Lille Tuborg", Strandvejen*
2 *Client: private*
3 *Architect: Charles I. Schou*
4 *Year built: 1932*
5 *Plot area: 27202.03 m²*
6 *Built-up area: 1648.67 m²*
7 *Number of main staircases: 7*
8 *Number of floors: 3, with habitable attic*

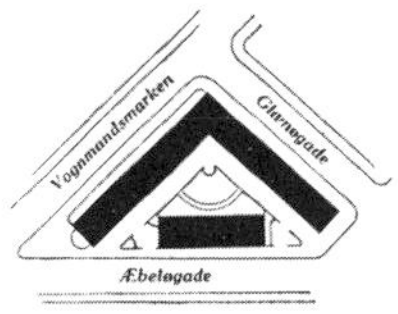

h 1 *Location: Vognmandsmarken*
2 *Client: A/S of 30–07–1933 "Solkrogen"*
3 *Architect: Tyge Hvass*
4 *Year built: 1933*
5 *Plot area: ca. 2000 m²*
6 *Built-up area: 1600 m²*
7 *Number of main staircases: 12*
8 *Number of floors: 5*

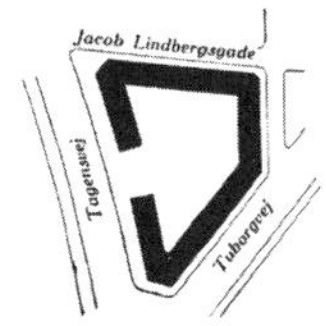

i 1 *Location: "Typografernes Stiftelse", Tagensvej*
2 *Client: Københavns almindelige Boligselskab (KAB)*
3 *Architect: P. Søgaard Petersen*
4 *Year built: 1933*
5 *Plot area: 6050 m²*
6 *Built-up area: 2480 m²*
7 *Number of main staircases: 20*
8 *Number of floors: 3, with habitable attic*

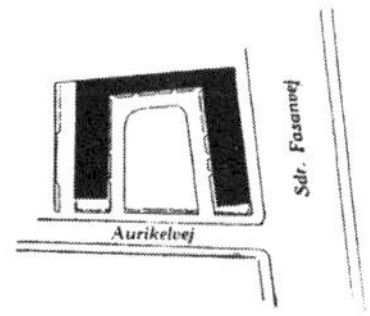

j 1 *Location: "Aurikelgården", Søndre Fasanvej*
2 *Client: private*
3 *Architect: Børge Ploumann, Hans Huusman*
4 *Year built: 1933*
5 *Plot area: -*
6 *Built-up area: 3100 m²*
7 *Number of main staircases: 5*
8 *Number of floors: 5*

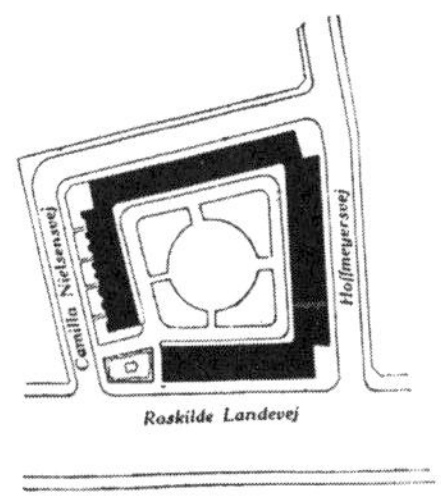

k 1 *Location: "Roskildegården", Roskildevej*
2 *Client: Frederiksberg Boligselskab*
3 *Architect: Henning Jørgensen*
4 *Year built: 1933–34*
5 *Plot area: 6467 m²*
6 *Built-up area: 2560 m²*
7 *Number of main staircases: 22*
8 *Number of floors: 5*

l 1 *Location: "Grønnehavegården", Godthåbsvej*
2 *Client: A/S of 26–4–34*
3 *Architect: Eske Kristensen and Mogens Meyling*
4 *Year built: 1934*
5 *Plot area: 3785 m²*
6 *Built-up area: 1420 m²*
7 *Number of main staircases: 7*
8 *Number of floors: 5*

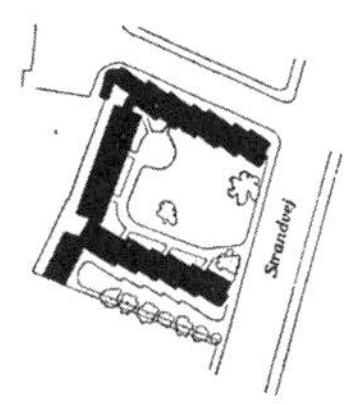

m 1 *Location: "Bellavista", Strandvejen*
2 *Client: private*
3 *Architect: Arne Jacobsen*
4 *Year built: 1934*
5 *Plot area: 7463 m²*
6 *Built-up area: 2701 m²*
7 *Number of main staircases: 12*
8 *Number of floors: 3*

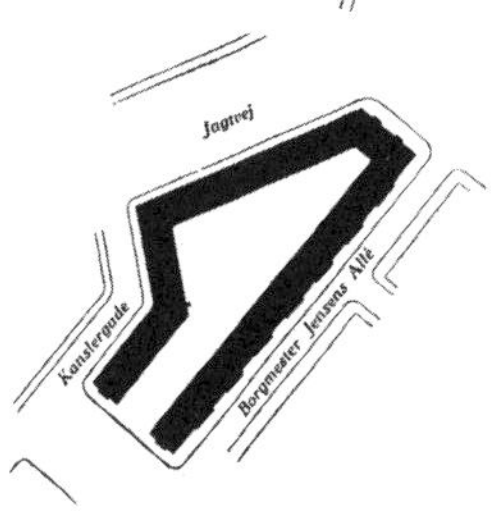

n 1 *Location: "Kanslergården", Jagtvej*
2 *Client: Arbejdernes Kooperative Byggeforening*
3 *Architect: E. Monberg and Henning Ortmann*
4 *Year built: 1935*
5 *Plot area: 6440 m²*
6 *Built-up area: 3196 m²*
7 *Number of main staircases: 18*
8 *Number of floors: 4, with habitable attic*

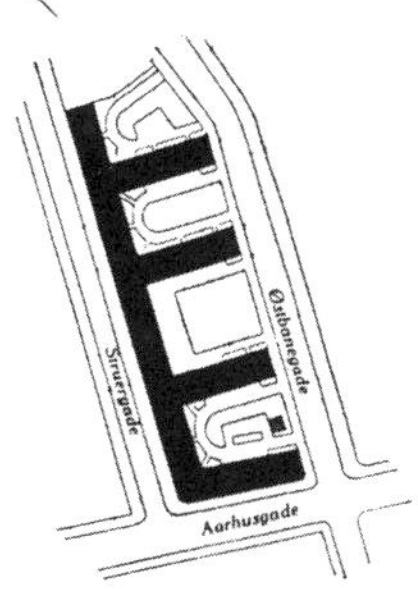

o 1 *Location: Østbanegade*
2 *Client: Nordhavnsgården A/S*
3 *Architect: Sven Risom*
4 *Year built: 1933*
5 *Plot area: 60173 m²*
6 *Built-up area: 2,860 m²*
7 *Number of main staircases: 20*
8 *Number of floors: 6*

Elaborated by I. Hansen Johnsen

Open complexes, *1:5,000. North is up*

C

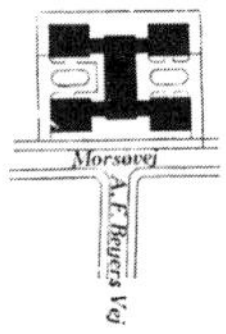

a
1 *Location: Morsøvej*
2 *Client: Master builder Kaj Rothe*
3 *Architect: Kaj Gottlob*
4 *Year built: 1930*
5 *Plot area: 2296 m²*
6 *Built-up area: 1014 m²*
7 *Number of main staircases: 6*
8 *Number of floors: 5*

b
1 *Location: Dyrehavevej, Klampenborg*
2 *Client: "Klampenborghus" A/S*
3 *Architect: Kooperative Arkitekter*
4 *Year built: 1935*
5 *Plot area: 1855 m²*
6 *Built-up area: 815 m²*
7 *Number of main staircases: 6*
8 *Number of floors: 3*

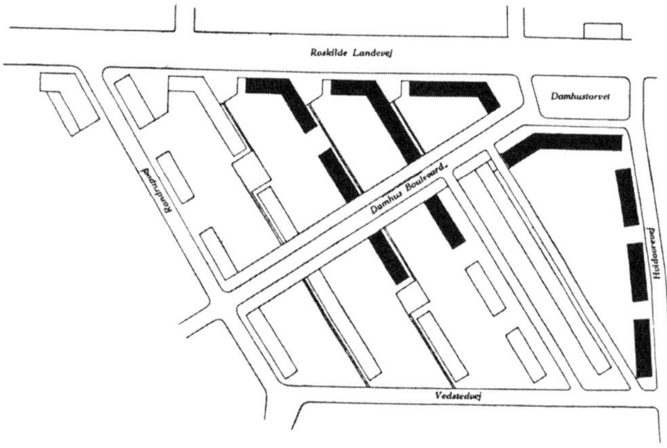

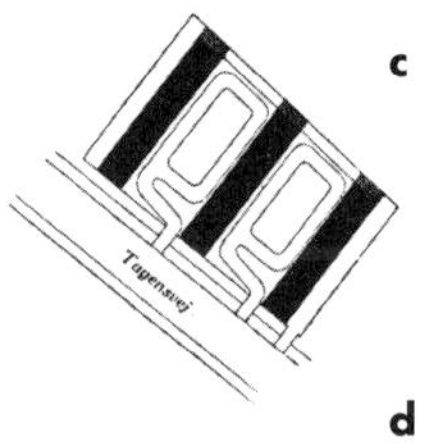

c
1 *Location: Tagensvej*
2 *Client: Tagensvej 152–180 A/S*
3 *Architect: Kay Fisker and C. F. Møller*
4 *Year built: 1932*
5 *Plot area: 5677 m²*
6 *Built-up area: 1818 m²*
7 *Number of main staircases: 15*
8 *Number of floors: 5*

g
1 *Location: Roskilde Landevej*
2 *Client: "Damtoften" A/S and "Damparken" A/S*
3 *Architect: Kooperative Arkitekter*
4 *Year built: 1931–32 and 1934*
5 *Plot area: 21292 m²*
6 *Built-up area: 4904 m²*
7 *Number of main staircases: 42*
8 *Number of floors: 3*

d
1 *Location: Corner of Godthåbsvej and Vagtelvej, Frederiksberg*
2 *Client: "Sano" A/S*
3 *Architect: Hans Hansen and Alva Lauritzen*
4 *Year built: 1934–35*
5 *Plot area: 5420 m²*
6 *Built-up area: 22 140 m²*
7 *Number of main staircases: 9*
8 *Number of floors: 4*

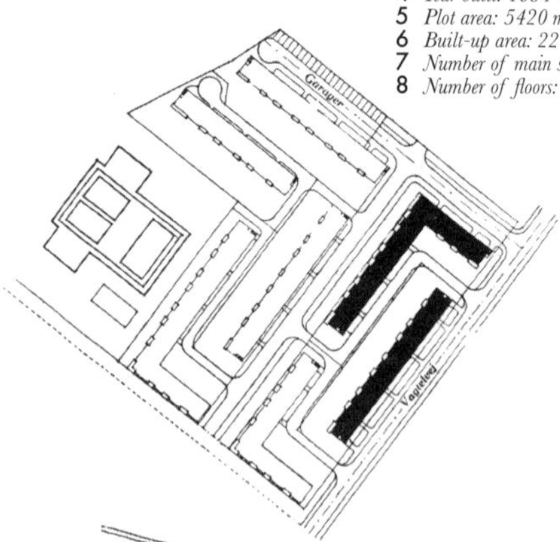

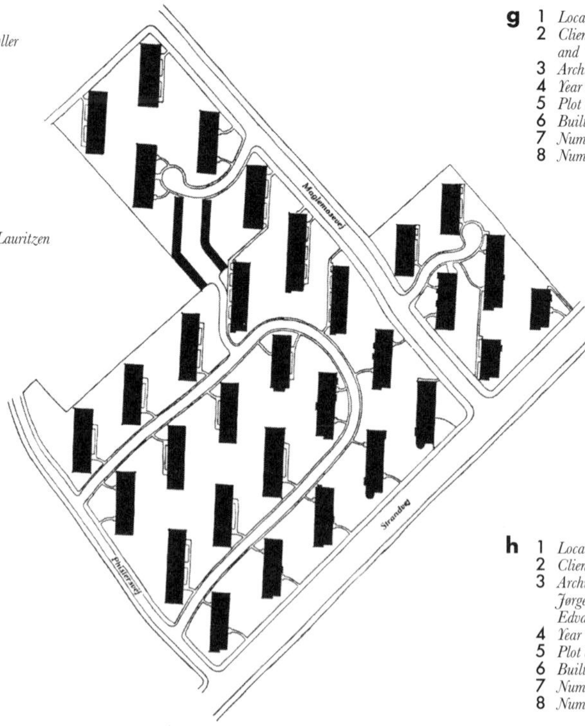

h
1 *Location: Strandvejen, Hellerup*
2 *Client: "Blidah" A/S*
3 *Architect: Skjøt-Pedersen, Ivar Bentsen, Jørgen V. Berg, Acton Bjørn, Edvard Heiberg, Karl Larsen*
4 *Year built: 1934*
5 *Plot area: 72217 m²*
6 *Built-up area: 12 711 m²*
7 *Number of main staircases: 62*
8 *Number of floors: 3*

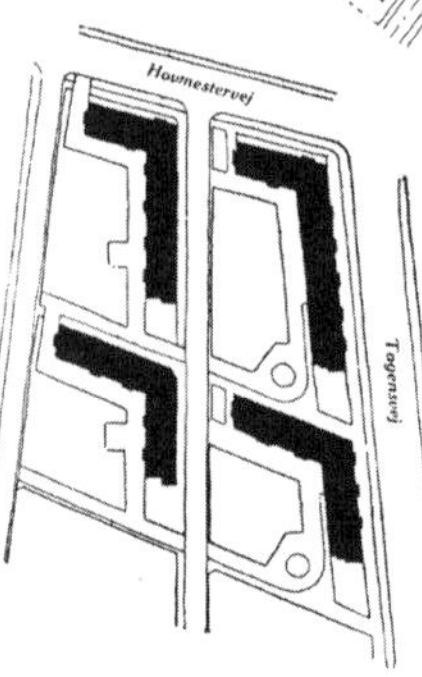

e
1 *Location: Tagensvej*
2 *Client: "Tagensbo" A/S*
3 *Architect: Chr. Krøyer and Valdemar Jørgensen*
4 *Year built: 1935–36*
5 *Plot area: 13914 m²*
6 *Built-up area: 3398 m²*
7 *Number of main staircases: 27*
8 *Number of floors: 5*

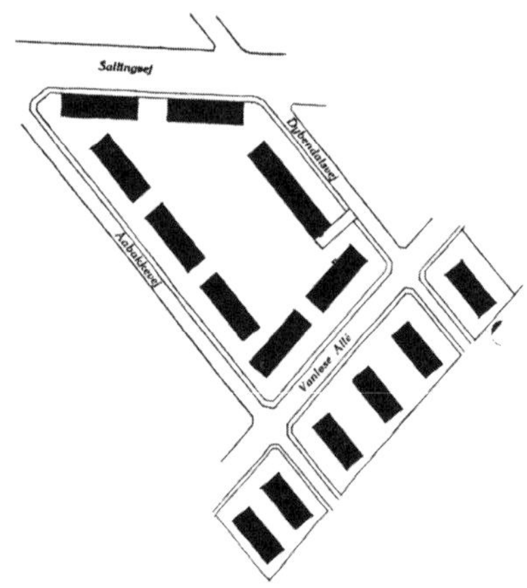

i
1 *Location: Vanløse Allé*
2 *Client: "Slettegaarden" A/S*
3 *Architect: A. Skjøt-Pedersen*
4 *Year built: 1933*
5 *Plot area: 21232 m²*
6 *Built-up area: 5185.29 m²*
7 *Number of main staircases: 37*
8 *Number of floors: 3*

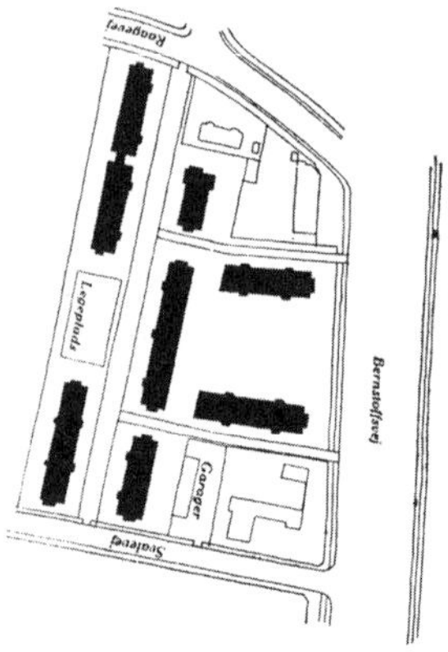

f
1 *Location: Bernstorffsvej*
2 *Client: "Høegsminde" A/S*
3 *Architect: Charles I. Schou*
4 *Year built: 1935–36*
5 *Plot area: 3400 m²*
6 *Built-up area: 1600 m²*
7 *Number of main staircases:16*
8 *Number of floors: 2 and 3*

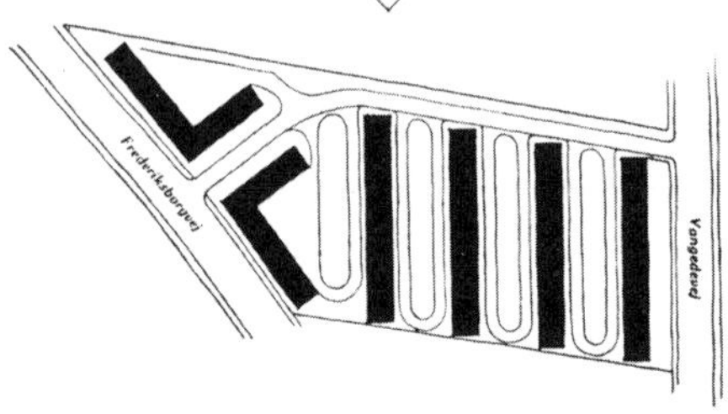

j
1 *Location: Frederiksborgvej*
2 *Client: "Gartnervænget" A/S*
3 *Architect: Anders P. Kirkerup*
4 *Year built: 1936*
5 *Plot area: 8003 m²*
6 *Built-up area: 1843 m²*
7 *Number of main staircases: 16*
8 *Number of floors: 5*

Elaborated by Hans Schack and Oscar Hansen

Open complexes, *1:5,000. North is up*

D

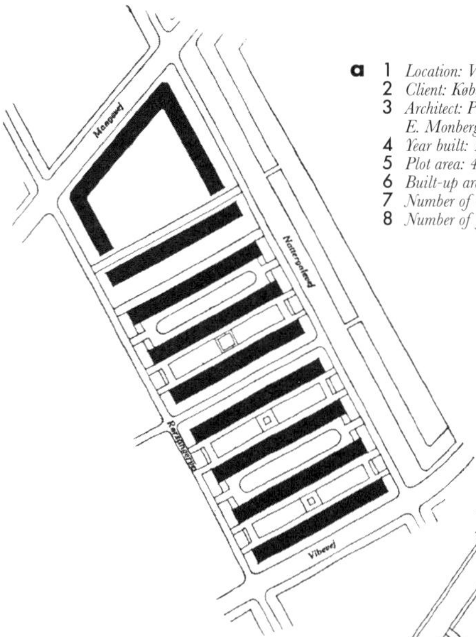

a
1 *Location: Vibevej, Mågevej, Utterslev*
2 *Client: Københavns almindelige Boligselskab (KAB)*
3 *Architect: Povl Baumann, E. Monberg, L. Hygom*
4 *Year built: 1928–29–31*
5 *Plot area: 47940 m²*
6 *Built-up area: 15 986 m²*
7 *Number of main staircases: 130*
8 *Number of floors: 3*

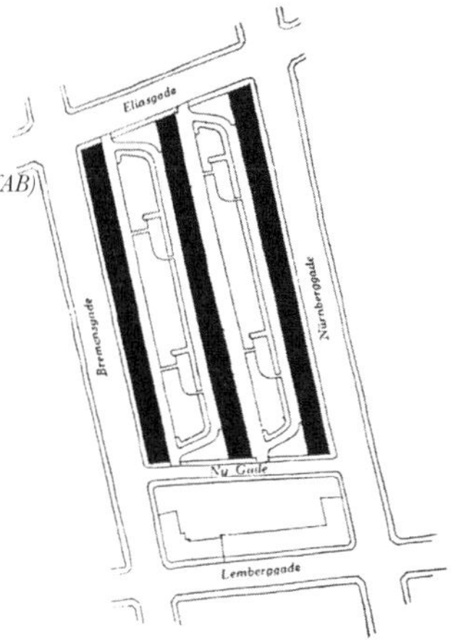

d
1 *Location: Lemberggade*
2 *Client: "Nürnberggaarden A/S"*
3 *Architect: Kay Fisker and C. F. Møller*
4 *Year built: 1933*
5 *Plot area: 17562 m²*
6 *Built-up area: 5840 m²*
7 *Number of main staircases: 42*
8 *Number of floors: 5*

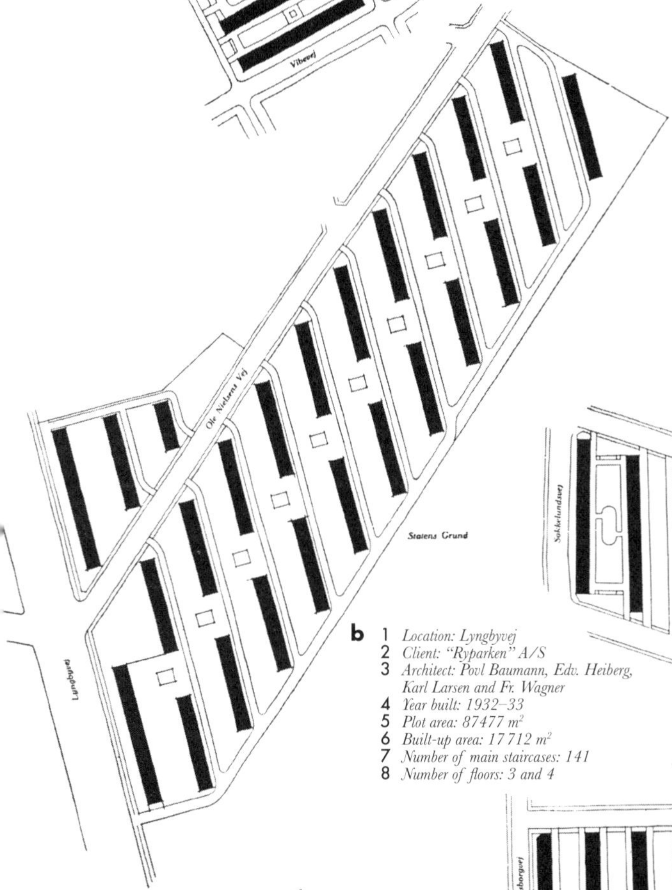

b
1 *Location: Lyngbyvej*
2 *Client: "Ryparken" A/S*
3 *Architect: Povl Baumann, Edv. Heiberg, Karl Larsen and Fr. Wagner*
4 *Year built: 1932–33*
5 *Plot area: 87477 m²*
6 *Built-up area: 17 712 m²*
7 *Number of main staircases: 141*
8 *Number of floors: 3 and 4*

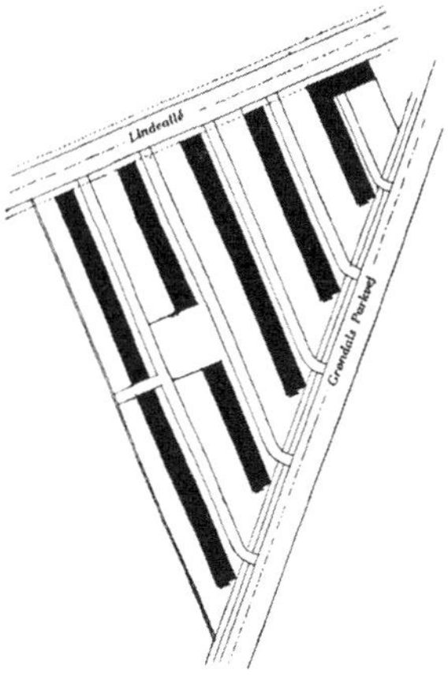

e
1 *Location: Grøndals Parkvej, Vanløse*
2 *Client: "Grøndalsparkvejens Haveby" A/S*
3 *Architect: Albinus Risom and Willy Isaksen*
4 *Year built: 1934–35*
5 *Plot area: 20360 m²*
6 *Built-up area: 8140.67 m²*
7 *Number of main staircases: 63*
8 *Number of floors: 3 + attic floor*

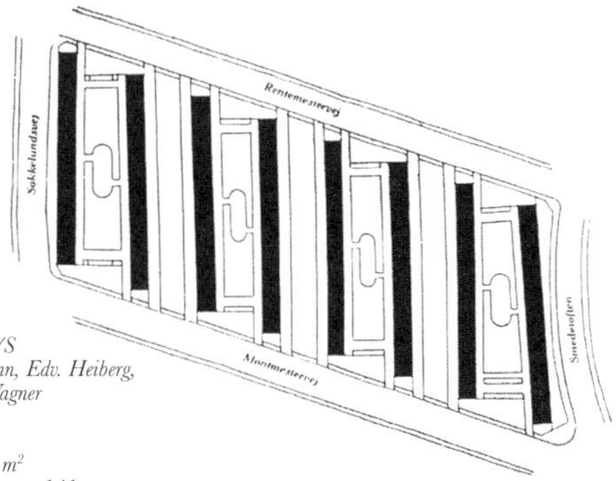

f
1 *Location: Rentemestervej*
2 *Client: Municipality of Copenhagen*
3 *Architect: E. Monberg*
4 *Year built: 1934*
5 *Plot area: 29163 m²*
6 *Built-up area: 8525 m²*
7 *Number of main staircases: 64*
8 *Number of floors: 3*

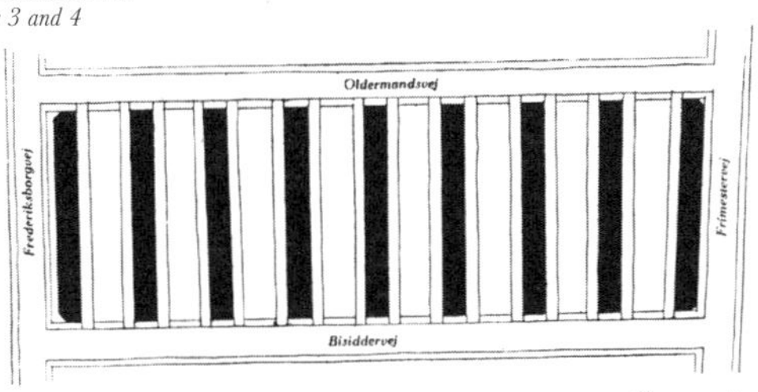

g
1 *Location: Frederiksborgvej*
2 *Client: "Boparken" A/S*
3 *Architect: Thorvald Dreyer*
4 *Year built: 1934–35*
5 *Plot area: 10899 m²*
6 *Built-up area: 2864.97 m²*
7 *Number of main staircases: 48*
8 *Number of floors: 5*

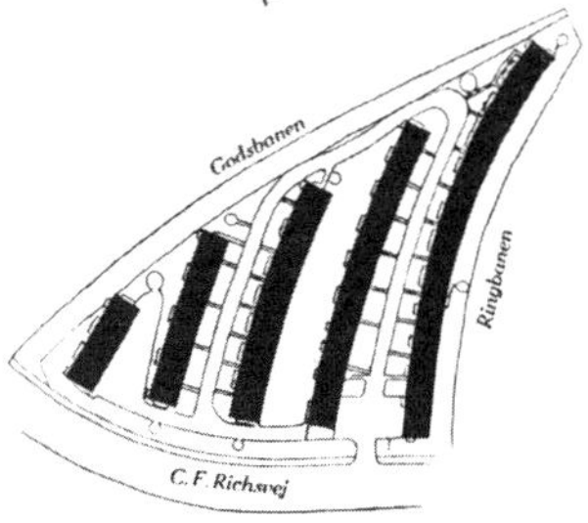

c
1 *Location: C. F. Richs Vej*
2 *Client: "Ringparken" A/S*
3 *Architect: A. Skjøt-Pedersen*
4 *Year built: 1934*
5 *Plot area: 14 703 m²*
6 *Built-up area: 4586.54 m²*
7 *Number of main staircases: 32*
8 *Number of floors: 3 and 4*

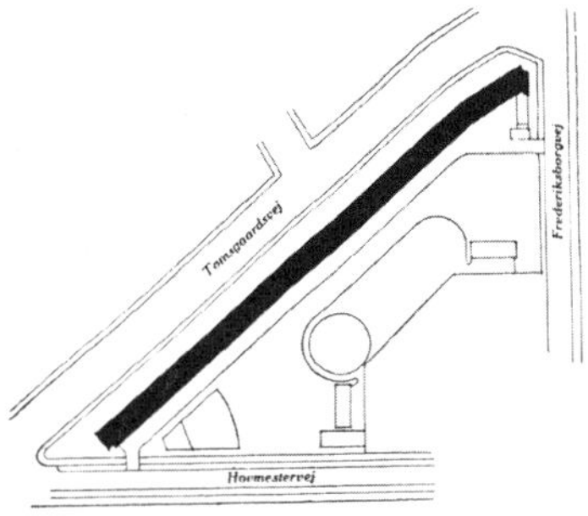

h
1 *Location: Tomsgårdsvej, Utterslev*
2 *Client: "Storgaarden" A/S*
3 *Architect: Povl Baumann and Knud Hansen*
4 *Year built: 1935*
5 *Plot area: ca. 10000 m²*
6 *Built-up area: 2453 m²*
7 *Number of main staircases: 21*
8 *Number of floors: 5*

Elaborated by Hans Schack and Oscar Hansen

Plan types

Two staircases located within the same party wall. *a–e: continuous main partition, f–i: discontinuous main partition. 1:200 and 1:500*

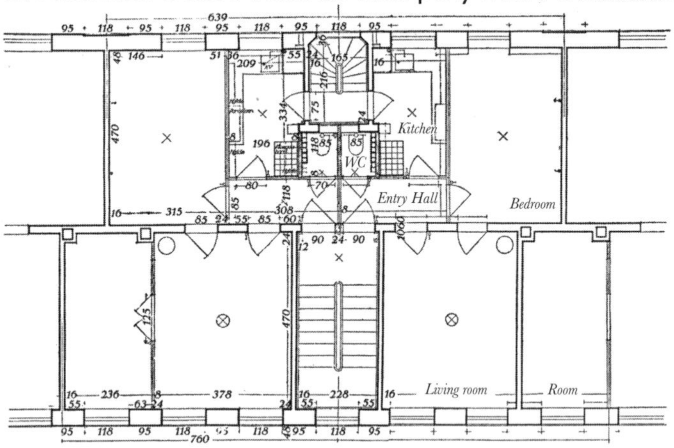

a
1 *Location: Struenseegade, Hans Tavsens Gade*
2 *Client: Municipality of Copenhagen*
3 *Architect: Povl Baumann*
4 *Year built: 1920*
5 *Building style: enclosed block*
6 *Number of rooms: 2 rooms + small room and 2 rooms*
7 *Gross area: 74 m²*
8 *Number of floors: 5 floors*
9 *Sanitary installations: WC, indirect lighting, no bath*
10 *Balcony system: none*
11 *Staircase system: 2 wooden staircases*
12 *Staircase location: symmetrical*
13 *Staircase orientation: west*
14 *Living room orientation: west*
15 *Number of flats per main staircase: 2*
16 *Remarks: The most commonly used Statsboligfond Period type with a continuous main partition, two large rooms with a width of 6° and 5°, respectively, and the small room placed next to the party wall, which in some respects is a weakness, since it cannot be accessed from the entry hall and thus can be difficult to sublet. The WC, which has a washbasin but not a shower, lies between the stairs and receives indirect light.*

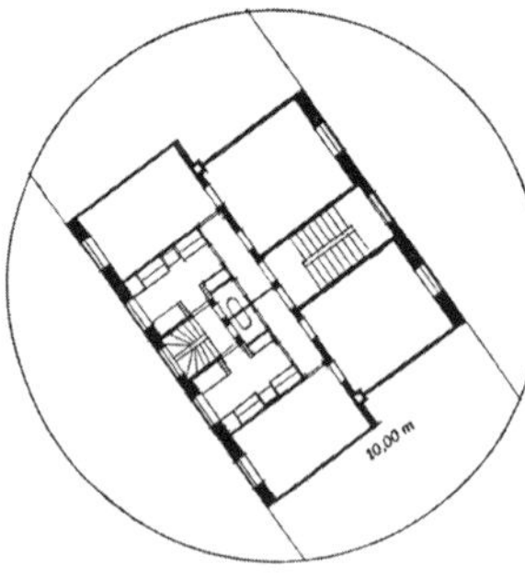

b
1 *Location: Borups Allé, Stefansgade*
2 *Client: Municipality of Copenhagen*
3 *Architect: Niels Rosenkjær and Alf Cock Clausen*
4 *Year built: 1924*
5 *Building style: enclosed block*
6 *Number of rooms: 2 rooms*
7 *Gross area: 56.50 m²*
8 *Number of floors: 5 floors*
9 *Sanitary installations: WC, indirect lighting*
10 *Balcony system: none*
11 *Staircase system: 2 wooden staircases*
12 *Staircase location: symmetrical*
13 *Staircase orientation: southeast*
14 *Living room orientation: southeast*
15 *Number of flats per main staircase: 2*
16 *Remarks: none*

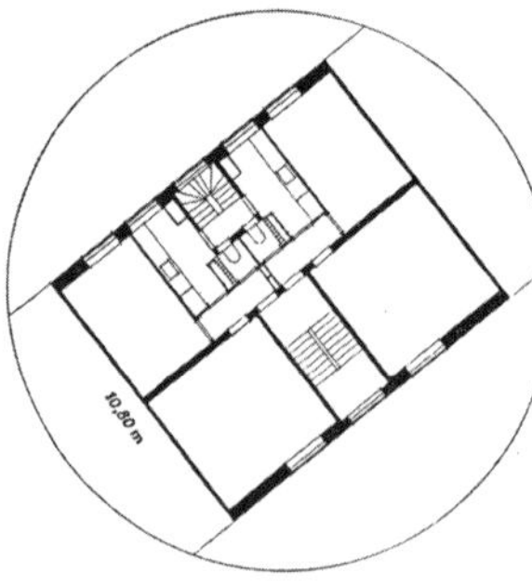

c
1 *Location: Artillerivej, Gullfossgade*
2 *Client: "Gullfosshus" A/S*
3 *Architect: Kay Fisker*
4 *Year built: 1927*
5 *Building style: enclosed block*
6 *Number of rooms: 2 rooms*
7 *Gross area: 63.5 m²*
8 *Number of floors: 6 floors*
9 *Sanitary installations: WC, indirect lighting*
10 *Balcony system: none*
11 *Staircase system: 2 wooden staircases*
12 *Staircase location: symmetrical*
13 *Staircase orientation: southeast*
14 *Living room orientation: southeast*
15 *Number of flats per main staircase: 2*
16 *Remarks: none*

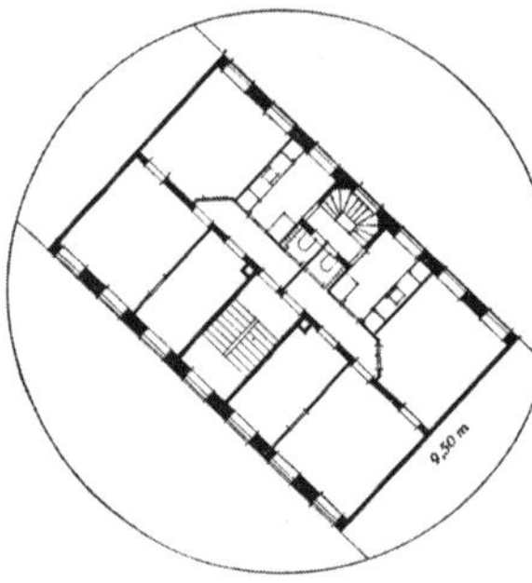

d
1 *Location: Borups Allé, Hornbækgade*
2 *Client: "Hornbækhus" Co-operative Housing Association*
3 *Architect: Kay Fisker*
4 *Year built: 1923*
5 *Building style: enclosed block*
6 *Number of rooms: 2 rooms + small room*
7 *Gross area: 68.9 m²*
8 *Number of floors: 5 floors*
9 *Sanitary installations: WC, indirect lighting*
10 *Balcony system: none*
11 *Staircase system: 2 wooden staircases*
12 *Staircase location: symmetrical*
13 *Staircase orientation: southwest*
14 *Living room orientation: southwest*
15 *Number of flats per main staircase: 2*
16 *Remarks: none*

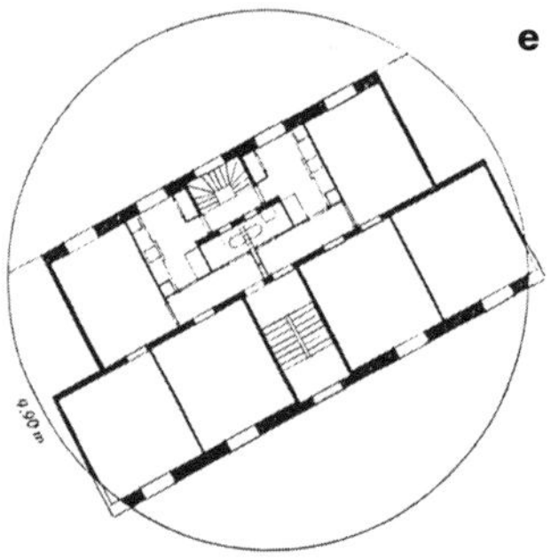

e
1 *Location: Vognmandsmarken, Venøgade*
2 *Client: Københavns Andelsbyggeforening*
3 *Architect: Kay Fisker*
4 *Year built: 1927*
5 *Building style: enclosed block*
6 *Number of rooms: 3 rooms*
7 *Gross area: 83.2 m²*
8 *Number of floors: 5 floors*
9 *Sanitary installations: combined bath and WC, indirect lighting*
10 *Balcony system: none*
11 *Staircase system: 2 wooden staircases*
12 *Staircase location: symmetrical*
13 *Staircase orientation: southeast*
14 *Living room orientation: southeast*
15 *Number of flats per main staircase: 2*
16 *Remarks: none*

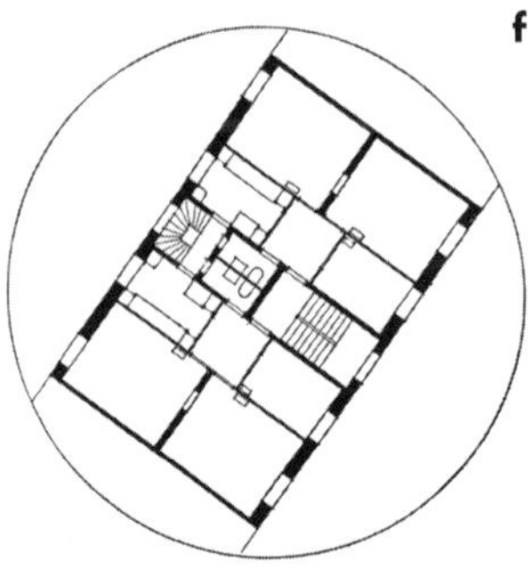

f
1 *Location: Jagtvej*
2 *Client: "Parkkvarterets Boligforening"*
3 *Architect: Kay Fisker and C. Holst*
4 *Year built: 1925*
5 *Building style: enclosed block*
6 *Number of rooms: 2 rooms + small room*
7 *Gross area: 79.50 m²*
8 *Number of floors: 5 floors*
9 *Sanitary installations: combined bath and WC, indirect lighting*
10 *Balcony system: none*
11 *Staircase system: 2 wooden staircases*
12 *Staircase location: symmetrical*
13 *Staircase orientation: west*
14 *Living room orientation: -*
15 *Number of flats per main staircase: 2*
16 *Remarks: none*

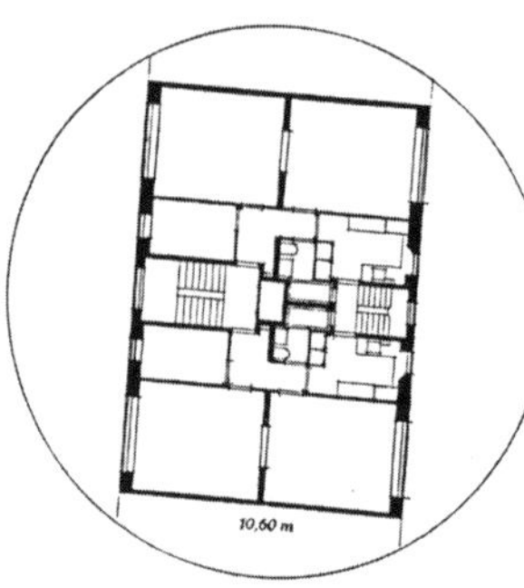

g
1 *Location: Søndre Fasanvej*
2 *Client: private*
3 *Architect: K. Gottlob, H. J. Kampmann and Aage Rafn*
4 *Year built: 1931*
5 *Building style: semi-enclosed block*
6 *Number of rooms: 2 rooms + small room*
7 *Gross area: 81.35 m²*
1 *Number of floors: 5 floors*
2 *Sanitary installations: bath, shared WC, indirect lighting*
3 *Balcony system: balconies on one side*
4 *Staircase system: 2 wooden staircases*
5 *Staircase location: symmetrical*
6 *Staircase orientation: west*
7 *Living room orientation: west*
8 *Number of flats per main staircase: 2*
9 *Remarks: lift*

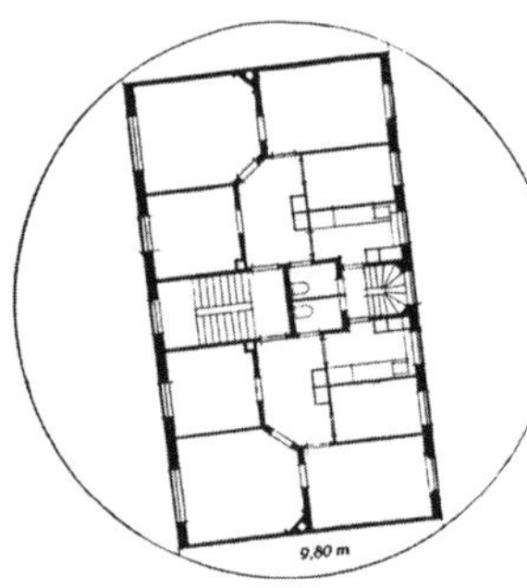

h
1 *Location: Borups Allé, Grønnegården*
2 *Client: Københavns almindelige Boligselskab (KAB)*
3 *Architect: Povl Baumann*
4 *Year built: 1930*
5 *Building style: enclosed block*
6 *Number of rooms: 3 rooms + small room*
7 *Gross area: 69.20 m²*
8 *Number of floors: 3 floors*
9 *Sanitary installations: WC, indirect lighting*
10 *Balcony system: none*
11 *Staircase system: 2 wooden staircases*
12 *Staircase location: symmetrical*
13 *Staircase orientation: west*
14 *Living room orientation: west*
15 *Number of flats per main staircase: 2*
16 *Remarks: none*

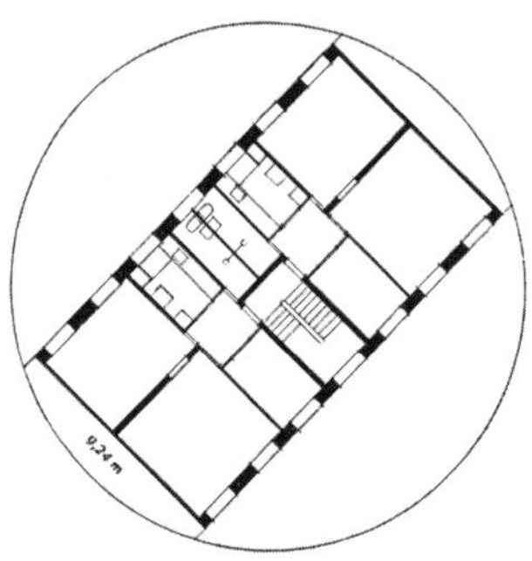

i
1 *Location: Hulgårdsvej*
2 *Client: Københavns almindelige Boligselskab (KAB)*
3 *Architect: Ivar Bentsen and Th. Henningsen*
4 *Year built: 1921*
5 *Building style: ribbon development*
6 *Number of rooms: 2 rooms and 2 rooms + small room and 3 rooms*
7 *Gross area: 75.7 m²*
8 *Number of floors: 3 floors*
9 *Sanitary installations: bath and WC, direct lighting*
10 *Balcony system: none*
11 *Staircase system: 1 wooden staircase*
12 *Staircase location: symmetrical*
13 *Staircase orientation: southeast*
14 *Living room orientation: southeast*
15 *Number of flats per main staircase: 2*
16 *Remarks: 3 floors, therefore only a single staircase system, plan type otherwise similar to the group's other variants*

Elaborated by Aage Madsen

Two staircases, located in opposing party walls. *1:200 and 1:500. a–f: staircases located on the same side, g–i: on opposite sides*

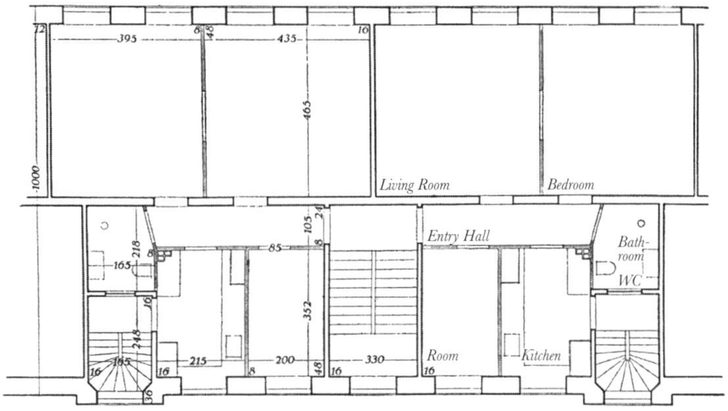

a
1 *Location: Amager Boulevard – Amagerfælledvej*
2 *Client: "Møllegaarden" Co-operative Housing Association*
3 *Architect: Povl Baumann*
4 *Year built: 1922*
5 *Building style: enclosed block*
6 *Number of rooms: 2 rooms + small room*
7 *Gross area: 80 m²*
8 *Number of floors: 6 floors*
9 *Sanitary installations: combined bath and WC, indirect lighting*
10 *Balcony system: none*
11 *Staircase system: 2 wooden staircases*
12 *Staircase location: single-side*
13 *Staircase orientation: east*
14 *Living room orientation: west*
15 *Number of flats per main staircase: 2*
16 *Remarks: State Housing Fund Period type similar to the IV plates, but with varying staircase location. Difficult to divide with fire parapets. One kitchen staircase per flat.*

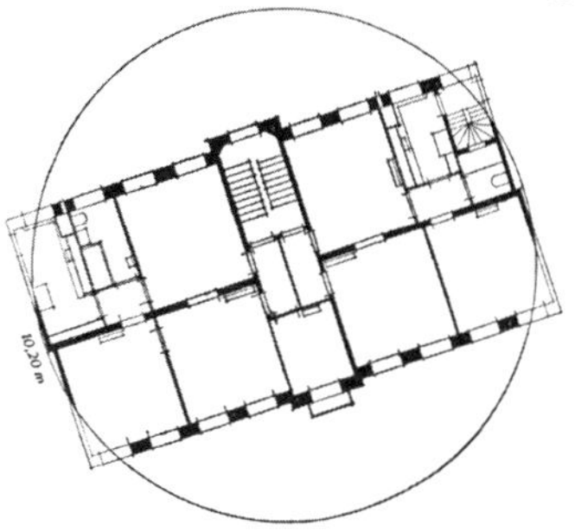

b
1 *Location: Strandboulevarden, Classensgade, Livjægergade, Arendalsgade*
2 *Client: Københavns almindelige Boligselskab (KAB)*
3 *Architect: Carl Petersen, O. Falkentorp, Peter Nielsen, Povl Baumann*
4 *Year built: 1934*
5 *Building style: semi-enclosed block*
6 *Number of rooms: 3 rooms and 3 rooms + small room*
7 *Gross area: 91 and 108 m²*
8 *Number of floors: 5*
9 *Sanitary installations: bath with tub and WC with indirect lighting, bath with tub, WC and sink with direct lighting*
10 *Balcony system: a small balcony in some flats*
11 *Staircase system: 2 wooden staircases*
12 *Staircase location: single-side*
13 *Staircase orientation: north facing*
14 *Living room orientation: north and south facing*
15 *Number of flats per main staircase: 2*
16 *Remarks: none*

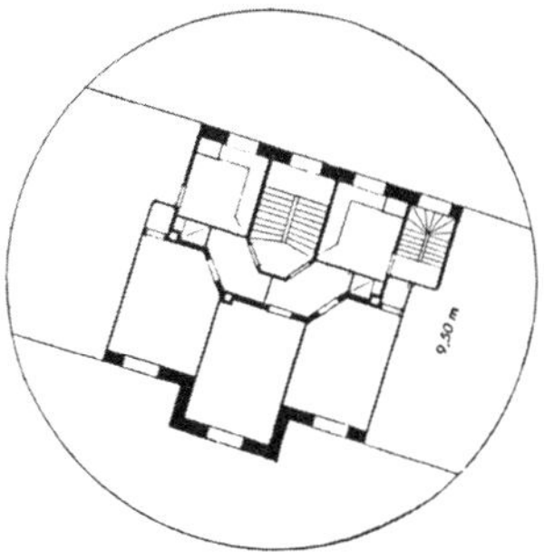

c
1 *Location: Genforeningsplads*
2 *Client: Landmandsbankens Byggeselskab*
3 *Architect:, n. Rosenkjær and T. H. Hjejle*
4 *Year built: 1920*
5 *Building style: enclosed block*
6 *Number of rooms: 1 and 2 rooms*
7 *Gross area: 42 and 63 m²*
8 *Number of floors: 3 floors*
9 *Sanitary installations: WC, indirect lighting*
10 *Balcony system: none*
11 *Staircase system: 2 wooden staircases*
12 *Staircase location: single-side*
13 *Staircase orientation: north*
14 *Living room orientation: south*
15 *Number of flats per main staircase: 2*
16 *Remarks: none*

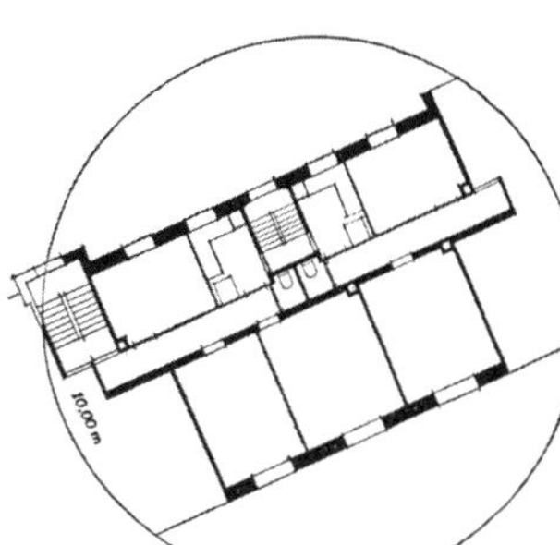

d
1 *Location: Strandvejen*
2 *Client: Arbejdernes Kooperative Byggeforening*
3 *Architect: Frederik Wagner*
4 *Year built: 1923*
5 *Building style: open and enclosed block*
6 *Number of rooms: 2 and 3 rooms + small room*
7 *Gross area: 58 and 78 m²*
8 *Number of floors: 5 floors*
9 *Sanitary installations: WC, indirect lighting*
10 *Balcony system: none*
11 *Staircase system: 2 wooden staircases*
12 *Staircase location: single-side*
13 *Staircase orientation: north*
14 *Living room orientation: south*
15 *Number of flats per main staircase: 2*
16 *Remarks: none*

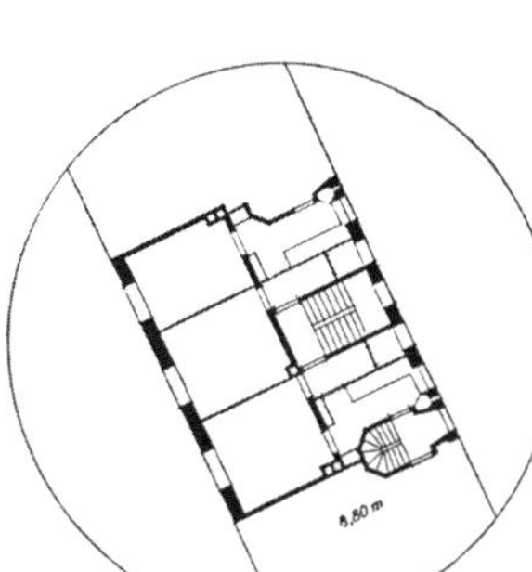

e
1 *Location: Sjællandsgade, Refsnæsgade, Fensmarkgade and Nøddebogade*
2 *Client: Municipality of Copenhagen*
3 *Architect: City architect Poul Holsøe*
4 *Year built: 1927*
5 *Building style: semi-enclosed block*
6 *Number of rooms: 1 and 2 rooms*
7 *Gross area: 39 and 52 m²*
8 *Number of floors: 5 floors*
9 *Sanitary installations: WC, direct lighting*
10 *Balcony system: none*
11 *Staircase system: 2 wooden staircases*
12 *Staircase location: single-side*
13 *Staircase orientation: northeast - southwest*
14 *Living room orientation: northwest - southeast*
15 *Number of flats per main staircase: 2*
16 *Remarks: none*

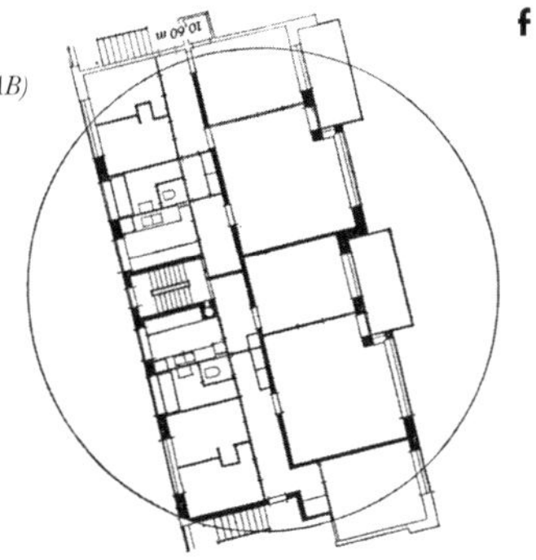

f
1 *Location: Gothåbsvej*
2 *Client: "Godthaabsvænge" A/S*
3 *Architect: Hans Hansen and Alvar Lauritzen*
4 *Year built: 1934–35*
5 *Building style: parallel block*
6 *Number of rooms: 3 rooms or 2 rooms + 2 small rooms, 4 rooms or 3 rooms + 2 small rooms*
7 *Gross area: 95–110 m²*
8 *Number of floors: 4 floors*
9 *Sanitary installations: separate bath and WC, bath with direct lighting*
10 *Balcony system: balcony on one side*
11 *Staircase system: 2 wooden staircases*
12 *Staircase location: single-side*
13 *Staircase orientation: east*
14 *Living room orientation: west*
15 *Number of flats per main staircase: 2*
16 *Remarks: size of the dining and living rooms may vary. Partitions between small rooms can be removed and the small rooms converted into a bedroom.*

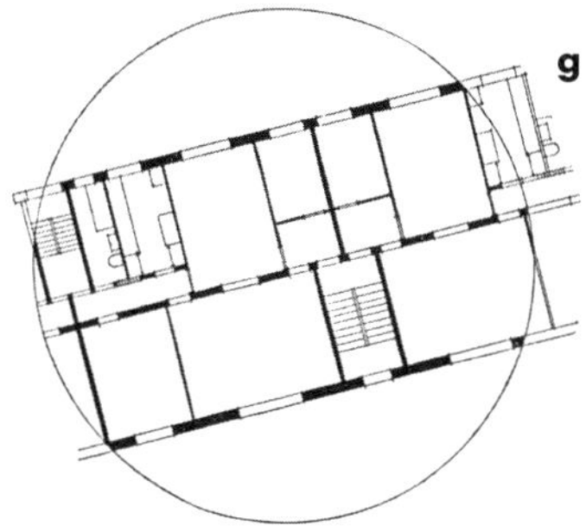

g
1 *Location: Rosenørns Allé*
2 *Client: 1 juli 1929 A/S*
3 *Architect: A. Skjøt-Pedersen*
4 *Year built: 1930*
5 *Building style: block development*
6 *Number of rooms: 5 rooms + small room*
7 *Gross area: 180 m²*
8 *Number of floors: 6 floors*
9 *Sanitary installations: bath and WC*
10 *Balcony system: none*
11 *Staircase system: 2 wooden staircases*
12 *Staircase location: staggered*
13 *Staircase orientation: south*
14 *Living room orientation: south*
15 *Number of flats per main staircase: 2*
16 *Remarks: none*

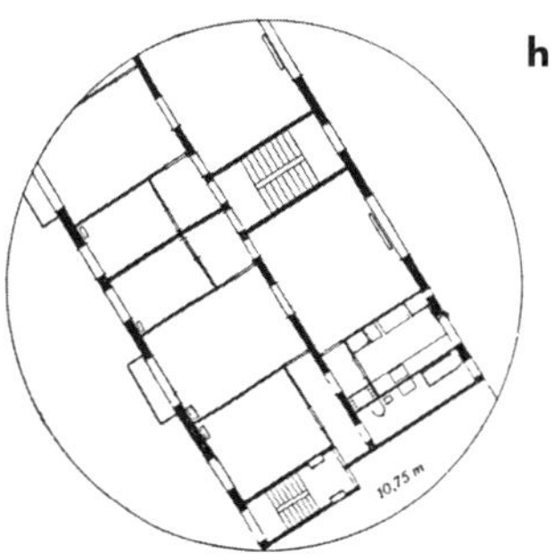

h
1 *Location: Gentofte Torv*
2 *Client: private*
3 *Architect: Hilda Rømer and P. Nyboe-Pedersen*
4 *Year built: 1932*
5 *Building style: enclosed block*
6 *Number of rooms: 3 rooms + 1 small room*
7 *Gross area: 120 m²*
8 *Number of floors: 5 floors*
9 *Sanitary installations: combined bath and WC, direct lighting*
10 *Balcony system: 1 balcony*
11 *Staircase system: 2 wooden staircases*
12 *Staircase location: staggered*
13 *Staircase orientation: northeast*
14 *Living room orientation: northeast*
15 *Number of flats per main staircase: 2*
16 *Remarks: none*

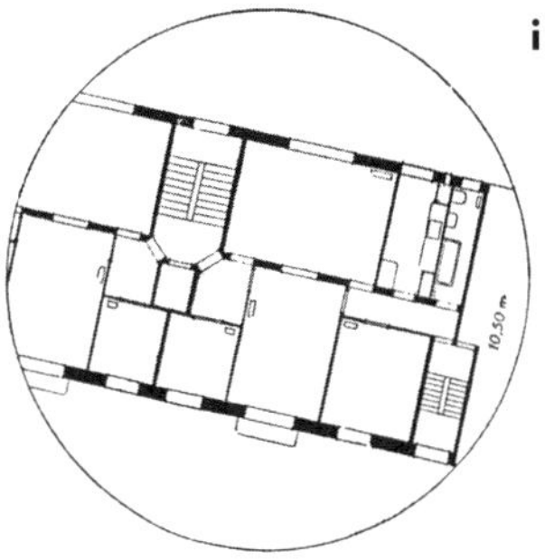

i
1 *Location: Kastelsvej*
2 *Client: Københavns almindelige Boligselskab (KAB)*
3 *Architect: Ivar Bentsen and Peter Nielsen*
4 *Year built: 1928*
5 *Building style: enclosed block*
6 *Number of rooms: 3 rooms and 1 small room*
7 *Gross area: 125 m²*
8 *Number of floors: 6 floors*
9 *Sanitary installations: combined bath and WC, direct lighting*
10 *Balcony system: 1 balcony*
11 *Staircase system: 2 wooden staircases*
12 *Staircase location: staggered*
13 *Staircase orientation: north*
14 *Living room orientation: north*
15 *Number of flats per main staircase: 2*
16 *Remarks: none*

Elaborated by B. Waagepetersen

Single staircase. Kitchen next to staircase. *Connected rooms. 1:200 and 1:500*

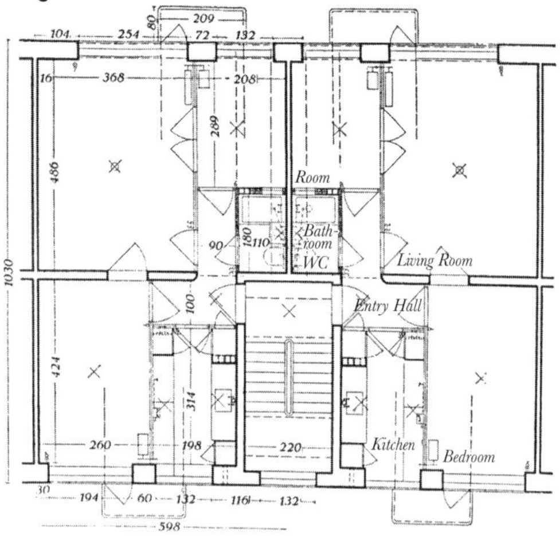

a
1 *Location: Vognmandsmarken*
2 *Client: Københavns almindelige Boligselskab (KAB)*
3 *Architect: Kay Fisker and C. F. Møller*
4 *Year built: 1933*
5 *Building style: semi-enclosed block*
6 *Number of rooms: 2 rooms + small room*
7 *Gross area: 58 m²*
8 *Number of floors: 5 floors*
9 *Sanitary installations: combined bath and WC, indirect lighting*
10 *Balcony system: fire escape balcony on two sides*
11 *Staircase system: 1 concrete staircase*
12 *Staircase location: symmetrical*
13 *Staircase orientation: north-northeast*
14 *Living room orientation: south-southwest*
15 *Number of flats per main staircase: 2*
16 *Remarks: Very concentrated type, but unattractive entry hall solution. The main partition is heavily intersected. Cost-effective bathroom installation*

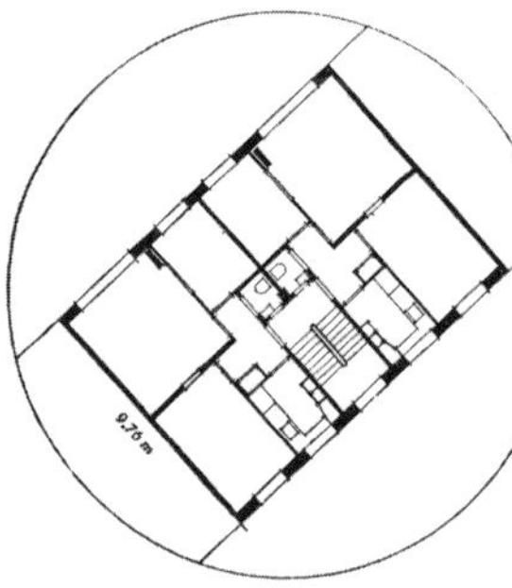

b
1 *Location: Hillerødgade, Vibevej*
2 *Client: Københavns almindelige Boligselskab (KAB)*
3 *Architect: Louis Hygom and E. Monberg*
4 *Year built: 1931*
5 *Building style: parallel and semi-enclosed blocks*
6 *Number of rooms: 2 rooms + small room*
7 *Gross area: 64.8 m²*
8 *Number of floors: 3 floors*
9 *Sanitary installations: combined bath and WC, indirect lighting*
10 *Balcony system: none*
11 *Staircase system: 1 wooden staircase*
12 *Staircase location: symmetrical*
13 *Staircase orientation: southeast*
14 *Living room orientation: northwest*
15 *Number of flats per main staircase: 2*
16 *Remarks: none*

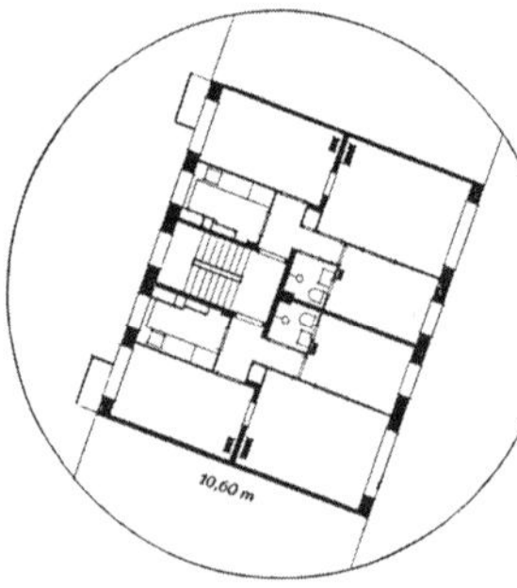

c
1 *Location: Enghavevej*
2 *Client: Københavns almindelige Boligselskab (KAB)*
3 *Architect: Wittmaack and Hvalsøe*
4 *Year built: 1932*
5 *Building style: semi-enclosed blocks*
6 *Number of rooms: 2 rooms + small room*
7 *Gross area: 66.25 m²*
8 *Number of floors: 5 floors*
9 *Sanitary installations: combined bath and WC, indirect lighting*
10 *Balcony system: connecting balconies*
11 *Staircase system: 1 concrete staircase*
12 *Staircase location: symmetrical*
13 *Staircase orientation: west-northwest*
14 *Living room orientation: east-southeast*
15 *Number of flats per main staircase: 2*
16 *Remarks: The connecting balconies, which are only required on one side, alternate on both sides, so that on each side there are only balconies on every other floor.*

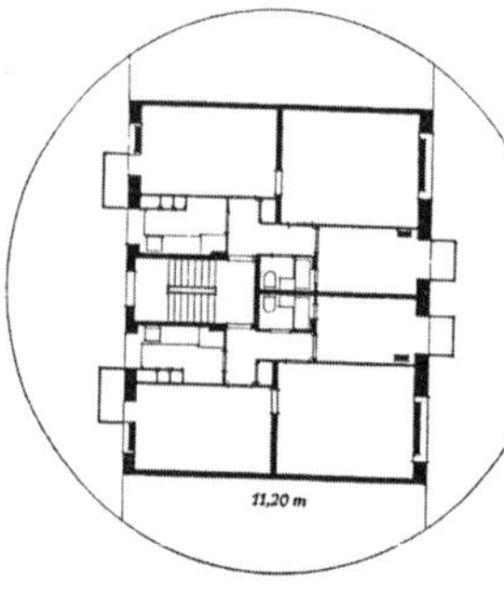

d
1 *Location: Evanstonevej 8*
2 *Client: private*
3 *Architect: P. Søgaard-Pedersen*
4 *Year built: 1933*
5 *Building style: ribbon development*
6 *Number of rooms: 2 rooms + small room*
7 *Gross area: 72.8 m²*
8 *Number of floors: 5 floors*
9 *Sanitary installations: combined bath and WC, indirect lighting*
10 *Balcony system: fire escape balconies on two sides*
11 *Staircase system: 1 concrete staircase*
12 *Staircase location: symmetrical*
13 *Staircase orientation: north*
14 *Living room orientation: south*
15 *Number of flats per main staircase: 2*
16 *Remarks: none*

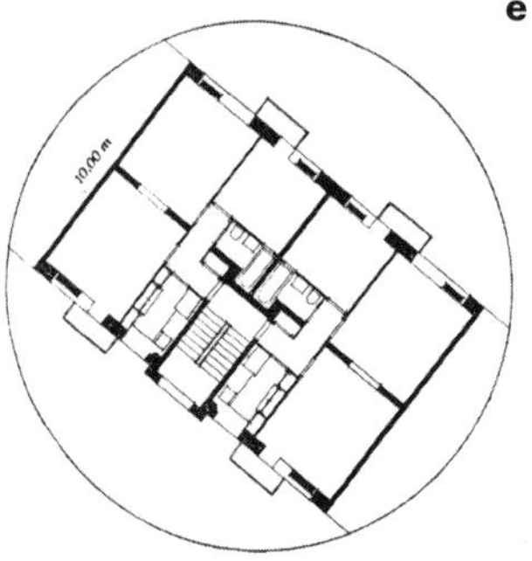

e
1 *Location: Frankrigsgade*
2 *Client: Københavns almindelige Boligselskab (KAB)*
3 *Architect: P. Søgaard-Pedersen*
4 *Year built: 1935*
5 *Building style: ribbon development*
6 *Number of rooms: 3 rooms*
7 *Gross area: 72.7 m²*
8 *Number of floors: 5 floors*
9 *Sanitary installations: combined bath and WC, indirect lighting*
10 *Balcony system: fire escape balconies on two sides*
11 *Staircase system: 1 concrete staircase*
12 *Staircase location: symmetrical*
13 *Staircase orientation: southwest*
14 *Living room orientation: southwest*
15 *Number of flats per main staircase: 2*
16 *Remarks: none*

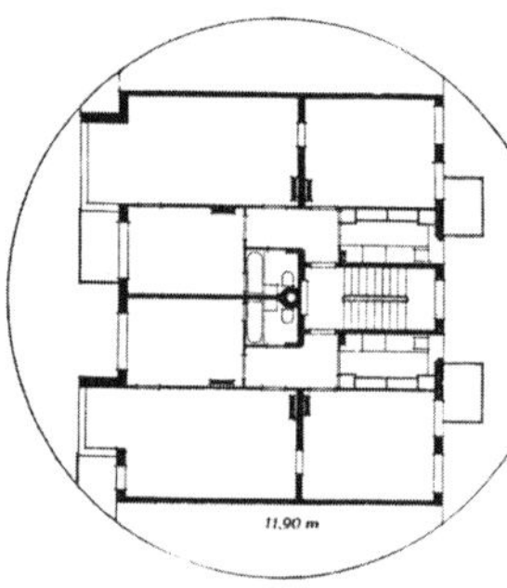

f
1 *Location: Strandvejen*
2 *Client: "Blidah II" A/S*
3 *Architect: Cooperative architect for the following type*
4 *Year built: 1934*
5 *Building style: linear block*
6 *Number of rooms: 2 rooms + small room*
7 *Gross area: 90.91 m²*
8 *Number of floors: 3 floors*
9 *Sanitary installations: combined bath and WC, indirect lighting*
10 *Balcony system: balconies on one side*
11 *Staircase system: 1 wooden staircase*
12 *Staircase location: symmetrical*
13 *Staircase orientation: east*
14 *Living room orientation: west*
15 *Number of flats per main staircase: 2*
16 *Remarks: asymmetrical south-facing bay windows and balconies, refuse chute*

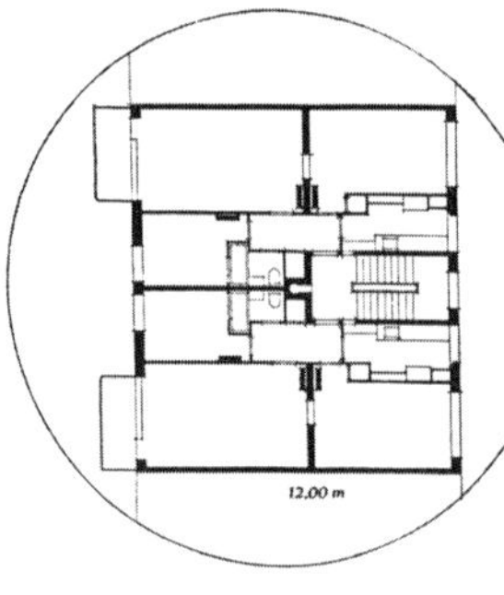

g
1 *Location: Strandvejen*
2 *Client: "Blidah II" A/S*
3 *Architect: for the following type A. Skjøt-Pedersen*
4 *Year built: 1934*
5 *Building style: linear block*
6 *Number of rooms: 2 rooms + small room*
7 *Gross area: 77.5 m²*
8 *Number of floors: 3 floors*
9 *Sanitary installations: combined bath and WC, indirect lighting*
10 *Balcony system: balconies on one side*
11 *Staircase system: 1 wooden staircase*
12 *Staircase location: symmetrical*
13 *Staircase orientation: east*
14 *Living room orientation: west*
15 *Number of flats per main staircase: 2*
16 *Remarks: none*

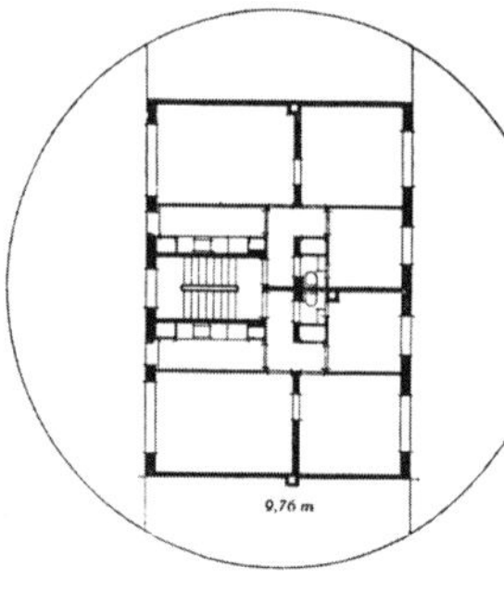

h
1 *Location: Rentmestervej*
2 *Client: Municipality of Copenhagen*
3 *Architect: E. Monberg*
4 *Year built: 1934*
5 *Building style: linear block*
6 *Number of rooms: 2 rooms + small room*
7 *Gross area: 61.8 m²*
8 *Number of floors: 3 floors*
9 *Sanitary installations: WC without bath, indirect lighting*
10 *Balcony system: none*
11 *Staircase system: 1 wooden staircase*
12 *Staircase location: symmetrical*
13 *Staircase orientation: west*
14 *Living room orientation: west*
15 *Number of flats per main staircase: 2*
16 *Remarks: none*

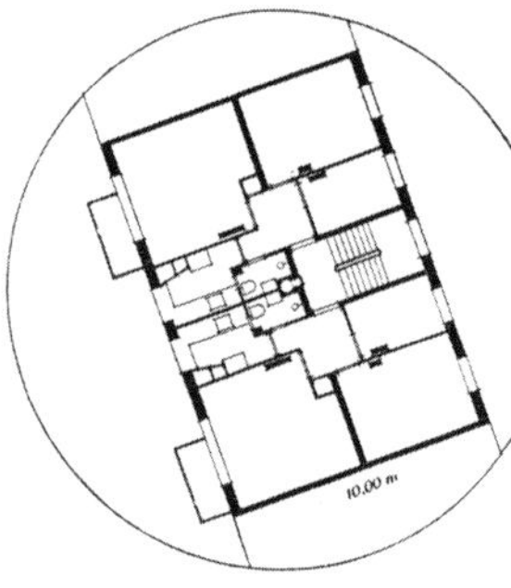

i
1 *Location: Lyngbyvej*
2 *Client: "Lundevænget" A/S*
3 *Architect: for the following type Frederik Wagner*
4 *Year built: 1934*
5 *Building style: linear block*
6 *Number of rooms: 2 rooms + small room*
7 *Gross area: 70 m²*
8 *Number of floors: 3 floors*
9 *Sanitary installations: combined bath and WC, indirect lighting*
10 *Balcony system: connecting balconies*
11 *Staircase system: 1 wooden staircase*
12 *Staircase location: symmetrical*
13 *Staircase orientation: east-northeast*
14 *Living room orientation: west-southwest*
15 *Number of flats per main staircase: 2*
16 *Remarks: The type is varied by interchanging the kitchen and small room, providing more advantageous installations. The type continues in IV_{38}. Refuse chute*

Elaborated by C. J. Ammitzbøll

Single staircase. Kitchen next to staircase. *Separated rooms. 1:200 and 1:500*

IV$_{36}$

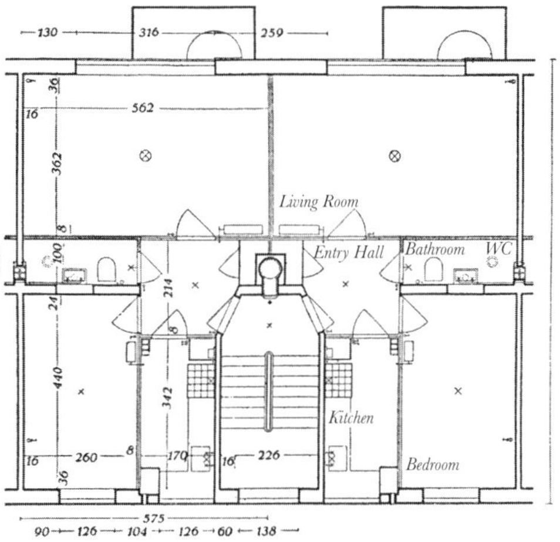

a
1 *Location: Lyngbyvej, Ole Nielsens Vej*
2 *Client: "Ryparken" A/S*
3 *Architect: Edvard Heiberg and Karl Larsen*
4 *Year built: 1934*
5 *Building style: parallel block*
6 *Number of rooms: 2 rooms*
7 *Gross area: 55.93 m²*
8 *Number of floors: 4 floors*
9 *Sanitary installations: bath with shower and WC, indirect lighting*
10 *Balcony system: 1 fire escape balcony*
11 *Staircase system: 1 wooden staircase*
12 *Staircase location: symmetrical*
13 *Staircase orientation: east*
14 *Living room orientation: west*
15 *Number of flats per main staircase: 2*
16 *Remarks: Because the two rooms are separated by the bathroom, this type presupposes the distinct use of these as living rooms and bedrooms or as two separate combined living and bedrooms. The type contains a large living room. The location of the bath by the main partition necessitates concentrated facilities. On the other hand, the kitchen installations are spread out.*

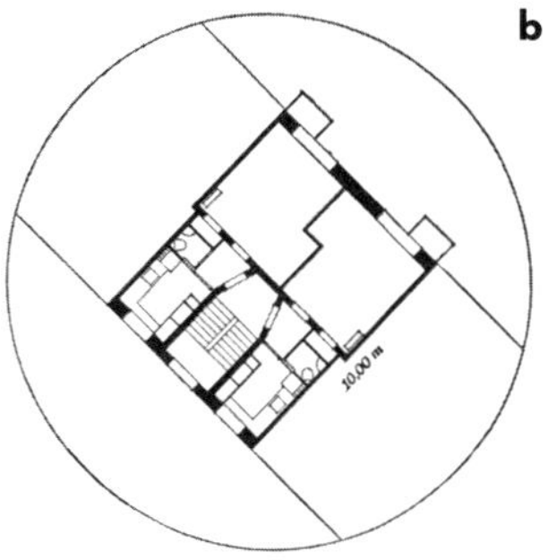

b
1 *Location: Utterslev, Copenhagen*
2 *Client: "Teklahus" A/S*
3 *Architect: P. Ambye*
4 *Year built: 1935*
5 *Building style: semi-enclosed block*
6 *Number of rooms: 1 room with alcove*
7 *Gross area: 38.85 m²*
8 *Number of floors: 5 floors*
9 *Sanitary installations: WC, indirect lighting*
10 *Balcony system: connecting balconies*
11 *Staircase system: 1 concrete staircase*
12 *Staircase location: symmetrical*
13 *Staircase orientation: southwest*
14 *Living room orientation: northeast*
15 *Number of flats per main staircase: 2*
16 *Remarks: none*

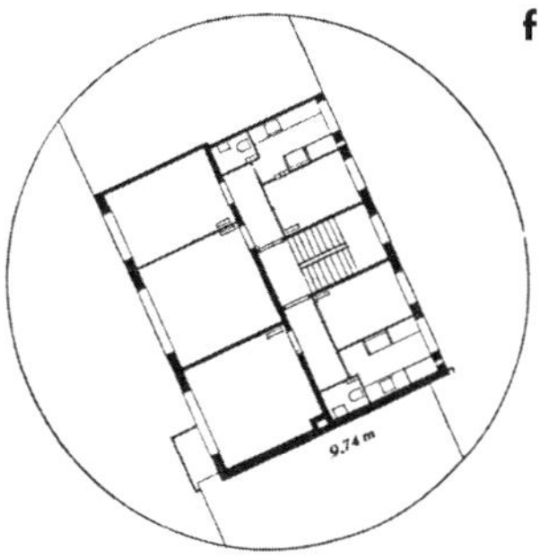

f
1 *Location: Sundby*
2 *Client: "Amager Haveby" A/S*
3 *Architect: Svend G. Hørup and Albinus Risom*
4 *Year built: 1935*
5 *Building style: linear block*
6 *Number of rooms: 2 rooms + 1 small room or 1 room + 1 small room*
7 *Gross area: 62 m² and 51.46 m²*
8 *Number of floors: 3 floors*
9 *Sanitary installations: WC, indirect lighting*
10 *Balcony system: left side flat with balcony*
11 *Staircase system: 1 wooden staircase*
12 *Staircase location: asymmetrical*
13 *Staircase orientation: east*
14 *Living room orientation: west*
15 *Number of flats per main staircase: 2*
16 *Remarks: none*

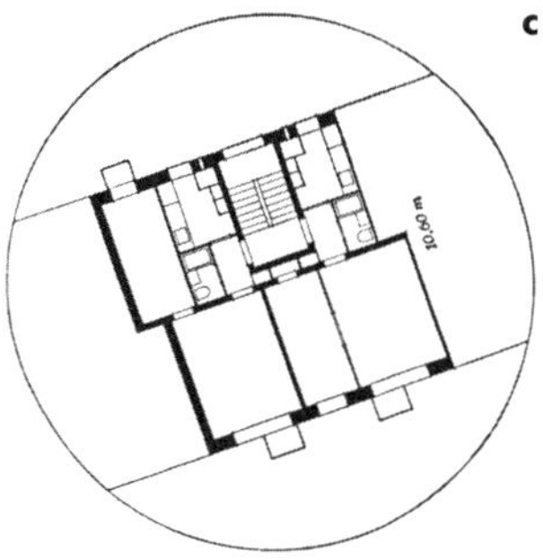

c
1 *Location: Sundby, Copenhagen*
2 *Client: "Kretahus I" A/S*
3 *Architect: Thorvald Dreyer*
4 *Year built: 1935*
5 *Building style: semi-enclosed block*
6 *Number of rooms: 1 room + 1 small room*
7 *Gross area: flat on the left 49.93 m², flat on the right 51.51 m²*
8 *Number of floors: 5 floors*
9 *Sanitary installations: combined bath with WC, indirect lighting*
10 *Balcony system: 2 balconies*
11 *Staircase system: 1 concrete staircase*
12 *Staircase location: asymmetrical*
13 *Staircase orientation: north*
14 *Living room orientation: south*
15 *Number of flats per main staircase: 2*
16 *Remarks: none*

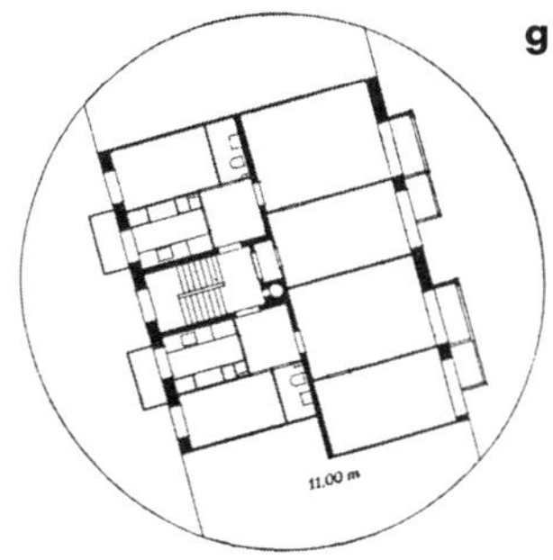

g
1 *Location: Brønshøj*
2 *Client: "Kløvergaarden" A/S*
3 *Architect: M. J. Kelde*
4 *Year built: 1935*
5 *Building style: ribbon development*
6 *Number of rooms: 2 rooms + 1 small room*
7 *Gross area: 72.49 m² and 60.45 m²*
8 *Number of floors: 5 floors*
9 *Sanitary installations: combined bath and WC, indirect lighting*
10 *Balcony system: 2 balconies*
11 *Staircase system: 1 concrete staircase*
12 *Staircase location: asymmetrical*
13 *Staircase orientation: west*
14 *Living room orientation: east*
15 *Number of flats per main staircase: 2*
16 *Remarks: refuse chute*

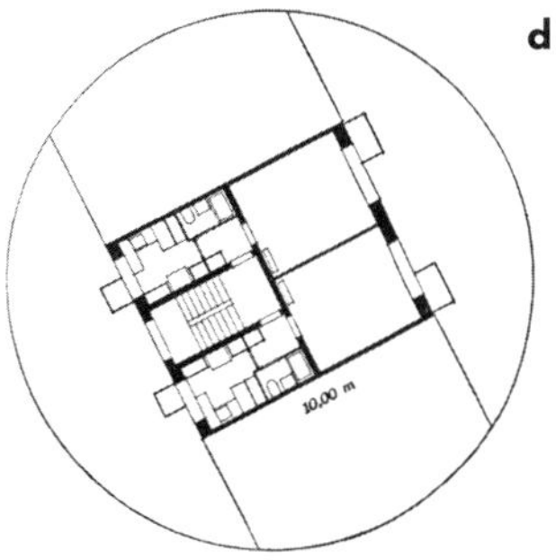

d
1 *Location: Sundby, Copenhagen*
2 *Client: "Kretahus I" A/S*
3 *Architect: Thorvald Dreyer*
4 *Year built: 1935*
5 *Building style: semi-enclosed block*
6 *Number of rooms: 1 room and dining kitchen*
7 *Gross area: 39.3 m²*
8 *Number of floors: 5*
9 *Sanitary installations: combined bath and WC, indirect lighting*
10 *Balcony system: 2 balconies*
11 *Staircase system: 1 concrete staircase*
12 *Staircase location: symmetrical*
13 *Staircase orientation: east*
14 *Living room orientation: west*
15 *Number of flats per main staircase: 2*
16 *Remarks: none*

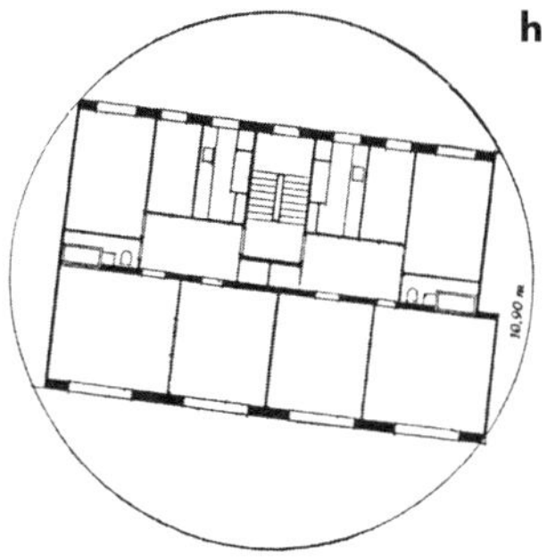

h
1 *Location: Frederiksberg*
2 *Client: "Normas Have" A/S*
3 *Architect: Holger Blytman*
4 *Year built: 1935*
5 *Building style: semi-enclosed block*
6 *Number of rooms: 3 rooms + 1 small room*
7 *Gross area: 83.12 m² and 85.07 m²*
8 *Number of floors: 3*
9 *Sanitary installations: combined bath and WC, indirect lighting*
10 *Balcony system: none*
11 *Staircase system: 1 wooden staircase*
12 *Staircase location: asymmetrical*
13 *Staircase orientation: north*
14 *Living room orientation: south*
15 *Number of flats per main staircase: 2*
16 *Remarks: none*

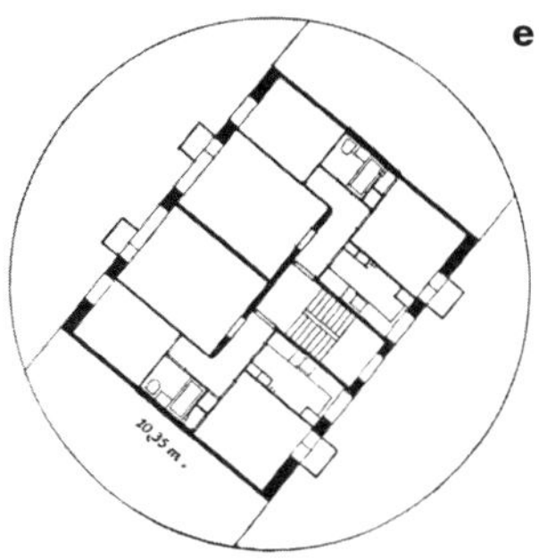

e
1 *Location: Tagensvej 159*
2 *Client: "Tagensvej 152" A/S*
3 *Architect: Kay Fisker and C. F. Møller*
4 *Year built: 1931*
5 *Building style: linear block*
6 *Number of rooms: 2 rooms + 1 small room*
7 *Gross area: 65.21 m²*
8 *Number of floors: 5 floors*
9 *Sanitary installations: combined bath and WC, indirect lighting*
10 *Balcony system: 2 balconies*
11 *Staircase system: 1 concrete staircase*
12 *Staircase location: symmetrical*
13 *Staircase orientation: southeast*
14 *Living room orientation: northwest*
15 *Number of flats per main staircase: 2*
16 *Remarks: none*

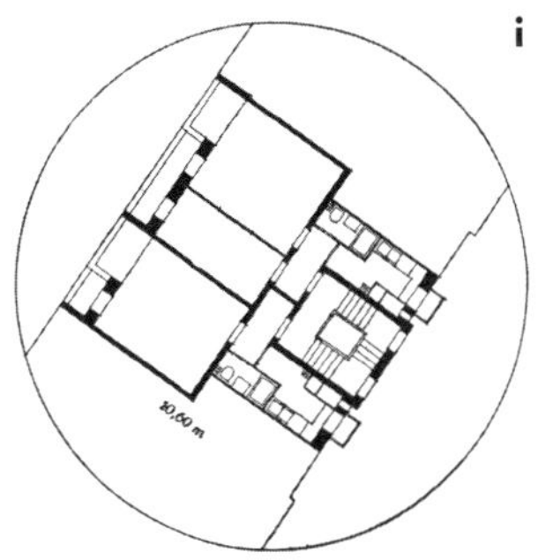

i
1 *Location: Christianshavn*
2 *Client: "Voldgaarden" A/S*
3 *Architect: Jens Nielsen and Thorvald Dreyer*
4 *Year built: 1933*
5 *Building style: enclosed block*
6 *Number of rooms: 1 room + small room or 1 room*
7 *Gross area: 54.71 and 42.95 m²*
8 *Number of floors: 6*
9 *Sanitary installations: combined bath and WC, indirect lighting*
10 *Balcony system: 2 balconies*
11 *Staircase system: 1 concrete staircase*
12 *Staircase location: asymmetrical*
13 *Staircase orientation: southeast*
14 *Living room orientation: northwest*
15 *Number of flats per main staircase: 2*
16 *Remarks: none*

Elaborated by Esben Klint

Single staircase. Kitchen opposite staircase. *Connected rooms. 1:200 and 1:500*

IV

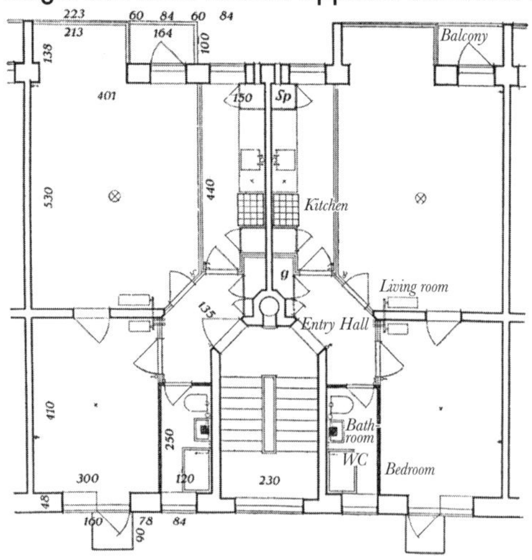

a
1 *Location: Struergade*
2 *Client: private*
3 *Architect: Th. Dreyer*
4 *Year built: 1935*
5 *Building style: ribbon development*
6 *Number of rooms: 2 rooms*
7 *Gross area: 64 m²*
8 *Number of floors: 6 floors*
9 *Sanitary installations: combined bath and WC, direct lighting*
10 *Balcony system: fire escape balconies*
11 *Staircase system: 1 staircase*
12 *Staircase location: symmetrical*
13 *Staircase orientation: west*
14 *Living room orientation: east*
15 *Number of flats per main staircase: 2*
16 *Remarks: The characteristic feature of this plan is the location of the kitchen next to the living room and the bathroom's direct lighting. This placement of the kitchen necessitates its narrow and very long dimensions with the worktop along one wall, and potentially narrow cabinets on the opposite wall. As with the living room, the kitchen also faces the sun.*

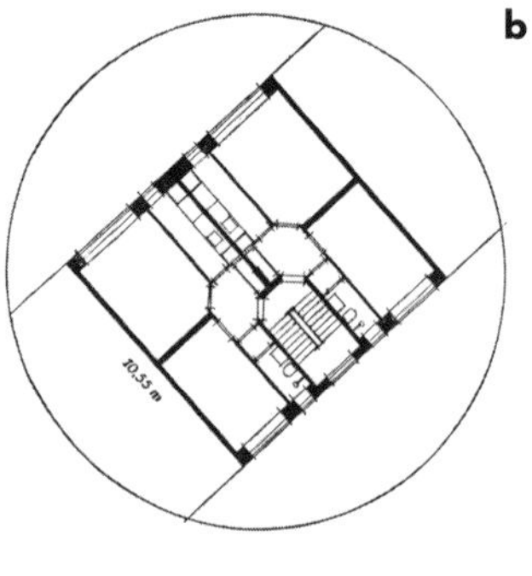

b
1 *Location: Vognmandsmarken*
2 *Client: "Ejendomsselskabet af 30. juni 1933" A/S*
3 *Architect: Tyge Hvass*
4 *Year built: 1934*
5 *Building style: semi-enclosed block*
6 *Number of rooms: 2 rooms*
7 *Gross area: 58 m²*
8 *Number of floors: 5 floors*
9 *Sanitary installations: combined shower and WC, direct lighting*
10 *Balcony system: fire escape balconies*
11 *Staircase system: 1 staircase*
12 *Staircase location: symmetrical*
13 *Staircase orientation: southeast*
14 *Living room orientation: northwest*
15 *Number of flats per main staircase: 2*
16 *Remarks: none*

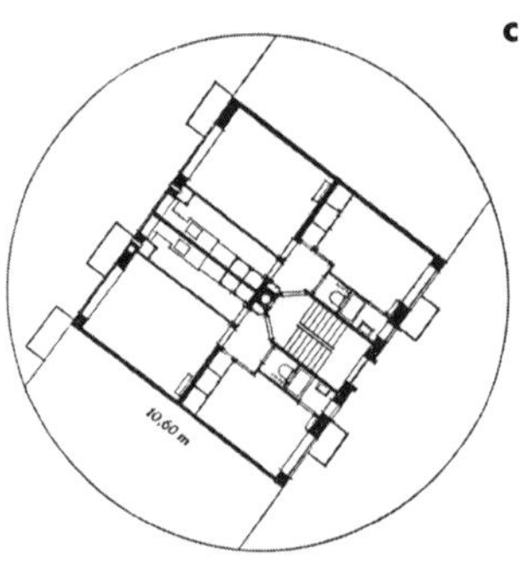

c
1 *Location: Søborg Hovedgade*
2 *Client: "Gartnervænget" A/S*
3 *Architect: Andreas P. Kirkerup*
4 *Year built: 1936*
5 *Building style: linear block*
6 *Number of rooms: 2 rooms*
7 *Gross area: 59 m²*
8 *Number of floors: 5 floors*
9 *Sanitary installations: bath with direct lighting, WC with indirect lighting*
10 *Balcony system: fire escape balconies*
11 *Staircase system: 1 staircase*
12 *Staircase location: symmetrical*
13 *Staircase orientation: east*
14 *Living room orientation: west*
15 *Number of flats per main staircase: 2*
16 *Remarks: refuse chute*

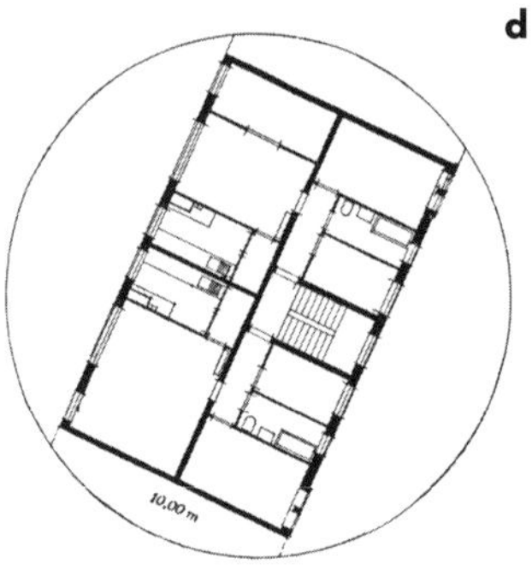

d
1 *Location: Ordrupvej*
2 *Client: private*
3 *Architect: A. Skjøt-Pedersen*
4 *Year built: 1934*
5 *Building style: linear block*
6 *Number of rooms: 2 rooms + 1 small room or 2 rooms + 2 small rooms*
7 *Gross area: 62 m²*
8 *Number of floors: 3 floors*
9 *Sanitary installations: combined bath and WC, direct lighting*
10 *Balcony system: living room balcony*
11 *Staircase system: 1 staircase*
12 *Staircase location: symmetrical*
13 *Staircase orientation: east*
14 *Living room orientation: west*
15 *Number of flats per main staircase: 2*
16 *Remarks: balcony not shown on the plan*

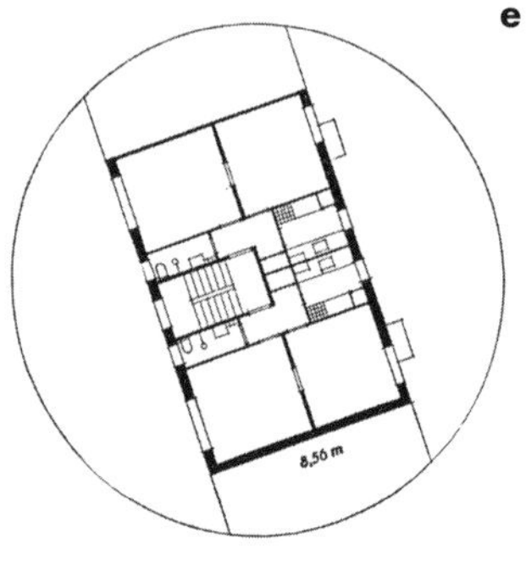

e
1 *Location: Emil Pipers Vej, Lyngby*
2 *Client: private*
3 *Architect: Thilo*
4 *Year built: 1933–34–35*
5 *Building style: semi-enclosed block*
6 *Number of rooms: 2 rooms*
7 *Gross area: 54 m²*
8 *Number of floors: 3 floors*
9 *Sanitary installations: combined shower and WC, direct lighting*
10 *Balcony system: balcony in the living room*
11 *Staircase system: 1 staircase*
12 *Staircase location: symmetrical*
13 *Staircase orientation: west*
14 *Living room orientation: west*
15 *Number of flats per main staircase: 2*
16 *Remarks: none*

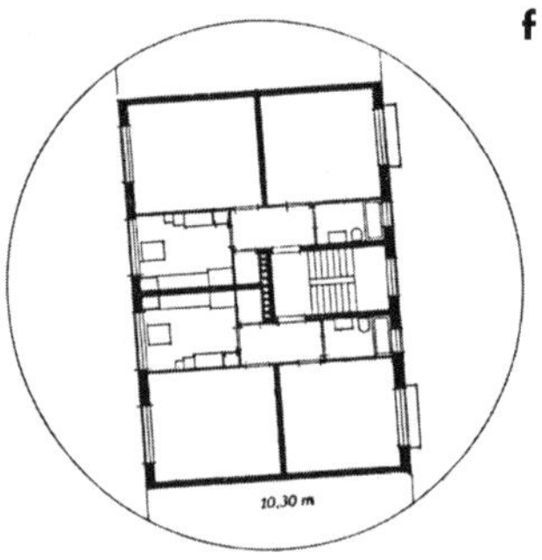

f
1 *Location: Oslo*
2 *Client: private*
3 *Architect: Sverre Poulsen*
4 *Year built: 1932*
5 *Building style: open block*
6 *Number of rooms: 2 rooms*
7 *Gross area: 74 m²*
8 *Number of floors: 4 floors*
9 *Sanitary installations: combined bath and WC, direct lighting*
10 *Balcony system: balcony in the bedroom*
11 *Staircase system: 1 staircase*
12 *Staircase location: symmetrical*
13 *Staircase orientation: east*
14 *Living room orientation: west*
15 *Number of flats per main staircase: 2*
16 *Remarks: none*

g
1 *Location: Frankfurt am Main*
2 *Client: Municipality of Frankfurt*
3 *Architect: Building department by Ernst May*
4 *Year built: 1929*
5 *Building style: linear block*
6 *Number of rooms: 1 room + 2 small rooms*
7 *Gross area: 61 m²*
8 *Number of floors: 3 floors*
9 *Sanitary installations: combined bath and WC, direct lighting*
10 *Balcony system: none*
11 *Staircase system: 1 staircase*
12 *Staircase location: symmetrical*
13 *Staircase orientation: west*
14 *Living room orientation: east*
15 *Number of flats per main staircase: 2*
16 *Remarks: bath located between small rooms*

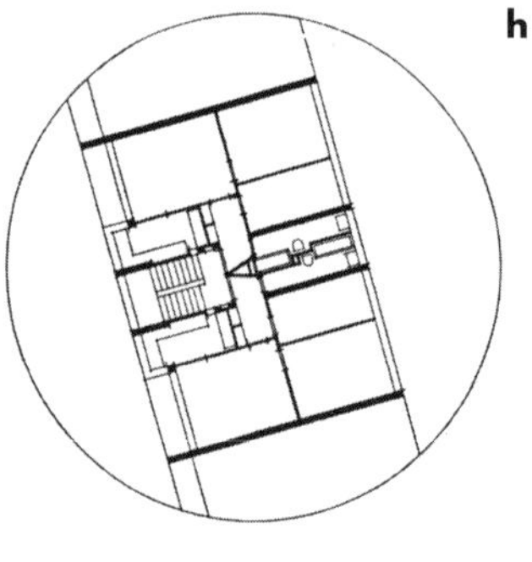

h
1 *Location: Frankfurt am Main*
2 *Client: Municipality of Frankfurt*
3 *Architect: Building department by Ernst May*
4 *Year built: 1929*
5 *Building style: linear block*
6 *Number of rooms: 2 room + 1 small room*
7 *Gross area: 64.5 m²*
8 *Number of floors: 3 floors*
9 *Sanitary installations: combined bath and WC, direct lighting*
10 *Balcony system: balcony in the living room*
11 *Staircase system: 1 staircase*
12 *Staircase location: symmetrical*
13 *Staircase orientation: west*
14 *Living room orientation: west*
15 *Number of flats per main staircase: 2*
16 *Remarks: load-bearing cross partition*

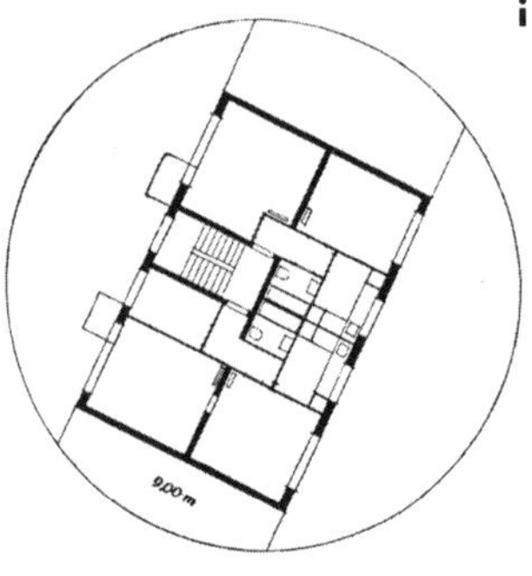

i
1 *Location: Himmerlandsvej*
2 *Client: private*
3 *Architect: Harald Larsen and Simon Henningsen*
4 *Year built: 1935*
5 *Building style: linear block*
6 *Number of rooms: 2 rooms*
7 *Gross area: 53.3 m²*
8 *Number of floors: 3 floors and habitable attic*
9 *Sanitary installations: combined bath and WC, indirect lighting*
10 *Balcony system: balconies on one side*
11 *Staircase system: concrete*
12 *Staircase location: asymmetrical*
13 *Staircase orientation: north*
14 *Living room orientation: north*
15 *Number of flats per main staircase: 2*
16 *Remarks: none*

Elaborated by Helmer Rèmark

Single staircase. Kitchen opposite staircase. *Separated rooms. 1:200 and 1:500* **IV 38**

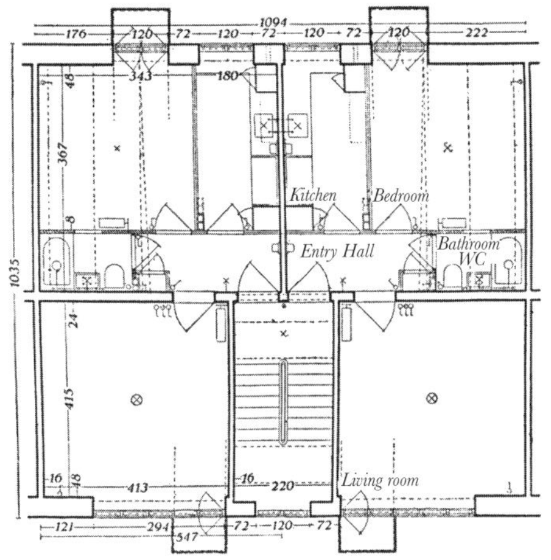

a
1 *Location: Tagensvej 152–180*
2 *Client: private*
3 *Architect: Kay Fisker and C. F. Møller*
4 *Year built: 1931*
5 *Building style: parallel block*
6 *Number of rooms: 2 rooms*
7 *Gross area: 56 m²*
8 *Number of floors: 5 floors*
9 *Sanitary installations: combined bath and WC, indirect lighting*
10 *Balcony system: fire escape balconies*
11 *Staircase system: 1 concrete staircase*
12 *Staircase location: symmetrical*
13 *Staircase orientation: west*
14 *Living room orientation: west*
15 *Number of flats per main staircase: 2*
16 *Remarks: Sizeable separation between living room and bedroom, making the type suitable for subletting. It can also be characterised by the kitchen's location opposite the staircase, while the entry hall, WC and bath form a kind of middle corridor. The type should be oriented east-west, but can be used with the living room facing south, if necessary. The continuous main partition is constructively advantageous.*

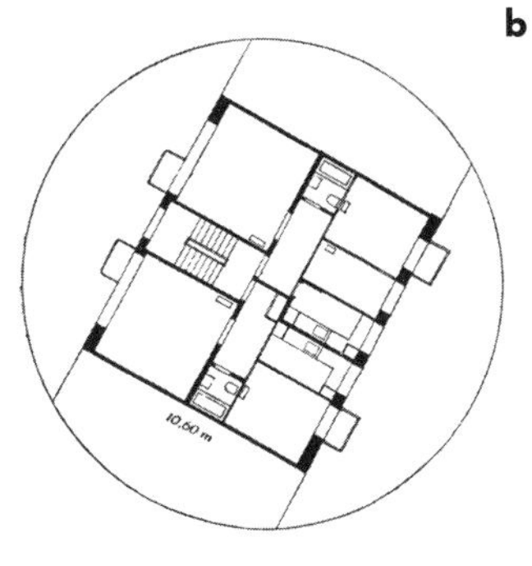

b
1 *Location: Tagensvej 152–180*
2 *Client: private*
3 *Architect: Kay Fisker and C. F. Møller*
4 *Year built: 1931*
5 *Building style: linear block*
6 *Number of rooms: 2 rooms and 2 rooms + small room*
7 *Gross area: 2 rooms 59.4 m², 2 rooms + small room 67 m²*
8 *Number of floors: 5 floors*
9 *Sanitary installations: combined bath and WC, indirect lighting*
10 *Balcony system: fire escape balconies*
11 *Staircase system: 1 concrete staircase*
12 *Staircase location: asymmetrical*
13 *Staircase orientation: west*
14 *Living room orientation: west*
15 *Number of flats per main staircase: 2*
16 *Remarks: linear block asymmetrical type, the same as the basic type with larger living room, smaller bedroom and small room on one side*

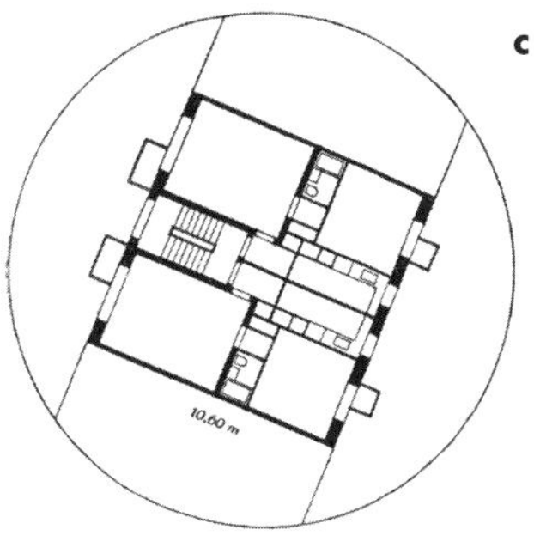

c
1 *Location: Frederiksborgvej*
2 *Client: "Bispehusene" and "Boparken" A/S*
3 *Architect: Th. Dreyer*
4 *Year built: 1935*
5 *Building style: linear block*
6 *Number of rooms: 2 rooms*
7 *Gross area: 56 m²*
8 *Number of floors: 5 floors*
9 *Sanitary installations: combined bath and WC, indirect lighting*
10 *Balcony system: fire escape balconies*
11 *Staircase system: 1 concrete staircase*
12 *Staircase location: symmetrical*
13 *Staircase orientation: west*
14 *Living room orientation: east-west*
15 *Number of flats per main staircase: 2*
16 *Remarks: The strict separation between bedroom and kitchen is beneficial*

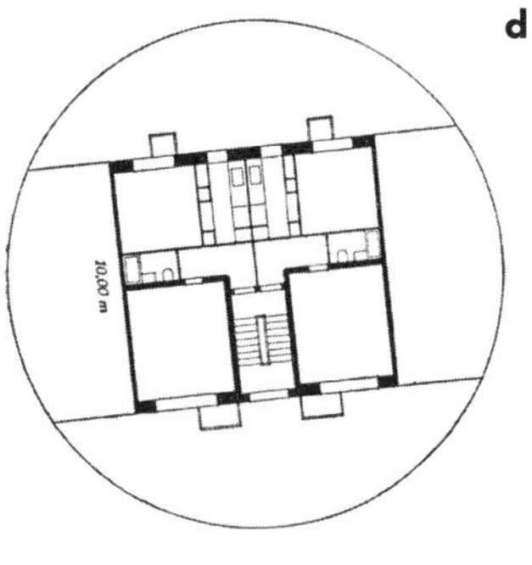

d
1 *Location: Grækenlandsvej, Kretavej, Kastrupvej*
2 *Client: "Kretahusene" II*
3 *Architect: Th. Dreyer*
4 *Year built: 1934–35*
5 *Building style: enclosed block*
6 *Number of rooms: 2 rooms*
7 *Gross area: 60 m²*
8 *Number of floors: 5 floors*
9 *Sanitary installations: combined bath and WC, indirect lighting*
10 *Balcony system: fire escape balconies*
11 *Staircase system: 1 concrete staircase*
12 *Staircase location: symmetrical*
13 *Staircase orientation: west*
14 *Living room orientation: west*
15 *Number of flats per main staircase: 2*
16 *Remarks: none*

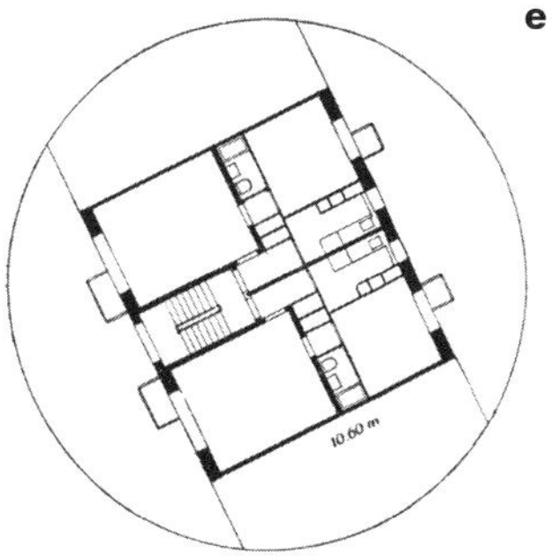

e
1 *Location: Grækenlandsvej, Kretavej, Kastrupvej*
2 *Client: "Kretahusene" III*
3 *Architect: Th. Dreyer*
4 *Year built: 1934–35*
5 *Building style: enclosed block*
6 *Number of rooms: 2 rooms*
7 *Gross area: 60 m²*
8 *Number of floors: 5 floors*
9 *Sanitary installations: combined bath and WC, indirect lighting*
10 *Balcony system: fire escape balconies*
11 *Staircase system: 1 concrete staircase*
12 *Staircase location: symmetrical*
13 *Staircase orientation: southwest*
14 *Living room orientation: southwest*
15 *Number of flats per main staircase: 2*
16 *Remarks: none*

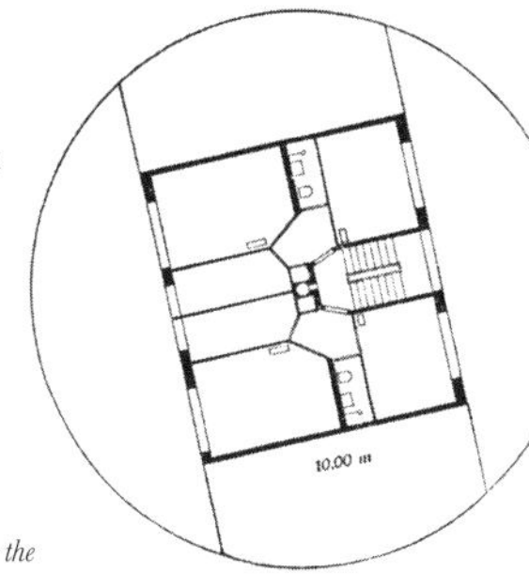

f
1 *Location: Ole Nielsens Vej*
2 *Client: "Lundevænget" A/S*
3 *Architect: Frederik Wagner*
4 *Year built: 1935*
5 *Building style: parallel block*
6 *Number of rooms: 4 rooms*
7 *Gross area: 54 m²*
8 *Number of floors: 3 floors*
9 *Sanitary installations: combined shower and WC, indirect lighting*
10 *Balcony system: balconies on the west side*
11 *Staircase system: 1 concrete staircase*
12 *Staircase location: symmetrical*
13 *Staircase orientation: west*
14 *Living room orientation: west*
15 *Number of flats per main staircase: 2*
16 *Remarks: none*

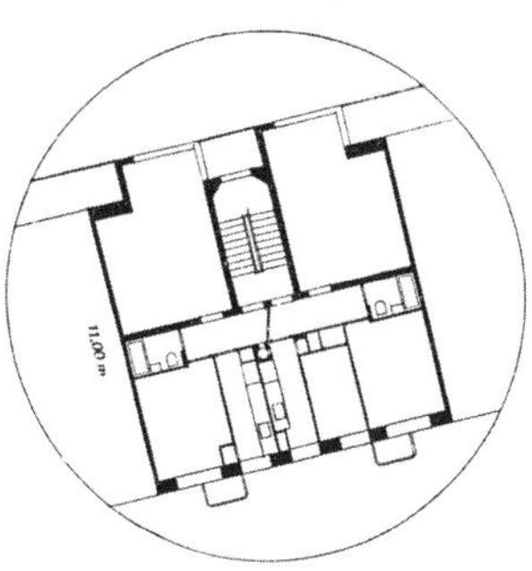

1 *Location: Højdevej, Elbagade*
2 *Client: "Jacobsgaard" A/S*
3 *Architect: F. Galatius*
4 *Year built: 1934*
5 *Building style: enclosed block*
6 *Number of rooms: 2 rooms and 2 rooms + small room*
7 *Gross area: 65 m² and 71 m²*
8 *Number of floors: 5*
9 *Sanitary installations: combined shower and WC, indirect lighting*
10 *Balcony system: fire escape balconies*
11 *Staircase system: 1 concrete staircase*
12 *Staircase location: symmetrical*
13 *Staircase orientation: south*
14 *Living room orientation: south*
15 *Number of flats per main staircase: 2*
16 *Remarks: none*

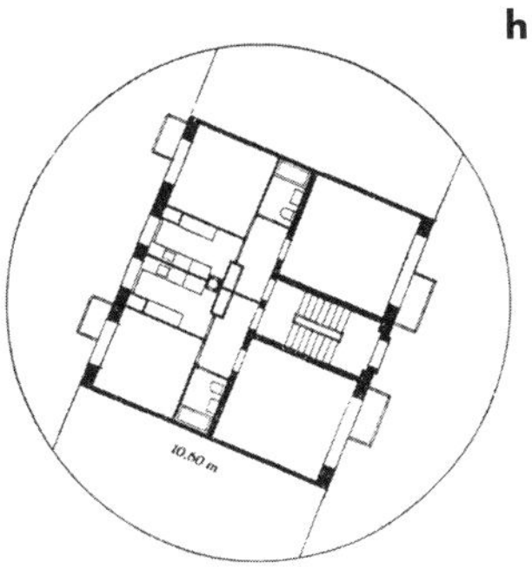

h
1 *Location: Englandsvej, Lærdalsgade*
2 *Client: private*
3 *Architect: F. Galatius*
4 *Year built: 1935*
5 *Building style: enclosed block*
6 *Number of rooms: 2 rooms*
7 *Gross area: 58 m²*
8 *Number of floors: 5 floors*
9 *Sanitary installations: combined bath and WC, indirect lighting*
10 *Balcony system: fire escape balconies*
11 *Staircase system: 1 concrete staircase*
12 *Staircase location: asymmetric*
13 *Staircase orientation: east*
14 *Living room orientation: west*
15 *Number of flats per main staircase: 2*
16 *Remarks: none*

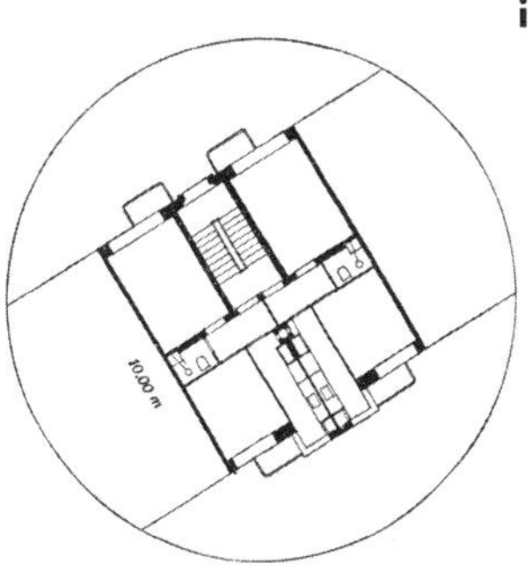

i
1 *Location: Højdevej, Elbagade*
2 *Client: "Jacobsgaard" A/S*
3 *Architect: F. Galatius*
4 *Year built: 1934*
5 *Building style: enclosed block*
6 *Number of rooms: 2 rooms*
7 *Gross area: 47.5 m²*
8 *Number of floors: 5 floors*
9 *Sanitary installations: combined shower and WC, indirect lighting*
10 *Balcony system: fire escape balconies*
11 *Staircase system: 1 concrete staircase*
12 *Staircase location: symmetrical*
13 *Staircase orientation: west*
14 *Living room orientation: west*
15 *Number of flats per main staircase: 2*
16 *Remarks: none*

Elaborated by Chr. Suhrlykke Petersen

One or two staircases. Dining area. *1:200 and 1:500*

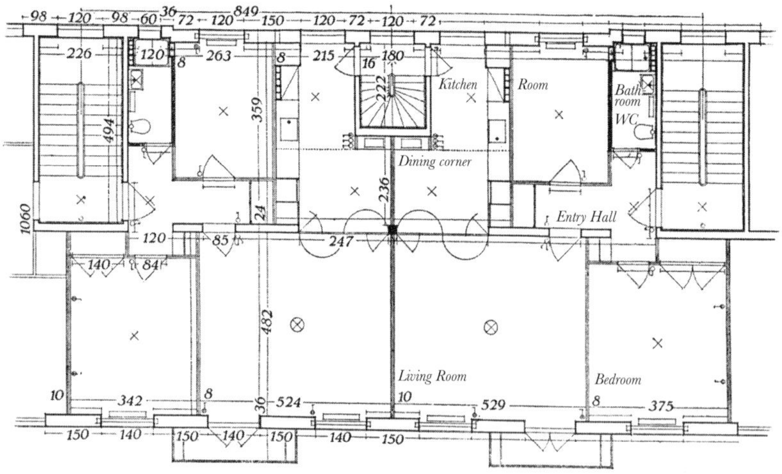

a 1 *Location: Torvegade*
2 *Client: Municipality of Copenhagen*
3 *Architect: B. Helweg-Møller*
4 *Year built: 1933*
5 *Building style: enclosed block*
6 *Number of rooms: 3 rooms and dining area*
7 *Gross area: 91.50 m²*
8 *Number of floors: 5*
9 *Sanitary installations: bath and WC, direct lighting*
10 *Balcony system: balconies only on one side*
11 *Staircase system: 2 wooden staircases*
12 *Staircase location: symmetrical*
13 *Staircase orientation: north*
14 *Living room orientation: south*
15 *Number of flats per main staircase: 2*
16 *Remarks: A compromise solution between "living room with dining area" and "dining kitchen". Against custom, the kitchen does not have access from the entry hall. The type is also described in the article (*Arkitekten Maanedshæfte *vol. XXXIV, No. 1, 1932, p. 1).*

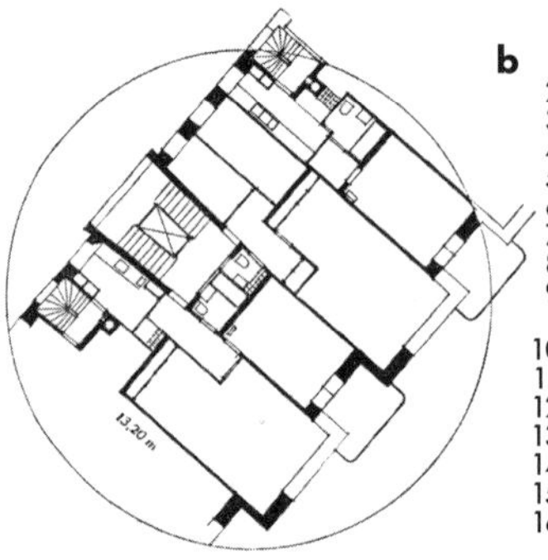

b 1 *Location: Gyldenløvesgade 21, Vestersøgade 60–78*
2 *Client: "Vestersøhus" A/S*
3 *Architect: Kay Fisker and C. F. Møller*
4 *Year built: 1935–36*
5 *Building style: block development*
6 *Number of rooms: 2 rooms and dining area*
7 *Gross area: 80 m²*
8 *Number of floors: 7 floors*
9 *Sanitary installations: combined bath and WC, separated for larger flats, indirect lighting*
10 *Balcony system: balconies on one side*
11 *Staircase system: 2 wooden staircases*
12 *Staircase location: asymmetrical*
13 *Staircase orientation: east*
14 *Living room orientation: west*
15 *Number of flats per main staircase: 2*
16 *Remarks: refuse chute, lift, great house depth*

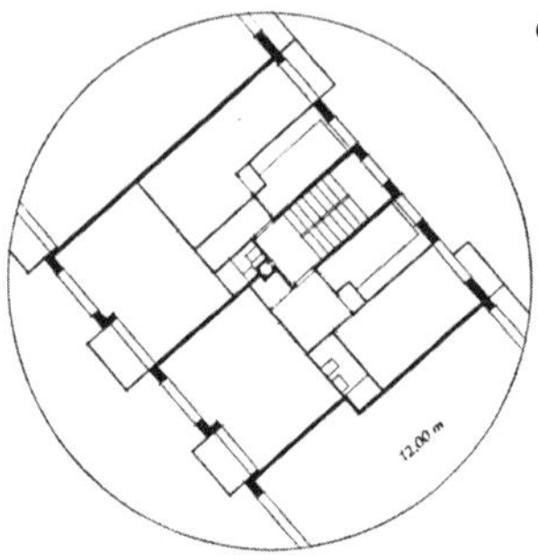

e 1 *Location: Sallingvej, Ådalsvej*
2 *Client: "Aadalshusene" A/S*
3 *Architect: J. Houmøller Klemmensen*
4 *Year built: 1936*
5 *Building style: semi-enclosed block*
6 *Number of rooms: 2 rooms*
7 *Gross area: 67 m², 72 m²*
8 *Number of floors: 4 floors*
9 *Sanitary installations: combined shower and WC, indirect lighting*
10 *Balcony system: connecting balconies on one side, fire escape balconies on the other side*
11 *Staircase system: 1 concrete staircase*
12 *Staircase location: asymmetrical*
13 *Staircase orientation: east*
14 *Living room orientation: west*
15 *Number of flats per main staircase: 2*
16 *Remarks: The east-facing room can be used as a living room with dining area or as a bedroom with dressing room or children's area*

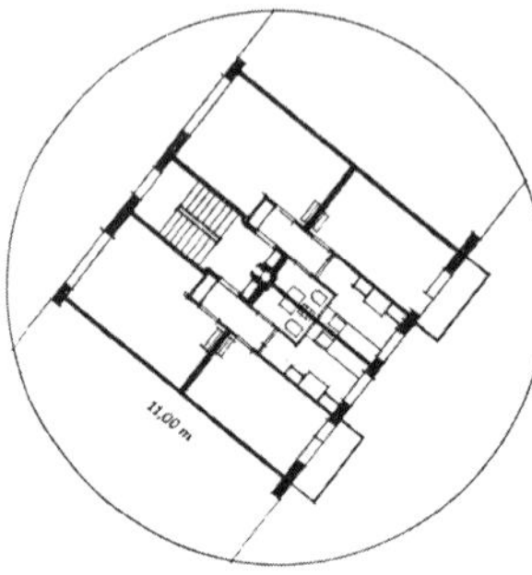

c 1 *Location: C. F. Richs Vej*
2 *Client: "Ringparken" A/S*
3 *Architect: A. Skjøt-Pedersen*
4 *Year built: 1935*
5 *Building style: parallel block*
6 *Number of rooms: 2 rooms and dining area*
7 *Gross area: 57.7 m²*
8 *Number of floors: 3 floors*
9 *Sanitary installations: combined bath and WC, indirect lighting*
10 *Balcony system: connecting balconies with separators*
11 *Staircase system: 1 concrete staircase*
12 *Staircase location: symmetrical*
13 *Staircase orientation: east*
14 *Living room orientation: east*
15 *Number of flats per main staircase: 2*
16 *Remarks: refuse chute*

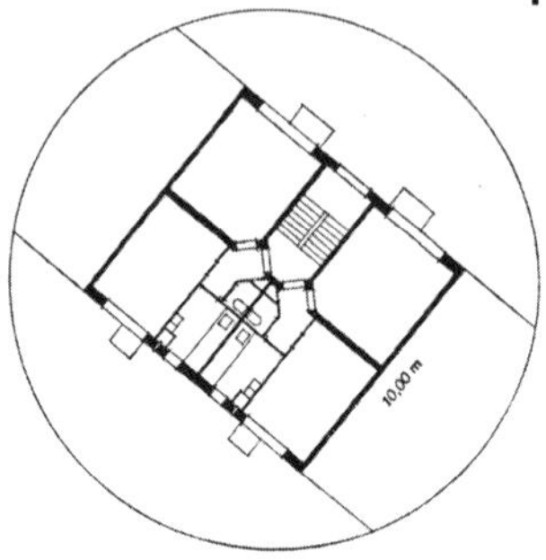

f 1 *Location: Kretavej and Kastrupvej*
2 *Client: "Kretahusene" A/S*
3 *Architect: Th. Dreyer*
4 *Year built: 1935*
5 *Building style: semi-enclosed block*
6 *Number of rooms: 2 rooms*
7 *Gross area: 50.7 m² per flat*
8 *Number of floors: 5 floors*
9 *Sanitary installations: combined shower and WC, indirect lighting*
10 *Balcony system: fire escape balconies*
11 *Staircase system: 1 concrete staircase*
12 *Staircase location: symmetrical*
13 *Staircase orientation: east and west*
14 *Living room orientation: east and west*
15 *Number of flats per main staircase: 2*
16 *Remarks: The possibility of a distinct dining area is basically eliminated by the oblique cut corner*

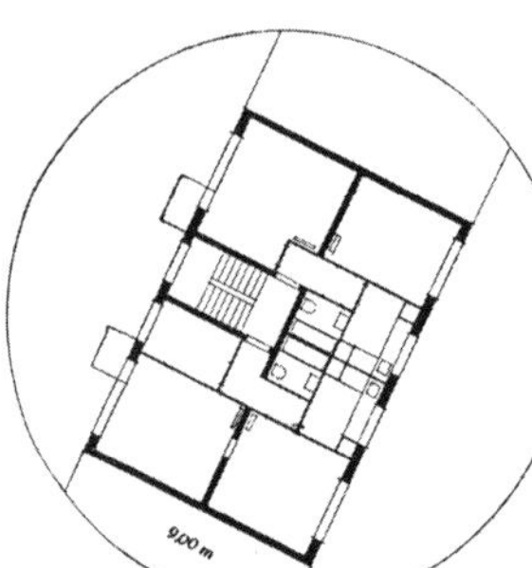

d 1 *Location: Himmerlandsvej*
2 *Client: private*
3 *Architect: Harald Larsen and Simon Henningsen*
4 *Year built: 1935*
5 *Building style: parallel block*
6 *Number of rooms: 2 rooms*
7 *Gross area: 53.3 m²*
8 *Number of floors: 3 rooms and attic floor*
9 *Sanitary installations: combined bath and WC, indirect lighting*
10 *Balcony system: balconies on one side*
11 *Staircase system: concrete*
12 *Staircase location: asymmetrical*
13 *Staircase orientation: north*
14 *Living room orientation: north*
15 *Number of flats per main staircase: 2*
16 *Remarks: none*

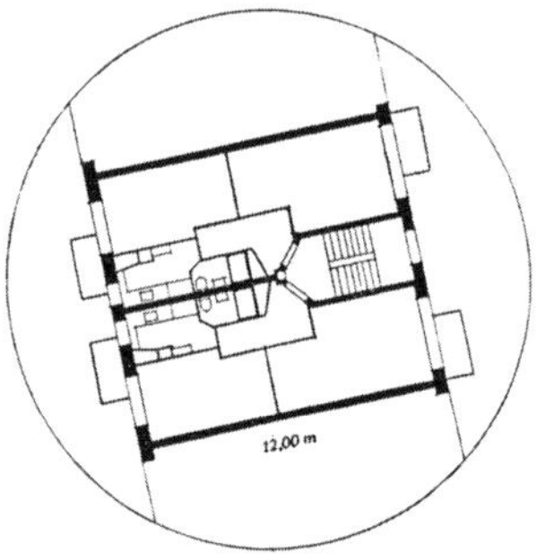

g 1 *Location: Roskildevej*
2 *Client: Københavns almindelige Boligselskab (KAB) "Roskildegaarden"*
3 *Architect: Henning Jørgensen*
4 *Year built: 1935*
5 *Building style: semi-enclosed block*
6 *Number of rooms: 2 rooms and dining area*
7 *Gross area: 60 m²*
8 *Number of floors: 5 floors*
9 *Sanitary installations: combined bath and WC, indirect lighting*
10 *Balcony system: fire escape balcony*
11 *Staircase system: 1 concrete staircase*
12 *Staircase location: symmetrical*
13 *Staircase orientation: east*
14 *Living room orientation: east*
15 *Number of flats per main staircase: 2*
16 *Remarks: refuse chute, load-bearing cross partition. The type continues in IX_{40}*

Elaborated by Eivind Dietz

Single staircase. Large floor depth. Load-bearing cross partition *(over 10.50 m). 1:200 and 1:500*

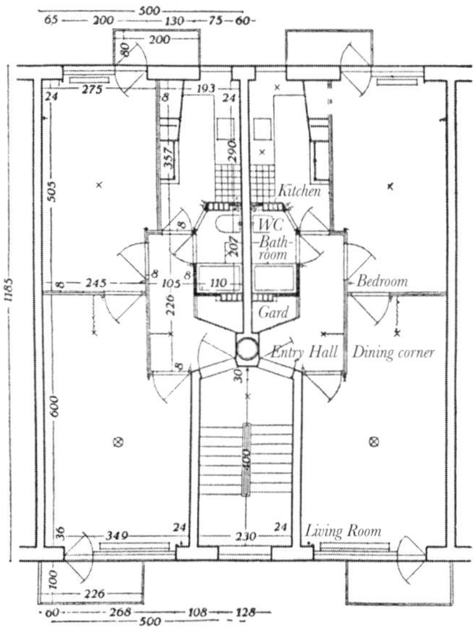

a
1 *Location: Roskildevej – Hoffmeyersvej*
2 *Client: Københavns almindelige Boligselskab (KAB)*
3 *Architect: Henning Jørgensen*
4 *Year built: 1935*
5 *Building style: semi-enclosed block*
6 *Number of rooms: 2 rooms and dining area*
7 *Gross area: 59.3 m²*
8 *Number of floors: 5 floors*
9 *Sanitary installations: combined bath and WC, indirect lighting*
10 *Balcony system: fire escape balconies on one side and connecting balcony on the other side*
11 *Staircase system: 1 concrete staircase*
12 *Staircase location: symmetrical*
13 *Staircase orientation: south and west*
14 *Living room orientation: south and west*
15 *Number of flats per main staircase: 2*
16 *Remarks: Load-bearing cross partitions offer several advantages over regular main partitions in the middle of the flat, including greater strength since they do not have door or window openings. For buildings with large floor depths, the use of load-bearing cross partitions can keep a timber floor joist system within reasonable dimensions. With this construction, individual flats are very distinct in terms of sound. It can be difficult to find a satisfactory solution for balconies, since in many cases they have to be confined, and as a result, they cannot be very wide. Load-bearing partitions can only be used for small flat types and in order to avoid beams with excessive spans, the rooms are often long and narrow; in the combined living and dining room, this is addressed with the rear part designed to accommodate the dining area and the lighted space in front of the window is maintained as a living area.*

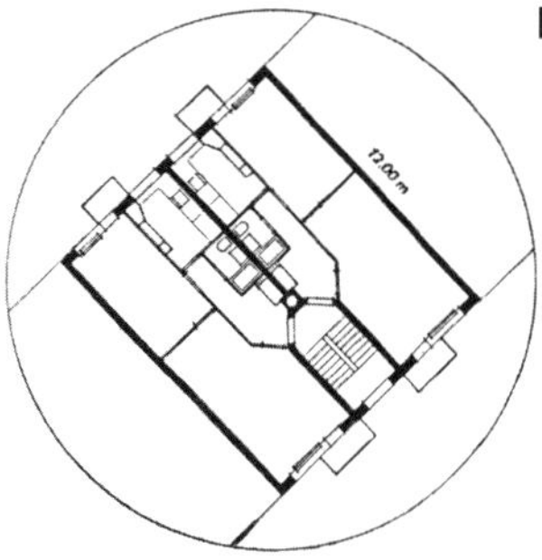

b
1 *Location: Ordrupvej 76*
2 *Client: Københavns almindelige Boligselskab (KAB)*
3 *Architect: P. Søgaard-Pedersen*
4 *Year built: 1934*
5 *Building style: ribbon development*
6 *Number of rooms: 2 rooms*
7 *Gross area: 61.2 m²*
8 *Number of floors: 5 floors*
9 *Sanitary installations: combined bath and WC, indirect lighting*
10 *Balcony system: fire escape balconies on two sides*
11 *Staircase system: 1 concrete staircase*
12 *Staircase location: symmetrical*
13 *Staircase orientation: southwest*
14 *Living room orientation: southwest*
15 *Number of flats per main staircase: 2*
16 *Remarks: dining area, refuse chute*

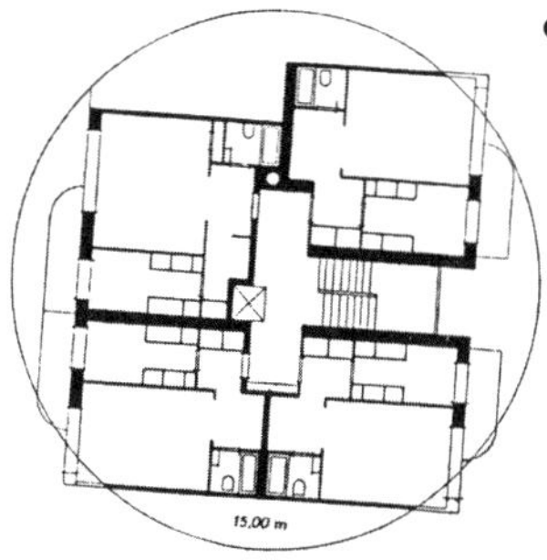

e
1 *Location: Stockholm*
2 *Client: unknown*
3 *Architect: unknown*
4 *Year built: 1928*
5 *Building style: enclosed block*
6 *Number of rooms: 2 rooms + 2 small rooms*
7 *Gross area: 41.80 m²*
8 *Number of floors: 4 floors*
9 *Sanitary installations: combined bath and WC, indirect lighting*
10 *Balcony system: no balconies*
11 *Staircase system: 1 concrete staircase*
12 *Staircase location: symmetrical*
13 *Staircase orientation: west*
14 *Living room orientation: west and east*
15 *Number of flats per main staircase: 4*
16 *Remarks: 4 flat per staircase, all walls are load-bearing, lift, refuse chute*

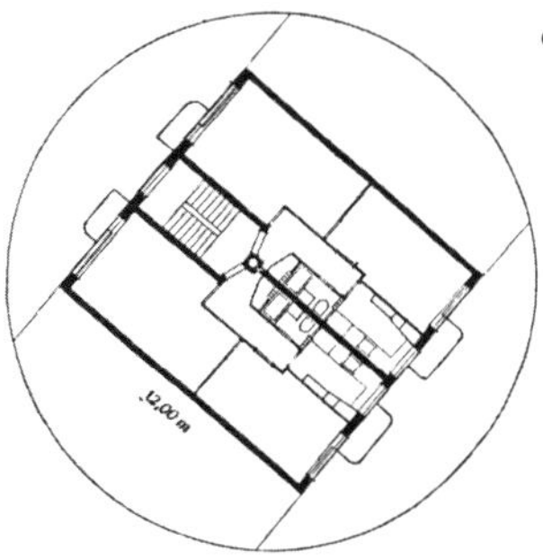

c
1 *Location: Ordrupvej 75 and 83*
2 *Client: Københavns almindelige Boligselskab (KAB)*
3 *Architect: Henning Jørgensen*
4 *Year built: 1934*
5 *Building style: ribbon development*
6 *Number of rooms: 2 rooms*
7 *Gross area: 63 m²*
8 *Number of floors: 5 floors*
9 *Sanitary installations: combined bath and WC, indirect lighting*
10 *Balcony system: fire escape balconies on two sides*
11 *Staircase system: 1 concrete staircase*
12 *Staircase location: symmetrical*
13 *Staircase orientation: northwest*
14 *Living room orientation: northwest*
15 *Number of flats per main staircase: 2*
16 *Remarks: dining area, refuse chute*

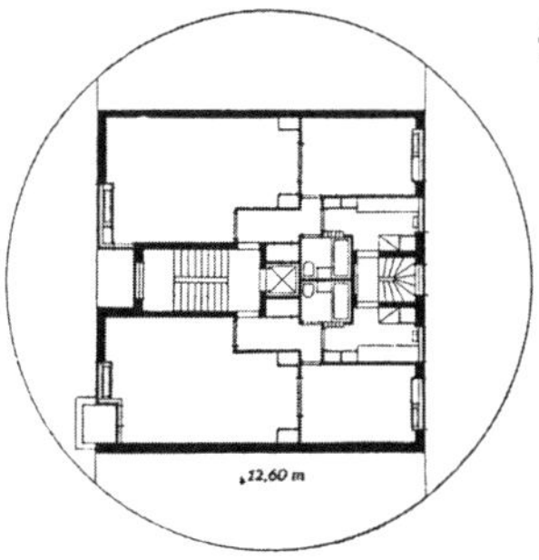

f
1 *Location: Rolighedsvej, Falkoner Allé, Sankt Nikolaj Vej, Hostrupsvej*
2 *Client: "Hostrups Have" A/S*
3 *Architect: H. Dahlerup Bertelsen*
4 *Year built: 1935–36*
5 *Building style: semi-enclosed block*
6 *Number of rooms: 2 rooms*
7 *Gross area: 78.4 m²*
8 *Number of floors: 6 floors*
9 *Sanitary installations: combined bath and WC, indirect lighting*
10 *Balcony system: some flats with balcony*
11 *Staircase system: 2 wooden staircases*
12 *Staircase location: symmetrical*
13 *Staircase orientation: west*
14 *Living room orientation: west*
15 *Number of flats per main staircase: 2*
16 *Remarks: lift*

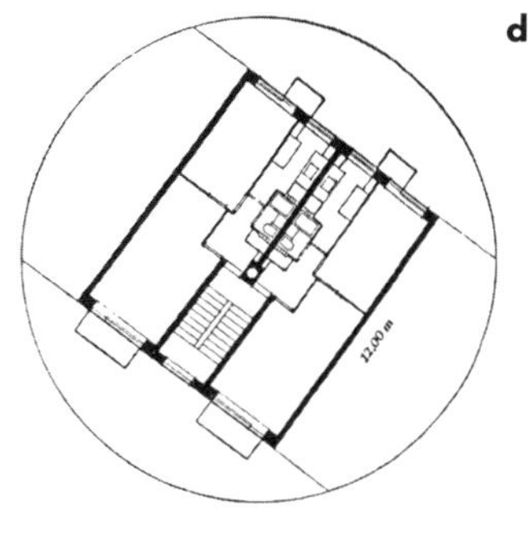

d
1 *Location: Torvegade, Prinsessegade, Skt. Annægade and Ved Volden*
2 *Client: Københavns almindelige Boligselskab (KAB)*
3 *Architect: Tyge Hvass*
4 *Year built: 1936*
5 *Building style: semi-enclosed block*
6 *Number of rooms: 2 rooms*
7 *Gross area: 60.0 m²*
8 *Number of floors: 6 floors*
9 *Sanitary installations: combined bath and WC, indirect lighting*
10 *Balcony system: fire escape balconies on two sides*
11 *Staircase system: 1 concrete staircase*
12 *Staircase location: symmetrical*
13 *Staircase orientation: southwest*
14 *Living room orientation: southwest*
15 *Number of flats per main staircase: 2*
16 *Remarks: dining area, refuse chute*

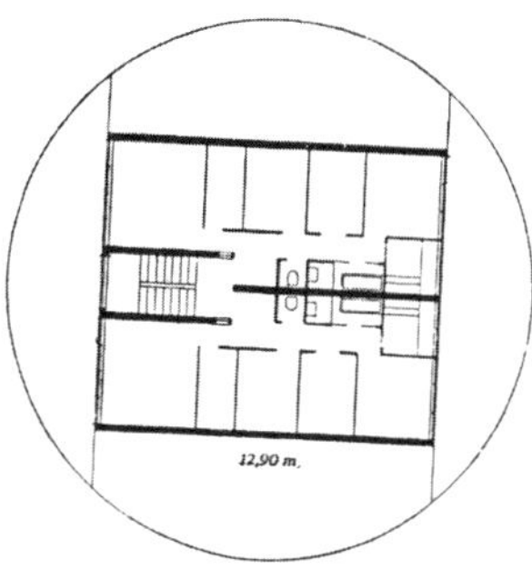

g
1 *Location: Stuttgart*
2 *Client: unknown*
3 *Architect: unknown*
4 *Year built: 1928*
5 *Building style: linear block*
6 *Number of rooms: 2 rooms + 3 small rooms*
7 *Gross area: 69.00 m²*
8 *Number of floors: 5 floors*
9 *Sanitary installations: combined bath and WC, indirect lighting*
10 *Balcony system: no balconies*
11 *Staircase system: 1 concrete staircase*
12 *Staircase location: symmetrical*
13 *Staircase orientation: west*
14 *Living room orientation: west*
15 *Number of flats per main staircase: 2*
16 *Remarks: load-bearing cross partitions, glass in upper walls over bedrooms*

Elaborated by Knud Bartholdy

Single staircase. Asymmetrical. *1:200 and 1:500*

IV

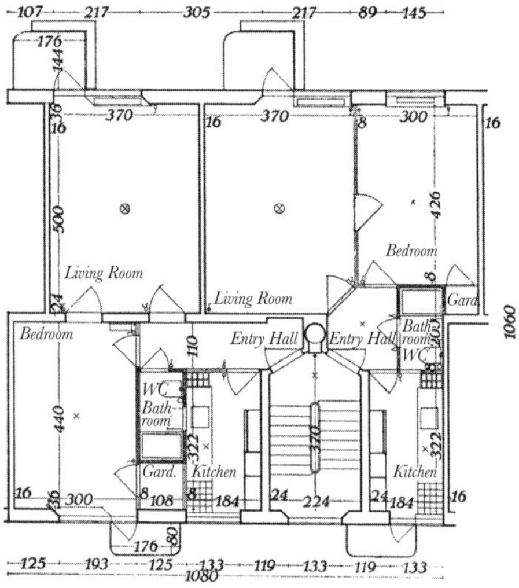

a
1 *Location: Tomsgårdsvej, Frederiksborgvej*
2 *Client: Storgaarden A/S*
3 *Architect: Povl Baumann and Knud Hansen*
4 *Year built: 1935*
5 *Building style: linear block*
6 *Number of rooms: 2 rooms*
7 *Gross area: 59.22 m² and 55.26 m²*
8 *Number of floors: 5 floors*
9 *Sanitary installations: combined bath and WC, indirect lighting*
10 *Balcony system: fire escape balconies on two sides*
11 *Staircase system: 1 concrete staircase*
12 *Staircase location: asymmetrical*
13 *Staircase orientation: northwest*
14 *Living room orientation: southeast*
15 *Number of flats per main staircase: 2*
16 *Remarks: asymmetrical type with different flats around the staircase; distinctive south facing type, further emphasised by the balcony screens on the north side.*

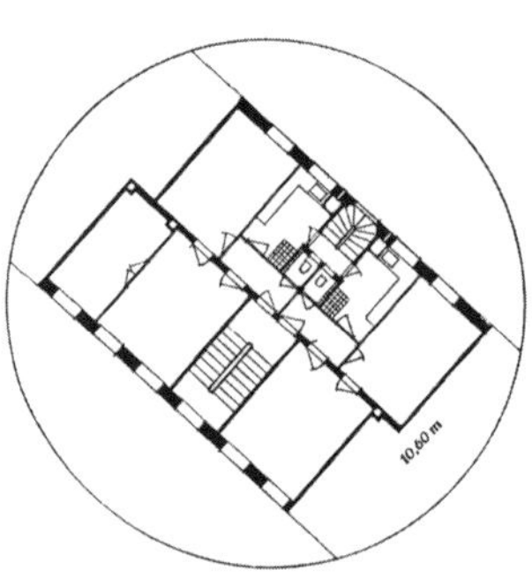

b
1 *Location: Struenseegade*
2 *Client: Municipality of Copenhagen*
3 *Architect: Povl Baumann*
4 *Year built: 1918*
5 *Building style: enclosed block*
6 *Number of rooms: 2 rooms + small room as well as 2 rooms*
7 *Gross area: 74.15 m² and 61.22 m²*
8 *Number of floors: 5 floors*
9 *Sanitary installations: WC, indirect lighting*
10 *Balcony system: none*
11 *Staircase system: 2 wooden staircases*
12 *Staircase location: symmetrical*
13 *Staircase orientation: southwest*
14 *Living room orientation: southwest*
15 *Number of flats per main staircase: 2*
16 *Remarks: the oldest and most widely used form of asymmetric flat groups*

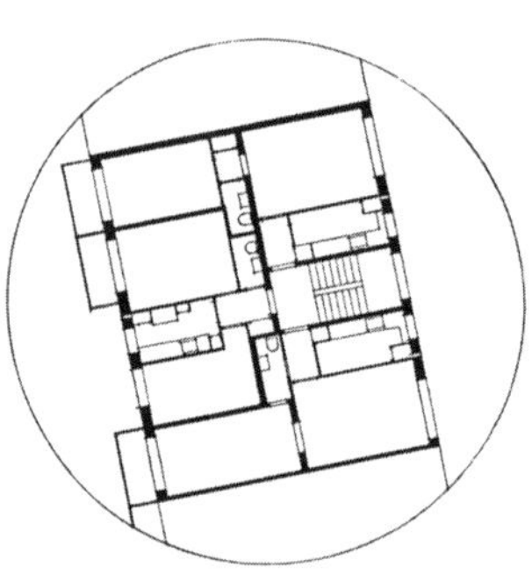

f
1 *Location: Vanløse Allé*
2 *Client: "Dalhusene" A/S*
3 *Architect: A. Skjøt-Pedersen*
4 *Year built: 1936*
5 *Building style: linear block*
6 *Number of rooms: 2 rooms*
7 *Gross area: 45.25 m², 50 m², 50.50 m²*
8 *Number of floors: 3 floors*
9 *Sanitary installations: combined bath and WC, shower, indirect lighting*
10 *Balcony system: balconies on one side*
11 *Staircase system: 1 concrete staircase*
12 *Staircase location: asymmetrical*
13 *Staircase orientation: east*
14 *Living room orientation: east and west*
15 *Number of flats per main staircase: 3*
16 *Remarks: type with 3 flats per staircase. Types of this kind will generally be asymmetrical. The type continues in IV_{45}*

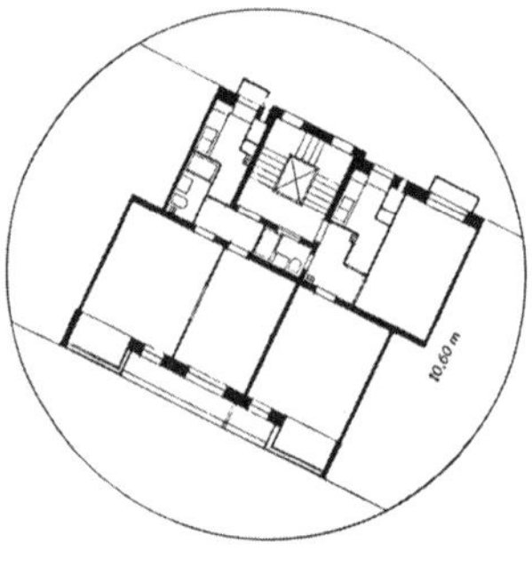

c
1 *Location: Langebrogade, Overgaden Oven Vandet*
2 *Client: "Voldgaarden" A/S*
3 *Architect: Jens Nielsen and Thorvald Dreyer*
4 *Year built: 1932*
5 *Building style: enclosed block*
6 *Number of rooms: 2 rooms*
7 *Gross area: 62 m²*
8 *Number of floors: 6 floors*
9 *Sanitary installations: combined bath and WC, indirect lighting*
10 *Balcony system: fire escape balcony on two sides*
11 *Staircase system: 1 concrete staircase*
12 *Staircase location: asymmetrical*
13 *Staircase orientation: north*
14 *Living room orientation: south*
15 *Number of flats per main staircase: 2*
16 *Remarks: lift*

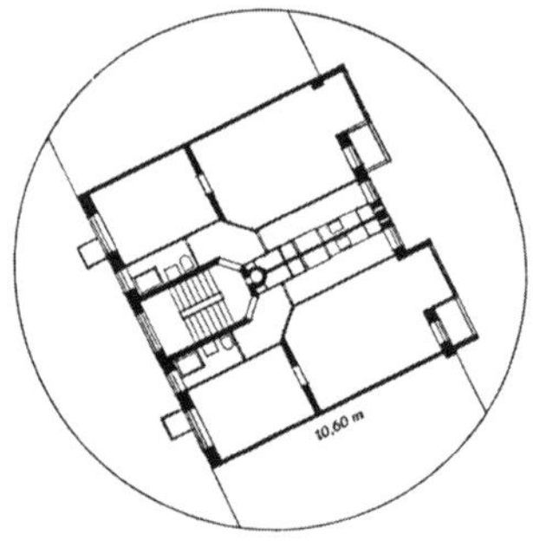

g
1 *Location: Struergade*
2 *Client: "Struergaarden" A/S*
3 *Architect: Thorvald Dreyer*
4 *Year built: 1935*
5 *Building style: ribbon development*
6 *Number of rooms: 2 rooms*
7 *Gross area: 64 m²*
8 *Number of floors: 6 floors*
9 *Sanitary installations: combined bath and WC, direct lighting*
10 *Balcony system: fire escape balconies on two sid*
11 *Staircase system: 1 concrete staircase*
12 *Staircase location: symmetrical*
13 *Staircase orientation: west*
14 *Living room orientation: east*
15 *Number of flats per main staircase: 2*
16 *Remarks: refuse chute*

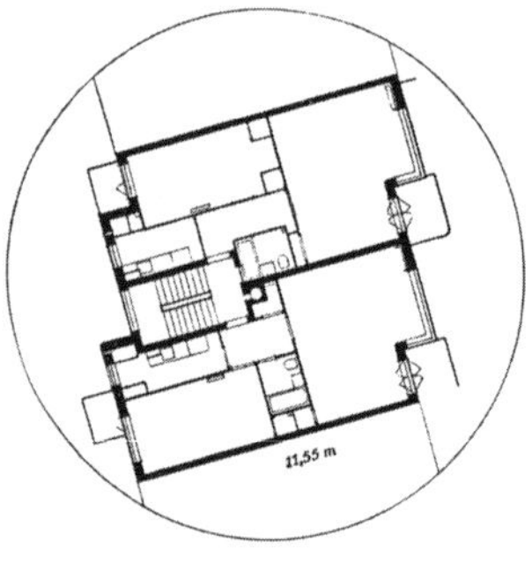

d
1 *Location: Skodsborg Strandvej*
2 *Client: "Høje Skodsborg" A/S*
3 *Architect: A. Wittmaack and V. Hvalsøe*
4 *Year built: 1936*
5 *Building style: linear block*
6 *Number of rooms: 2 rooms*
7 *Gross area: 72.2 m² and 73.5 m²*
8 *Number of floors: 3 floors*
9 *Sanitary installations: combined bath and WC, indirect lighting*
10 *Balcony system: balconies on two sides*
11 *Staircase system: 1 concrete staircase*
12 *Staircase location: symmetrical*
13 *Staircase orientation: west*
14 *Living room orientation: east*
15 *Number of flats per main staircase: 2*
16 *Remarks: refuse chute*

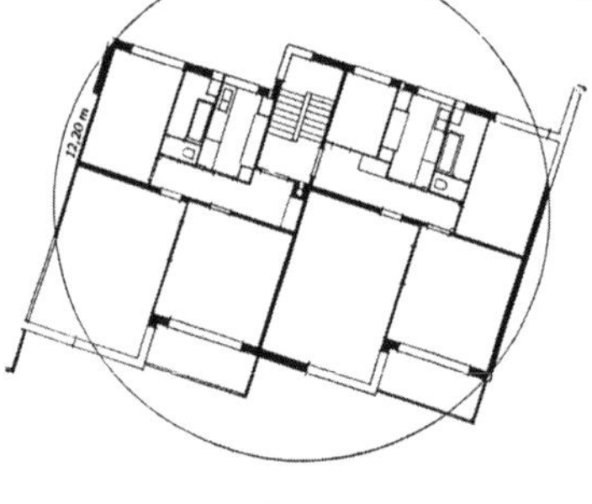

h
1 *Location: Klampenborg Strandvej*
2 *Client: "Bellavista" A/S*
3 *Architect: Arne Jacobsen*
4 *Year built: 1934*
5 *Building style: semi-enclosed block*
6 *Number of rooms: 3 room, 3 rooms + small ro*
7 *Gross area: 110 m² and 122 m²*
8 *Number of floors: 3*
9 *Sanitary installations: separate bath and WC, bath with direct lighting, WC with indirect ligh*
10 *Balcony system: balcony on one side*
11 *Staircase system: 1 concrete staircase*
12 *Staircase location: asymmetrical*
13 *Staircase orientation: north*
14 *Living room orientation: south*
15 *Number of flats per main staircase: 2*
16 *Remarks: refuse chute*

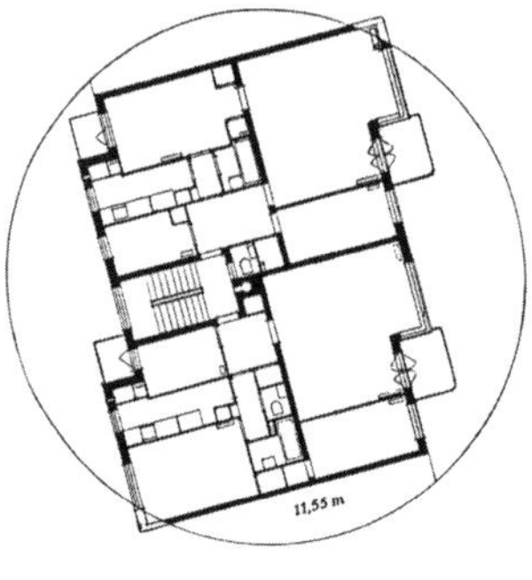

e
1 *Location: Skodsborg Strandvej*
2 *Client: "Høje Skodsborg" A/S*
3 *Architect: A. Wittmaack and V. Hvalsøe*
4 *Year built: 1936*
5 *Building style: linear block*
6 *Number of rooms: 2 rooms + 2 small rooms*
7 *Gross area: 95 m² and 94.3 m²*
8 *Number of floors: 3 floors*
9 *Sanitary installations: combined bath and WC, indirect lighting*
10 *Balcony system: balconies on two sides*
11 *Staircase system: 1 concrete staircase*
12 *Staircase location: symmetrical*
13 *Staircase orientation: west*
14 *Living room orientation: east*
15 *Number of flats per main staircase: 2*
16 *Remarks: refuse chute*

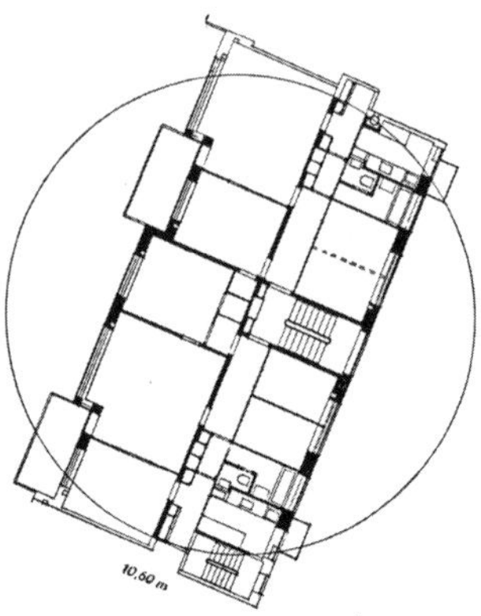

i
1 *Location: Vagtelvej*
2 *Client: "Godthaabsvænge" A/S*
3 *Architect: Hans Hansen and Alvar Lauritzen*
4 *Year built: 1935*
5 *Building style: linear block*
6 *Number of rooms: variable*
7 *Gross area: 118 m² and 100 m²*
8 *Number of floors: 4 floors*
9 *Sanitary installations: separate bath and WC, bath with direct lighting, WC with indirect ligh*
10 *Balcony system: balcony on one side*
11 *Staircase system: 2 wooden staircases*
12 *Staircase location: asymmetrical*
13 *Staircase orientation: east*
14 *Living room orientation: west*
15 *Number of flats per main staircase: 2*
16 *Remarks: concrete floor division, refuse chute*

Elaborated by Erik Dahl

Single staircase. Reduced floor depth *(under 9.50 m.)*

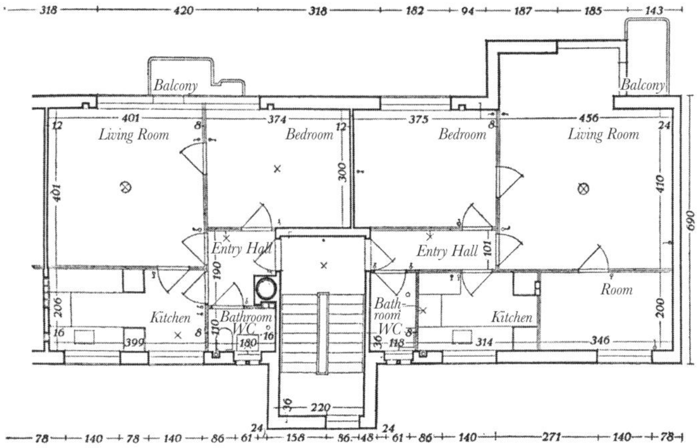

a
1 *Location: Tuborgvej*
2 *Client: Journalistforbundet*
3 *Architect: Vilhelm Lauritzen*
4 *Year built: 1935*
5 *Building style: linear block*
6 *Number of rooms: 2 rooms and 2 rooms + small room*
7 *Gross area: 50.2 m² and 88.5 m²*
8 *Number of floors: 3 floors*
9 *Sanitary installations: combined bath and WC, direct lighting*
10 *Balcony system: south-facing balcony*
11 *Staircase system: 1 wooden staircase*
12 *Staircase location: symmetrical*
13 *Staircase orientation: north*
14 *Living room orientation: south*
15 *Number of flats per main staircase: 2*
16 *Remarks: The type is a distinct north-south facing type, with all secondary rooms, such as kitchen, bath, WC, as well as main stairwell, facing north. In this location, the bathroom receives direct light. In the two-room type, the dining area of the kitchen is very well lit. As the floor depth is reduced, the traditional longitudinal main partition space can be avoided, allowing room planning in the floor plan to be much more elastic. The type allows for living rooms with windows in the longitudinal wall. The large outer wall area is partially offset by the small free-standing spans of the joist systems. The shallow floor depth often requires the staircases to be projected outward.*

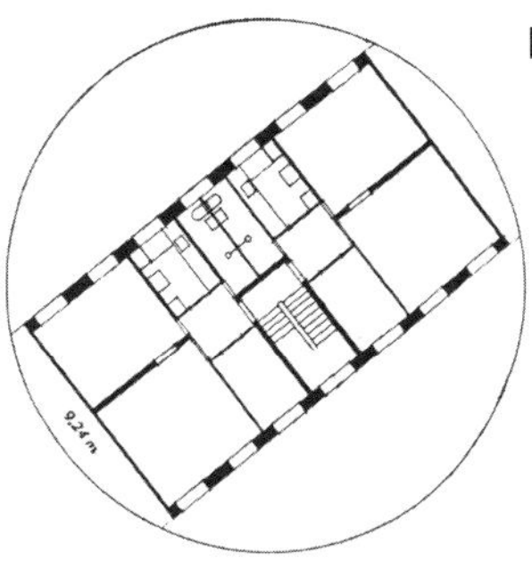

b
1 *Location: Hulgårdsvej*
2 *Client: Københavns almindelige Boligselskab (KAB)*
3 *Architect: Ivar Bentsen and Th. Henningsen*
4 *Year built: 1921*
5 *Building style: linear block*
6 *Number of rooms: 2 rooms + small room*
7 *Gross area: 75.7 m²*
8 *Number of floors: 3*
9 *Sanitary installations: bath and WC, direct lighting*
10 *Balcony system: none*
11 *Staircase system: 1 wooden staircase*
12 *Staircase location: symmetrical*
13 *Staircase orientation: southwest*
14 *Living room orientation: southwest*
15 *Number of flats per main staircase: 2*
16 *Remarks: 3 floors, therefore only a single staircase system*

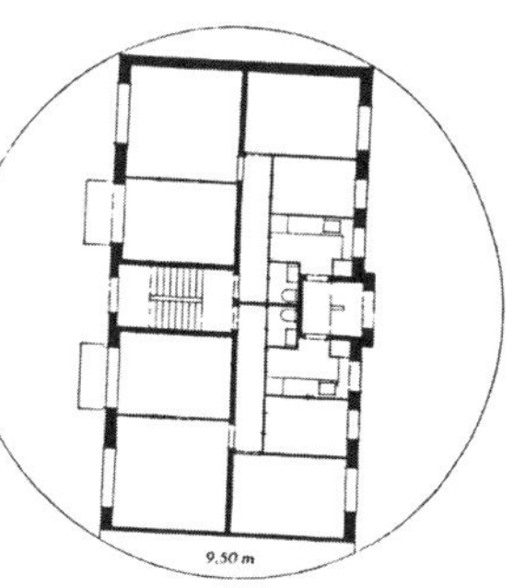

c
1 *Location: Frederiksborgvej*
2 *Client: "Boparken" A/S*
3 *Architect: Th. Dreyer*
4 *Year built: 1935*
5 *Building style: linear block*
6 *Number of rooms: 3 rooms + small room*
7 *Gross area: 80.80 m²*
8 *Number of floors: 5 floors*
9 *Sanitary installations: combined bath and WC, indirect lighting*
10 *Balcony system: west-facing balcony*
11 *Staircase system: 2 wooden staircases*
12 *Staircase location: symmetrical*
13 *Staircase orientation: west*
14 *Living room orientation: west*
15 *Number of flats per main staircase: 2*
16 *Remarks: none*

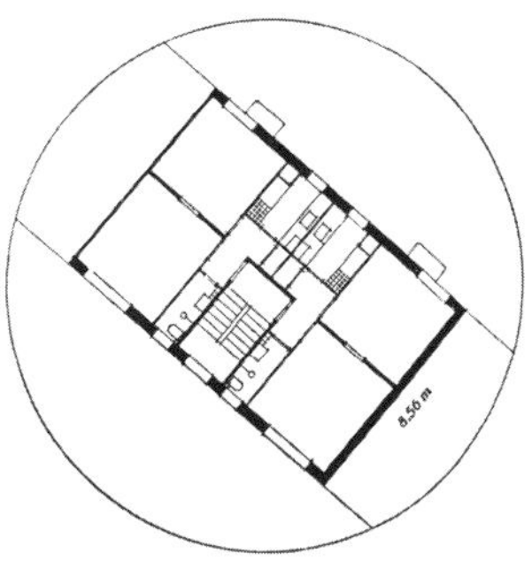

d
1 *Location: Emil Pipers Vej, Lyngby*
2 *Client: Privat*
3 *Architect: Aa. and F. Thilo*
4 *Year built: 1934*
5 *Building style: semi-enclosed block*
6 *Number of rooms: 2 rooms*
7 *Gross area: 54 m²*
8 *Number of floors: 3 floors*
9 *Sanitary installations: shower and WC, direct lighting*
10 *Balcony system: northeast-facing fire escape balcony*
11 *Staircase system: 1 wooden staircase*
12 *Staircase location: symmetrical*
13 *Staircase orientation: southwest*
14 *Living room orientation: southwest*
15 *Number of flats per main staircase: 2*
16 *Remarks: none*

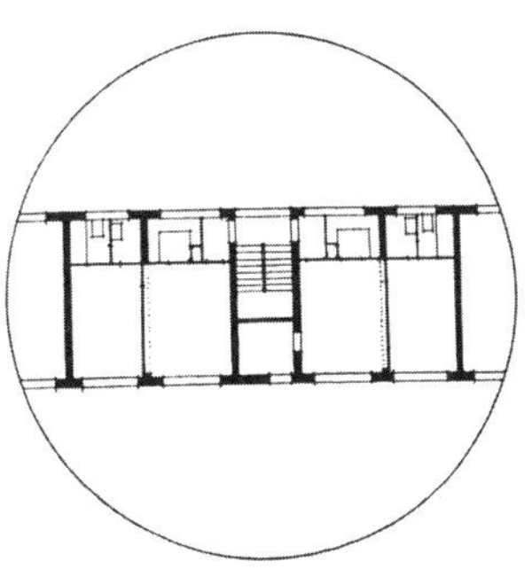

e
1 *Location: Frankfurt*
2 *Client: Municipality of Frankfurt*
3 *Architect: Ernst May*
4 *Year built: 1930*
5 *Building style: linear block*
6 *Number of rooms: 2 rooms and 2 rooms + small room*
7 *Gross area: 77.5 m²*
8 *Number of floors: 3 floors*
9 *Sanitary installations: bath and WC, direct lighting*
10 *Balcony system: none*
11 *Staircase system: 1 concrete staircase*
12 *Staircase location: symmetrical*
13 *Staircase orientation: west*
14 *Living room orientation: west*
15 *Number of flats per main staircase: 2*
16 *Remarks: none*

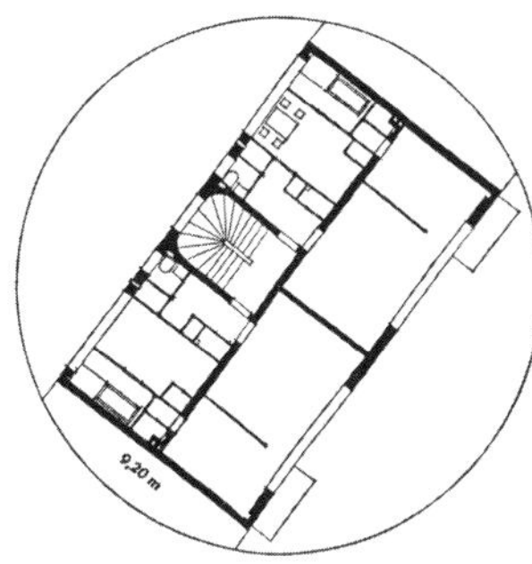

f
1 *Location: Hästholmen, Stockholm*
2 *Client: "Kooperativa Förbundet" (KF)*
3 *Architect: Eskil Sundahl*
4 *Year built: 1933*
5 *Building style: linear block*
6 *Number of rooms: 2 rooms and dining area*
7 *Gross area: 53 m²*
8 *Number of floors: 3 floors*
9 *Sanitary installations: separate bath and WC, direct lighting*
10 *Balcony system: connecting balconies*
11 *Staircase system: 1 concrete staircase*
12 *Staircase location: symmetrical*
13 *Staircase orientation: northwest*
14 *Living room orientation: southeast*
15 *Number of flats per main staircase: 2*
16 *Remarks: partition in living room*

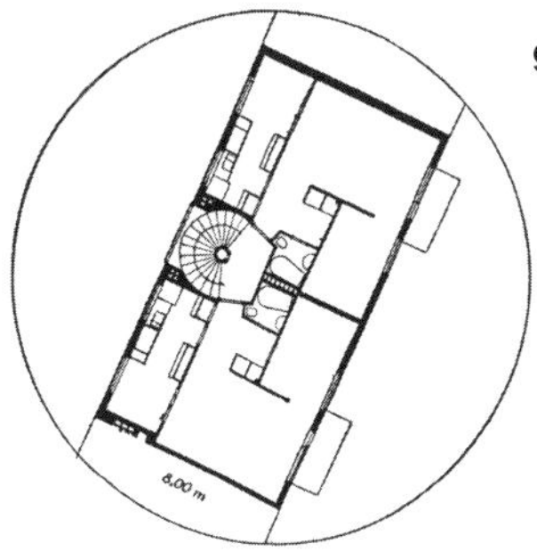

g
1 *Location: Traneberg, Stockholm*
2 *Client: Byggnadsfirman Lundberg & Blom*
3 *Architect: Holger Blom*
4 *Year built: 1935*
5 *Building style: linear block*
6 *Number of rooms: 2 rooms and 3 rooms*
7 *Gross area: 60.8 m²*
8 *Number of floors: 3 floors*
9 *Sanitary installations: combined bath and WC, direct lighting*
10 *Balcony system: balcony on one side*
11 *Staircase system: 1 concrete staircase*
12 *Staircase location: symmetrical*
13 *Staircase orientation: west*
14 *Living room orientation: west*
15 *Number of flats per main staircase: 2*
16 *Remarks: none*

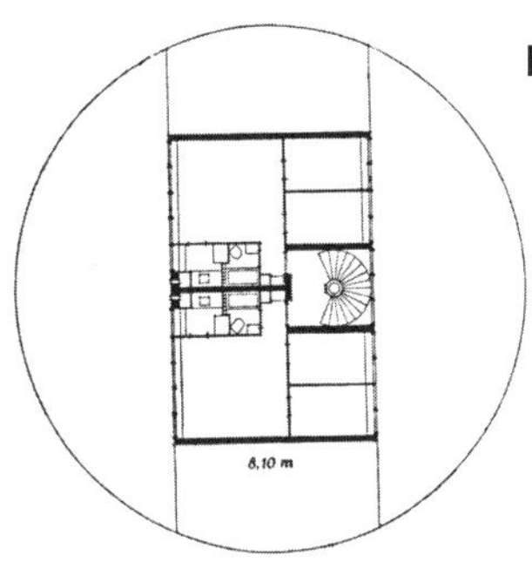

h
1 *Location: "Hjorthagen", Stockholm*
2 *Client: private*
3 *Architect: Hakon Ahlberg*
4 *Year built: 1935*
5 *Building style: linear block*
6 *Number of rooms: 1 room + small room*
7 *Gross area: 36 and 41 m²*
8 *Number of floors: 3 floors*
9 *Sanitary installations: combined bath and WC, direct lighting*
10 *Balcony system: none*
11 *Staircase system: 1 staircase*
12 *Staircase location: symmetrical*
13 *Staircase orientation: northeast*
14 *Living room orientation: southwest*
15 *Number of flats per main staircase: 2*
16 *Remarks: none*

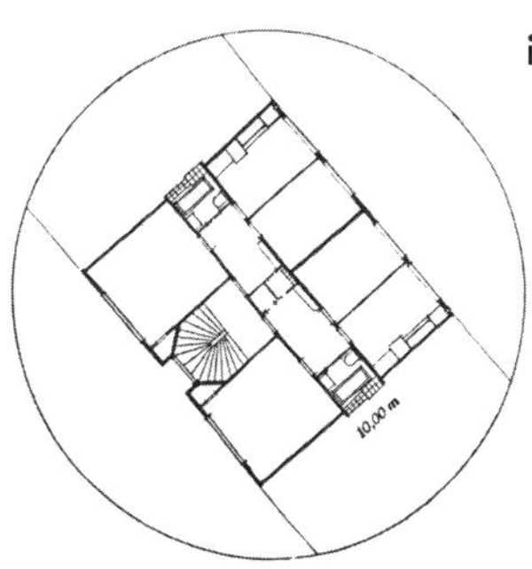

i
1 *Location: Gothenburg*
2 *Client: "H. S. B."*
3 *Architect: unknown*
4 *Year built: 1931*
5 *Building style: linear block*
6 *Number of rooms: 1 room + small room*
7 *Gross area: 52 m²*
8 *Number of floors: 2 floors*
9 *Sanitary installations: combined bath and WC, indirect lighting*
10 *Balcony system: none*
11 *Staircase system: 1 staircase*
12 *Staircase location: symmetrical*
13 *Staircase orientation: southwest*
14 *Living room orientation: southwest*
15 *Number of flats per main staircase: 2*
16 *Remarks: 'Governor's House', (1 brick floor with 2 upper floors of wood)*

Elaborated by Poul Møller

Single staircase. Several small rooms. *1:200 and 1:500*

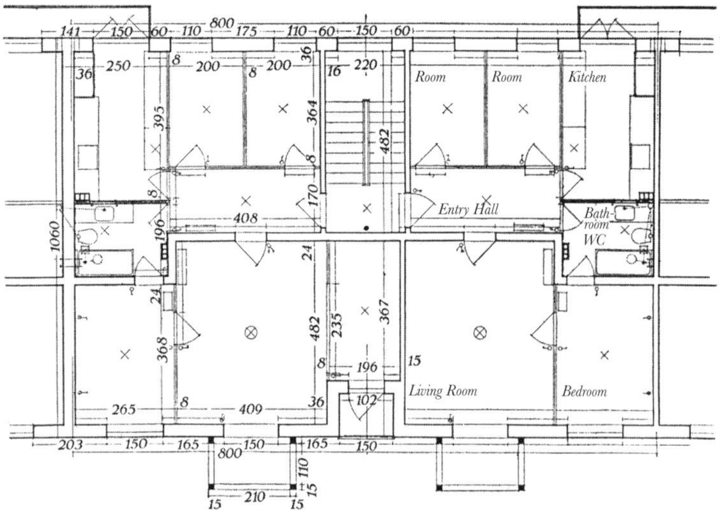

a
1 *Location: Sankt Kjelds Gade – Ourøgade – Langøgade – Vejrøgade*
2 *Client: Københavns almindelige Boligselskab (KAB), "Solgaarden"*
3 *Architect: Henning Hansen*
4 *Year built: 1929–30*
5 *Building style: semi-enclosed block*
6 *Number of rooms: 2 rooms + 2 small rooms*
7 *Gross area: 78.45 m²*
8 *Number of floors: 5 floors*
9 *Sanitary installations: combined bath and WC, indirect lighting*
10 *Balcony system: connecting balconies, loggia*
11 *Staircase system: 1 concrete staircase*
12 *Staircase location: symmetrical*
13 *Staircase orientation: east*
14 *Living room orientation: west*
15 *Number of flats per main staircase: 2*
16 *Remarks: South-facing oriel windows and balconies. One of the small rooms can be used as a dining room because of its location near the living room with connecting doors. If they are used as bedrooms, then it is useful that all doors from the small rooms lead only to the entry hall, but it would have been more advantageous to have them grouped independently. The small rooms are under the legal minimum size.*

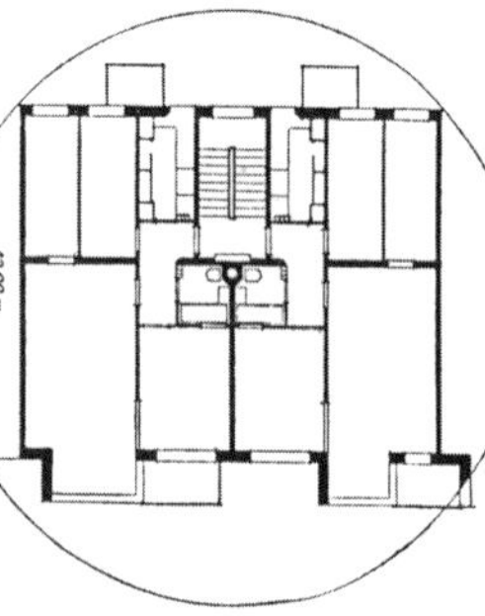

b
1 *Location: Strandvejen, Hellerup*
2 *Client: "Blidah" A/S*
3 *Architect: Kooperative Arkitekter for the following type*
4 *Year built: 1934*
5 *Building style: linear block*
6 *Number of rooms: 2 rooms + 2 small rooms*
7 *Gross area: 93 m²*
8 *Number of floors: 3 floors*
9 *Sanitary installations: combined bath and WC, indirect lighting*
10 *Balcony system: balcony on both sides*
11 *Staircase system: 1 wooden staircase*
12 *Staircase location: symmetrical*
13 *Staircase orientation: east*
14 *Living room orientation: west*
15 *Number of flats per main staircase: 2*
16 *Remarks: refuse chute, south-facing oriel windows, large house width*

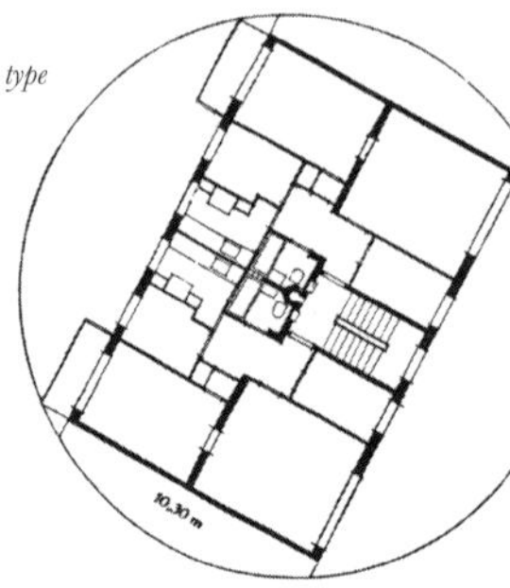

f
1 *Location: C. F. Richs Vej*
2 *Client: "Ringparken" A/S*
3 *Architect: A. Skjøt-Pedersen*
4 *Year built: 1935*
5 *Building style: linear block*
6 *Number of rooms: 2 rooms + 2 small rooms*
7 *Gross area: 79 m²*
8 *Number of floors: 3 floors*
9 *Sanitary installations: combined bath and WC, indirect lighting*
10 *Balcony system: connecting balconies*
11 *Staircase system: 1 wooden staircase*
12 *Staircase location: symmetrical*
13 *Staircase orientation: east*
14 *Living room orientation: east*
15 *Number of flats per main staircase: 2*
16 *Remarks: refuse chute*

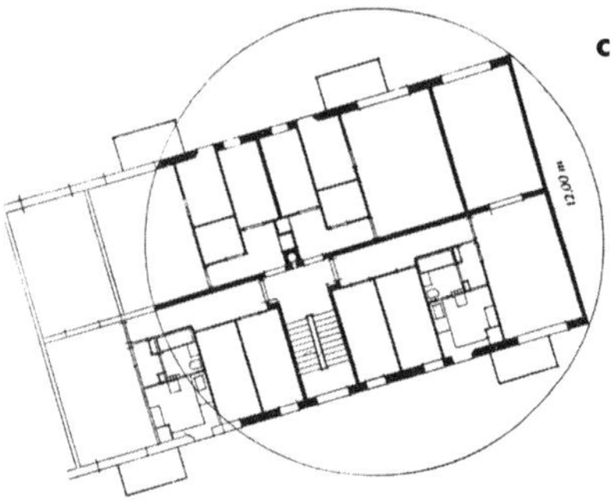

c
1 *Location: Strandvejen, Hellerup*
2 *Client: "Blidah" A/S*
3 *Architect: Ivar Bentsen, Jørgen U. Berg, Acton Bjørn*
4 *Year built: 1933*
5 *Building style: linear block*
6 *Number of rooms: 2 rooms + 2 small room*
7 *Gross area: 91 m²*
8 *Number of floors: 3 floors*
9 *Sanitary installations: combined bath and WC, indirect lighting*
10 *Balcony system: balcony on one side*
11 *Staircase system: 1 wooden staircase*
12 *Staircase location: symmetrical*
13 *Staircase orientation: west*
14 *Living room orientation: west*
15 *Number of flats per main staircase: 4*
16 *Remarks: 4 flats per staircase, refuse chute*

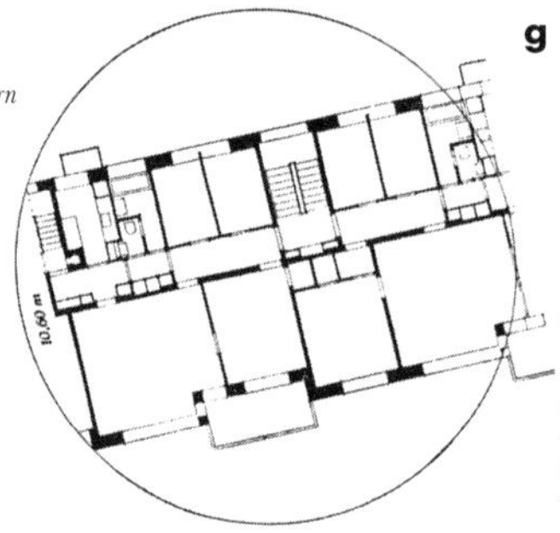

g
1 *Location: Vagtelvej*
2 *Client: "Godthaabsvænget" A/S*
3 *Architect: Hans Hansen, Alvar Lauritzen*
4 *Year built: 1935*
5 *Building style: linear block*
6 *Number of rooms: 2 rooms + 2 small rooms*
7 *Gross area: 102 m²*
8 *Number of floors: 4 floors*
9 *Sanitary installations: bath, direct lighting, WC, indirect lighting*
10 *Balcony system: balcony on both sides*
11 *Staircase system: 2 wooden staircases*
12 *Staircase location: symmetrical*
13 *Staircase orientation: east*
14 *Living room orientation: west*
15 *Number of flats per main staircase: 2*
16 *Remarks: concrete floor division, refuse chute*

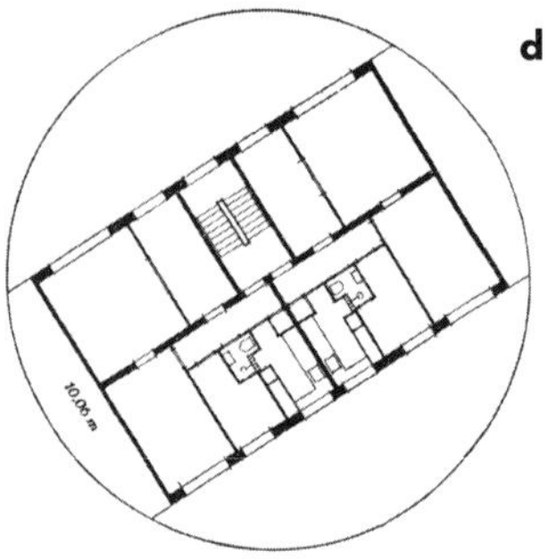

d
1 *Location: Vibevej*
2 *Client: Københavns almindelige Boligselskab (KAB)*
3 *Architect: E. Monberg*
4 *Year built: 1930*
5 *Building style: semi-enclosed block*
6 *Number of rooms: 2 rooms + 2 small rooms*
7 *Gross area: 81 m²*
8 *Number of floors: 3 floors with habitable attic*
9 *Sanitary installations: combined shower and WC, indirect lighting*
10 *Balcony system: none*
11 *Staircase system: 1 wooden staircase*
12 *Staircase location: symmetrical*
13 *Staircase orientation: northwest*
14 *Living room orientation: southwest*
15 *Number of flats per main staircase: 2*
16 *Remarks: none*

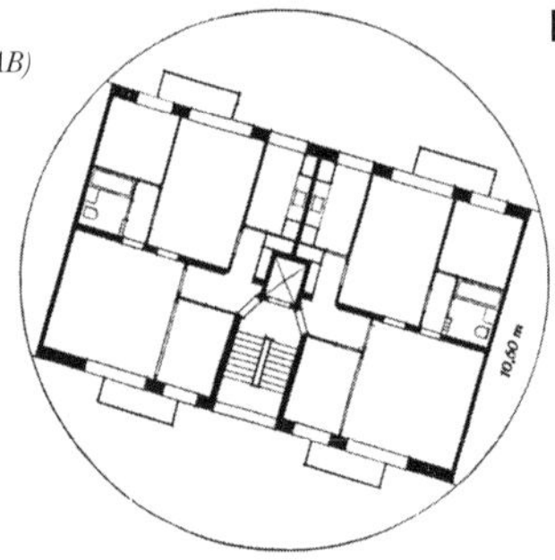

h
1 *Location: Godthåbsvej*
2 *Client: "Grønnehavegaard" A/S*
3 *Architect: Eske Kristensen and Mogens Meyling*
4 *Year built: 1934*
5 *Building style: semi-enclosed block*
6 *Number of rooms: 2 rooms + 2 small rooms*
7 *Gross area: 87 m²*
8 *Number of floors: 5 floors*
9 *Sanitary installations: combined bath and WC, indirect lighting*
10 *Balcony system: fire escape balcony on both sides*
11 *Staircase system: 1 concrete staircase*
12 *Staircase location: symmetrical*
13 *Staircase orientation: south*
14 *Living room orientation: south*
15 *Number of flats per main staircase: 2*
16 *Remarks: lift*

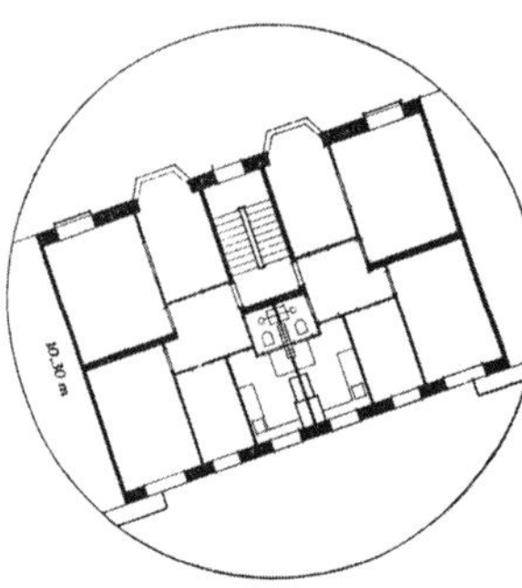

e
1 *Location: Vigerslev Allé*
2 *Client: Københavns almindelige Boligselskab (KAB)*
3 *Architect: Wittmaack and Hvalsøe*
4 *Year built: 1930*
5 *Building style: semi-enclosed block*
6 *Number of rooms: 2 rooms + 2 small rooms*
7 *Gross area: 78 m2*
8 *Number of floors: 5 floors*
9 *Sanitary installations: WC and shower, indirect lighting*
10 *Balcony system: connecting balconies*
11 *Staircase system: 1 concrete staircase*
12 *Staircase location: symmetrical*
13 *Staircase orientation: south*
14 *Living room orientation: south*
15 *Number of flats per main staircase: 2*
16 *Remarks: none*

i
1 *Location: Vester Søgade*
2 *Client: "Vestersøhus" A/S*
3 *Architect: Kay Fisker and C. F. Møller*
4 *Year built: 1936*
5 *Building style: enclosed block*
6 *Number of rooms: 2 rooms + 2 small rooms*
7 *Gross area: 106 m²*
8 *Number of floors: 7 floors*
9 *Sanitary installations: separate bath and WC, indirect lighting*
10 *Balcony system: 1 balcony*
11 *Staircase system: 2 wooden staircases*
12 *Staircase location: asymmetrical*
13 *Staircase orientation: east*
14 *Living room orientation: west*
15 *Number of flats per main staircase: 2*
16 *Remarks: lift, refuse chute, concrete floor division, large house depth*

Elaborated by Peter Sandholt

Single staircase. Easily modifiable. *1:200 and 1:500*

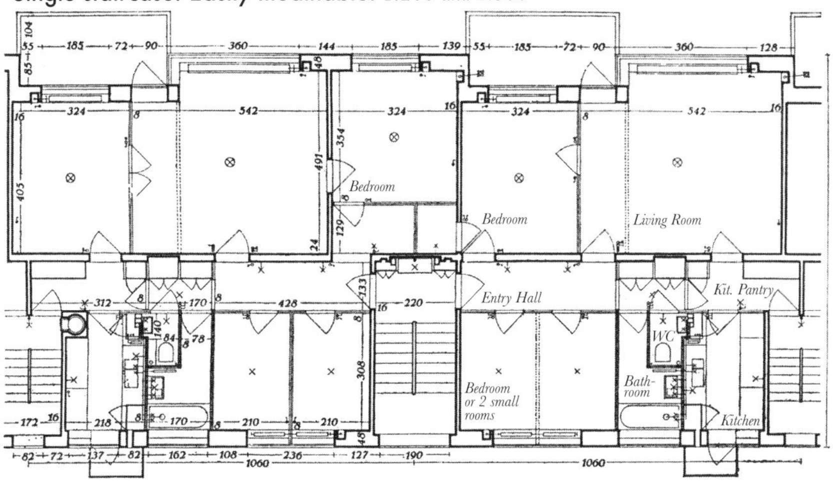

1 *Location: Godthåbsvej, Frederiksberg*
2 *Client: "Godthaabsvænget" A/S*
3 *Architect: Hans Hansen and Alvar Lauritzen*
4 *Year built: 1935*
5 *Building style: parallel block*
6 *Number of rooms: 3 rooms or 2 rooms + 2 small rooms, 4 rooms or 3 rooms + 2 small rooms*
7 *Gross area: 95–110 m²*
8 *Number of floors: 4 floors*
9 *Sanitary installations: separate bath and WC, bath with direct lighting*
10 *Balcony system: balcony on one side*
11 *Staircase system: 2 wooden staircases*
12 *Staircase location: asymmetrical*
13 *Staircase orientation: east*
14 *Living room orientation: west*
15 *Number of flats per main staircase: 2*
16 *Remarks: the size of the dining and living rooms can be modified. The partition between the small rooms can be removed and they can be transformed into a single large bedroom.*

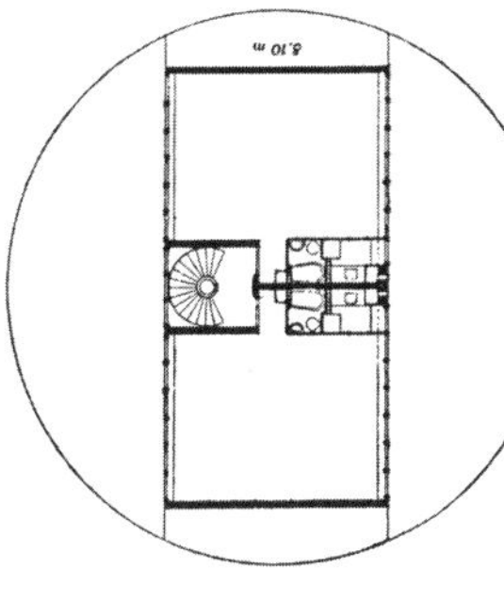

b
1 *Location: Stockholm*
2 *Client: exhibition project*
3 *Architect: Niels Ahrbom, Helge Zimdahl*
4 *Year built: 1933*
5 *Building style: linear block*
6 *Number of rooms: variable*
7 *Gross area: 62.78 m²*
8 *Number of floors: 3 floors*
9 *Sanitary installations: combined bath and WC, indirect lighting*
10 *Balcony system: none*
11 *Staircase system: 1 concrete staircase*
12 *Staircase location: symmetrical*
13 *Staircase orientation: southeast*
14 *Living room orientation: northwest*
15 *Number of flats per main staircase: 2*
16 *Remarks: none*

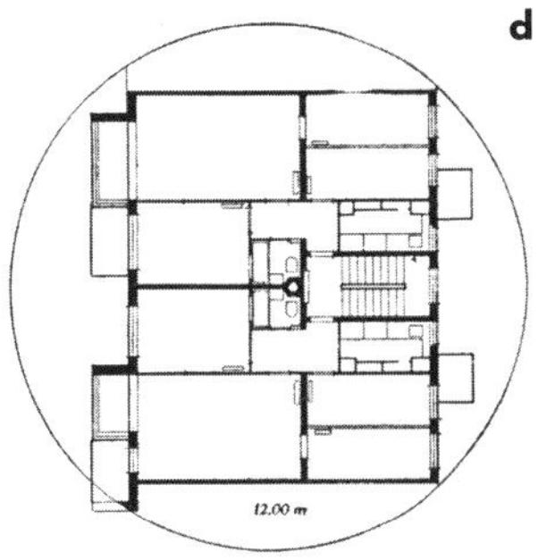

d
1 *Location: Strandvejen, Copenhagen*
2 *Client: "Blidah" A/S*
3 *Architect: Kooperative Arkitekter*
4 *Year built: 1934*
5 *Building style: row houses*
6 *Number of rooms: 2 rooms + 2 small rooms (3 rooms)*
7 *Gross area: 92.85 m²*
8 *Number of floors: 3 floors*
9 *Sanitary installations: combined bath and WC, indirect lighting*
10 *Balcony system: balconies on two sides*
11 *Staircase system: 1 wooden staircase*
12 *Staircase location: symmetrical*
13 *Staircase orientation: east*
14 *Living room orientation: west*
15 *Number of flats per main staircase: 2*
16 *Remarks: none*

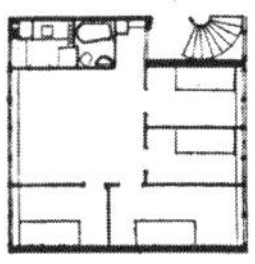
1

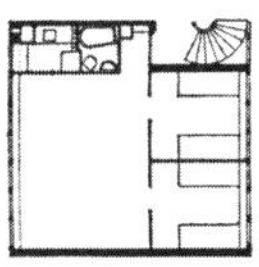
2

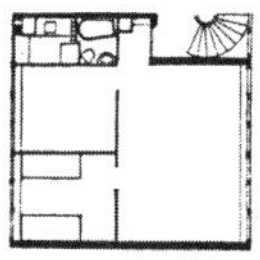
3

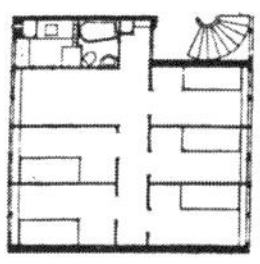
4

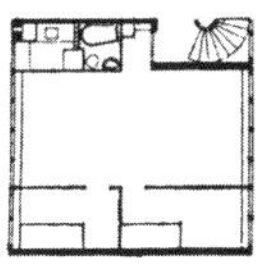
5

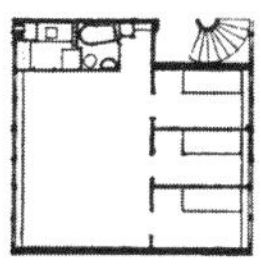
6

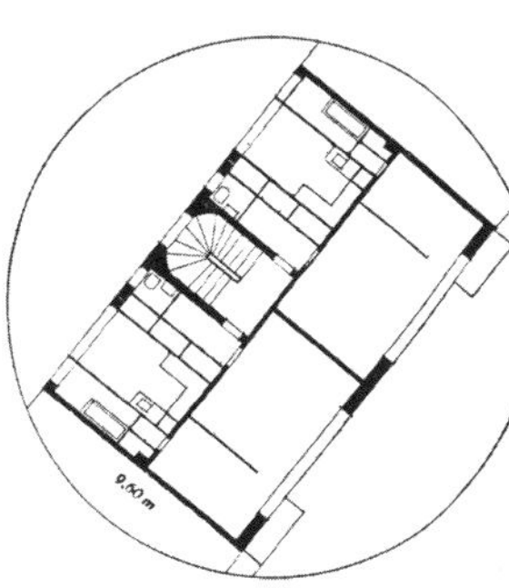

e
1 *Location: Hästholmen Stockholm*
2 *Client: Kooperativa Förbundet (KF)*
3 *Architect: Eskil Sunddahl*
4 *Year built: 1933*
5 *Building style: linear block*
6 *Number of rooms: 1 room + small room*
7 *Gross area: 74 m²*
8 *Number of floors: 3 floors*
9 *Sanitary installations: separate WC and bath, direct lighting*
10 *Balcony system: connecting balconies*
11 *Staircase system: 1 concrete staircase*
12 *Staircase location: symmetrical*
13 *Staircase orientation: north*
14 *Living room orientation: south*
15 *Number of flats per main staircase: 2*
16 *Remarks: combined bath and laundry room, variable location of partitions in the living room*

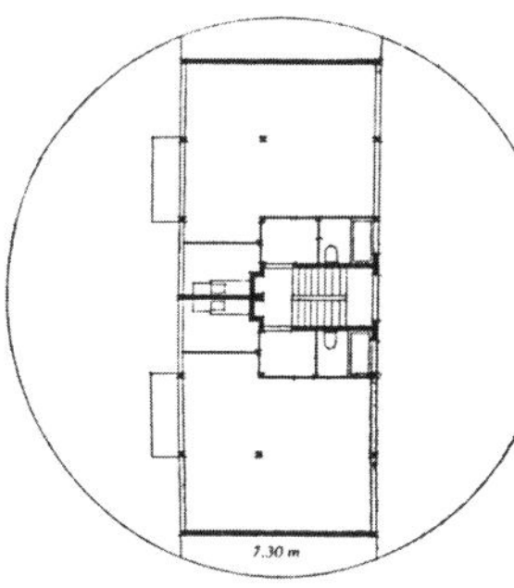

c
1 *Location: Stuttgart*
2 *Client: Weissenhofsiedlung*
3 *Architect: Mies van der Rohe*
4 *Year built: 1927*
5 *Building style: linear block*
6 *Number of rooms: variable*
7 *Gross area: 56.84 m²*
8 *Number of floors: 3 floors*
9 *Sanitary installations: combined bath and WC, direct lighting*
10 *Balcony system: balcony on one side*
11 *Staircase system: 1 concrete staircase*
12 *Staircase location: symmetrical*
13 *Staircase orientation: east*
14 *Living room orientation: west*
15 *Number of flats per main staircase: 2*
16 *Remarks: none*

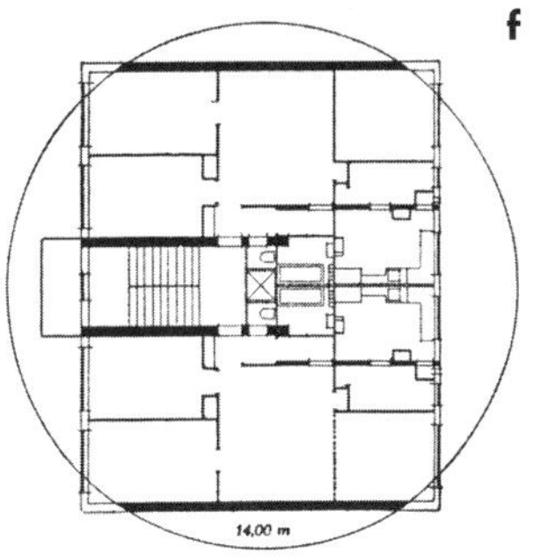

f
1 *Location: Åbo, Finland*
2 *Client: private*
3 *Architect: Aino and Alvar Aalto*
4 *Year built: 1927*
5 *Building style: linear block*
6 *Number of rooms: variable*
7 *Gross area: 116.9 m²*
8 *Number of floors: 6 floors*
9 *Sanitary installations: separate WC and bath, direct lighting*
10 *Balcony system: none*
11 *Staircase system: 1 concrete staircase*
12 *Staircase location: symmetrical*
13 *Staircase orientation: west*
14 *Living room orientation: -*
15 *Number of flats per main staircase: 2*
16 *Remarks: load-bearing cross partitions, all other partitions variable. Refuse chute.*

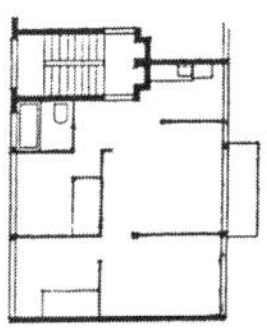
1

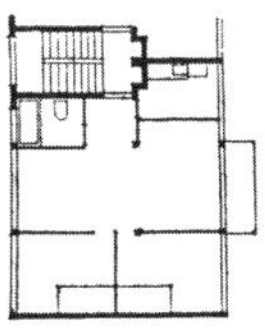
2

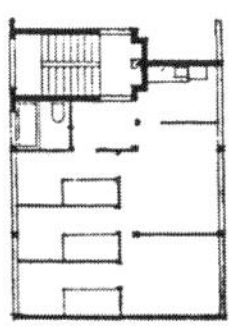
3

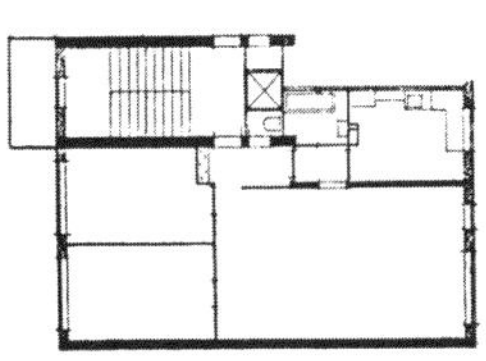
1

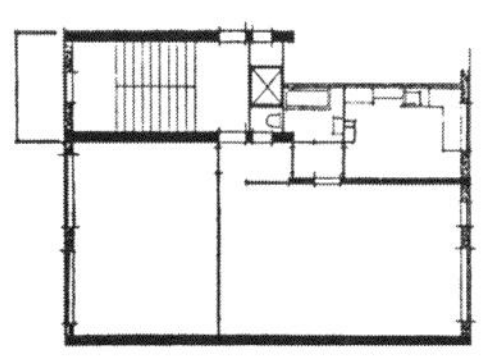
2

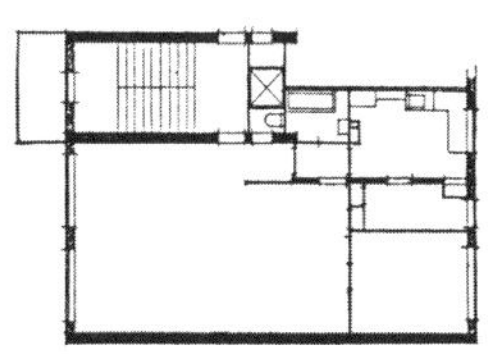
3

Single staircase. Three flats per staircase. *1:200 and 1:500*

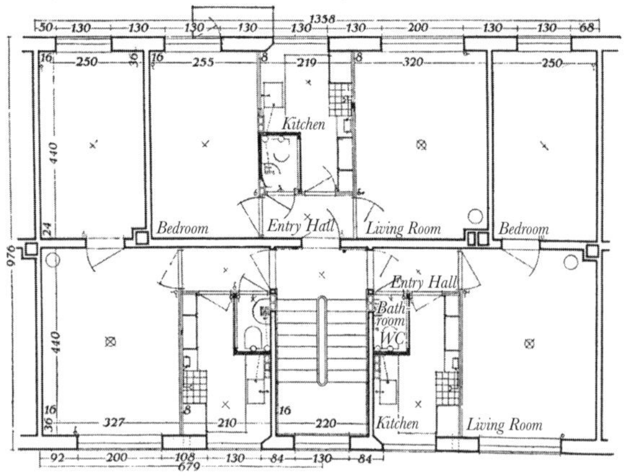

a
1 *Location: Rentemestervej*
2 *Client: Municipality of Copenhagen*
3 *Architect: E. Monberg*
4 *Year built: 1934*
5 *Building style: linear block*
6 *Number of rooms: 2 rooms*
7 *Gross area: 35 m²*
8 *Number of floors: 3 floors*
9 *Sanitary installations: combined bath and WC, indirect lighting*
10 *Balcony system: single-side flat with 1 balcony*
11 *Staircase system: 1 wooden staircase*
12 *Staircase location: symmetric*
13 *Staircase orientation: east and west*
14 *Living room orientation: east and west*
15 *Number of flats per main staircase: 3*
16 *Remarks: cost-effective concentration relative to the staircase. The single-side flat ought to have artificial ventilation. Its separation of the two rooms requires a distinct use of these as a living room and a bedroom.*

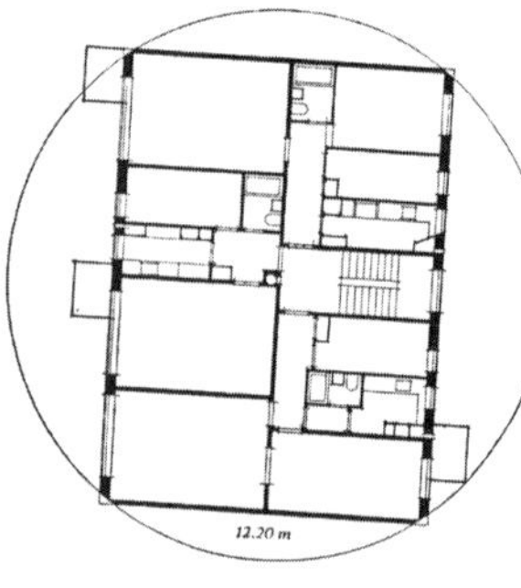

b
1 *Location: Maglemosevej, Hellerup*
2 *Client: "Blidah" A/S*
3 *Architect: Ivar Bentsen, Jørgen U. Berg, Acton Bjørn*
4 *Year built: 1933*
5 *Building style: linear block*
6 *Number of rooms: 2 rooms + small room or 1 room + small room*
7 *Gross area: 76 m² and 56 m²*
8 *Number of floors: 3 floors*
9 *Sanitary installations: combined bath and WC, indirect lighting*
10 *Balcony system: balcony on one side*
11 *Staircase system: 1 concrete staircase*
12 *Staircase location: asymmetrical*
13 *Staircase orientation: east*
14 *Living room orientation: west*
15 *Number of flats per main staircase: 3*
16 *Remarks: refuse chute*

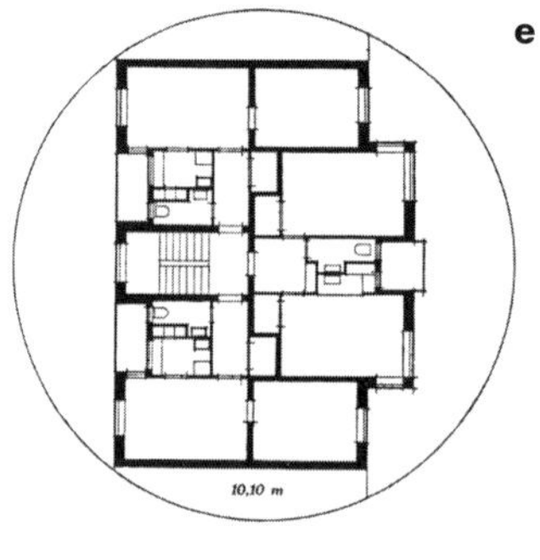

e
1 *Location: Breslau*
2 *Client: private*
3 *Architect: Hans Scharoun*
4 *Year built: 1929*
5 *Building style: enclosed block*
6 *Number of rooms: 2 rooms + small room*
7 *Gross area: 40 m²*
8 *Number of floors: 8*
9 *Sanitary installations: sink and WC, direct lighti*
10 *Balcony system: loggia*
11 *Staircase system: 1 concrete staircase*
12 *Staircase location: symmetrical*
13 *Staircase orientation: west*
14 *Living room orientation: west on the left and right, east in the middle*
15 *Number of flats per main staircase: 3*
16 *Remarks: none*

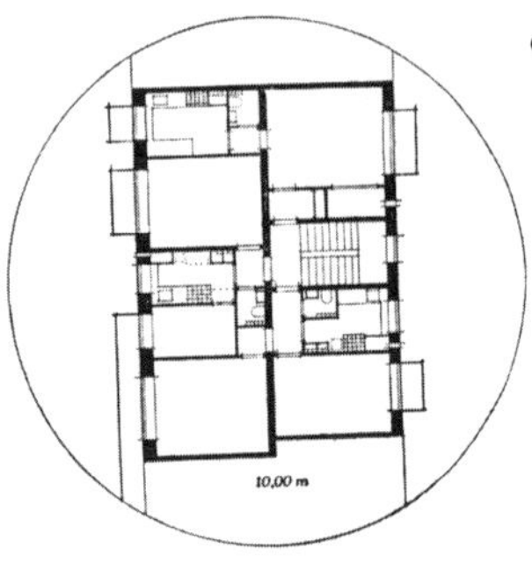

c
1 *Location: Frederikssundsvej 68*
2 *Client: "Boparken" A/S*
3 *Architect: Thorvald Dreyer*
4 *Year built: 1931*
5 *Building style: linear block*
6 *Number of rooms: 2 rooms and 1 room + small room*
7 *Gross area: 41 m² and 58 m²*
8 *Number of floors: 5 floors*
9 *Sanitary installations: combined shower and WC, indirect lighting*
10 *Balcony system: connecting balconies*
11 *Staircase system: 1 concrete staircase*
12 *Staircase location: asymmetrical*
13 *Staircase orientation: east*
14 *Living room orientation: west*
15 *Number of flats per main staircase: 3*
16 *Remarks: none*

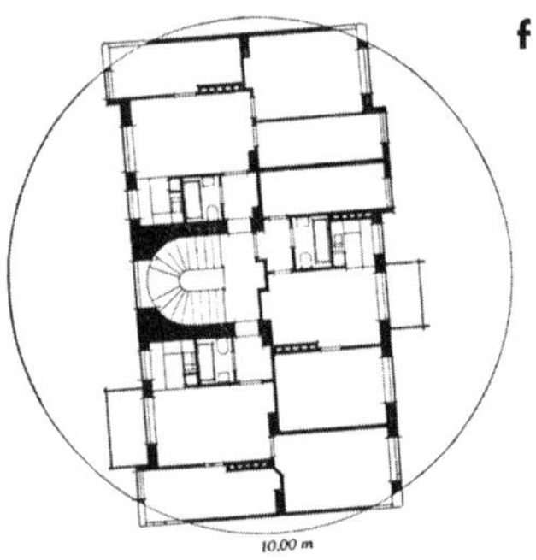

f
1 *Location: Wien*
2 *Client: unknown*
3 *Architect: unknown*
4 *Year built: ca. 1930*
5 *Building style: linear block*
6 *Number of rooms: 2 rooms + 2 small rooms and 2 rooms + 1 small room*
7 *Gross area: 43 m²*
8 *Number of floors: 3 floors*
9 *Sanitary installations: combined bath and WC*
10 *Balcony system: 1 balcony per flat*
11 *Staircase system: 1 concrete staircase*
12 *Staircase location: asymmetrical*
13 *Staircase orientation: west*
14 *Living room orientation: west on the left and right, east in the middle*
15 *Number of flats per main staircase: 3*
16 *Remarks: none*

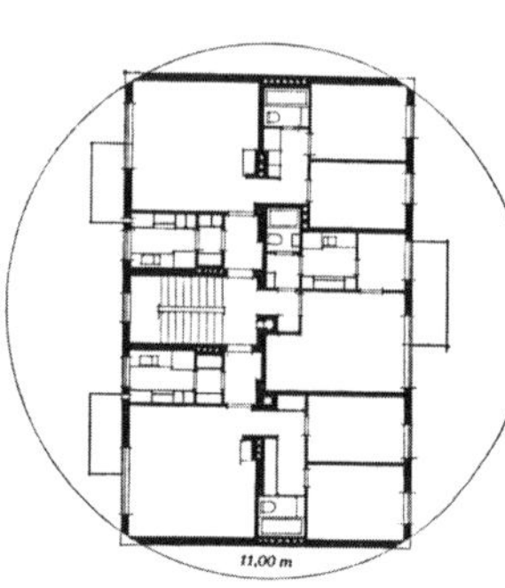

d
1 *Location: Stockholm*
2 *Client: private*
3 *Architect: Sture Frölén*
4 *Year built: 1933*
5 *Building style: linear block*
6 *Number of rooms: 1 and 3 rooms*
7 *Gross area: 33 and 65 m²*
8 *Number of floors: 3 floors*
9 *Sanitary installations: combined bath and WC, bathtub, indirect lighting*
10 *Balcony system: 1 balcony per flat*
11 *Staircase system: 1 concrete staircase*
12 *Staircase location: symmetrical*
13 *Staircase orientation: west*
14 *Living room orientation: west on the right and left, east in the middle*
15 *Number of flats per main staircase: 3*
16 *Remarks: refuse chute*

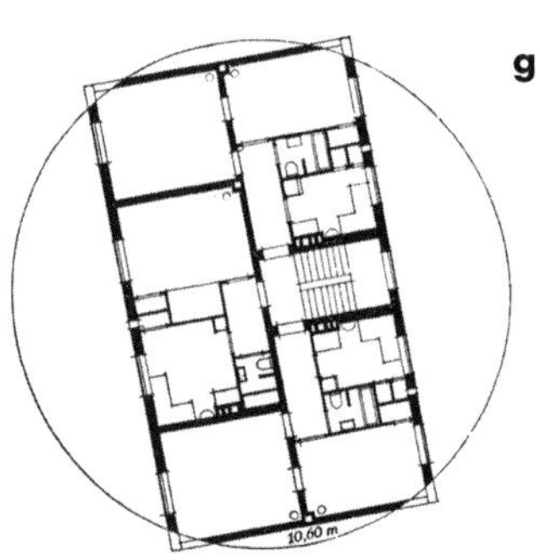

g
1 *Location: Oslo*
2 *Client: unknown*
3 *Architect: unknown*
4 *Year built: 1928*
5 *Building style: -*
6 *Number of rooms: 2 rooms and 1 room*
7 *Gross area: 54 m²*
8 *Number of floors: -*
9 *Sanitary installations: combined bath and WC, indirect lighting*
10 *Balcony system: none*
11 *Staircase system: 1 concrete staircase*
12 *Staircase location: symmetrical*
13 *Staircase orientation: east*
14 *Living room orientation: west*
15 *Number of flats per main staircase: 3*
16 *Remarks: none*

Elaborated by Reinhold Jensen

Single staircase or two staircases. Four flats per staircase. *1:200 and 1:500*

IV$_{46}$

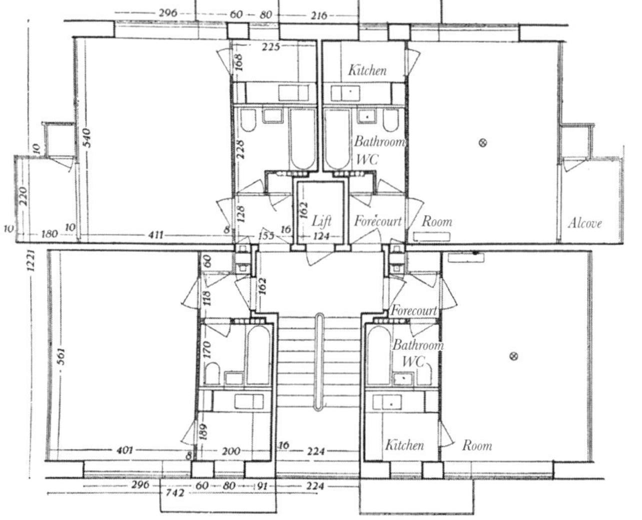

a 1 *Location: Herman Triers Plads*
2 *Client: private*
3 *Architect: Kay Fisker and C. F. Møller*
4 *Year built: 1930*
5 *Building style: enclosed block*
6 *Number of rooms: 1 room and 1 room with alcove*
7 *Gross area: 42 m²*
8 *Number of floors: 6 floors*
9 *Sanitary installations: combined bath and WC, indirect lighting*
10 *Balcony system: balcony in each flat*
11 *Staircase system: 1 concrete staircase*
12 *Staircase location: symmetrical*
13 *Staircase orientation: northeast*
14 *Living room orientation: northeast and southwest*
15 *Number of flats per main staircase: 4*
16 *Remarks: Very concentrated type. Building laws previously permitted single staircases. After 1932, two staircases were required. The kitchen is below the legal limit which was allowed until 1934 when it had electric heating instead of gas.*

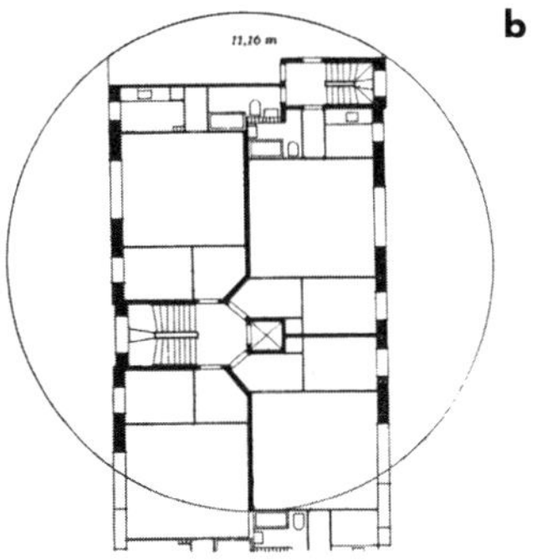

b 1 *Location: Strandboulevarden*
2 *Client: private*
3 *Architect: Th. Henningsen*
4 *Year built: 1929*
5 *Building style: enclosed block*
6 *Number of rooms: 1 room + small room*
7 *Gross area: 58 m²*
8 *Number of floors: 5 floors*
9 *Sanitary installations: combined bath and WC, indirect lighting*
10 *Balcony system: none*
11 *Staircase system: 2 wooden staircases*
12 *Staircase location: symmetrical*
13 *Staircase orientation: west*
14 *Living room orientation: west and east*
15 *Number of flats per main staircase: 4*
16 *Remarks: lift, access to kitchen staircase through bath*

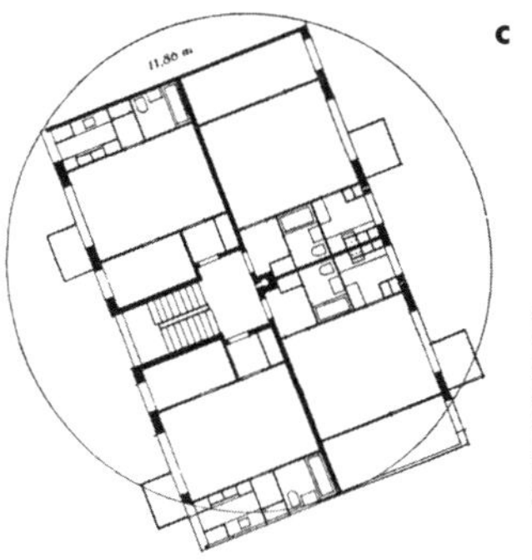

c 1 *Location: Strandvej 221*
2 *Client: "Blidah" A/S*
3 *Architect: Edvard Heiberg and Karl Larsen*
4 *Year built: 1934*
5 *Building style: linear block*
6 *Number of rooms: 1 room + small room*
7 *Gross area: 52 m²*
8 *Number of floors: 3*
9 *Sanitary installations: combined bath and WC, indirect lighting*
10 *Balcony system: balcony in each flat*
11 *Staircase system: 1 concrete staircase*
12 *Staircase location: symmetrical*
13 *Staircase orientation: west*
14 *Living room orientation: west and east*
15 *Number of flats per main staircase: 4*
16 *Remarks: refuse chute*

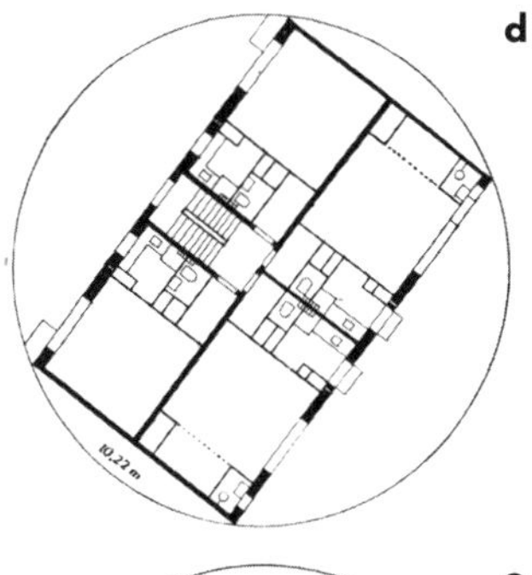

d 1 *Location: Vigerslev Allé, Kjeldsgårdsvej*
2 *Client: Københavns almindelige Boligselskab (KAB)*
3 *Architect: Wittmack and Hvalsøe*
4 *Year built: 1931*
5 *Building style: enclosed block*
6 *Number of rooms: 1 room and alcove*
7 *Gross area: 47 m²*
8 *Number of floors: 5 floors*
9 *Sanitary installations: combined bath and WC without direct lighting*
10 *Balcony system: connecting balconies*
11 *Staircase system: 1 concrete staircase*
12 *Staircase location: symmetrical*
13 *Staircase orientation: northeast*
14 *Living room orientation: northwest and southeast*
15 *Number of flats per main staircase: 4*
16 *Remarks: refuse chute*

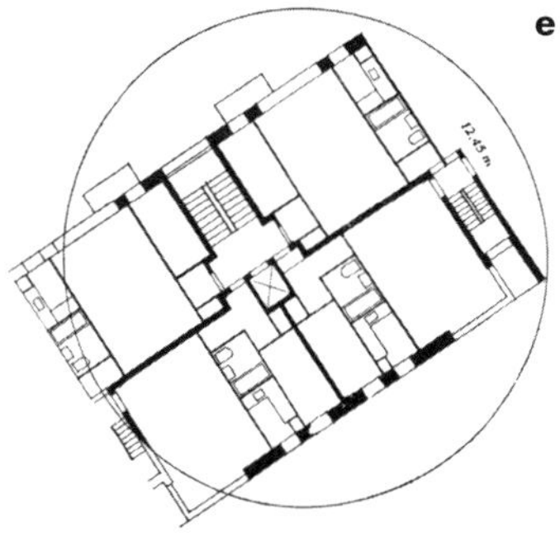

e 1 *Location: Rosenørs Allé, Åboulevarden*
2 *Client: private*
3 *Architect: Kay Fisker and C. F. Møller*
4 *Year built: 1932*
5 *Building style: enclosed block*
6 *Number of rooms: 1 room + small room*
7 *Gross area: 48.5 m²*
8 *Number of floors: 6 floors*
9 *Sanitary installations: combined bath and WC, indirect lighting*
10 *Balcony system: balcony in each flat*
11 *Staircase system: 2 staircases*
12 *Staircase location: symmetrical*
13 *Staircase orientation: northwest*
14 *Living room orientation: northwest and southwest*
15 *Number of flats per main staircase: 4*
16 *Remarks: lift*

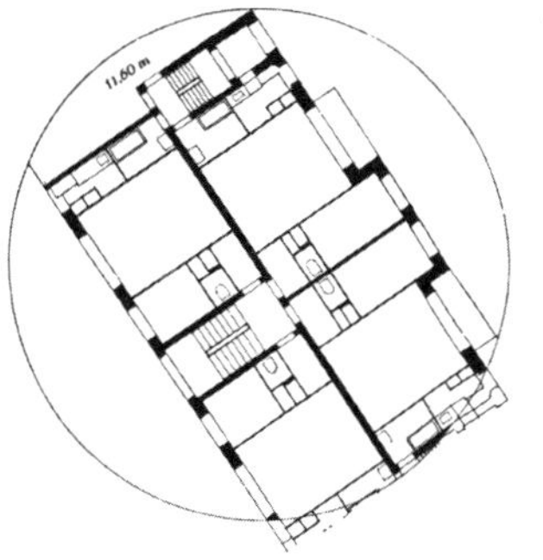

f 1 *Location: Ane Katrines Vej, Kronprinsesse Sofies Vej and Borups Allé*
2 *Client: Københavns almindelige Boligselskab (KAB)*
3 *Architect: Wittmack and Hvalsøe, P. Søgaard Petersen*
4 *Year built: 1933*
5 *Building style: enclosed block*
6 *Number of rooms: 1 room + small room*
7 *Gross area: 41 m²*
8 *Number of floors: 5 floors*
9 *Sanitary installations: separate bath and WC, bathtub, indirect lighting*
10 *Balcony system: balcony on one side*
11 *Staircase system: 2 wooden staircases*
12 *Staircase location: symmetrical*
13 *Staircase orientation: southwest*
14 *Living room orientation: southwest and northeast*
15 *Number of flats per main staircase: 4*
16 *Remarks: access to kitchen staircase through bath*

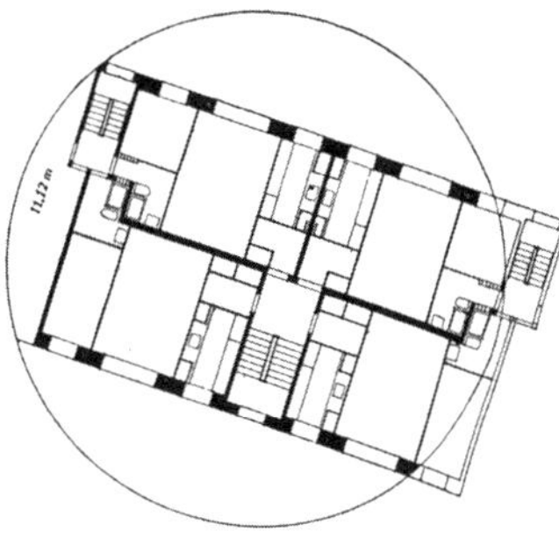

g 1 *Location: Æbeløgade*
2 *Client: private*
3 *Architect: Tyge Hvass*
4 *Year built: 1934*
5 *Building style: enclosed block*
6 *Number of rooms: 1 room + small room*
7 *Gross area: 48 m²*
8 *Number of floors: 5*
9 *Sanitary installations: combined bath and WC, bathtub, indirect lighting*
10 *Balcony system: none*
11 *Staircase system: 2 wooden staircases*
12 *Staircase location: symmetrical*
13 *Staircase orientation: southwest*
14 *Living room orientation: southwest and northwest*
15 *Number of flats per main staircase: 4*
16 *Remarks: access to kitchen staircase through bath*

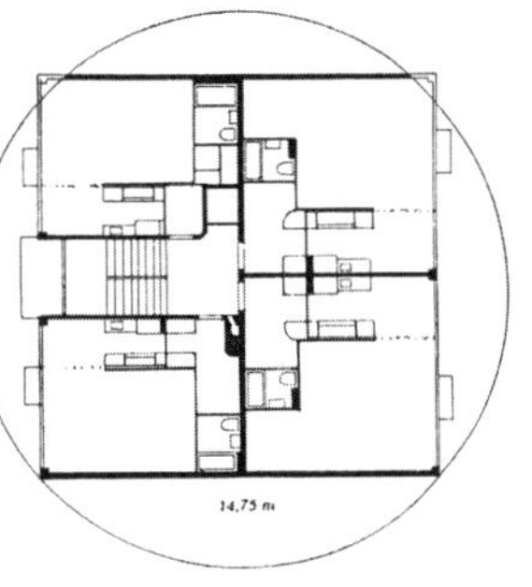

h 1 *Location: Gothenburg*
2 *Client: private*
3 *Architect: Anders Funkquist*
4 *Year built: 1935*
5 *Building style: linear block*
6 *Number of rooms: 1 room and 1 room with alcove*
7 *Gross area: 46.8 m² and 34.7 m²*
8 *Number of floors: 5 floors*
9 *Sanitary installations: combined bath and WC, bathtub, indirect lighting*
10 *Balcony system: balconies on both sides*
11 *Staircase system: 1 concrete staircase*
12 *Staircase location: -*
13 *Staircase orientation: west*
14 *Living room orientation: west and east*
15 *Number of flats per main staircase: 4*
16 *Remarks: concrete house*

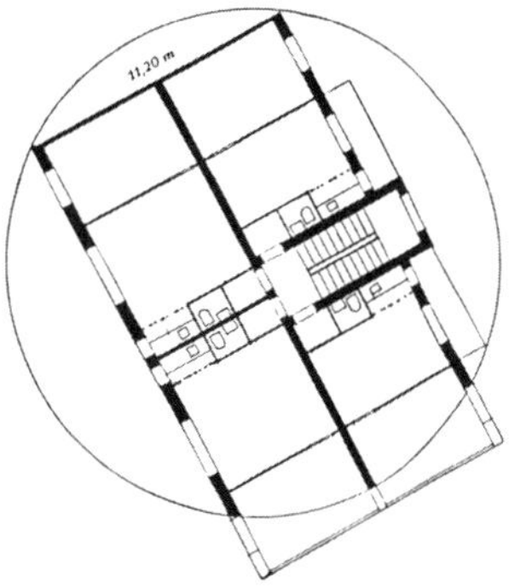

i 1 *Location: Wien*
2 *Client: unknown*
3 *Architect: Franz Schuster*
4 *Year built: 1927*
5 *Building style: linear block*
6 *Number of rooms: 3 rooms*
7 *Gross area: 58 m² and 50 m²*
8 *Number of floors: -*
9 *Sanitary installations: WC, indirect light*
10 *Balcony system: balcony on one side*
11 *Staircase system: 1 concrete staircase*
12 *Staircase location: symmetrical*
13 *Staircase orientation: northeast*
14 *Living room orientation: northeast and southwest*
15 *Number of flats per main staircase: 4*
16 *Remarks: No bath. Kitchenette in living room.*

Elaborated by Erling Paludan

Single staircase. Three flats per staircase. Central staircase. *1:200 and 1:500*

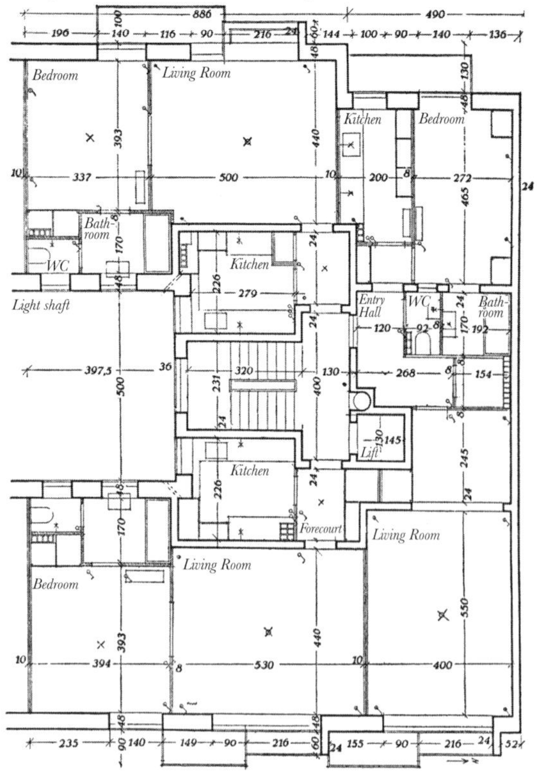

a
1 *Location: Harsdorffsvej 3*
2 *Client: private*
3 *Architect: Louis Hygom*
4 *Year built: 1935*
5 *Building style: double linear block*
6 *Number of rooms: 2 rooms*
7 *Gross area: 75 m²*
8 *Number of floors: 5 floors*
9 *Sanitary installations: separate bath and WC, direct lighting*
10 *Balcony system: fire escape balconies*
11 *Staircase system: 1 concrete staircase*
12 *Staircase location: symmetrical*
13 *Staircase orientation: south-north*
14 *Living room orientation: east-west*
15 *Number of flats per main staircase: 3*
16 *Remarks: Plan type that is particularly advantageous for extensive plot utilisation. The plan form conditions positioning along the north-south longitudinal axis. The type continues in current central staircase systems with skylights.*

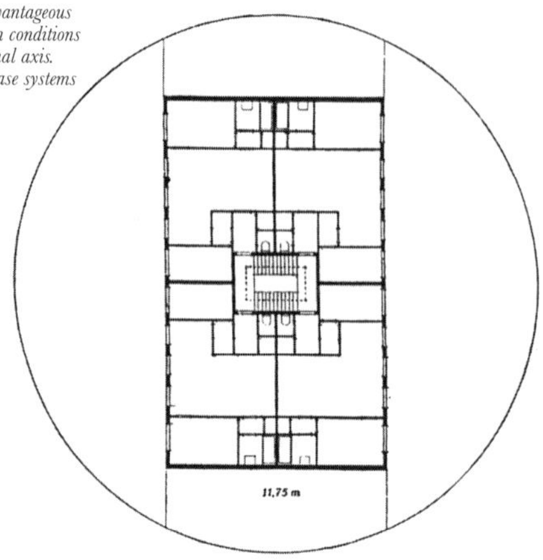

d
1 *Location: Norrmälarstrand, Stockholm*
2 *Client: private*
3 *Architect: Ture Rydberg, Stockholm*
4 *Year built: 1932*
5 *Building style: linear block*
6 *Number of rooms: 1 room + small room and dining area*
7 *Gross area: 60 m²*
8 *Number of floors: 10 floors*
9 *Sanitary installations: combined WC and bath, indirect lighting*
10 *Balcony system: none*
11 *Staircase system: 1 concrete staircase*
12 *Staircase location: symmetrical*
13 *Staircase orientation: east-west*
14 *Living room orientation: east-west*
15 *Number of flats per main staircase: 4*
16 *Remarks: staircase illuminated only from skylight*

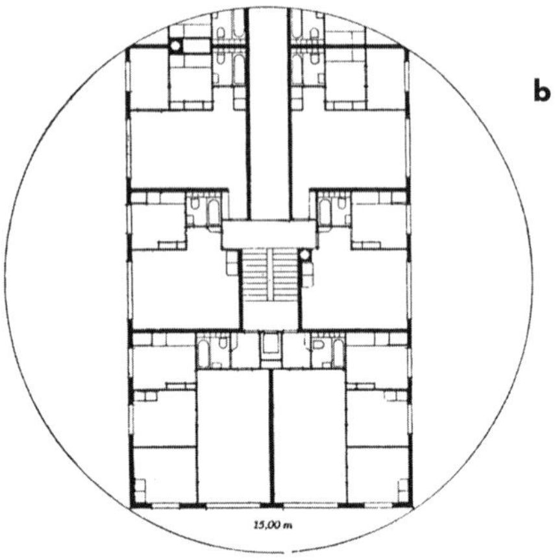

b
1 *Location: Ringvägen, Stockholm*
2 *Client: "H.S.B." (Hyresgästernas sparkasse - och byggnadsförening)*
3 *Architect: Niels Einar Eriksson*
4 *Year built: 1932*
5 *Building style: linear block*
6 *Number of rooms: 1 room with one or more small rooms*
7 *Gross area: 50 m²*
8 *Number of floors: 6 floors*
9 *Sanitary installations: combined WC and bath, indirect lighting*
10 *Balcony system: none*
11 *Staircase system: 1 concrete staircase illuminated from light well*
12 *Staircase location: symmetrical*
13 *Staircase orientation: north-south*
14 *Living room orientation: east-west*
15 *Number of flats per main staircase: 6*
16 *Remarks: Staircase illuminated from light well*

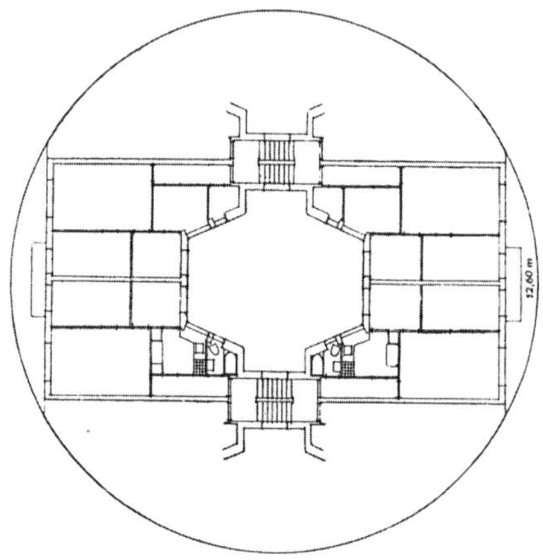

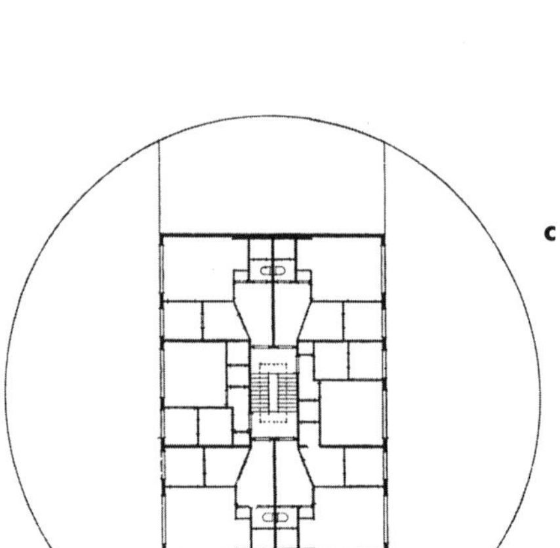

c
1 *Location: Eriksdal, Stockholm*
2 *Client: private*
3 *Architect: Sven Markelius*
4 *Year built: 1932*
5 *Building style: linear block*
6 *Number of rooms: 1 room with dining area*
7 *Gross area: 48 m²*
8 *Number of floors: 3 floors*
9 *Sanitary installations: combined shower and WC, indirect lighting*
10 *Balcony system: none*
11 *Staircase system: 1 concrete staircase*
12 *Staircase location: symmetrical*
13 *Staircase orientation: south-north*
14 *Living room orientation: east-west*
15 *Number of flats per main staircase: 6*
16 *Remarks: staircase illuminated only from skylight*

e
1 *Location: theoretical project*
2 *Client: -*
3 *Architect: Hilda Rømer and P. Nyboe-Petersen*
4 *Year built: -*
5 *Building style: linear block*
6 *Number of rooms: 2 rooms + small room*
7 *Gross area: 50 m²*
8 *Number of floors: 6 rooms*
9 *Sanitary installations: combined bath and WC, direct lighting*
10 *Balcony system: connecting balconies*
11 *Staircase system: 1 concrete staircase*
12 *Staircase location: symmetrical*
13 *Staircase orientation: east-west*
14 *Living room orientation: east-west*
15 *Number of flats per main staircase: 4*
16 *Remarks: stairs and secondary rooms are illuminated from light well*

Elaborated by Gudmund Rafn and Edmund Hansen

Residential neighbourhood circa 1870. *The neighbourhood around Gasværksvej and Viktoriagade as viewed towards Sønder Boulevard. Examples of building forms with extensive land utilisation.*

Residential neighbourhood circa 1923. *The neighbourhood around Enghavevej and Ny Carlsbergvej. Examples of the Statsboligfond Period's block developments. In the foreground four residential blocks built by Copenhagen municipality and designed by the City Architects, E. Monberg and Strøm Tejsen.*

Residential neighbourhood circa 1926. *The neighbourhood around Australiensvej and Vennemindevej. Example from the last year of the State Housing Fund Period with the semi-enclosed block Solgården by Henning Hansen behind an enclosed municipal housing block by L. Hygom. In the foreground, a building complex by Poul Henningsen, and furthest to the right, as comb house with row development from before 1914.*

Residential neighbourhood circa 1926. *The neighbourhood around Borups Allé and Hillerødgade. Typical neighbourhood with an easement (mid-rise buildings). In the middle of the picture, the parallel block complex Vibevænget by Povl Baumann and L. Hygom, the semi-enclosed Vibehusene by E. Monberg; in the foreground at Borups Allé Grønnegården by Povl Baumann and at the very front Hvidkildegård by Ivar Bentsen, all built by Københavns almindelige Boligselskab (KAB). Below left, a corner of the residential building around Genforeningsplads by Henning Hansen and L. Hygom; on the right a municipal housing block by F. C. Harboe.*

Residential neighbourhood circa 1935. *The neighbourhood around Frederiksborgvej and Oldermandsvej with Boparken parallel development of linear blocks by Th. Dreyer.*

Residential neighbourhood circa 1935. *The neighbourhood around Strandvejen and Maglemosevej with the Blidah parallel development of linear blocks by Ivar Bentsen, A. Skjøt-Pedersen, Achton Bjørn, Jørgen U. Berg, Edvard Heiberg & Karl Larsen and Cooperative's architects.*

Hornbækhus *on Borups Allé-Ågade. Built by Copenhagen's Andelsbyggeforening, 1922. Typical State Housing Fund Period block with street-facing living rooms. Architect: Kay Fisker, Garden: G., N. Brandt. Plant type* III_{33d}

Hornbækhus. *Façade towards Ågade*

Ved Classens Have. *Classensgade-Strandboulevarden. Built in 1924 by Københavns almindelige Boligselskab (KAB). Semi-enclosed block surrounding a municipal park.*
Transitional form towards open block forms, but with living rooms facing the street and service areas towards the park. Architects: Carl Petersen, Povl Baumann, Ole Falkentorp and Peter Nielsen. Gardens: municipal head gardener Fabricius Hansen.
Plan type III_{34b}

Solgården *on Vennemindevej. Built in 1926 by Københavns almindelige Boligselskab (KAB). Semi-enclosed block. Main entrances and living rooms facing the courtyard. Architect: Henning Hansen. Plan type* IV_{43a}

Vibevænget *between Vibevej and Mågevej. Built in 1926 by Københavns almindelige Boligselskab (KAB). The first parallel development of linear blocks of Copenhagen's modern estates. The wings are turned symmetrically so that the areas between them are alternately used for access roads and service areas. Three-storey type with single staircase system and fire balconies on the top floor. Some attic flats have access to two staircases. Architects: Povl Baumann, E. Monberg, L. Hygom. Development plan* D_a*. Plan type* IV_{35b}

Tagensvej, Rådmandsgade. *Built in 1931. Yellow brick estate with concrete balcony parapets. Architects: Edvard Thomsen and Knud Thorball.*

Treleddet *on Finsensvej. Built in 1930. Flamed brick block with reinforced balcony parapets. Architects: Th. Dreyer and Palle Suenson.*

Lykkens Gave *on Ordrupvej. Built in 1934 by Københavns almindelige Boligselskab (KAB). Semi-enclosed five-storey block with single staircase system and balconies on both sides with open wrought iron railings. Architect: Henning Jørgensen.*
Plan Type IV_{40c}

Roskildegården *on Roskildevej. Built in 1934 by Københavns almindelige Boligselskab (KAB). Five-storey, semi-enclosed block with single staircase system, balconies with closed parapet in connection with south-facing bay windows. Architect: Henning Jørgensen. Development plan* B_k*, Plan type* IV_{39g}

Vestervænget *on Enghavevej. Built in 1935 by Københavns almindelige Boligselskab (KAB). Parallel development of linear blocks with single staircase system and balconies on two sides. The street-facing balconies are designed with folding windows so that they can be used as sun lounges. Architect: P. Søegaard Pedersen*

Storgården *on Tomsgårdsvej and Frederiksborgvej. Built in 1935. Yellow brick estate with balcony parapets of corrugated iron and, on the north side with screens. Architects: Povl Baumann and Knud Hansen. Development plan D_{k}, plan type IV_{41a}*

Kanslergården *on Jagtvej and Kanslergade. Built in 1936. Red brick estate. Wrought iron balcony railings. Architects: E. Monberg and Henning Ortmann. Development plan B_{n}.*

Svanemøllebo *on Strandvejen. Built in 1935. Red brick block. Balcony parapets of coloured Eternit. Architects: Wittmaack and V. Hvalsøe*

Herman Triersplads. *Built in 1934. Enclosed triangular block with the main façade facing the open space with old vegetation from the former workhouse grounds. Roof terrace from load-bearing external wall to main partition, which extends over the terrace as an outer wall with posterior roof space. Two-flight-staircase system with four flats per staircase. Architects: Kay Fisker and C. F. Møller. Development plan* A_k*, Plan type* IV_{46a} *and* IV_{46e}

Ringparken *on Tesdorpfsvej and C. F. Richs Vej. Built in 1935. Three-storey parallel development with linear blocks on steeply sloping terrain. Architect: A. Skjøt-Pedersen. Development plan* D_c*, Plan type* IV_{39c}

Jørgenshave *on Ordrupvej. Built in 1934. Three-storey parallel development with linear blocks in old park. Architect: A. Skjøt-Pedersen. Plan type* IV_{37d}

Bellavista *on Strandvejen, Klampenborg. Built in 1935. Three-storey, three-winged building in old park, open towards the Øresund. Architect: Arne Jacobsen. Development plan* B_m*, Plan type* IV_{41h}

Blidah *on Strandvejen and Maglemosevej. Built by Blidah A/S in 1934 and 1935. Three-storey buildings in old park. Architect of the pictured buildings: A. Skjøt-Pedersen. Development plan* C_k*, Plan type* IV_{35g}

Blidah. *Architect of the pictured buildings: Kooperative Arkitekter.*
Development plan C_h*, Plan type* IV_{43b} *and* IV_{43c}

Lille Tuborg *at Stradvejen-Gl. Vartovvej. Built in 1934. Detached irregular three-storey building in an old park. Architect: Charles I. Schou.*
Development plan Bg

RÆKKEHUSTYPER

En oversigt udarbejdet paa Kunstakademiets Arkitekturskole

under ledelse af professor Kay Fisker

Udgivet af Tidsskriftet ARKITEKTEN, Akademisk Arkitektforening, København 1941

Two-storey row house in Keats Grove, Hampstead, London, around 1780
As an opening image, from Steen Eiler Rasmussen's book on London, this small modest terraced house, a house from the time of George III, has been chosen, as the finest example I could find of an ancient building type that was refined during a distinguished cultural period, completely natural in its relationship between construction and form, firm in its facade structure, and at the same time unbiased in its fulfillment of functional requirements.

On row, comb, chained and other types of contiguous houses

By architect, professor Kay Fisker

The following designs of row house types and other forms of contiguous construction are extracts from a study carried out in the Academy's School of Architecture under my supervision. This research is a continuation of previous studies on residential buildings, an excerpt of which has been published here in the journal in 1936.*

The study has involved collecting material, sorting it into types and then recording it based on existing projects or blueprints, in some cases by reproductions from books and periodicals. In a few cases, we have sought to reconstruct a missing façade, basement or roof plan. Therefore, some

* Volume XXXVIII p. 113, as well as the separate book *Copenhagen Housing Types* 1936.

misrepresentations may occur. Yet the main characteristics of the plan types, which are of particular interest, are faithfully reproduced. For the purpose of comparison, a consistent form of presentation has been used for all the recorded projects.

The material has been collected for both Danish as well as foreign buildings, both projected and completed, and includes a total of 120 types. The drawings reproduced here are extracts from the very extensive material and the intention is only to demonstrate the present situation against the backdrop of a few older types. For the sake of current local circumstances, I have placed an emphasis on Danish row houses that have been built in the last few years or are currently under construction. Furthermore, I have been interested in reproducing examples of less used and less familiar forms of contiguous construction, such as the types we refer to as comb row houses, double comb row houses, patio row houses, chain row houses and other, more detached forms, which are transitional to the completely detached house, which I think will be dealt with more in the future.

The study is limited to contiguous construction forms in which the dwellings are located *next to each other*, regardless of the number of floors. House forms in which dwellings are situated *on top of each other* are considered multi-storey buildings, even though they consist of only two-stories. Examples have been chosen due to their type being considered of particular interest and less because of their architectural value. In some cases, I even feel compelled to distance myself from the design.

The material was collected and this text was written before the Academic Architectural Association Crisis Construction Competition was launched. The work at the Academy based on these types may have affected some of the works that emerged from the competition, especially within the group of chain row houses. After the results of the competition were available, I supplemented this overview with a few typical competition proposals, redrawn in the standard form we have used so that, although they have been made public, they are reproduced here in a new context.

The reproduced material has been examined and recorded by the following architecture students: *Jørgen Bo, Frederik Boyesen, Sven Boyesen, Kai Christensen, Vagn Christensen, Ebbe Clemmensen, Otto Frankild, Hans Frederiksen, Gunnar Garde, Albert Gehrke Hansen, Erik Glud, Karen Margrethe Gravesen, Jørgen Grønborg Hansen, Hans Hannibal, Knud Hansen Møller, Ove Hove, Jens Høhne, Carl Hylling Larsen, Henning Jacobsen, Heiberg Jensen, Hans Jensen, Marius Johansen, Poul Jochumsen, Hack Kampmann, Arne Kjær, Jens Kjær, Kjeld Kjeldsen, Ole Kornerup Bang , Kai Kørbing, Mogens Leth, Mogens Lilie, Svend Lindholm, Jens Malling Petersen, Jørgen Maahr, Holger Mygind, Ib Møgelvang Nielsen, Kai Børge Nielsen, Henning Noes Petersen, Jørgen Nordskov, Aage Paludan, Mogens Black Petersen, Mogens Petterson, Niels Ole Poulsen, Max Boje Rasmussen, Niels Jacob Rasmussen, Knud Rohbrandt, Bent Salicath, Flemming Schüter, Kjártan Sigurdson and Wendelboe Jensen.* Leaders of the study team were, in the first year, *Jørgen Bo and Hans Frederiksen*, and in the last year *Niels Ole Poulsen*. In the final revision of the drawings and adaptation of material, the architects *Kaj Børge Nielsen and Mogens Leth* have provided me with very valuable help.

The traditional row house type that we are familiar with from old provincial towns fell into decline as the individualistic villa emerged at the end of the last century and reached its peak during Herholdt's generation. At that time, one could not imagine living in row houses, except in a few conservative and stagnant small towns, such as Rønne and Stege for example, where the type continued to be popular. The streets of these provincial towns with their individually varied three and four bay houses, with adjoining back gardens and common back paths, still show some of the row houses' best features. But in Copenhagen one did not live in row houses. Buildings such as *Lægeforening*'s row houses on Øster Allé and Strandvejen, *Classen's* row houses on Nyelandsvej and *Arbejdernes Byggeforening's* houses between Øster Farimagsgade and the lakes were not very reputable forms of residential development. Only a very few of the older housing associations like *Arbejdernes Byggeforening* continued to build row houses. The cooperative building organisations and the small building associations, which flourished especially in the Sundby neighbourhoods and in Valby, preferred uniform detached, and sometimes semi-detached, houses.

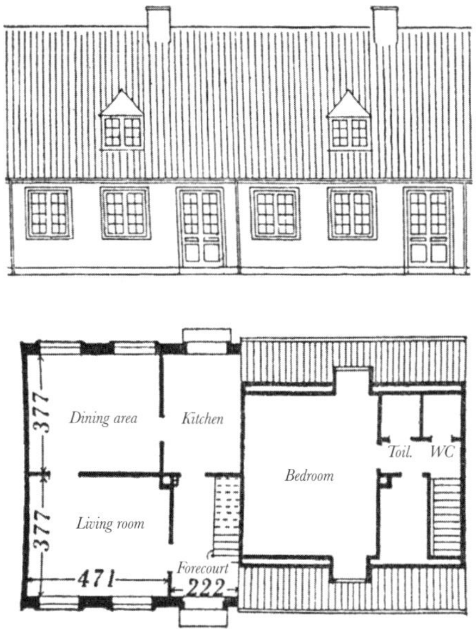

Ivar Bentsen and Thorkild Henningsen:
Bakkehusene, Bellahøj. Built in 1922 by KAB. 1:400

In 1922, when *K.A.B* undertook the valiant effort to build *Ivar Bentsen's* and *Thorkild Henningsen*'s row houses, Bakkehusene, the housing association encountered neither understanding from the public nor the authorities. No one wanted to live in barracks. For a number of years, these houses were the most important part of a better way of living. Housing preferences were too ingrained.

The Bakkehusene were thus not inhabited by the social class they were intended for, i.e. the working class, but became rather, as Bentsen once put it, a haunt for open-minded intellectuals with many children. Now, twenty years later, on a summer evening wandering among the lush gardens, the life lived in these houses and gardens seems like the best vindication of the type, especially when compared to the five-storey blocks built during the same period from the beginning of 1920s.

But back then row houses did not succeed as workers' housing. The next advance for row houses was Thorkild Henningsen's tireless work, which was also not intended for the working class, but rather the middle class. In the latter half of the 1920s, thanks mainly to the master masons G. C. and A. V. Andersen, Henningsen succeeded in completing one such a middle-class block of large, expensive row houses. For a short period, it became fashionable to live in row houses rather than in villas.

In the history of the Danish row house, Thorkild Henningsen's work is a chapter in itself, the story of a man's constant and obstinate struggle. He was able to build a row housing estate which was extensive under the circumstances, but only succeeded in realising his real goal, building workers' housing (Damvænget by Damhussøen), shortly before his death.

Poul Henningsen once* gave an excellent characterisation of the Thorkild Henningsen types, pointing out their strengths and weaknesses and describing their evolution in architectural terms. In those years, Thorkild Henningsen, as well as all of his contemporaries, evolved gradually from the split-bay house with equal-sized living rooms where the window is the smallest unit in the row of houses, to the more strongly accented house with an emphasis on functionality, where the house itself eventually becomes the smallest unit.

**Arkitekten*, Vol. XXXIII, p. 17.

The row houses that followed in Henningsen's footsteps, with projects by *Povl Haumann, Hygom, Dahlerup-Berthelsen* and others, did not differ much

from his own. They also waned in popularity quickly after his death. Others either lacked his energy to keep them alive or, at that time in the early 1930s, the market, perhaps due simply to a passing fashion, was suddenly saturated. In any case, interest in row housing ceased until it resurfaced in the last few years. Now on a whole new basis, *the affordable row house*, serving as workers' housing and housing for families with many children, and which was forced onto the housing market by social housing associations, has been made possible first and foremost by the interest the authorities are now showing in these forms of housing. It seems that the architects' efforts over twenty years in the field are now suddenly leading to results.
The housing types have evolved a lot since Bakkehusene was built. There is a greater connection between Bakkehusene's plans and architectural forms and the Fuggersiedlung in Augsburg which was built in 1519 and which has many, if not more, similarities with our Nyboder row houses, than between Bakkehusene and the types of row houses we see being built this year. The conditions have completely changed. Housing requirements are different now and the urge to move further out has become stronger. Over the years, developments in urban construction and building technology have given low-rise buildings greater opportunities, and the well-established high-rise housing development will undoubtedly be gradually replaced by higher 10 to 12-storey housing blocks on the one hand and scattered low-rise buildings, on the other. The present acute situation has given the last group, low-rise, technically simplified housing, a special chance.
Row housing has not yet been cultivated and refined as much as the multi-storey and low-rise detached dwellings have in recent years. In the propaganda of modern architects around the world at large exhibitions with model cities that have been held around Europe for the last fifteen years, row housing has been a major topic. But in the real estate market, it has been pushed into the background. It is true that the form has been experimented with, but the types have not been adapted and fine-tuned in the way that the demands of everyday reality have forced upon multi-storey dwellings.

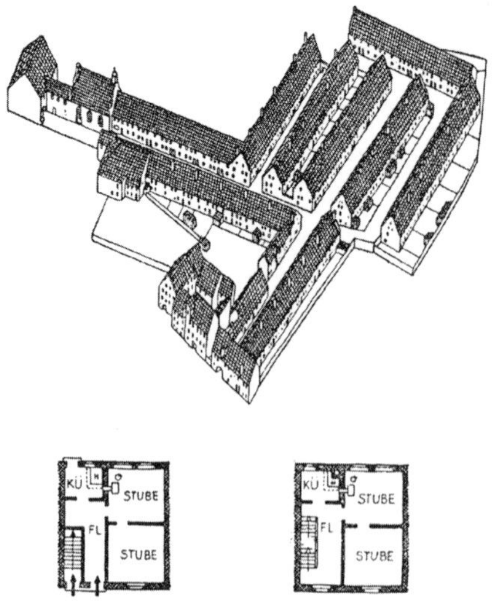

The Fuggerei in Augsburg, built in 1519 by the merchant Jacob Fugger as workers' housing. Two-storey dwelling with the houses one above the other. 1:500

Development systems

In a methodological study of modern row housing types, the relationship to access roads is one of the most important prerequisites.
A number of development forms that have been used so far are reproduced on page 6 and 7.
Of these, the ordinary two-sided road (6 d, e, etc.) is, of course, the most used, but is nonetheless the most inhibiting road system for the housing's plan design. The difficulty is the same as with ordinary two-sided developments with detached houses, where houses north of the road have a garden to the south and access the house through the garden. Technically and economically, the long and expensive service lines in this case are an additional difficulty. Most of Thorkild Henningsen's buildings, e.g. Sundvænget in Hellerup, have this development form and also display its weaknesses.
The same two-sided system as the southern buildings in Sundvænget with small courtyards on the north side was also used in an old project by *Baillie Scott* from 1902, which I enjoyed finding and include here. Incidentally, there are many striking similarities between several of Henningsen's works and these old model projects from the period

M. H. Baillie Scott, *Comb row house project, Bedford 1902. See similar house type p. 35 a*

around the turn of the century when English architecture was of great importance for developments in the rest of Europe. Inferior in terms of function but cheaper to construct is the double road system with a two-sided access road and a back path (6 a), which is the common form in older provincial buildings and which is used in newer buildings, such as in Bakkehusene.

Most advantageous for the housing plan form itself, however, are the one-sided roads on the north side of the housing rows (6 b, etc.). The system requires a large road area, which can be countered somewhat by the reduced requirements for the road's width and quality, made possible by the reduced amount of traffic. This road system is not yet found very often in completed buildings, but once developments discover their proper form and we learn how to build narrow, cheap roads with easy paving and simplified sewerage systems, it will probably be more widely used. The remaining examples from the site layout plan on the same page show different road systems, of which the combinations with blind byroads are perhaps most interesting (6 h, 7 l and m).

Two-storey type

Among the housing forms, the *two-storey types* have so far been utilised the most. They are predominant in both the older residential buildings as well as in projects from recent years.

Of course, these types have indisputable economic advantages construction-wise as well as in terms of plot use, but on the other hand, their functional weaknesses are so preponderant that they should fade into the background. Stairless housing generally has the most advantages in functional terms, and in the case of row houses, the view from the overlooking first-floor windows of the neighbouring houses, especially when there are balconies, significantly reduces the value of the garden. Furthermore, outdoor areas are overshadowed more than with low houses. Apart from these fundamental weaknesses, many of the two-storey buildings from recent years reveal beautiful solutions. Some of these have been included here, including *Suenson and Ib Martin Jensen's* buildings at Bernstorffsvej, *Milther and Søndergaard's* Hasselvænget near Damhussøen, *Herald G. Petersen's* buildings on Ammentorpsvej in Gentofte, *Kooperative Arkitekter's* row houses around Kantorparken and Emdrupvej, and *Søgaard Pedersen* and *Albinus'* K.A.B, among others.

One-storey types

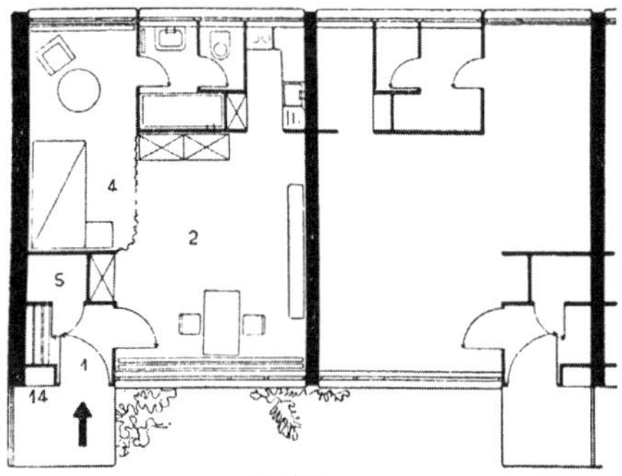

1 Vorplatz
2 Wohnraum
4 Schlafnische
5 Abstellraum
14 Zählerkasten
23 Garage

Roth, Artaria et al.: *One-storey row house type, Neubühl, Zürich 1935*

In addition to the aforementioned advantages, *one-storey types* make the most sense for very small flats. Most row housing developments built on the basis of the Housing Allowance Act for large families are therefore one-storey homes. Within this category, reproduced here are *Ivar Bentsen's* homes for the municipality of Copenhagen on Vigerslev Allé and some of the *Foreningen Socialt Boligbyggeri's* residential buildings in the rest of the country. One-storey buildings of this kind are also under construction by *Københavns Almindelige Boligselskab* in Helsingør.

On a slightly higher economic and social level, we include other one-storey buildings, such as *Remark and Svend Aage Petersen's* beautiful red houses on Kongevejen in Holte, *Frans Jastrau's* buildings in Ørholm as well as types by *Harald G. Petersen*. The one-storey type reproduced here from Neubühl near Zurich by *Roth, Artaria, Haefeli* et al. seems to me to be one of the most beautiful and clear examples within this group.

Plan types with *semi-detached dwellings*, i.e. with only one free outer wall, placed "side by side", are not built in Denmark. They are found in

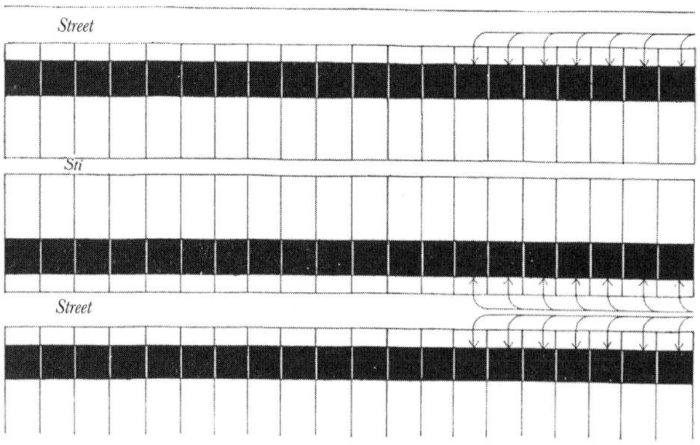

a. Row houses.
Two-sided roads with two-sided back path. Ivar Bentsen and Thorklid Henningsen: Bakkehusene, Copenhagen. House type, p. 3

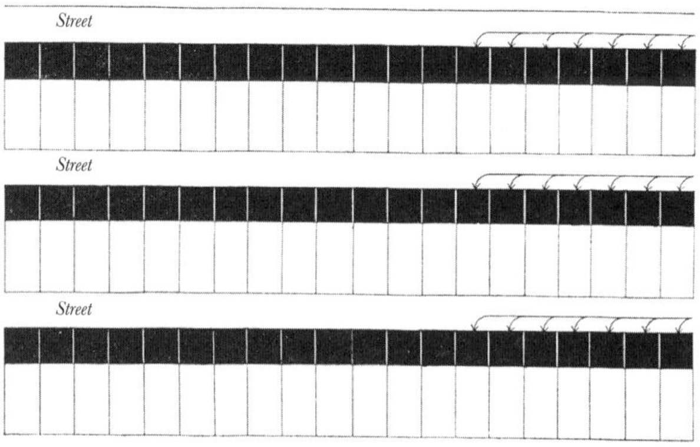

b. Row houses.
One-sided roads with the buildings on the south side

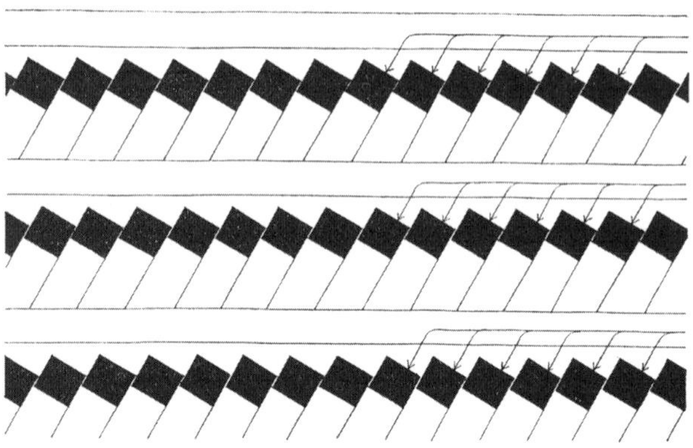

c. Row houses.
Z-shaped buildings. One-sided roads. Frederichsen and Poulsen: Æblevænget, Lyngby. Milthers and Søndergaard: Hasselvænget, Copenhagen, etc., house types, p. 15; p. 33 a and b

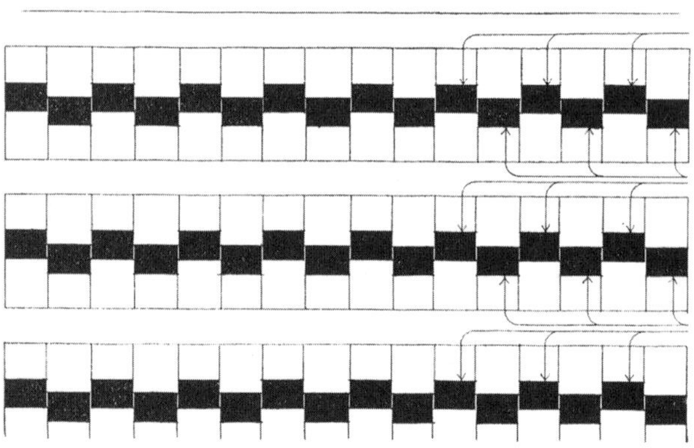

d. Row houses.
U-shaped buildings. Two-sided roads. Th. Henningsen: Vanløse Allé, Finn Juhl and Ole Hagen: The Crisis Construction Competition. House type, p. 10

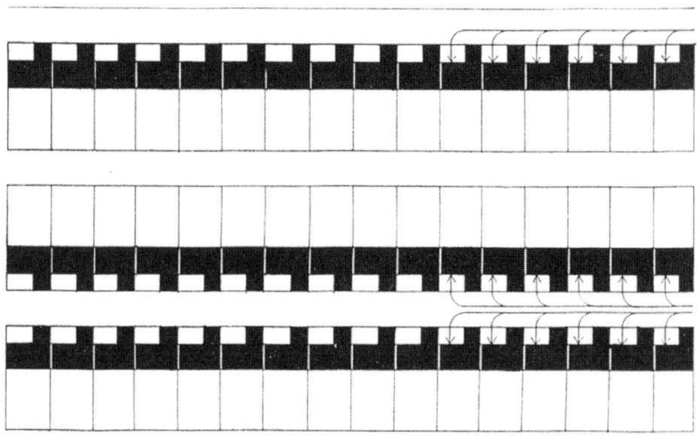

e. Comb row houses.
Double two-sided roads. M. H. Baillie Scott, Bedford. House type, pp. 4 and 35 a

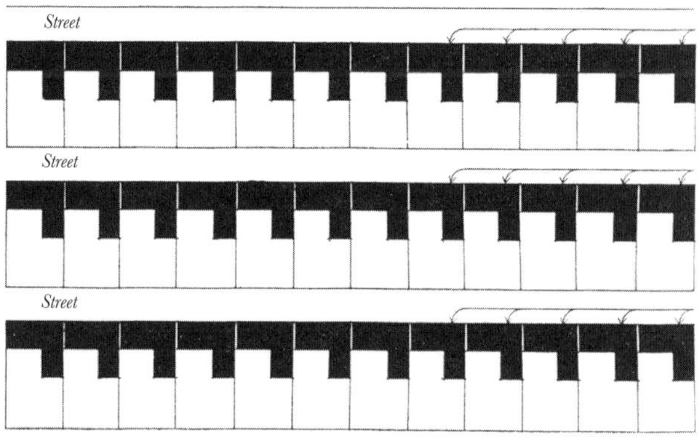

f. Comb row houses.
One-sided roads with dwellings on the south side. House type, p. 34 a and b

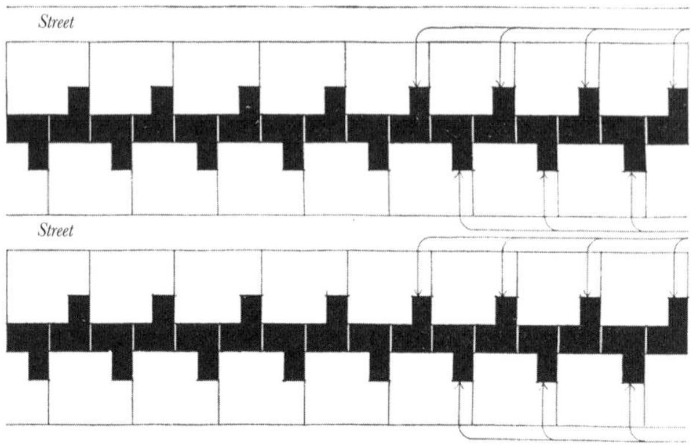

g. Double comb row houses.
Houses turned opposite each other. Double two-sided roads. Hilding Ekelund: Helsinki. House type p. 36 a

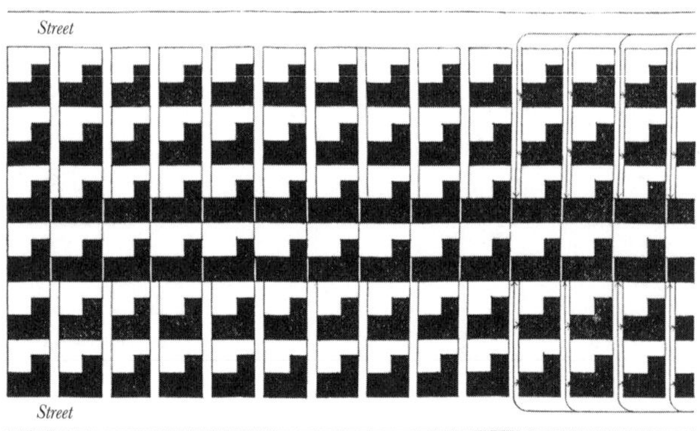

h. L-shaped and comb row houses.
Two-sided roads with byroads.

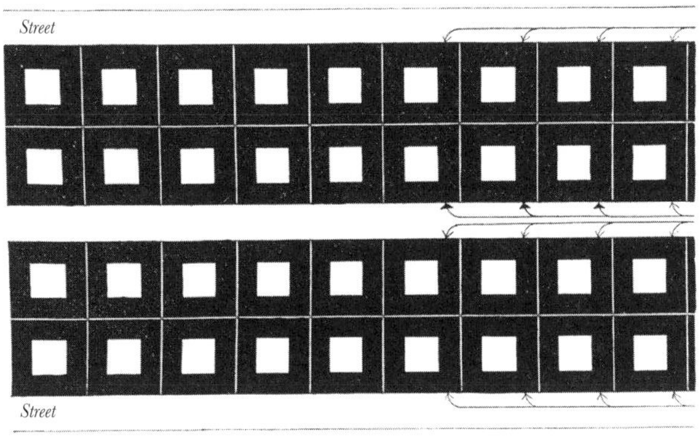

i. Patio houses.
1/1 houses. Two-sided roads. Independent patio. The houses receive exposure from one side. Poul Wiboe: The Crisis Construction Competition

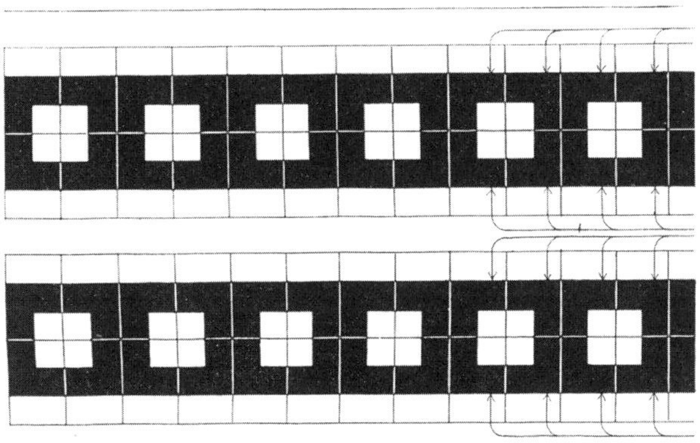

j. Patio houses.
¼ houses. Two-sided roads. Common patio or divided by fence. The system can include other divisions, e.g. ½. Bogenhausen, Munich. House type p. 18 and 38 b.

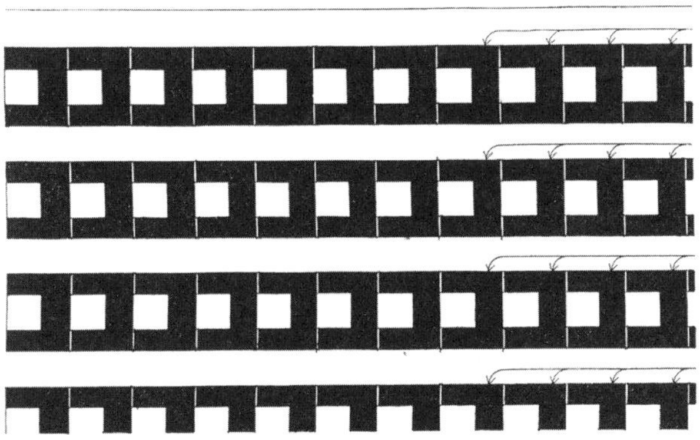

k. Patio houses.
¾ houses. One-sided roads. Independent patio. Erik Pfannschmidt, Ramersdorf, Munich

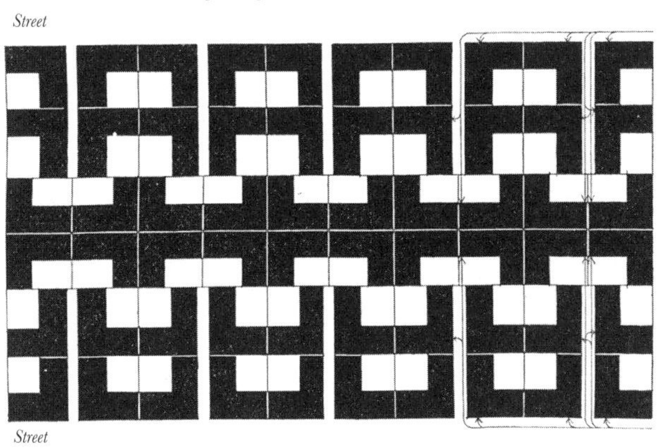

l. Patio houses.
¼ houses. Split patio. Two-sided roads with byroads. Howard Major, Palm Beach, Florida, U.S.A. House type, pp. 19 and 39 a

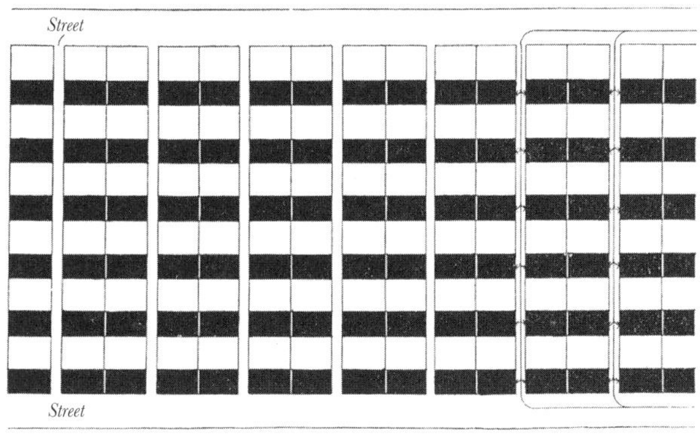

m. Semi-detached houses.
Two-sided roads with cross paths

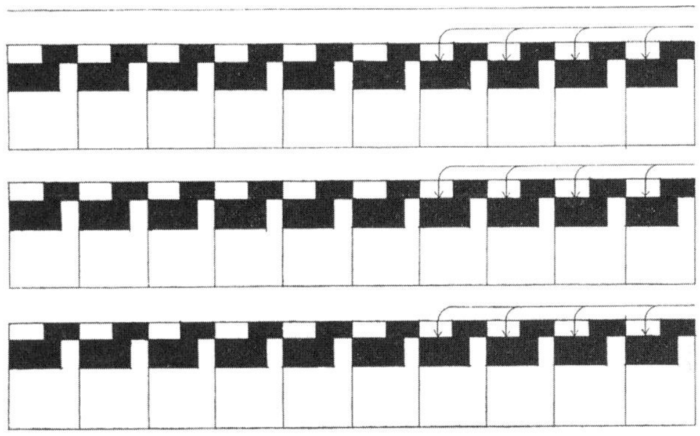

n. Chain row houses.
Semi-detached house type. One-sided roads with the buildings on the south side

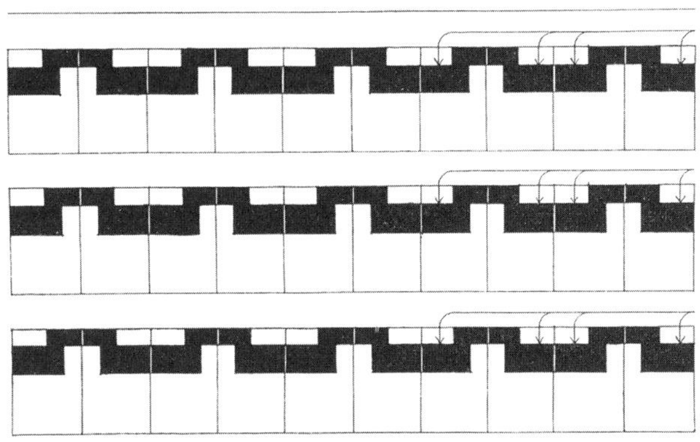

o. Chain row houses.
Symmetrical houses. One-sided roads with the buildings on the south side

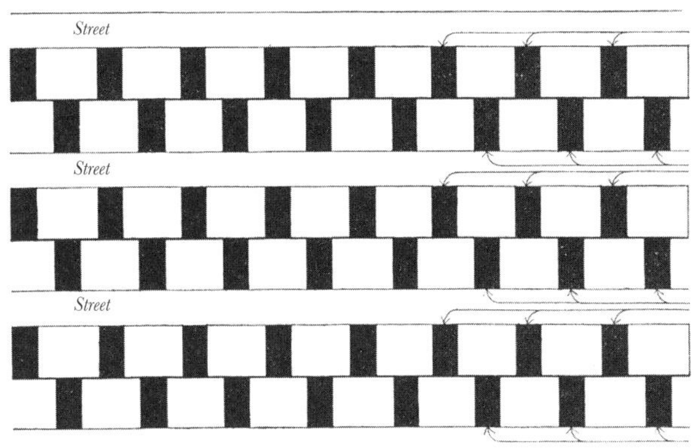

p. North boundary row houses.
Two-sided roads. Hilding Ekelund, Helsinki. House type p. 36 b

multi-storey dwellings, but have not been approved for low-rise ones by either the building or licensing authorities. To a certain extent this is unjustified. They have very significant economic advantages, are inexpensive to build, better insulated and easier to heat than the general types. One of their weaknesses is difficult ventilation, which can be remedied by special exhaust systems. But their location is obviously restricted to certain cardinal points.

Many such types have been built in Germany for a very long time. *Franz* has built a dwelling in Vienna which is reproduced in his book entitled "Ein eingerichtetes Siedlungshaus" (Jul. Hoflmann, Stuttgart).

Ib Lunding produced a project with semi-detached types for a competition in 1928 (*Arkitekten* vol. XXXIV, p. 57), just as he did for the Crisis Construction Competition. In recent years, the Swedes have also become interested in such forms. *Kooperativa Förbundets Arkitektkontor* in Stockholm has completed a very beautiful, two-storey, semi-detached project, which is reproduced here in its original form. A variant of this type can be found on p. 31 b. The project is remarkable for a variety of reasons, including the fact that it has managed to scale down to the minimum area of 4.5 × 6 m without rendering the plan meaningless. However, it helps that Swedish living habits allow the staircase to be placed in the living room. The only examples I know of here at home of such a staircase system which is, of course, an English tradition, are the types attempted by Th. Henningsen in Fuglebakken and in Kantorparken, and by Suenson and Ib Martin Jensen on Bernstorffsvej.

We are familiar with the *very deep house types* from neoclassical London houses, often three or four-storey dwellings, which on the narrow and very deep plots can create very large house depths, all the way up to around 30 m and far beyond what is justifiable in relation to light sources. In many cases, however, this can be remedied with small light wells, or creating L-shaped or U-shaped dwellings. This English tradition, which has also found expression in the United States is disappearing. In England in recent years, the distinctive London types have been abandoned and multi-storey blocks have been built. But the type can still be found in older urban neighbourhoods. Of recent American examples, I recall a house that *Howe* and *Lescaze* built a few years ago in New York as a fine modernist variant of an old tradition (reproduced, for example, in Pica: "Nuova architettura nel mondo", Milan 1938). The type is certainly almost never found in Scandinavia. An exception is a house that Professor *Erik Lallerstedt* built in Stockholm in 1918 as a residence for himself: a house where the style is distinctly Swedish, but the type is English.

The very deep row houses in Barcelona by *Le Corbusier* and *Pierre Jeanneret,* which I have included here (p. 32 b) are strange rather than architecturally convincing. These are very deep houses at 21 m and, moreover, built back-to-back. They are built under distant skies which impose a different set of housing requirements than ours, but even though the task is to create protection against the light to a certain extent, the solution with the strange covered courtyards is artificial, complicated and expensive. Perhaps it is based on a Spanish tradition. I do not know. From an objective point of view at least, it seems forced. The row houses in Pessac near Bordeaux on the same page are also by Le Corbusier and seem more real, especially after having been redrawn, even though they have the look of having been designed by a painter, not an

Semi-detached types

Kooperativa förbundets arkitektkontor (professor Eskil Sundahl) *Stockholm: Project for semi-detached row houses 1936. 1:200 House type, see also p. 31 b*

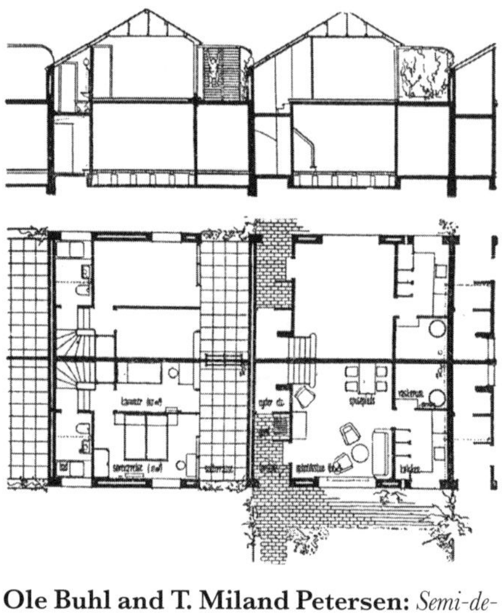

Ole Buhl and T. Miland Petersen: *Semi-detached row houses with large house depth and roof terraces. Crisis Construction Competition 1940. 1:400*

architect. The many roof terraces and large balconies are, as mentioned above, uncommon in row houses. However, the off-putting aspect of the neighbourhood is a bit offset by the fact that the front of the houses, and hence the roof terraces, alternately face opposite sides. Steen Eiler Rasmussen has previously written about these houses in this journal *(Arkitekten* , vol. XXVIII, 1926, pp. 409–414). They are included here as counter-examples.

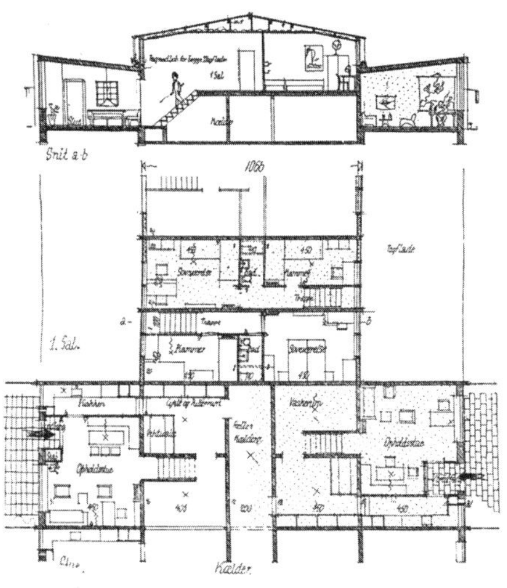

Ole Buhl and T. Miland Petersen: *Row houses with large house depth and roof terraces. Crisis Construction Competition 1940. 1:400*

For the Crisis Construction Competition, *Ole Buhl and Miland Petersen* had a couple of interesting, but complicated semi-detached projects with very large depths and narrow upper storeys so that roof terraces appear both in front of and between the houses.

Housing types with large depths also occur in some of our own residential buildings, including in Brønsparken in Brønshøj, which I am helping to build for *Foreningen Socialt Boligbyggeri*, and which is reproduced on p. 31 a. The two-storey type is 4.15 m wide and 11.20 m deep. In this case, the form is dictated by the high cost of the plot, but it also has some of the same advantages as the semi-detached plans, such as keeping construction costs down and providing good insulation. The staircase is located in the middle of the dwelling and receives natural light via the entrance hall and glass doors. It would probably have been more aesthetically pleasing if the stairs had been open towards the living room, but it was decided that it would be best to wait for the experiences from the experiment in Kantorparken before continuing with this solution. The fact that many such tenants have large families that generate a lot of traffic to the upper floor is perhaps a strike against having an open staircase in the living room.

One-and-a-half story types

Then there are a number of intermediate forms occurring in various guises from the pure two-storey to the pure one-storey row house, as well as *one-and-a-half-storey types*.

In the residential buildings built by co-operative architects and *Arbejdernes Andels-boligforening* at Emdrupvej and Lyngbyvejen (p. 25 a), the sloping terrain in connection with elevation regrading is utilised in such a way that one enters from the street onto an intermediate landing on the staircase with the living room downstairs and the cellar in the back facing north. Similar types have been used by *Foreningen Socialt Boligbyggeri* in some of the most recent residential buildings in provincial areas such as in Skive.

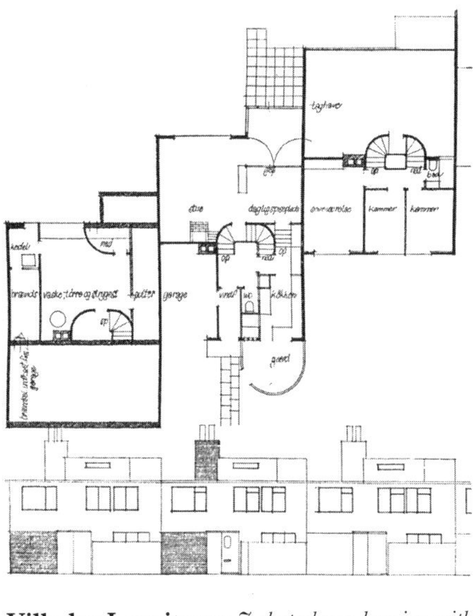

Vilhelm Lauritzen: *Z-shaped row housing with split-level floors.*
Concrete Housing Competition 1934. 1:400

Another type with *split-levels* and a basement under half of the house, so that the bedrooms are above the basement, while the living room and kitchen are half a floor lower, is used by *Harpøth and Kryger* in the interesting houses in Virum (p. 24 b), which is a further elaboration of the project that the two architects were awarded in the Bata competition in Czechoslovakia. The type is the same that has been used in recent years in single-family home types, probably first achieved by *Tyge Hvass* in a house on Heslehøj Allé. Later, the type was used in many places and featured heavily in *Politiken's* competition for single-family houses a few years ago. In his "Wohnbaufibel", *Otto Völckers* has two types based on this planning principle: one with transverse split-levels, the other with longitudinal ones (pp. 23 a and 24 a). In the latter solution, windows can be placed in the roof of the lower half. *Thorball, Stephensen and S. Nalbaldian* had produced a beautiful project with a similar structure for the Crisis Construction Competition (p. 23 b).

These plan solutions may have economic shortcomings, but they solve the basement problem in an advantageous way. A basement area is achieved that is no larger nor more expensive than necessary and avoids deep basement excavating while gaining garden-level living spaces, thus avoiding low-lying bedrooms, which in many people's eyes are a major weakness of one-storey homes.

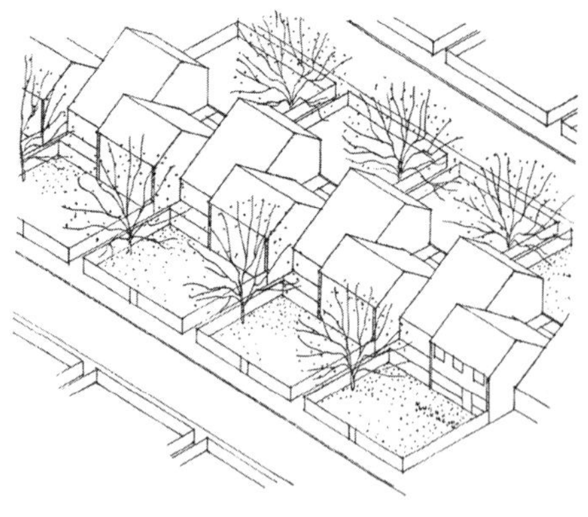

Finn Juhl and Ole Hagen: *U-shaped row housing. Crisis Construction Competition 1940*

Finally, this form attains an accentuation in architectural terms, which is now apparently desired by both the public and architects. Ever since the Bakkehusene period, there has been a bit of a reluctance to live in traditional, monotonous row houses. The same people who find it natural to be confined within a greater or lesser number of cells in multi-storey blocks have steadfastly rejected living in rows.

The old traditional provincial housing, unlike the new row houses, are not always monotonous. They consist of houses with the same profile and same principal materials, but within this limitation the size varies, the number of bays changes and details such as cornices, window shapes, colour, etc., are different and fulfil people's demands for individualisation.

It surprises me that such variation has not been tried to a greater extent in more recent residential buildings. Hygom has experimented along these lines in the large expensive row houses in Svanevænget, but there are no examples from smaller ones.

The possibility of division provided by these *vertical split-level types* allows architects to accommodate an increasing desire for greater expressiveness. Even the types of row houses that are more ordinary than this type have become more accentuated over the years. It began when Thorkild Henningsen's types were given the protruding bay window, providing the outdoor living space with protection from wind and peering neighbours. Gradually, there has been an effort to emphasise the homes' divisions through a pronounced grouping of rooms, varied floor heights and other ways of giving prominence to their external form.

Split-level types

The easiest and most inexpensive way to avoid monotonous rows of houses is through *horizontal displacement* in relation to each other, either, as in one of Henningsen's older buildings on Vanløse Allé, in a U shape or, as in many modern buildings, in a Z shape. In a competition for concrete houses, *Vilhem Lauritzen* once produced such a Z-shaped project which additionally had vertical split-level floors (*Arkitekten Ugehæfte*, vol. XXXVI, No. 12, 1934, p. 60). Professor *Poul Hedquist's* houses in Ålsten near Stockholm have a similar shape. *Harpøth* and *Kryger* have also used it in the aforementioned one-and-a-half storey houses, as did *Friderichsen and Poulsen* in Sorgenfri (p. 33 a), *Milthers and Søndergaard* in Hasselvænget (p. 33 b), and in many other places for that matter.

On the other hand, it is strange that *comb-shaped house types* are not used more. Both the single and double comb shapes meet all possible requirements for a row house in terms of division, shelter and variation. Furthermore, they rectify one of the shortcomings of almost all other forms of contiguous construction: the ability for extensions via additions.

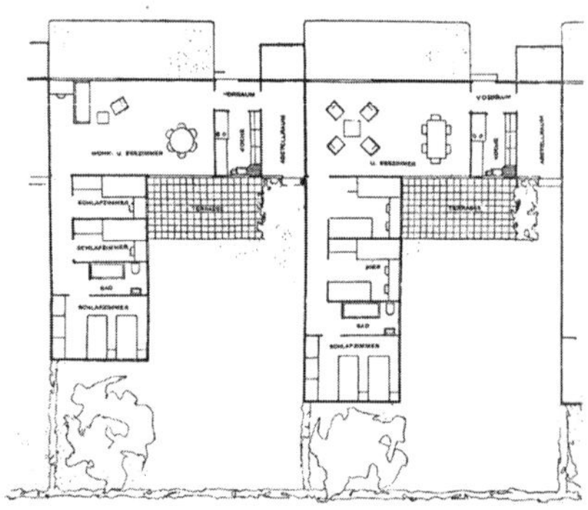

German comb row house type with varied lengths of transverse wings

Moderne Bauformen once published (XXXV p. 60) a comprehensive and interesting study of one-storey comb dwellings (6 f, g and h, p. 34 a and b). The plans are divided into living spaces in one wing and bedrooms in the other and the proposals contain two main types: one has the living space as a fixed element in the projecting wing and bedrooms in a

Northern boundary row houses

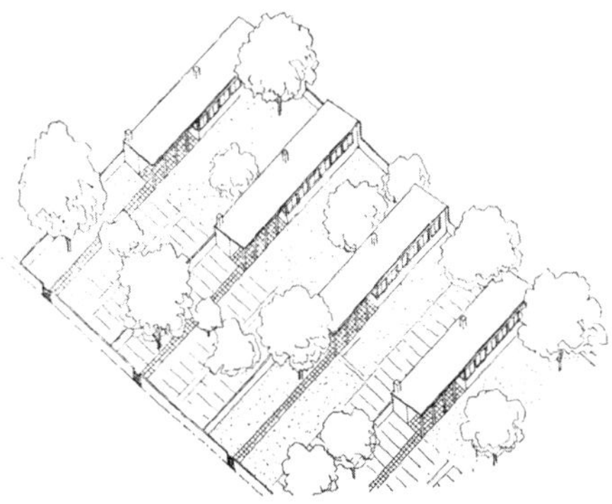

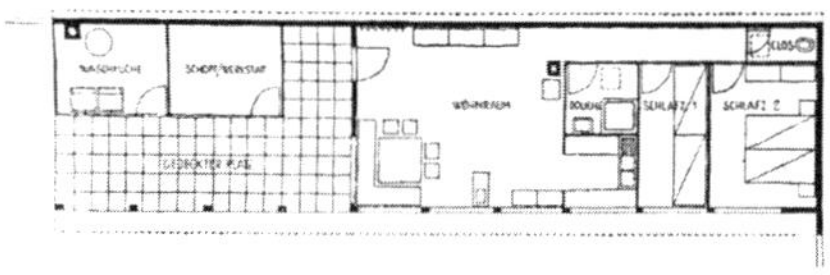

Paul Artaria, Zurich: *Project for northern boundary row houses with lighting from one side 1:200 Also house type, p. 37*

corner of the horizontal wing, and the other is the reverse. The types can vary in size, as the teeth in the comb can have irregular lengths.

At the Werkbund exhibition in Vienna in 1932 there were also a number of comb row houses. At the *Nordic Building Day* exhibition in 1932 in Helsinki, *Hilding Ekelund* had an interesting project with double comb row houses, which are reproduced here (pp. 6 g, 7 p and 36 a and b). It is a transitional form to the project reproduced on the same page, which seems to be a kind of comb building, but in reality, consists of detached houses, located on two sides of the plot boundaries, i.e. with exposure exclusively from the other two sides and with very small plots. The houses have street-facing gables and windows with the southern façade facing the small garden that is otherwise limited on one side by the closed north wall, on the south by another house and on the other side by the gable of the neighbouring house, extended with a short fence wall connecting all the houses. Since only the plan has been published, and since I have not been able to get in touch with Ekelund, we have drawn a structure ourselves. The possibilities that have been experimented with here should be adaptable, for example, along the lines of the semi-detached row house plans. In his recently published book "Vom Bauen und Wohnen", *Paul Artaria* from Zurich has a similar plan form with detached houses along the northern plot boundary line and one-sided exposure. The plan can also be used as a row house form and is therefore included here (p. 37 b). When development conditions and easements in Denmark have reached the point where we can parcel out very small plots and build on boundary lines, types of this kind will be of great importance.

In the plan shown on p. 6 h, comb row houses are combined in an interesting way with detached L-shaped row houses that are also situated with closed north walls along the plot boundary. This results in very extensive plot utilisation while preserving all the advantages of the low-rise house. Similarly, the scheme makes a very economical road system possible.

Patio row houses

Ekelund calls his aforementioned houses *patio row houses*.

It seems to me to be a misnomer, as a patio is surrounded by the housing block on all four sides. If one turns the teeth of comb row housing in towards each other, then they become patio row houses.

In Wassmuth's "Lexikon für Baukunst", these houses are listed as a special type, illustrated with a patio row house in Munich by *Ernst Pfannschmidt* (p. 7 k). It consists of two houses assembled around a courtyard. The system can also be used with two, four or more houses around the patio. The reproduced dwelling by *Uli Seeck*, also in Munich, shows a quarter system. In the Crisis Construction Competition, *Poul Wiboe* had a proposal with the patio surrounded by only a single house, but in some respects his plan is characterised by efforts to extend the plan so far in length that it can reach all the way around.

We have found an American example from Palm Beach in Florida by Howard *Major* (p. 39 a), which shows a contiguous construction around six closed and three open courtyards. It can be expanded to a whole complex of small courtyards, as shown in the site layout plan, p. 7 l.

These types constitute a transition to completely detached houses. Another transition to detached houses are the types the Germans call *chain row houses*, i.e. houses that are only contiguous through smaller sections of the actual house, garages, verandas and similar elements.

Chain row houses

These more detached forms of construction are found in a number of newer German residential buildings. In Ramersdorf near Munich, *Emil Freymuth* and *Guido Harbers* have built chain row houses, and in a number of competitions in which the Stuttgart school especially has been represented, such types have predominated, and very beautiful results have been achieved with these experiments. A few examples of such chain dwellings are included here (pp. 7 n and o, 40 a and b). In both of the plans shown, the garage forms the "chain link", in one case unidirectionally, in the other symmetrically. The types are neither new nor strange. Similar contiguous forms have been found in building society houses in the suburbs of Copenhagen since the turn of the century, but they have been out of production for many years.

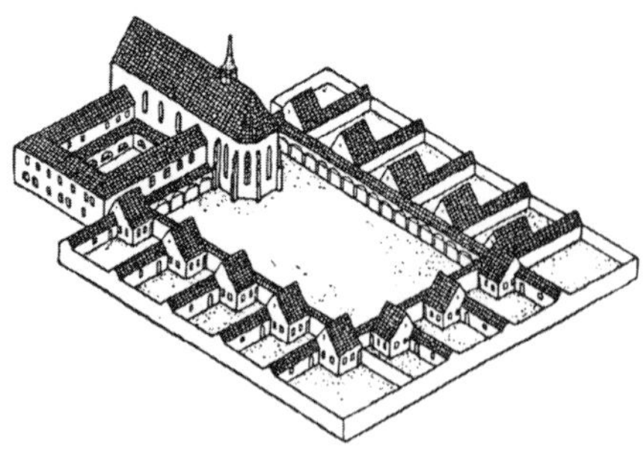

Carthusian monastery, Chain row house system

These many different contiguous construction forms from the familiar semi-detached house to more complicated house forms allow for more unusual development methods, many of which are of interest and should be experimented with here in Denmark. Pages 6 and 7 show a number of examples of such forms, some of which come from existing projects, while others are more theoretical, but they offer opportunities both for new urban forms and new housing forms. The most detached and arbitrary form of contiguous construction we find among the English, who in their garden city developments frequently build several houses together in a quite random way so that it is impossible to see where the individual houses join together. Around 1912, Baillie Scott built two groups of houses of this kind in Hampstead, which are probably familiar to many. The solution is beautiful and picturesque, but the method is not very logical based on its principle. Meanwhile, whether or not we prefer one contiguous form of construction over another, all of these more picturesque and detached types of coherent buildings allow for homes with individual emphasis. Once we reach the point where the wild, chaotic construction of detached small single-family houses is also planned according to broader outlines and executed under more fixed forms of organisation, then more varied, alternating and individually emphasised house types will surely develop, which will replace the uniform row housing we are working with now.

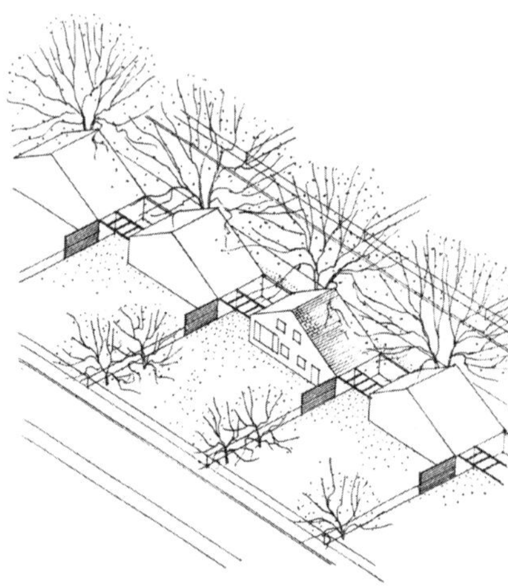

Finn Juhl and Ole Hagen: *Chain row house project. Crisis Construction Competition 1940*

Gardens

Finally, a few reflections on the gardens.

The most frequently common arrangement for row house gardens is a division with narrow, long gardens perpendicular to the row of houses, most often separated by spruce fencing planted with vines.

After a few years, when these vines have reached a suitable stage of growth, there is a risk that the fence will rot and fall over, and one starts all over again. Better fences and walls, for example, are generally too expensive, and picket fencing is not popular. In K.A.B's study town at Bernstorffsvej, the fences between the row gardens, which according to G.N. Brandt's theory are so high that one is hidden when sitting down, but can talk to the neighbours when standing up, are made of notched concrete posts with horizontal boards laid in the notches. When the bottom board becomes rotted, it can be kicked away and a new one placed at the top.

Ivar Bentsen has used a similar fence for the municipal building on Vigerslev Allé. It is a good and suitable fence, but this kind of division, which resembles pigsties, is not popular. The right kind of fence between row gardens has not really been invented yet.

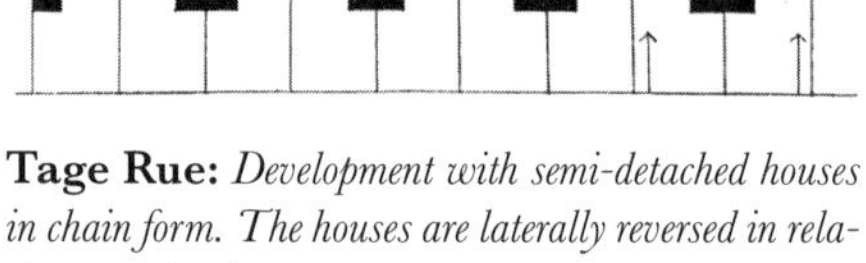

Tage Rue: *Development with semi-detached houses in chain form. The houses are laterally reversed in relation to each other.*
1:2500. (Arkitekten vol. XXIV, No. 17, 1922, p. 218 Housing type) see p. 40 a

How the garden area itself should be designed in detail is a question in and of itself, but would lead us too far astray to go into here, and thus must be left to landscape architects.
Its principal categorisation, on the other hand, concerns the architects.
In older developments the gardens are usually quite large, but there is a tendency in the newer ones to make them ever smaller. Everyone appreciates the open spaces, but many people do not have the time or the means to maintain fairly large gardens, and these areas are of little value for cultivating a kitchen garden. Although at the moment it is nice to be able to plant a few rows of potatoes, such home production under normal conditions has no economic significance.
The gardens are therefore made smaller: so small that they do not occupy the entire outdoor space, which in order to have a reasonable exposure must be between the rows of houses. Some of the larger buildings, therefore, have experimented with a special design of the space that creates a division between private gardens and a common park area. Such a solution has been attempted, for example, at Kantorparken and Hasselvænget.
An attempt has been made at Brønsparken, which includes approximately 200 houses, to divide the open-air areas so that the largest parts are laid out as a public park and the private garden is reduced to an area the size of a living room; an "open-air living room" where prams and sandboxes can be placed, clothes hung to dry and where people can do whatever they want without being gazed upon by strangers. These small gardens are fenced off by semicircular walls that hide the private arrangements so that the park-like character of the residential buildings is preserved.
The houses are positioned with the gardens alternately on each side, so that the small gardens are not directly adjoined. The common area has roads and paths paved with brick tiles and the green areas are planted with privets that form large puffs and are easier to maintain than grass. Along the length of the development is a sunken playground and sunken lane, framed by elders, hawthorn and wild roses. Children can access this playground without having to cross the road area.
As with most state-subsidised residential buildings where the houses are not owned but let like multi-storey dwellings, I think such a garden design is more fitting than the large gardens. Where residents do not have a sense of ownership in relation to the garden, they will most often neglect it. It should therefore be as small as possible and hidden from view as much as possible, and the largest feasible part of the area should, as with multi-storey houses, benefit all residents in the form of a common area.

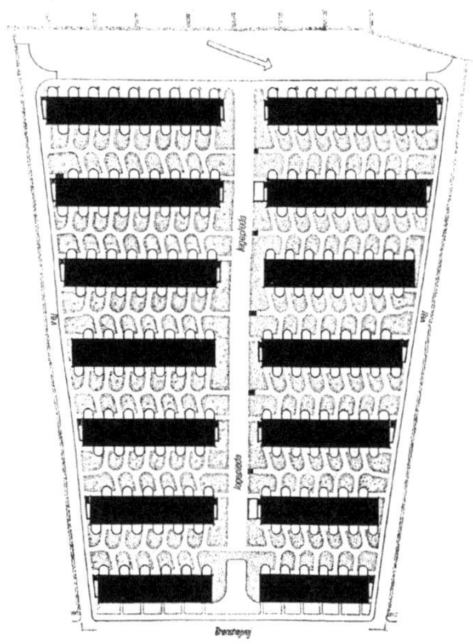

Kay Fisker, C.F. Møller and Erik Jensen: *Brønsparken, built around Brønshøjvej in 1941 by Social Boligbyggeri.*
Park by **C. Th. Sorensen**.
House type, p. 31 a

P. Søgaard-Pedersen:
42 row houses built in 1922 by Københavns Almindelige Boligselskab (KAB) on Hyldegaards Tværvej in Odrup.
The houses contain 2 living rooms and a kitchen on the ground floor and 2 large rooms and a small room on the 1st floor.
The houses are built of yellow brick and the roof is covered with red pantiles.

Ib Lunding:
27 row houses built in 1928 on Tranegaardsvej in Gentofte.
The houses contain 2 living rooms and a kitchen on the ground floor and 1 bedroom and 4 small rooms on the 1st floor.
The houses are built of yellow brick and the roof is covered with pantiles.

Thorkild Henningsen:
20 row houses built in 1927 on Bernstorffsvej.
The houses contain 2 living rooms and a kitchen on the ground floor and 1 bedroom and 3 small rooms on the 1st floor.
The houses are built of red brick. The roof is covered with red pantiles.

Henry Kryger and Erik Harpøth:
9 row houses built in 1938 on Rømmerødgaard's lands in Virum.
The houses contain a living room and a kitchen on the same level as the garden and 2 small, split-level rooms.
The houses are built of yellow brick and the roof is covered with Icopal.
Plan type p. 24 b

Knud Frederichsen and Arne Poulsen:
7 row houses built in 1938 at Æblevænget in Lyngby.
The houses contain a large living room and kitchen on the ground floor and 2 bedrooms and 1 small room on the 1st floor.
The houses are built of yellow machine-made brick and the roof is covered with Icopal.
Plan type p. 33 a

K. K. Søndergaard and Gunnar Milthers:
38 row houses built in 1939. on Hasselvej in Vanløse.
The type area is 55 m².
The houses contain 1 living room, 3 bedrooms, a kitchen and bathroom.
The houses are built of yellow and red hand-made brick.
The roof is covered with red pantiles. The former landowner of the site nursery owner Hastrup, has helped with the landscaping design of the garden area.
Plan type p. 33 b

Kooperative Arkitekter and Dan Fink:
213 row houses built by Arbejdernes Andels-Boligforening (AAB) on Emdrupvej in 1938–1940.
The houses contain a living room, kitchen and storeroom on the ground floor. On the 1st floor there are 2 bedrooms, 1 small room and a bathroom. There is a common heating plant and a laundry machine room.
The houses are built of yellow brick and the roof is covered with Icopal. The entrance to the houses is on the landing of the staircase.
Plan type p. 25 a

Kooperative Arkitekter:
109 row houses built by Foreningen Socialt Boligbyggeri (FSB) on Bispebjerg Parkallé in 1939–40.
The houses contain a living room and a kitchen, and and a bedroom and 2 small rooms, respectively.
The houses are supplied by a common heating plant.
The houses are built of yellow brick and the roof is covered with Icopal. There are load-bearing cross partition walls.
Plan type p. 28 b

Karl Almer Nielsen:
7 row houses built in 1938 on Kollegievej in Ordrup.
The type area is 88 m^2. The houses contain a living room, dining room, hall and kitchen on the ground floor. On the 1st floor, there is a bedroom, a guest room and two small rooms.
The houses are built of hand-made rubble stone. Roofs are covered with Icopal.
Plan type p. 26 b

Helmer Remark and Svend Aage Petersen:
30 row houses built in 1937 on the corner of Kongevejen and Nærumvejen in Virum. On the 1st floor, the houses contain a living room, dining room, bedroom, small room, kitchen and bathroom. The houses are built of red hand-made. brick and the roof is covered with Icopal.
Plan type p. 21 b

Ivar Bentsen in collaboration with Ole Buhl and T. Miland Petersen:
157 row houses built by the municipality of Copenhagen on Vigerslev Allé in 1938–39.
There are 112 houses with 2 large rooms and 1 small room and 45 houses with 2 large rooms and 2 small rooms.
There is a basement under one half of the houses.
The houses are built of red hand-made brick and the roof is covered with Icopal.
The storey partitions are made of reinforced concrete.
Plan type p. 22 a

Palle Suenson and Ib Martin Jensen:
25 row houses built on Svejagervej in Hellerup.
The floor-area of the two types is: 63 m² and 49 m².
The road network consists of a 10 m wide road in front of the houses and a 4 m wide path behind the houses.
The houses are built of red hand-made bricks. The roof is covered with Icopal.
The window frames are made of steel.
Plan type p. 27 b

Emil Freymuth:
On the ground floor, the houses contain a living room and a kitchen and on the 1st floor there are 2 bedrooms and a bath.
Row houses built in Ramersdorf near Munich in 1934.
The houses are built of brick and the roof is covered with pantiles.
Plan type p. 29 b

Uli Seeck:
Patio houses, built in Munich-Bogenhausen in 1931.
The houses are built of brick and the roof is covered with pantiles.
Plan type p. 38 b

Guido Harbers:
Chain row houses, built in Ramersdorf near Munich in 1934.
The houses are built of rendered brick. The roof is covered with pantiles.

Howard Major:
Patio houses built in Palm Beach in Florida, USA. The houses are built of rendered brick and the roof is covered with light-coloured slate. Plan type p. 39 a

Alvar Aalto:
Staggered row houses, built for Sunila cellulose factory in Finland as housing for senior employees. The houses are constructed in reinforced concrete and the roof is covered with roofing felt.

Kooperativa Förbundets Arkitektkontor (KFAI):
Row houses built on Hästholmen near Stockholm. The houses are built of wood with firewalls of gasbeton. The roof is covered with roofing felt. Plan type p. 20 a

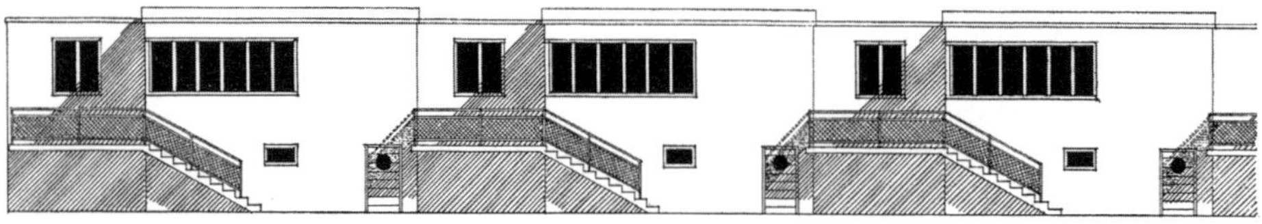

Façade facing the garden

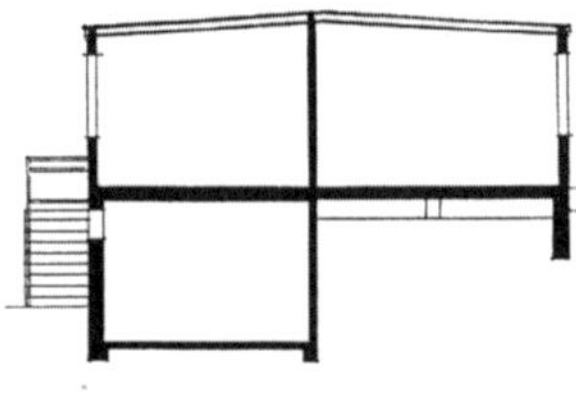

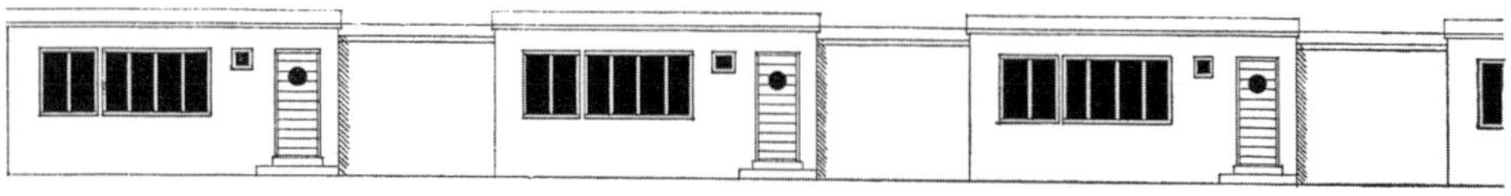

Façade facing the street

Basement floor

Ground floor

Location: *Hästholmen, Stockholm (Sweden)*
Builder: *Kooperativa Förbundet (KF)*
Architect: *Kooperativa Förbundets Arkitektkontor (KFAI)*
Year completed: *1930*
Road system: *one-side road*
Built up area: *72 m²*
Floor area: *72 m²*
Volume: *253 m³*
Materials etc.: *The houses are built of wood with firewalls in aerated concrete. Roof covered with roofing felt*

Elaborated by Aage Palludan
Redrawn from the working drawings

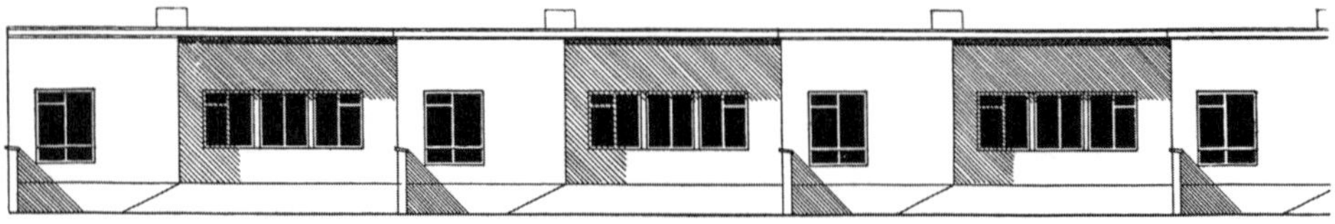

Façade facing the garden

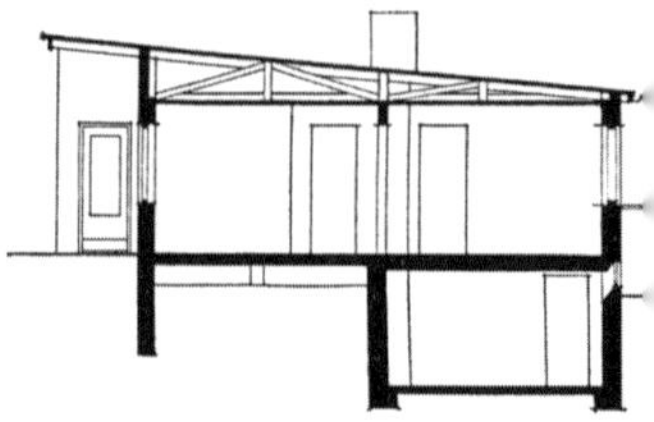

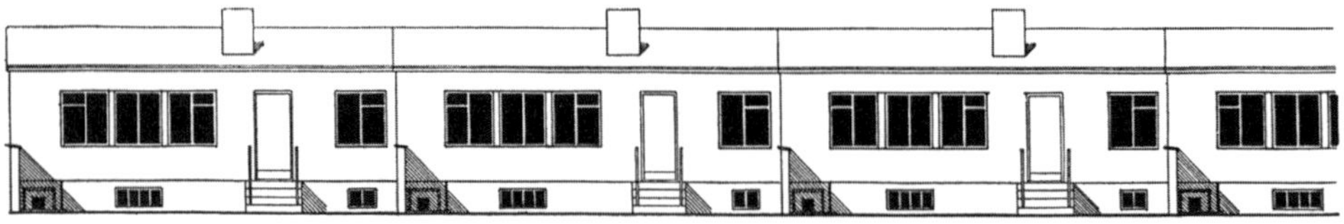

Façade facing the street

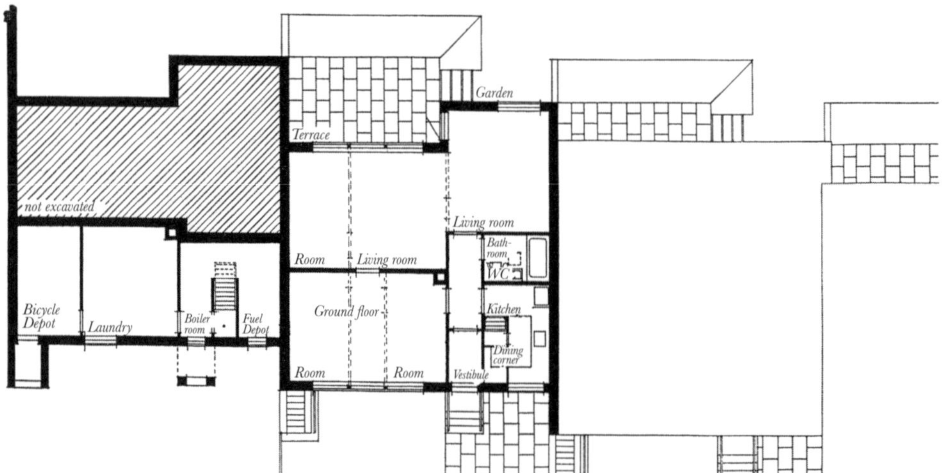

Basement floor

Ground floor

Location: *Ørholm near Copenhagen*
Architect: *Frans Fastrau*
Year completed: *1939*
Road system: *one-side road*
Built up area: *75 m²*
Plot area: *370 m²*
Volume: *330 m³*
Materials etc.: *The houses are built of yellow brick. The roof is covered with Icopal*

Elaborated by Mogens Lillie
Redrawn from the working drawings

Row houses. *One-storey types with semi-basement. 1:250*

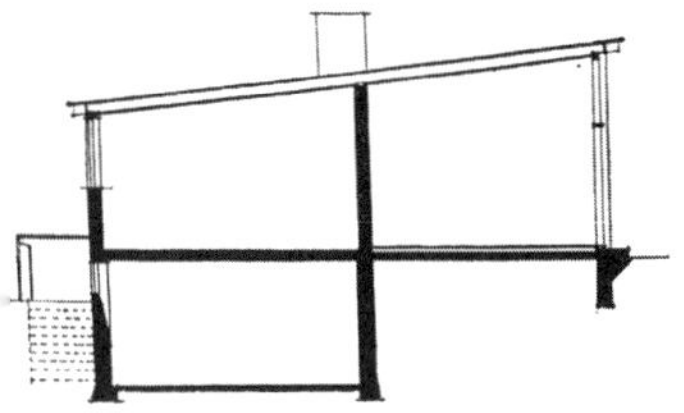

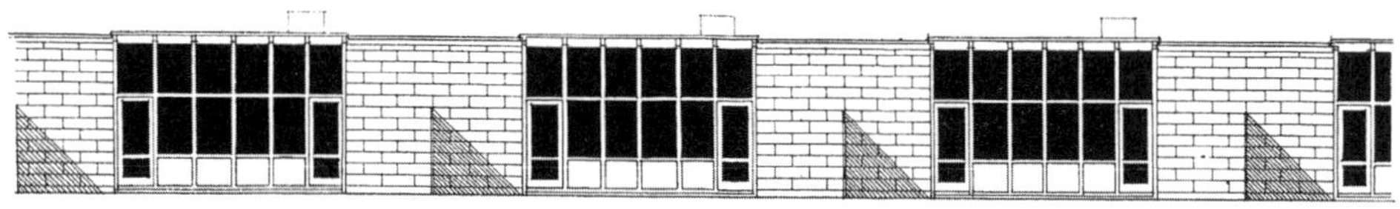

Façade facing the garden

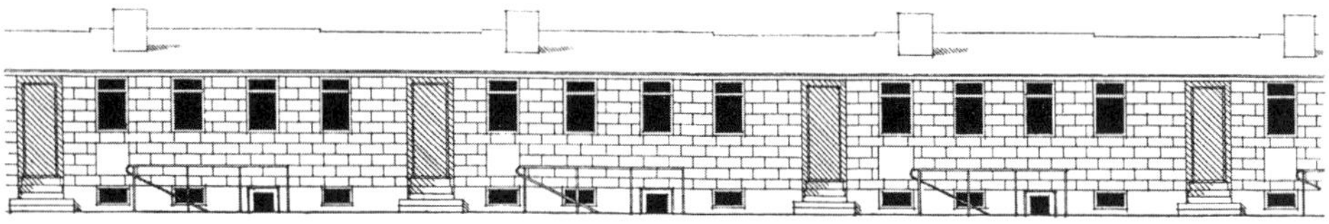

Façade facing the street

Location: *Project*
Architect: *Steen Eiler Rasmussen*
Road system: *one-side road*
Built up area: *84.5 m²*
Floor area: *84.5 m²*
Volume: *338 m³*
Materials etc.: *The houses are to be built of KH-blocks and covered with Icopal.*

Elaborated by Poul Jochumsen and Kai Børge Nielsen
Redrawn from the working drawings

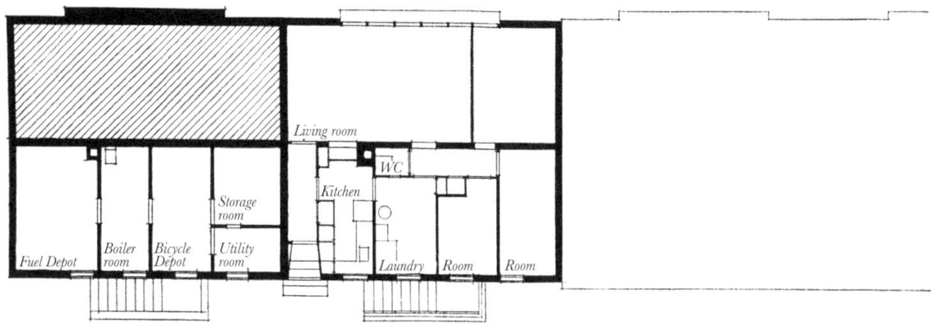

Basement floor *Ground floor*

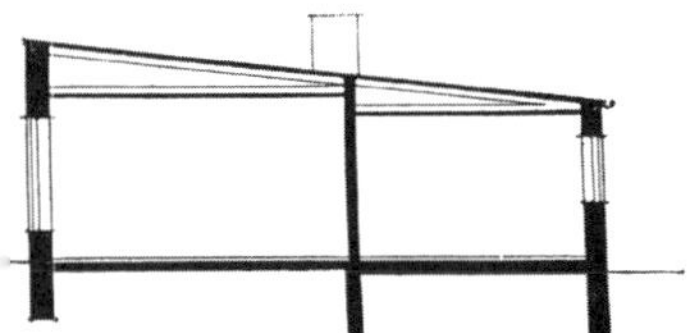

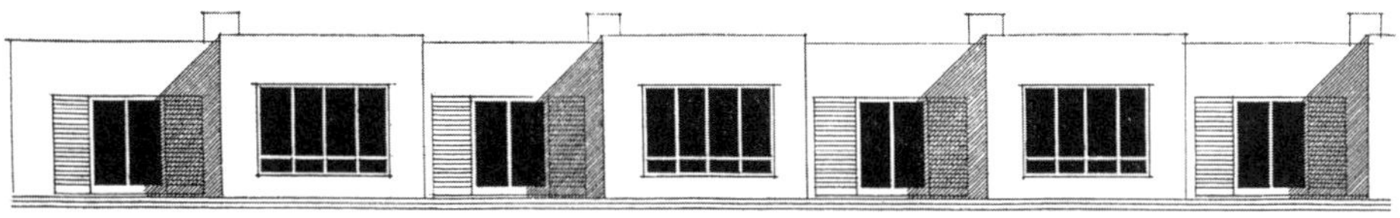

Façade facing the garden

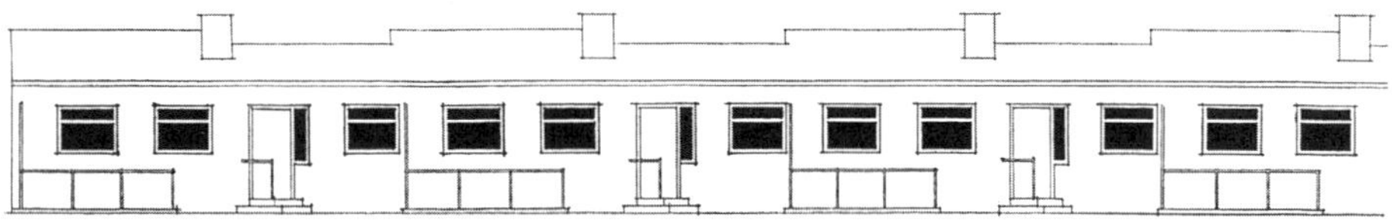

Façade facing the street

Location: *Virum near Copenhagen*
Architect: *Helmer Remark and Svend Aage Petersen*
Year completed: *1937*
Road system: *one-side road*
Built up area: *82 m²*
Plot area: *250 m²*
Volume: *356 m²*
Construction cost: *12'000 kr.*
Cost per m²: *146 kr.*
Cost per m³: *34 kr.*
Materials etc.: *The houses are built of red hand-made brick.*

Elaborated by Hans Jensen
Redrawn from the working drawings

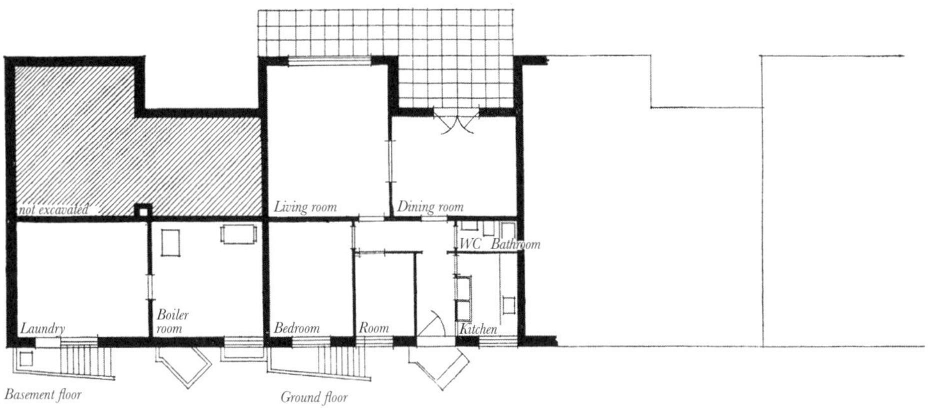

Basement floor *Ground floor*

Row houses. *One-storey types with semi-basement. 1:250*

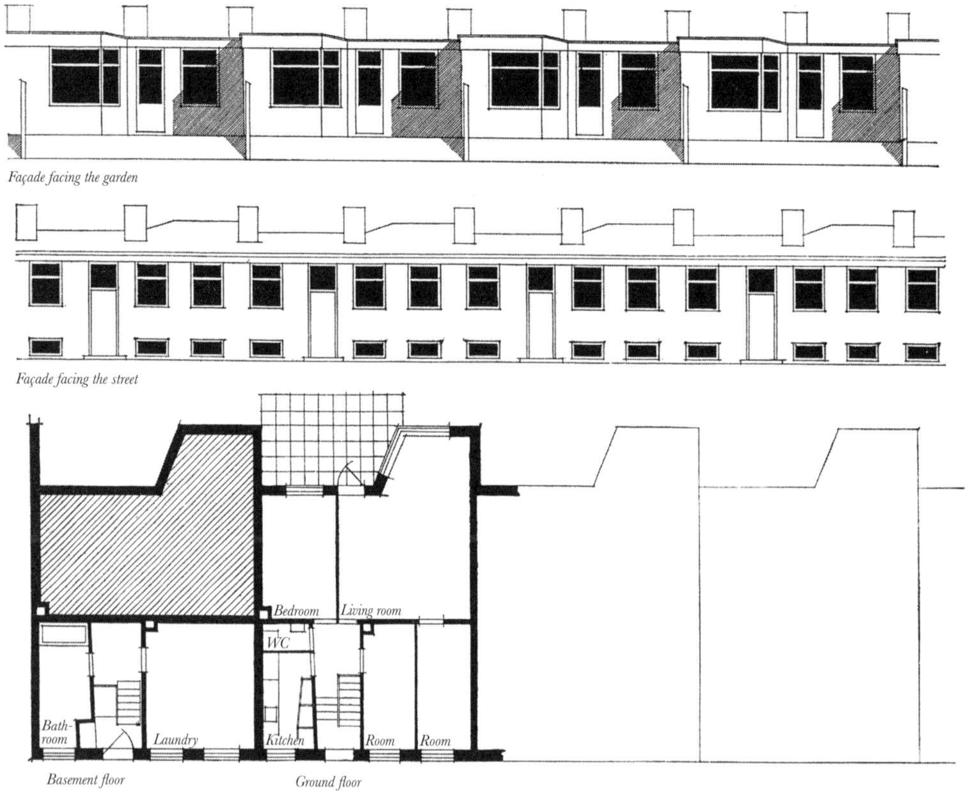

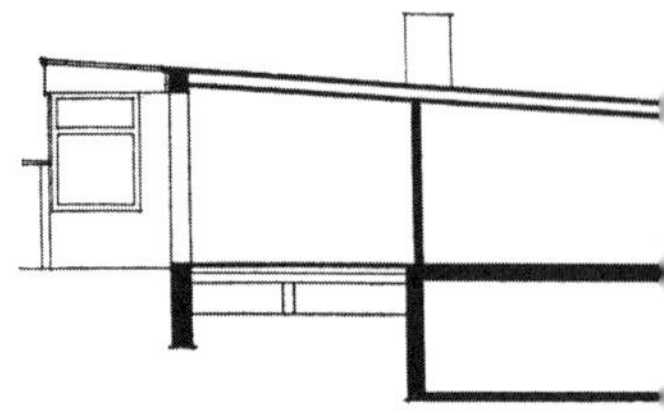

Location: *Vigerslev allé*
Client: *Copenhagen Municipality*
Architect: *Prof. Ivar Bentsen, Ole Buhl and T. Miland Petersen*
Year completed: *1938–39*
Road system: *4.5 m wide, two-sided roads with 2.5 m wide back path*
Built up area: *73.4 m²*
Volume: *273.4 m²*
Floor area: *73.4 m²*
Volume: *310 m³*
Construction cost: *10 445 kr.*
Cost per m²: *142 kr.*
Cost per m³: *34 kr.*
Materials etc.: *The houses are to be built of KH-blocks and covered with Icopal The houses are built of red hand-made brick. The roof is covered with Icopal. Iron heating stoves.*

Elaborated by Hans Jensen
Redrawn from the working drawings

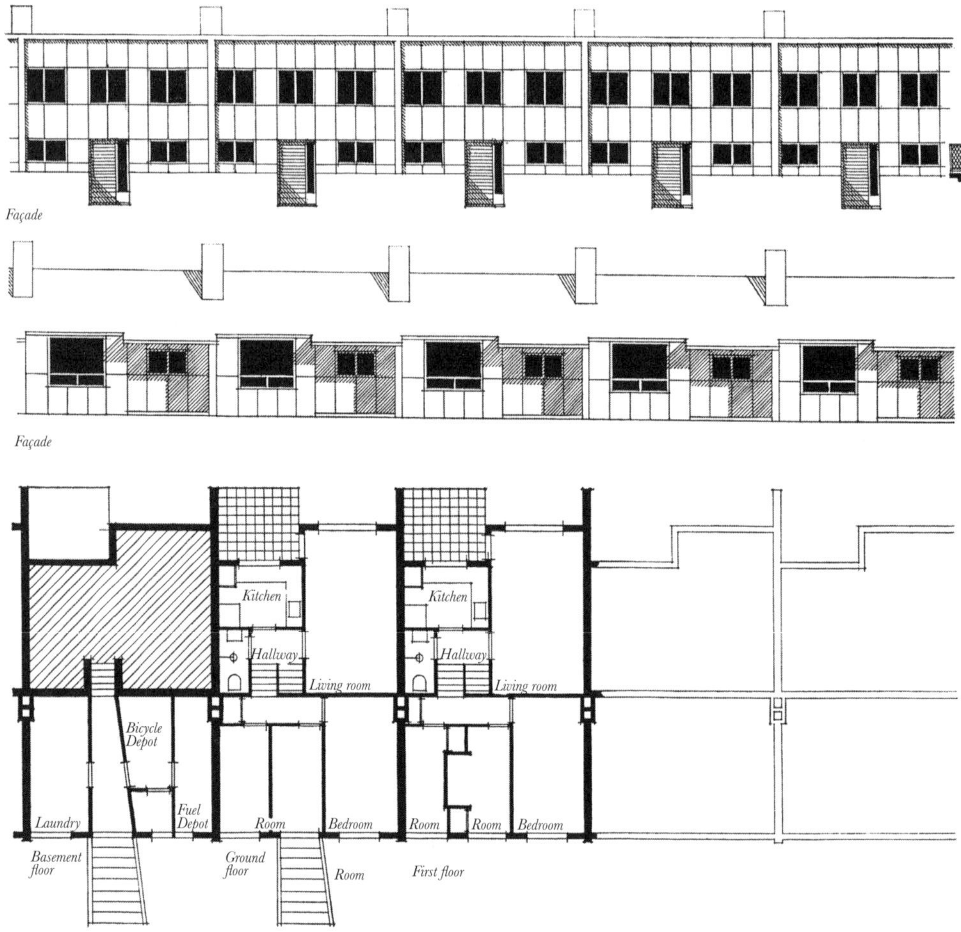

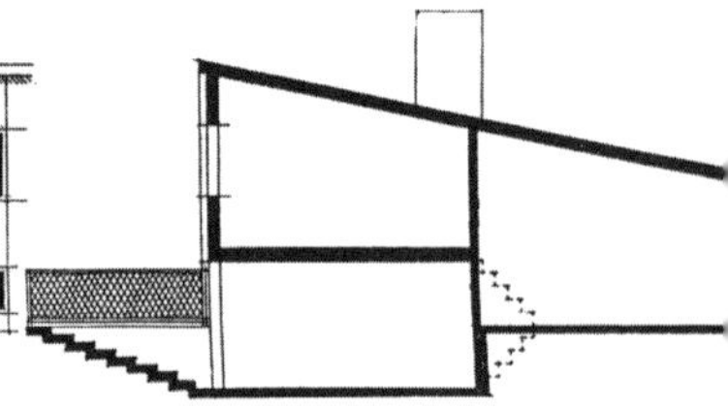

Location: *Project for the Academic Architectural Association Competition on construction crisis*
Architect: *J.C. Louring Nielsen*
Road system: *two-sided roads*
Built up area: *65 m²*
Floor area: *95 m²*
Volume: *260 m³*
Materials etc.: *The houses are planned to be built with brick gables and outer walls of skeleton construction covered with Eternit tiles. Roof covered with corrugated sheeting.*

Elaborated by Kjártan Sigurdsson
Redrawn from the competition project

Row houses. *One-storey type with semi-basement, and one-and-a-half storey type with split-levels along the length of the house and semi-basement. 1:250*

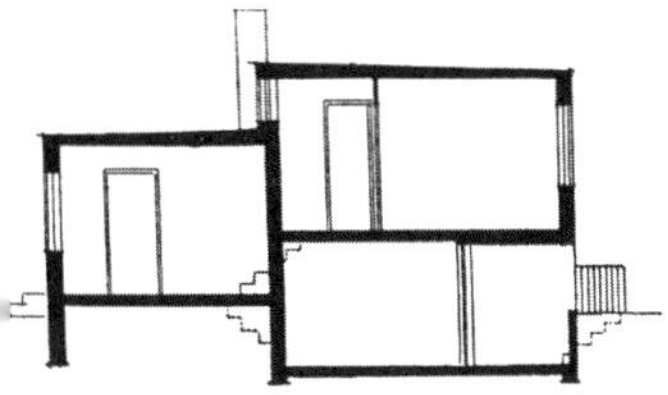

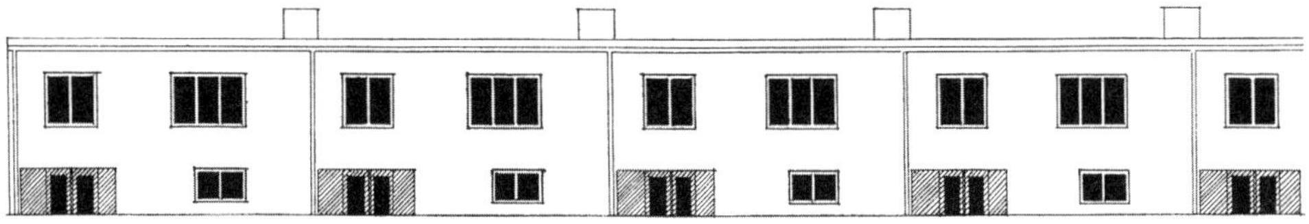

Façade facing the garden

Location: *Project*
Architect: *Munich*
Road system: *West-East two-sided walking roads*
Built up area: *64.82 m²*
Floor area: *102.02 m²*
Volume: *277 m³*
Materials etc.: *The houses are planned to be built of brick. The houses are split-level in the longitudinal direction. Bathroom and storage room lit from west with a window over the lower part of the house.*

Elaborated by Jørgen Jacobsen Drawn from Otto Völckers: "Wohnbaufibel". Jul. Hoffmanns Forlag, Stuttgart 1932.

Façade facing the street

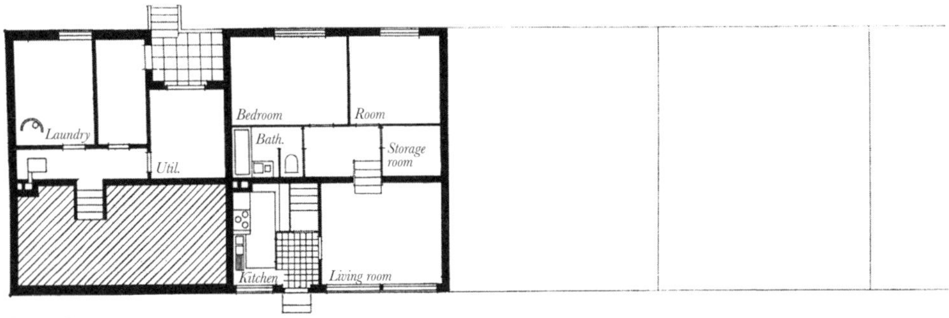

Basement floor

Ground floor

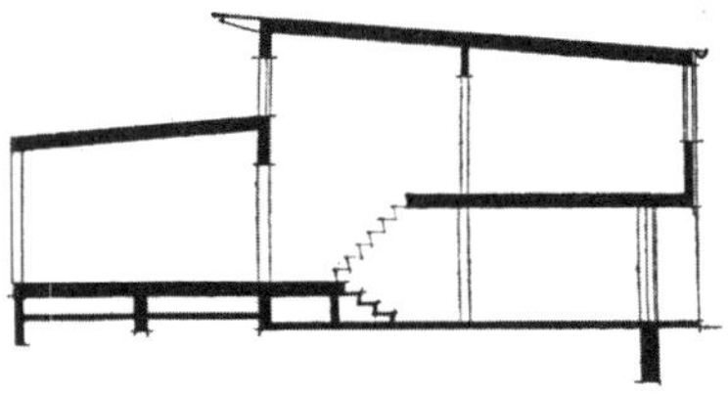

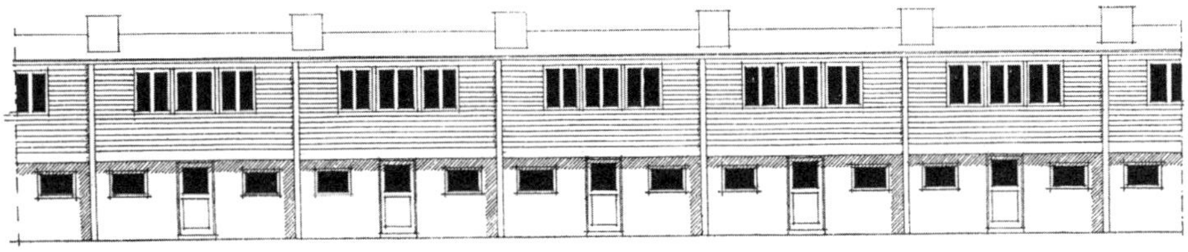

Façade

Location: *Project for the Akademisk Arkitekforening's Konkurrence om krisebyggeri*
Architect: *Magnus Stephensen, Knud Thorball and S. Nalbandian*
Built up area: *61.50 m²*
Floor area: *102 m²*
Volume: *282 m³*
Materials etc.: *The houses are planned to be built of brick and timber-framing. Roof covered with Icopal*

Elaborated by Ib Møgelvang Nielsen Redrawn from the project

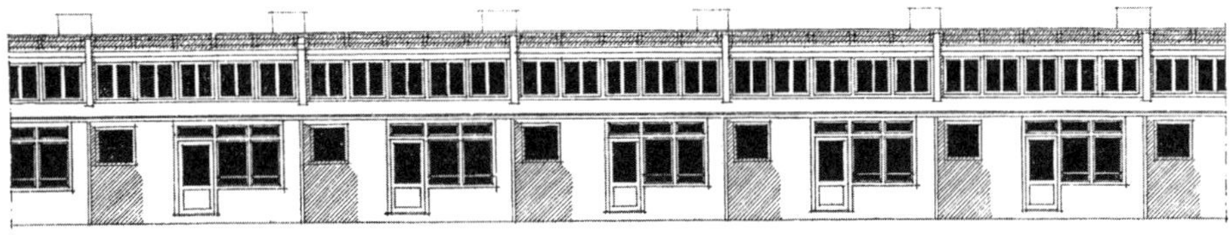

Façade

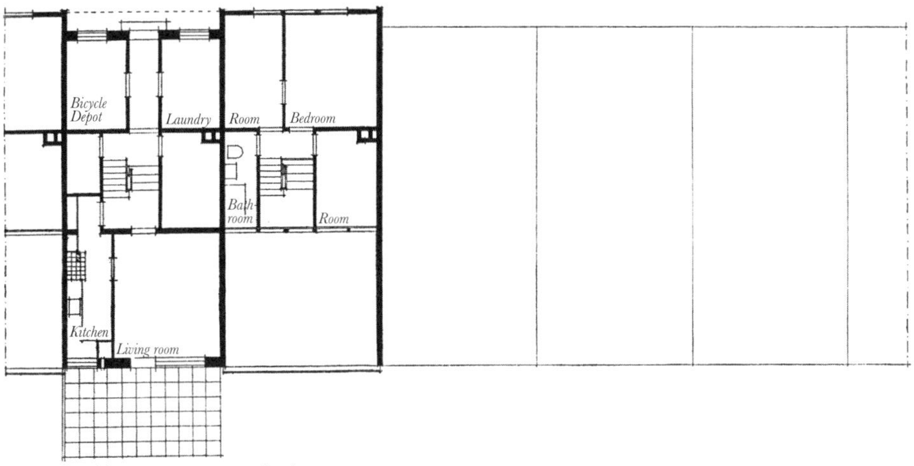

Ground floor

First floor

Row houses. *One-and-a-half storey types with the split-levels along the length of the house and semi-basement. 1:250*

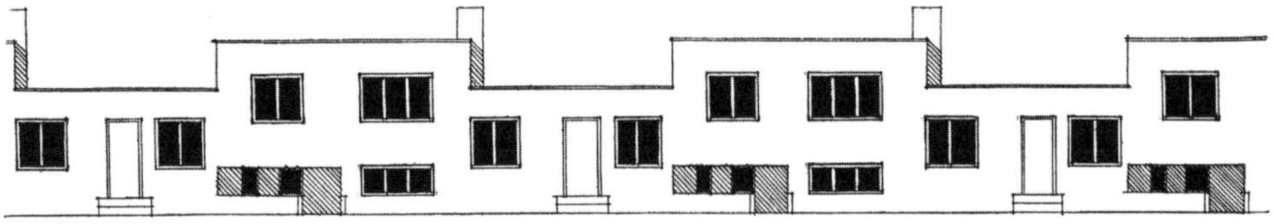

Façade facing the street

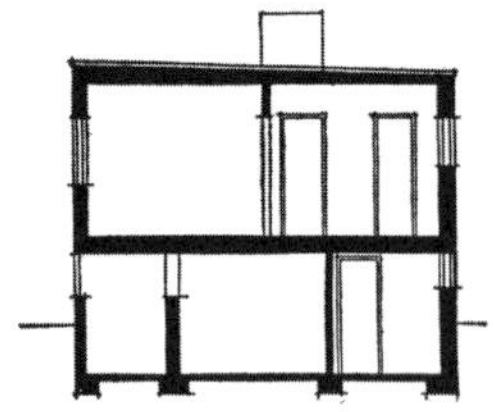

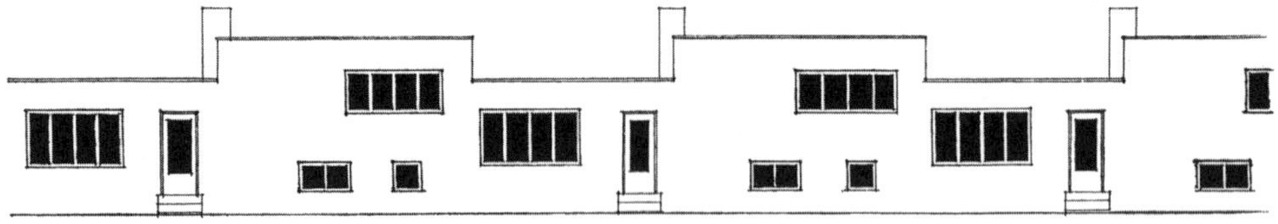

Façade

Location: Project
Architect: Otto Völckers, Munich
Built up area: 75 m²
Volume: 290 m³
Materials etc.: The houses are planned to be built of brick and the roof covered with roofing felt. Transverse-split-level floors. Semi-basement.

Elaborated by Henning Jacobsen
Drawn from Otto Völckers: "Wohnbaufibel". Jul. Hoffmanns Forlag, Stuttgart 1932

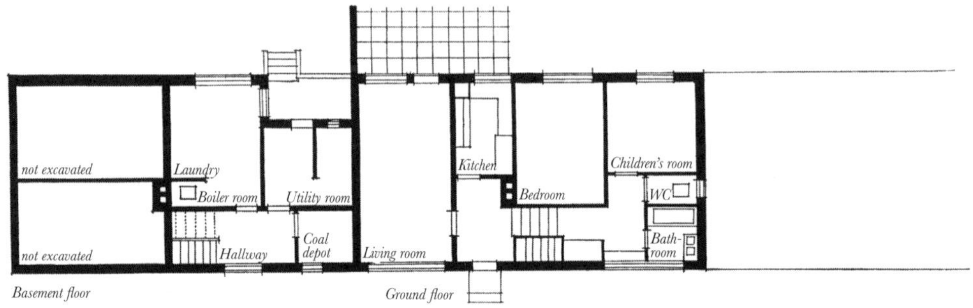

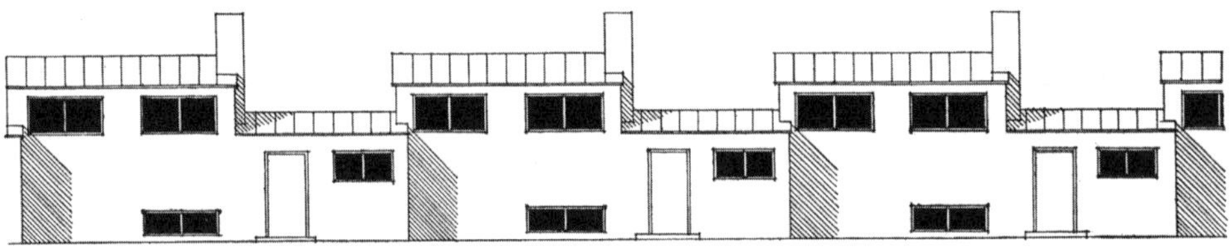

Façade facing the street

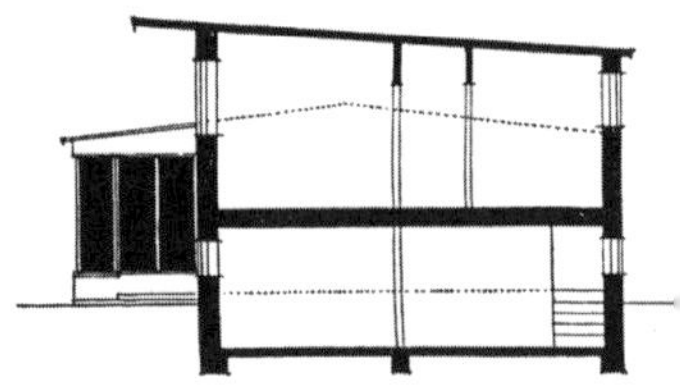

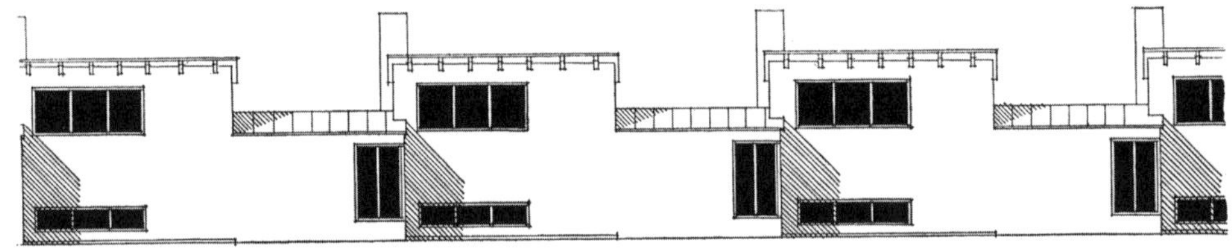

Façade facing the garden

Location: *Rømmerødgaards land, Virum near Copenhagen*
Builder: *Bricklayer master Th. Olsen*
Architect: *Henry Kryger and Erik Harpøth*
Year completed: *1937*
Road system: *one-side road*
Built up area: *81 m²*
Plot area: *335 m²*
Floor area: *84 m²*
Volume: *350 m³*
Construction cost: *19'000 kr.*
Cost per m²: *235 kr.*
Cost per m³: *54.30 kr.*
Materials etc.: *The houses are built of yellow brick with the roof covered with Icopal. Transverse split-level floors.*

Elaborated by Erik Glud
Redrawn from the working drawings

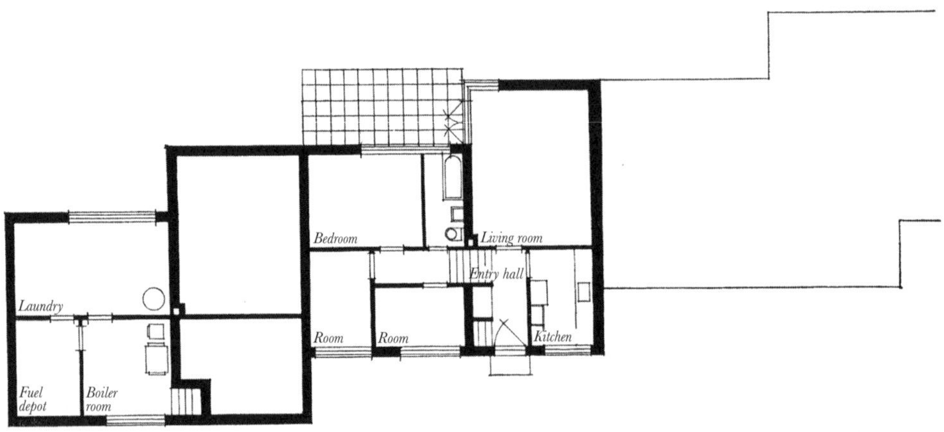

Row houses. *One-and-a-half storey types with transverse split-level floors and a semi-basement. 1:250*

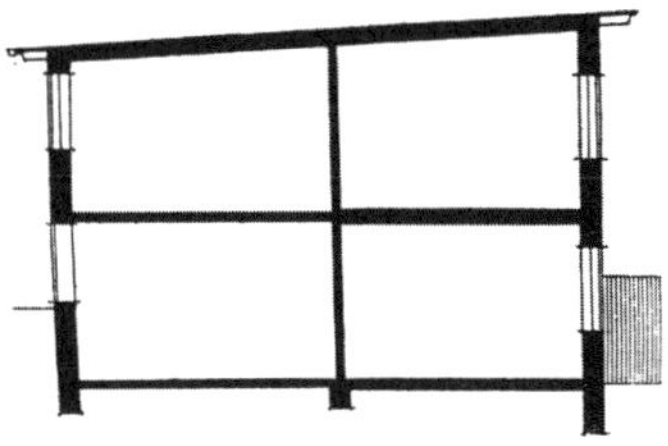

Façade facing the garden

Location: *Lyngbyvej and Emdrupvej, Copenhagen*
Builder: *The Workers' Cooperative Housing Association*
Architect: *Kooperative Arkitekter and Dan Fink*
Year completed: *1939–40*
Road system: *one-sided road 3m wide, reserved for general. driving, perpendicular to it, wide driveways with parking spaces*
Built up area: *47.84 m²*
Floor area: *95.68 m²*
Volume: *277 m³*
Construction cost: *8 300 kr.*
Cost per m²: *173.36 kr.*
Cost per m³: *30 kr.*
Materials etc.: *The houses are built of yellow brick and the roof is covered with Icopal. There is an entrance to the houses on the staircase's intermediate landing. Common heating plant*

Elaborated by Knud Hansen
Redrawn from the working drawings

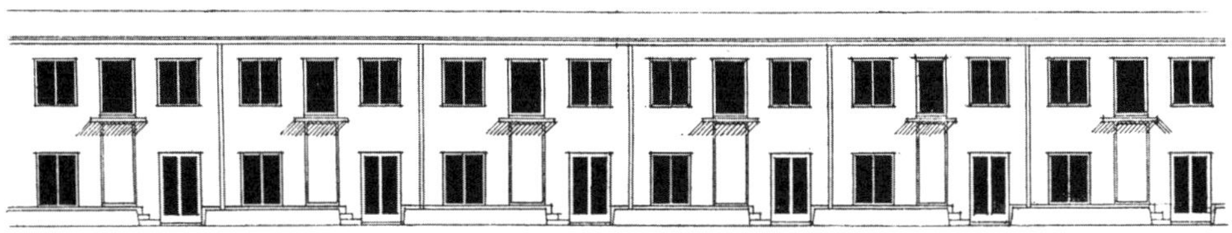

Façade facing the street

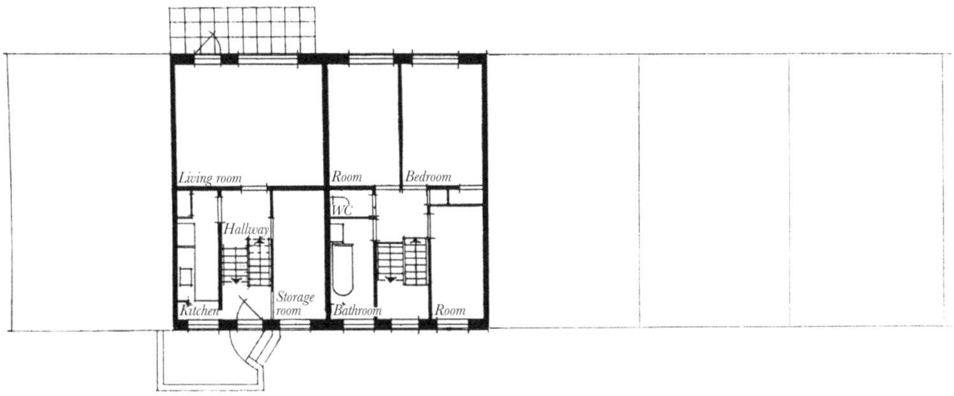

Ground floor First floor

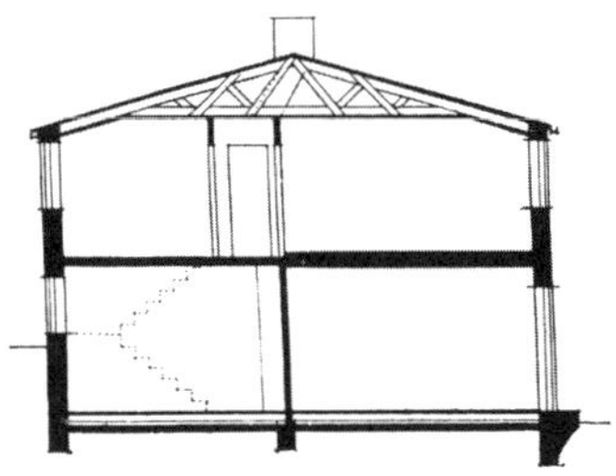

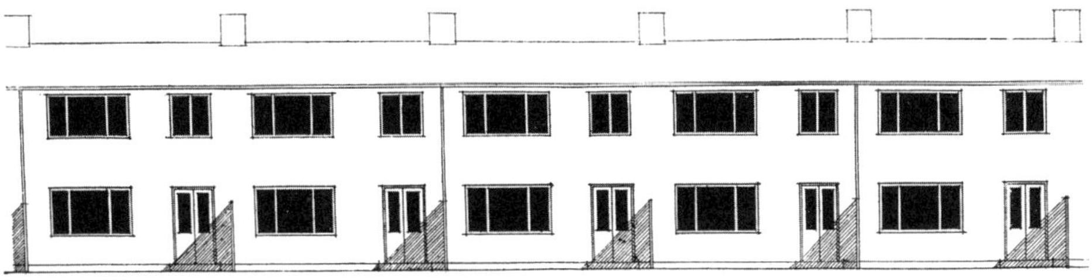

Façade facing the garden

Location: *Skive*
Builder: *Foreningen Socialt Boligbyggeri (FSB)*
Architect: *Erik V. Lind and Tage Hansen*
Year completed: *1940*
Road system: *two-sided road*
Built up area: *60 m²*
Plot area: *240 m²*
Floor area: *108 m²*
Volume: *366 m³*
Construction cost: *10 700 kr.*
Cost per m²: *179 kr.*
Cost per m³: *30 kr.*
Materials etc.: *The houses are built of brick and the roof is covered with Icopal. There is an entrance to the houses on the staircase's intermediate landing*

Elaborated by Ove Hove
Redrawn from the working drawings

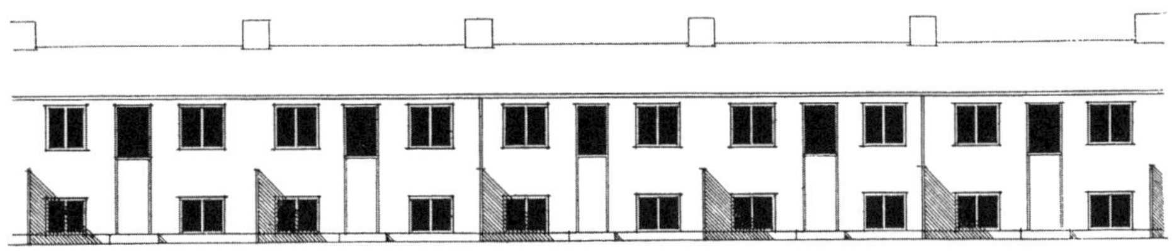

Façade facing the street

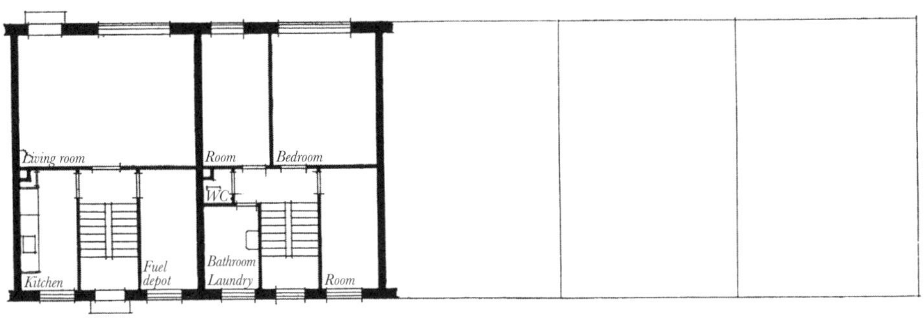

Ground floor First floor

Row houses. *Two-storey types on sloping terrain. Entrance on the staircase's intermediate landing. Half of the downstairs is a basement. 1:250*

Façade facing the garden

Façade facing the street

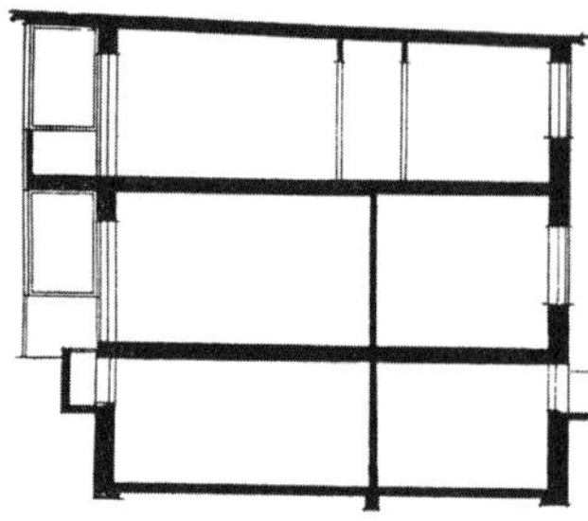

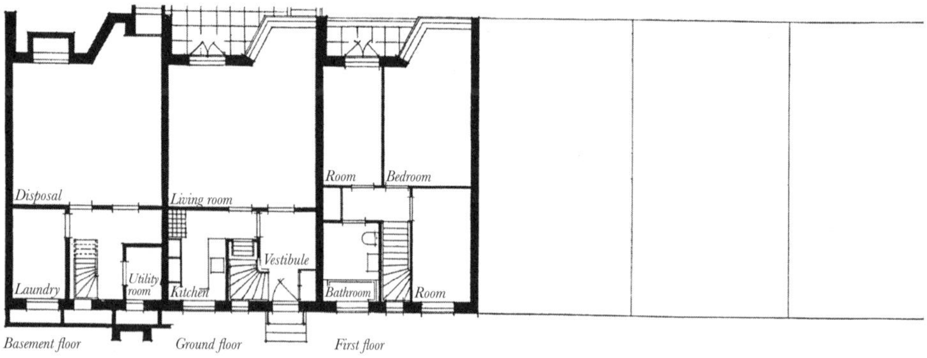

Basement floor Ground floor First floor

Location: *Hasle in Aarhus*
Builder: *Foreningen Socialt Boligbyggeri (FSB)*
Architect: *Architects of the Cooperative, Dan Fink and N. Chr. Skjøth, Aarhus*
Year completed: *1939*
Road system: *one-sided 3m wide road, reserved for general driving*
Built up area: *50.30 m²*
Floor area: *100.60 m²*
Volume: *402.40 m³*
Construction cost: *13 000 kr.*
Cost per m²: *258 kr.*
Cost per m³: *32.24 kr.*
Materials etc.: *The houses are built of yellow brick. Roof covered with Icopal.*

Elaborated by Knud Hansen
Redrawn from the working drawings

Façade facing the garden

Façade facing the street

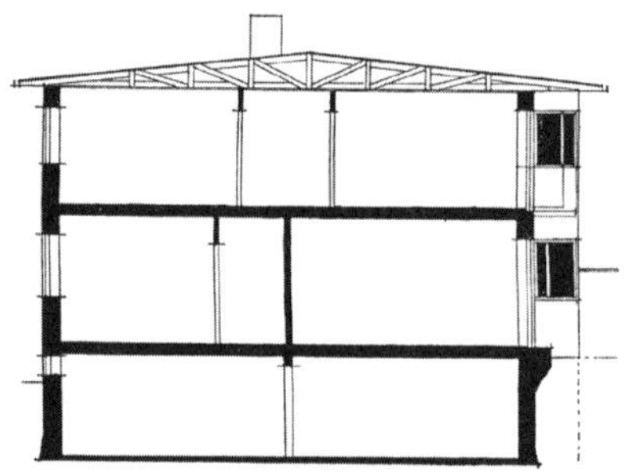

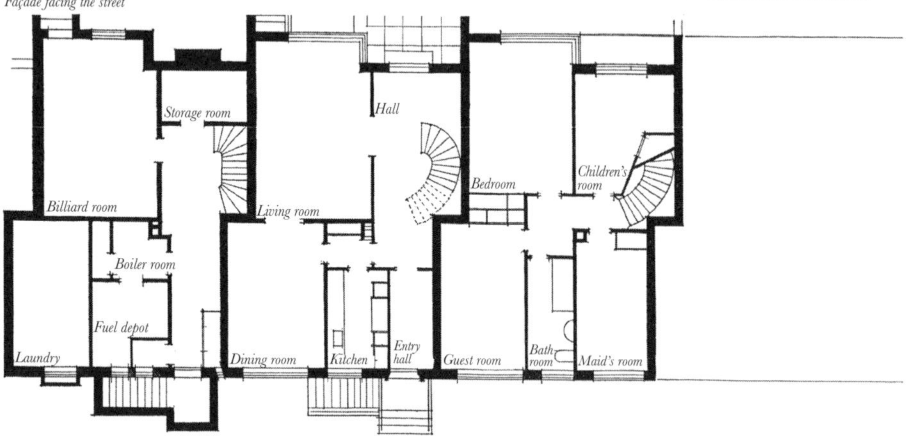

Location: *Kollegievej, Ordrup*
Architect: *Karl Almer Nielsen*
Year completed: *1938*
Road system: *one-sided road*
Built up area: *88 m²*
Plot area: *395 m²*
Floor area: *175.40 m²*
Volume: *705 m³*
Materials etc.: *The houses are built of hand-made rubble stone. The roof is covered with Icopal.*

Elaborated by Marius Johansen
Redrawn from the working drawings

Row houses. *Two-storey types with full basement. 1:250*

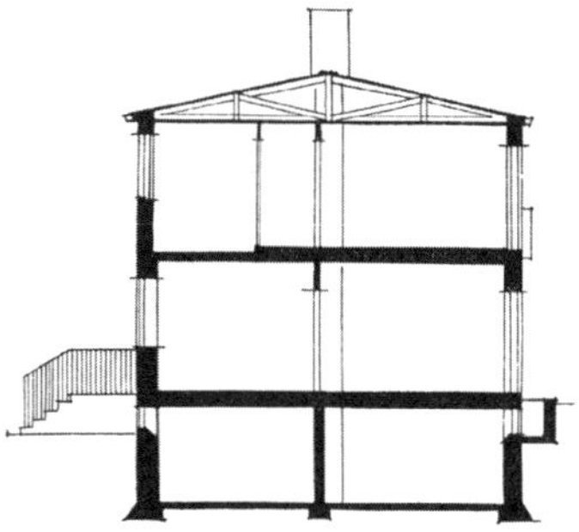

Location: *Ammentorpsvej, Gentofte*
Architect: *Harald G. Petersen*
Year completed: *1939–40*
Road system: *two-sided road*
Built up area: *49 m²*
Plot area: *174 m²*
Floor area: *144 m²*
Volume: *396 m³*
Materials etc.: *The houses are built of red machine-made brick. The roof is covered with Icopal*

Elaborated by Knud Rohbrandt
Redrawn from the working drawings

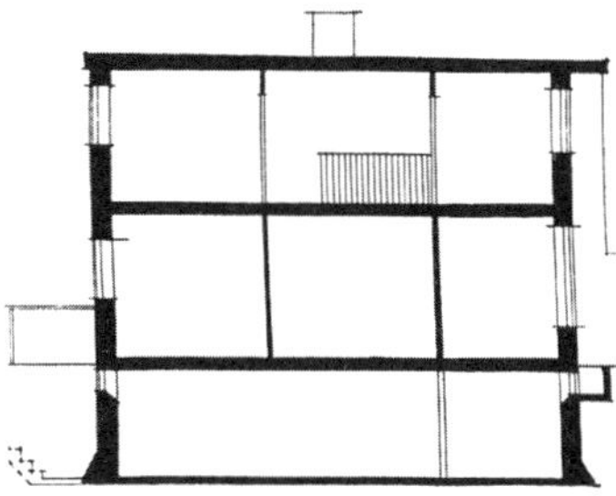

Location: *Svejaggervej, Hellerup*
Builder: *Bricklayer master I. Martin Jensen*
Architect: *Palle Suenson and Ib Martin Jensen*
Year completed: *1935*
Road system: *two-sided road*
Built up area: *63 m² and 49 m²*
Plot area: *240 m² and 195 m²*
Floor area: *171 m² and 132 m²*
Volume: *490 m³ and 380 m³*
Construction cost: *23'500 kr. and 18'400 kr.*
Cost per m²: *365 kr. and 375 kr.*
Cost per m³: *48 kr. and 49 kr.*
Materials etc.: *The houses are built of red hand-made brick. The roof is covered with Icopal.*

Elaborated by Karen Margrethe Gravesen
Redrawn from the working drawings

Row houses. *Two-storey types with full basement. 1:250*

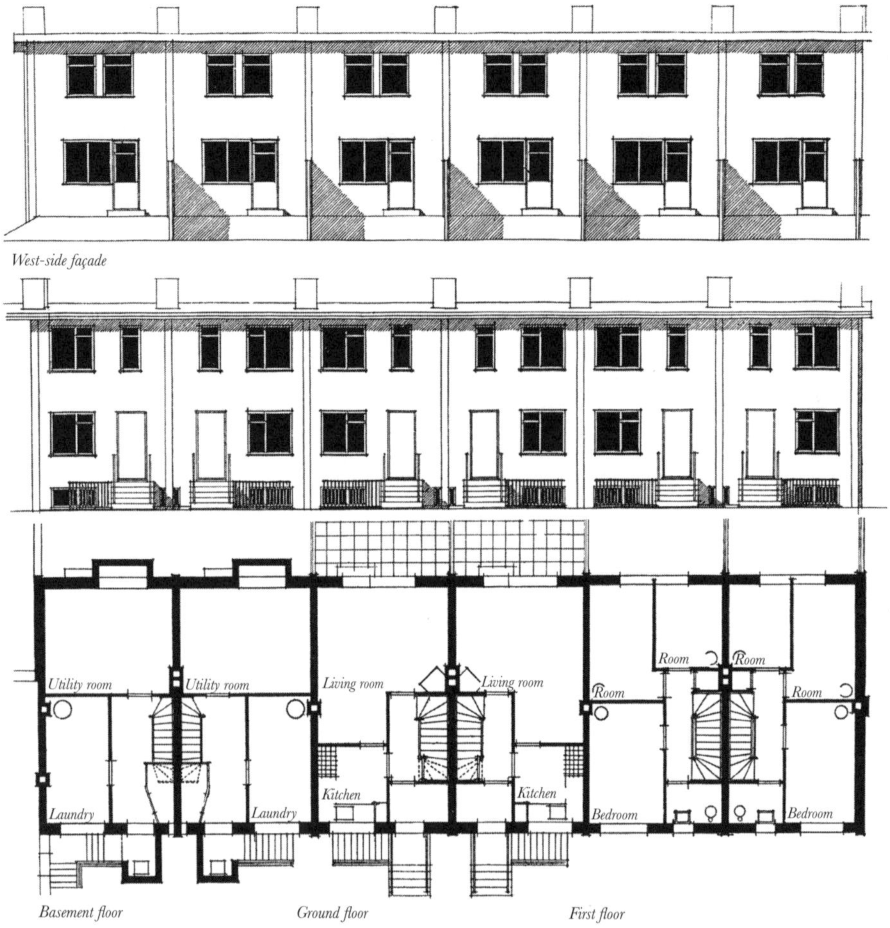

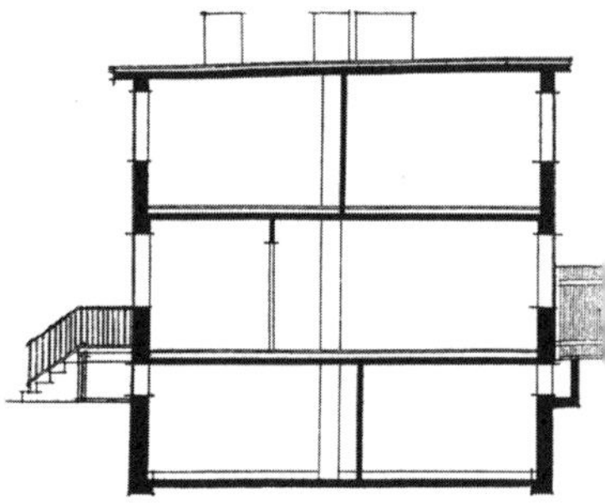

Location: *Korsør, Denmark*
Client: *Foreningen Socialt Boligbyggeri (FSB)*
Architect: *Aage Müller og August Ramussen*
Year completed: *1940*
Road system: *two-sided road*
Built up area: *58 m²*
Floor area: *99 m²*
Volume: *342 m³*
Construction cost: *9 720 kr.*
Cost per m²: *168 kr.*
Cost per m³: *28 kr.*
Materials etc.: *Brick construction. The front house, containing the vestibule, fuel, and bicycle depot, is made of wood.*

Elaborated by Ove Hove
Redrawn from the working drawings

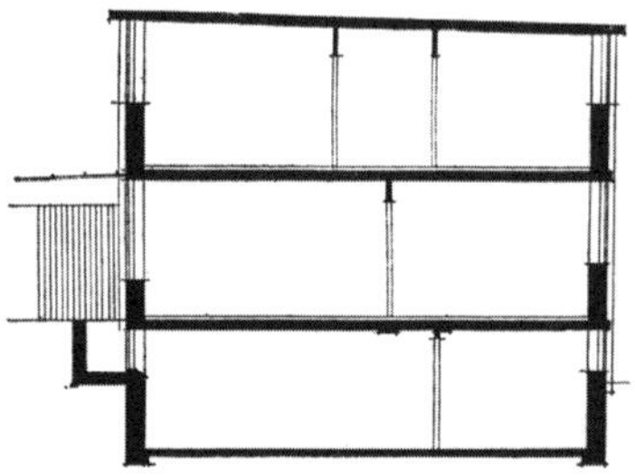

Location: *Kantorparken, Bispebjerg Parkhall, Copenhagen*
Builder: *Foreningen Socialt Boligbyggeri (FSB)*
Architect: *Architects of the Cooperative*
Year completed: *1939–40*
Road system: *two-sided road*
Built up area: *40 m²*
Floor area: *120 m²*
Construction cost: *8 900–10 500 kr.*
Cost per m²: *123 kr.*
Cost per m³: *31 kr.*
Volume: *315 m³*
Materials etc.: *The houses are built of yellow brick and the roof is covered with Icopal. There are load-bearing cross partitions. Heating is from a common plant.*

Elaborated by Mogens Petterson
Redrawn from the working drawings

Row houses. *Two-storey types with full basement. 1:250*
In the top type, every other house is reversed along the transverse axis. The bottom type has a staircase connection from the living room

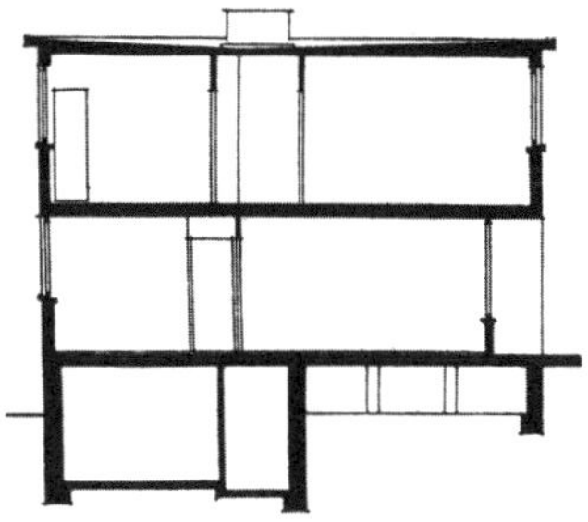

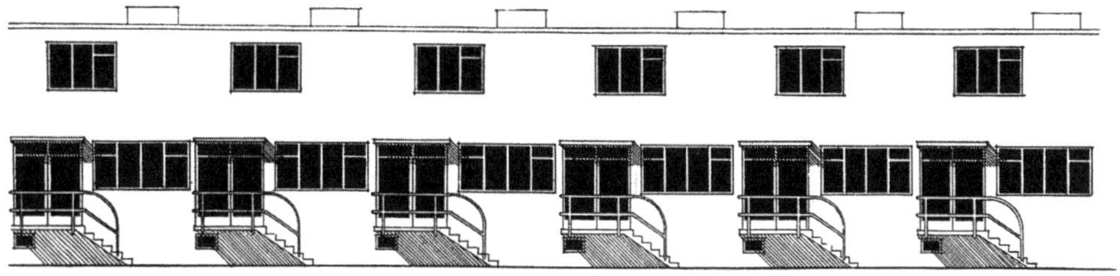

Façade facing the street

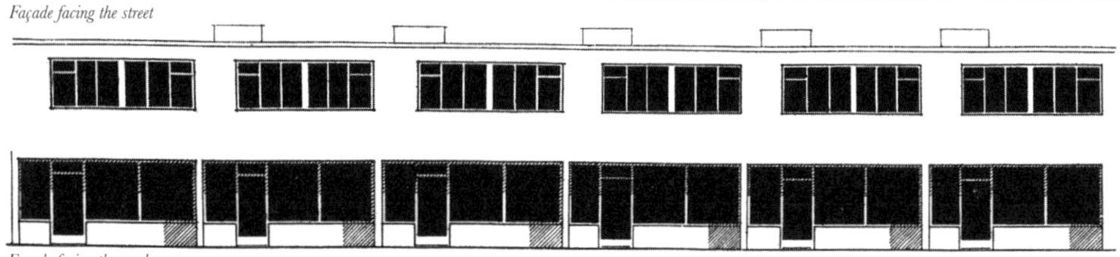

Façade facing the garden

Location: *Werkbundsiedlung Neubühl, Zurich*
Client: *Schweizerischer Werkbund*
Architect: *Max Haefeli, Rudolf Steiger, Werner Moser, Paul Artaria and Hans Schmidt*
Year completed: *1930–32*
Road system: *one-sided road*
Built up area: *48 m²*
Plot area: *135 m²*
Floor area: *96 m²*
Volume: *365 m³*
Materials etc.: *The houses are built of reinforced concrete.*

Elaborated by Mogens Lillie
Drawn from Alfred Roth "Die neue Architektur", Ginsbergers Forlag, Zürich 1939

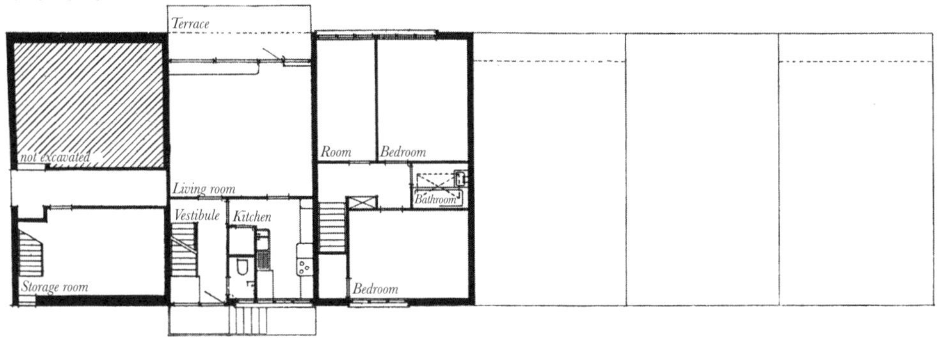

Basement floor *Ground floor* *First floor*

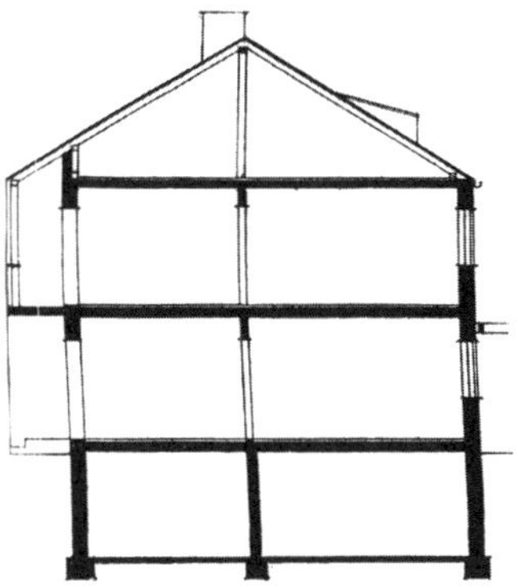

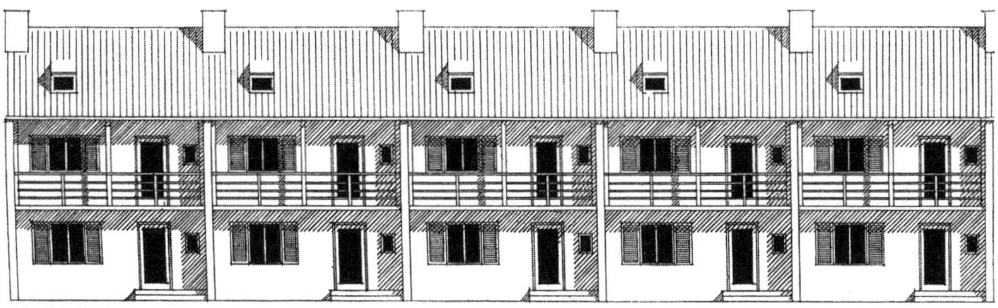

Façade facing the street

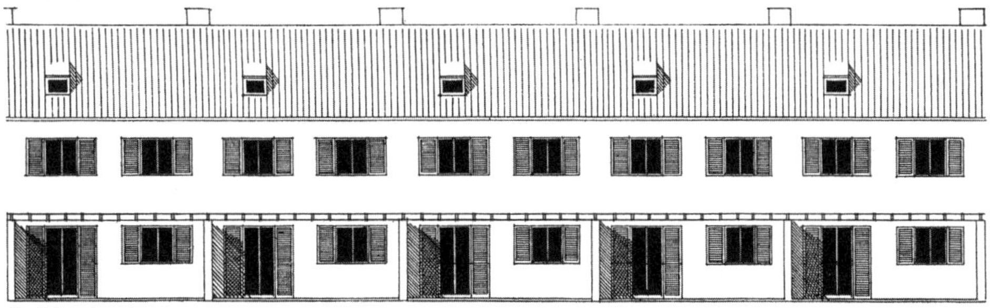

Façade facing the garden

Location: *Siedlung Ramersdorf, Munich*
Client: *German State*
Architect: *Emil Freymuth*
Year completed: *1934*
Road system: *two-sided road*
Built up area: *84.60 m²*
Plot area: *220 m²*
Floor area: *174 m²*
Volume: *432 m³*
Materials etc.: *The houses are built of rendered brick. The roof is covered with pantiles.*

Elaborated by Arne Kjær
Drawn from "Der Baumeister" XVI, p. 317

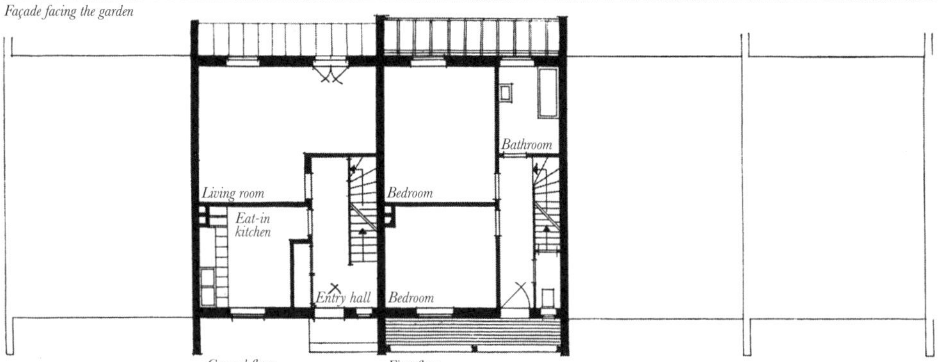

Ground floor *First floor*

Row houses. *Two-storey types with full basement. 1:250*

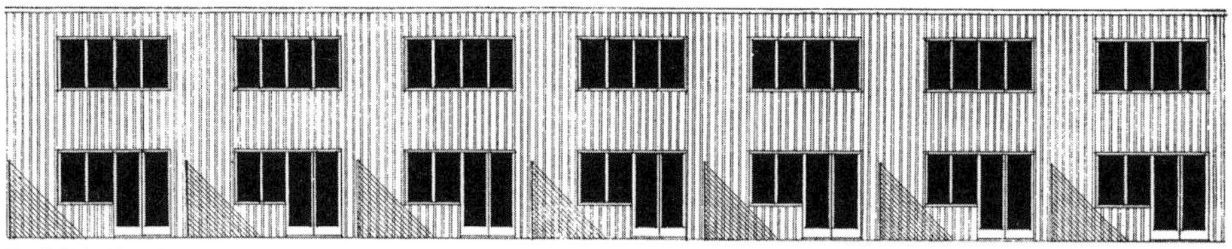

Façade facing the garden

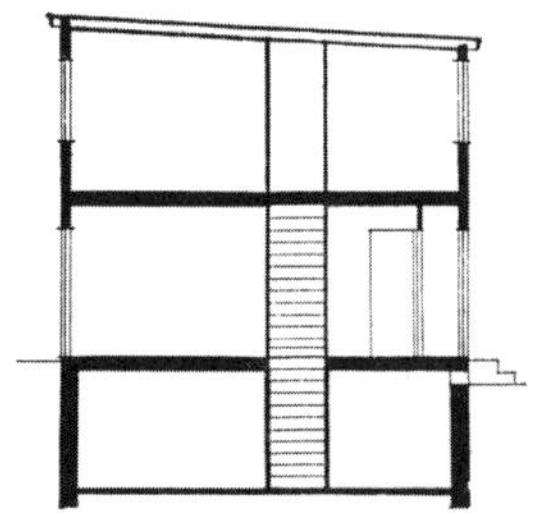

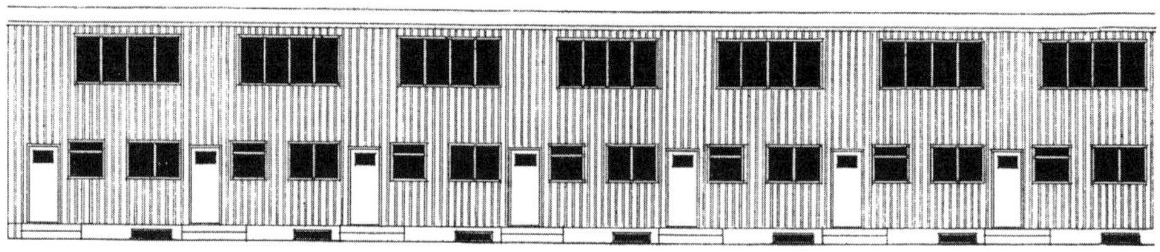

Façade facing the street

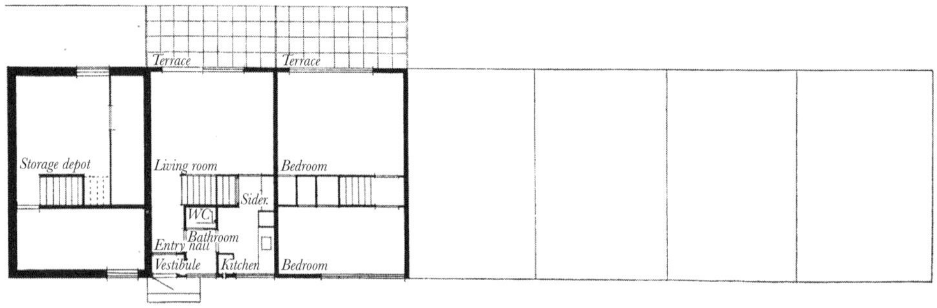

Location: *Stockholm*
Client: *Kooperativa Förbundet (KF)*
Architect: *Kooperativa Förbundets Arkitektkontor (KFAI), Eskil Sundhal*
Road system: *one-sided road*
Built up area: *30 m²*
Plot area: *67 m²*
Floor area: *67 m²*
Volume: *233 m³*
Materials etc.: *The houses are built of wood. The roof is covered with roofing felt. There is a common heating plant.*

Elaborated by Aage Paludan
Redrawn from the working drawings

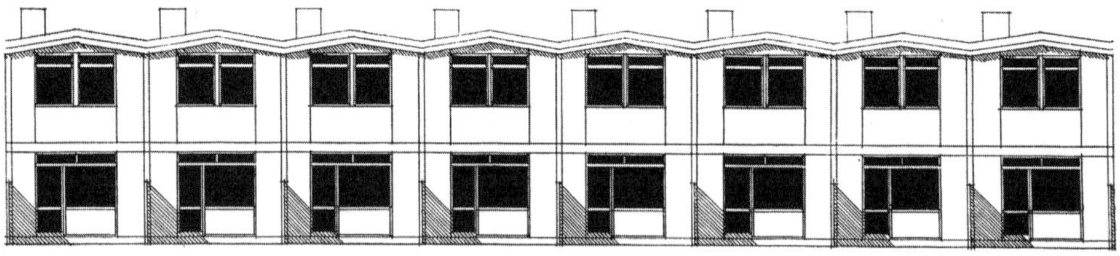

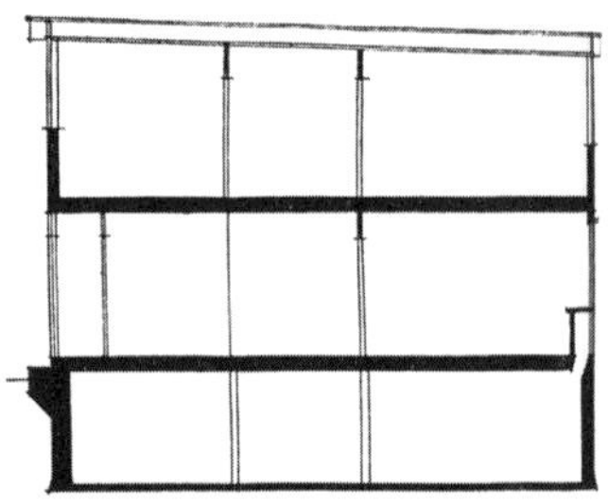

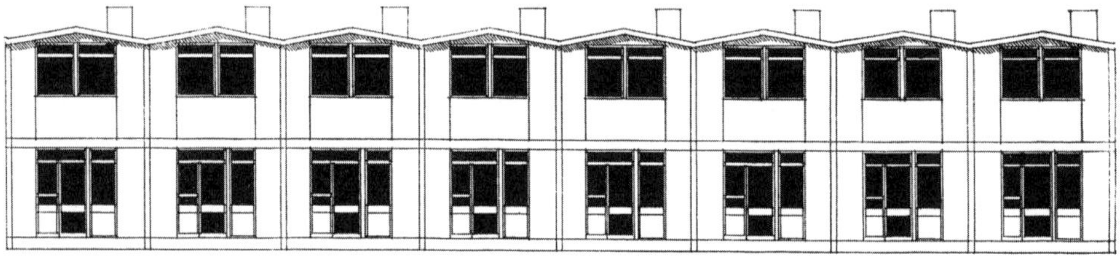

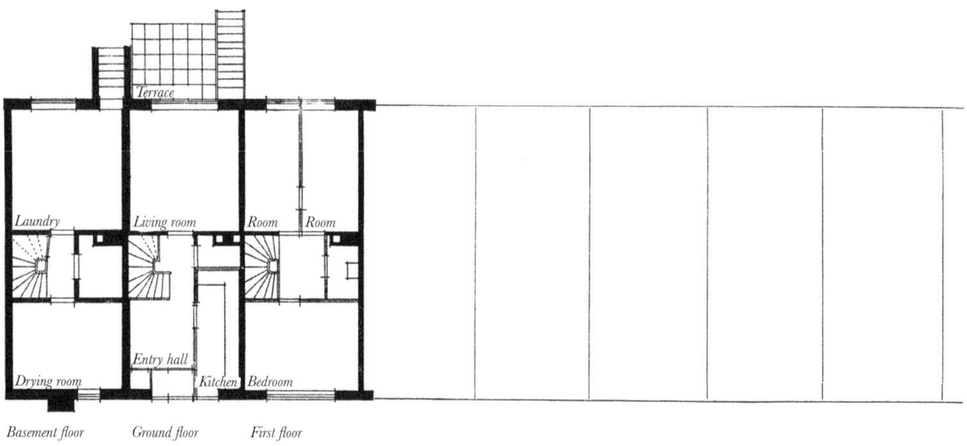

Basement floor *Ground floor* *First floor*

Location: *Stenmaglevej and Gislingevej, Husum Copenhagen*
Client: *Copenhagen Municipality*
Architect: *Magnus Stephensen*
Year completed: *1941*
Built up area: *40 m²*
Floor area: *120 m²*
Volume: *316 m³*
Materials etc.: *The houses are built of red brick and the roof is covered with Icopal. Parapets are made of rendered gasbeton. Iron heating stoves.*

Elaborated by Mogens Leth
Redrawn from the working drawings

Row houses. *Two-storey types with full basement. 1:250*

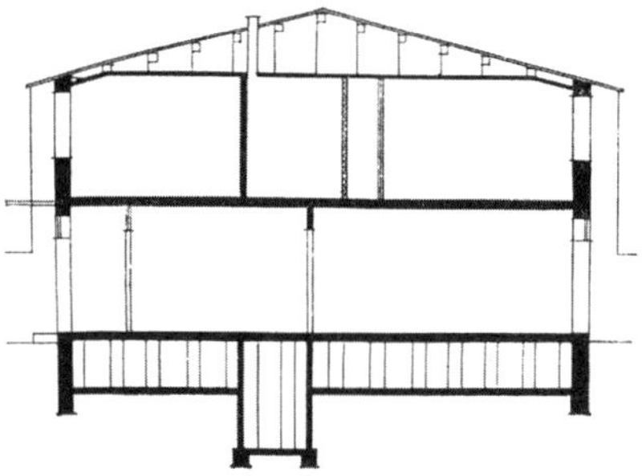

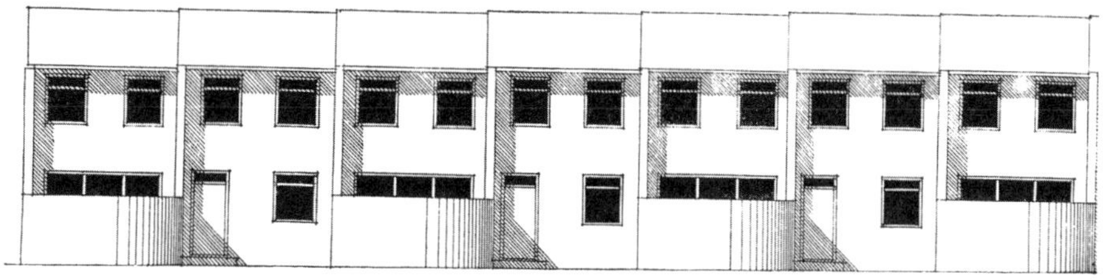

Façade

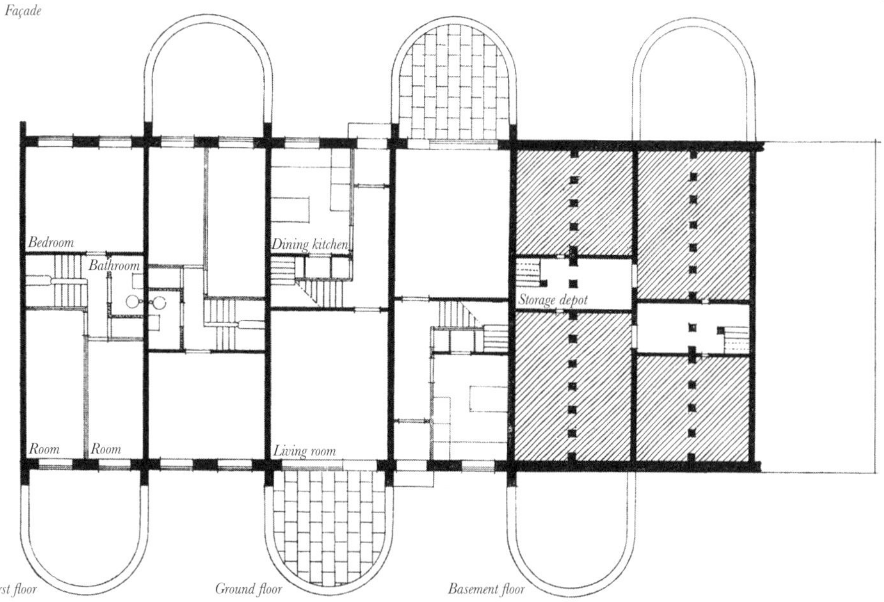

Location: *Brønsparken, Brønshøjvej, Copenhagen*
Builder: *Foreningen Socialt Boligbyggeri (FSB)*
Architect: *Kay Fisker, C. F. Møller and Erik Jensen*
Year completed: *1940–41*
Road system: *two-sided dead-end road*
Built up area: *45 m²*
Floor area: *95 m²*
Volume: *285 m³*
Materials etc.: *The houses are built of red brick and the roof is covered with Eternit corrugated sheeting. Each house is mirrored to the following one. There is a common heating plant and laundry machine rooms. No private garden, but an open-air living room. The buildings are grouped around a common park.*

Elaborated by Flemming Schlüter
Redrawn from the working drawings

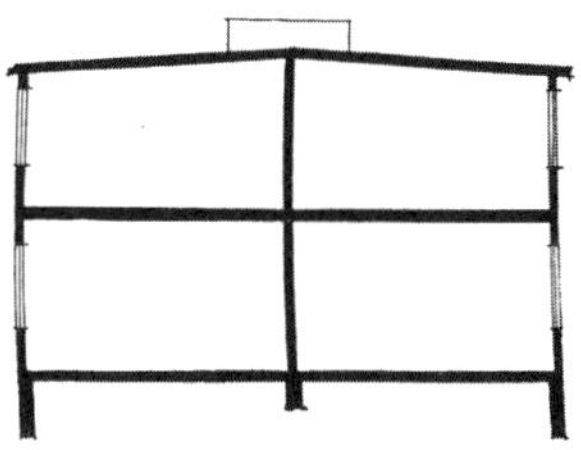

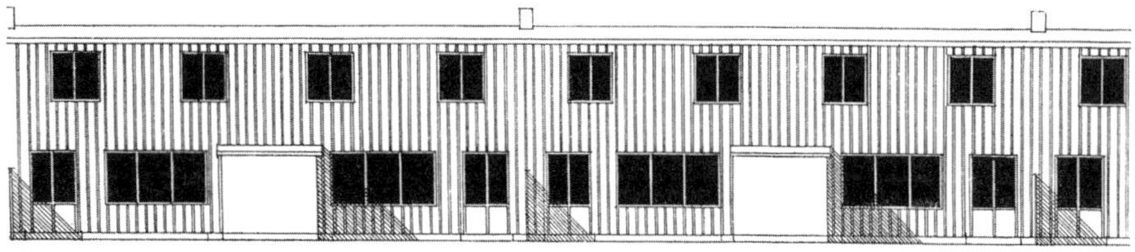

Façade

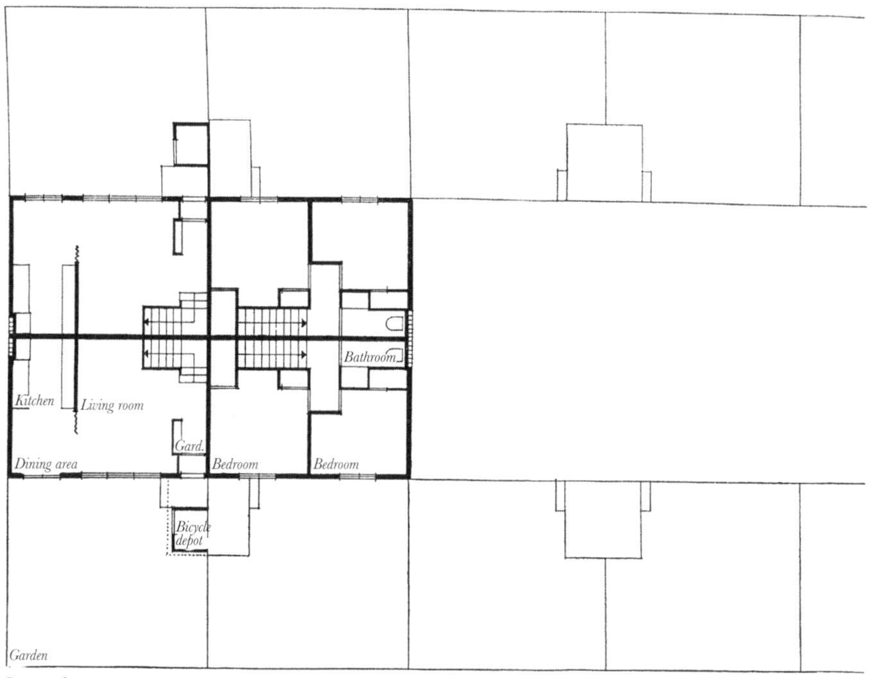

Basement floor

Location: *Project*
Architect: *Kooperativa Förbundets Arkitektkontor (KFAI), Eskil Sundhal*
Year completed: *1932*
Road system: *two-sided road*
Built up area: *31 m²*
Plot area: *75 m²*
Floor area: *62 m²*
Volume: *167 m³*
Materials etc.: *The houses are planned to be built of wood. The houses are single-sided and every other type is reversed. There is a common heating plant.*

Elaborated by Kai Christensen
Redrawn from the working drawings

Row houses. *Two-storey types without basement. 1:250. The top type has a crawl space for wires and storage under the stairs, with every other house reversed along the longitudinal axis. The bottom type consists of single-sided houses, reversed along the transverse axis.*

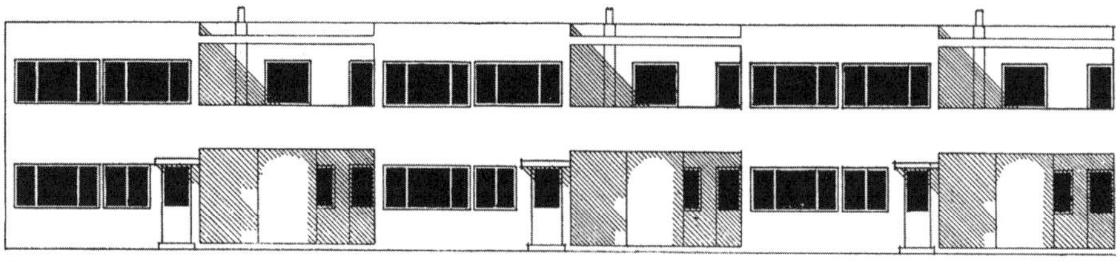

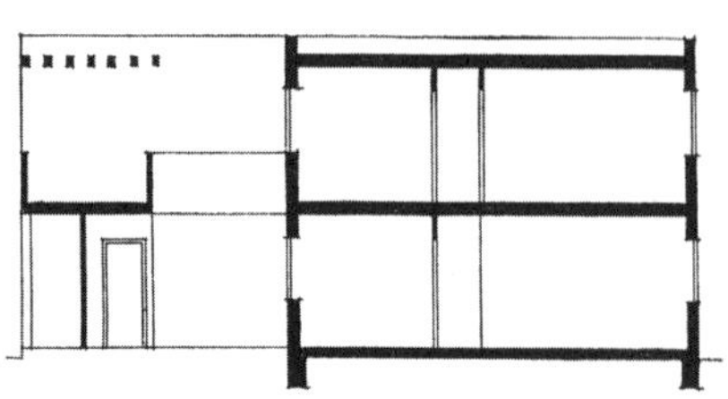

Façade

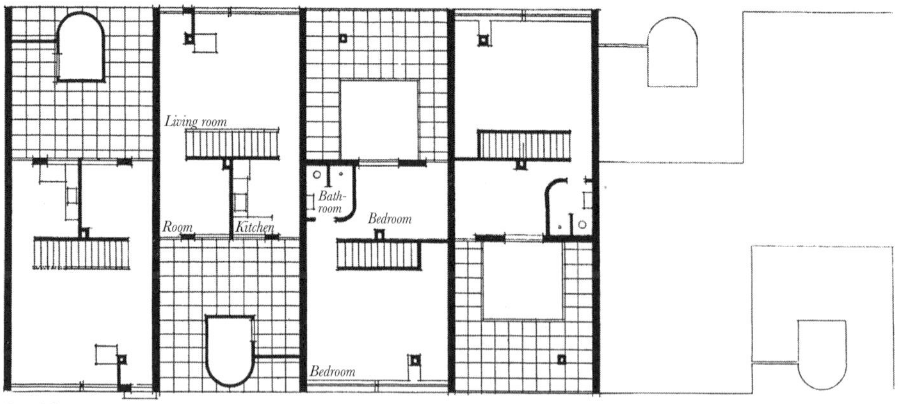

Ground floor *First floor*

Location: *Pessac near Bordeaux*
Architect: *Pierre Jeanneret*
Year completed: *1925*
Road system: *two-sided road*
Year completed: *1933*
Built up area: *63.5 m²*
Plot area: *145 m²*
Floor area: *127 m²*
Volume: *350 m³ including the terrace*
Materials etc.: *The houses are built of reinforced concrete. Every house is mirrored to the adjacent one.*

Elaborated by Mogens Black Petersen and Modens Leth Drawn from "Le Corbusier and Pierre Janneret: Oeuvre complète de 1910–1929", Ginsberger & Cie. Forlag, Zürich 1930

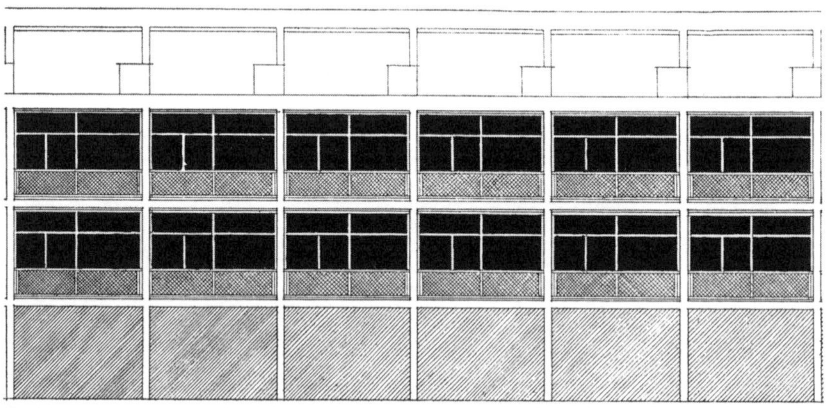

Façade

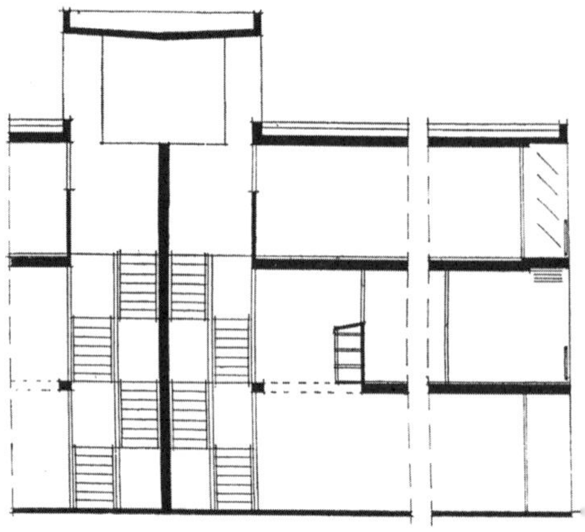

Bottom floor *Middle floor* *Top floor*

Location: *Barcelona*
Architect: *Le Corbusier and Pierre Jeanneret*
Year completed: *1933*
Built up area: *81 m²*
Floor area: *162 m²*
Volume: *ca 800 m³*
Materials etc.: *Concrete construction. Semi-detached, narrow house types.*

Elaborated by Mogens Black Petersen Drawn from "Le Corbusier and Pierre Janneret: Oeuvre complète de 1910–192", Ginsberger & Cie. Forlag, Zürich 1930

Row houses. *Two-storey types without basement. 1:250. In the top type, the houses are reversed along the longitudinal axis. The bottom type is single-sided with a covered courtyard on the lower floor*

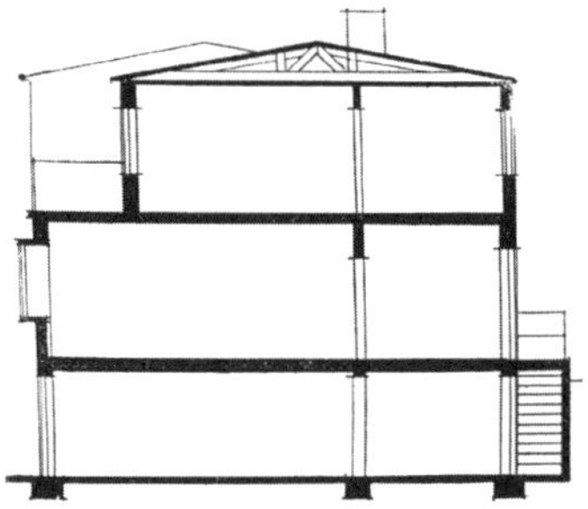

Location: *Æblevænget, Lyngby*
Builder: *Bricklayer master P. Marcussen and Schneidelbach*
Architect: *Knud Friderichsen and Arne Poulsen*
Year completed: *1936*
Road system: *one-sided road*
Built up area: *66 m²*
Plot area: *265 m²*
Floor area: *114 m²*
Volume: *378 m³*
Construction cost: *19 300 kr.*
Cost per m²: *290 kr.*
Cost per m³: *51 kr.*
Materials etc.: *Yellow machine-made brick. The roof is covered with Icopal.*

Elaborated by Karen Magrethe Gravesen
Redrawn from the working drawings

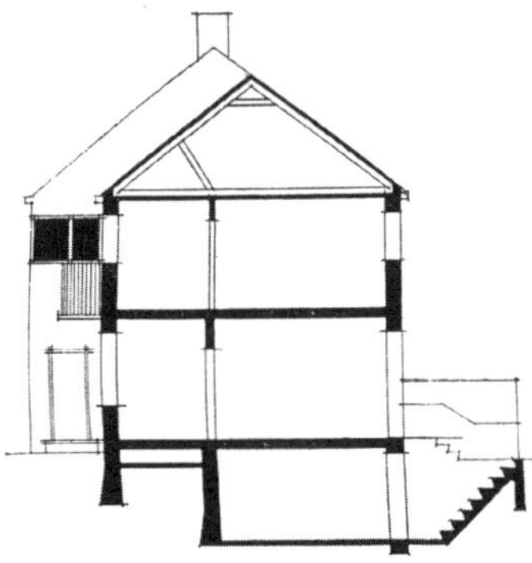

Location: *Hasselvej, Vanløse, Copenhagen*
Builder: *Akts. Hasselvænget*
Architect: *K. K. Søndergaard and Gunnar Milthers*
Year completed: *1939*
Road system: *one-sided road*
Built up area: *55 m²*
Plot area: *110–150 m²*
Floor area: *142 m²*
Volume: *440 m³*
Materials etc.: *38 houses have been built. The houses are built of red and yellow brick and the roof is covered with red pantiles. The dwellings are grouped around a common garden area.*

Elaborated by Kai Børge Nielsen
Redrawn from the working drawings

Row houses. *Two-storey types with horizontal Z-shape displacements. 1:250.*

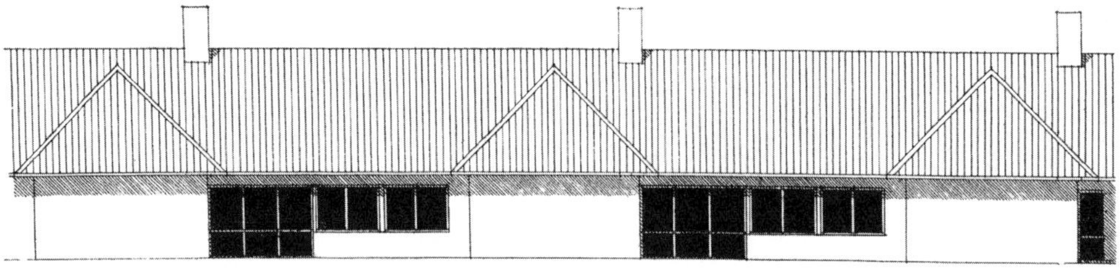

Façade facing the garden

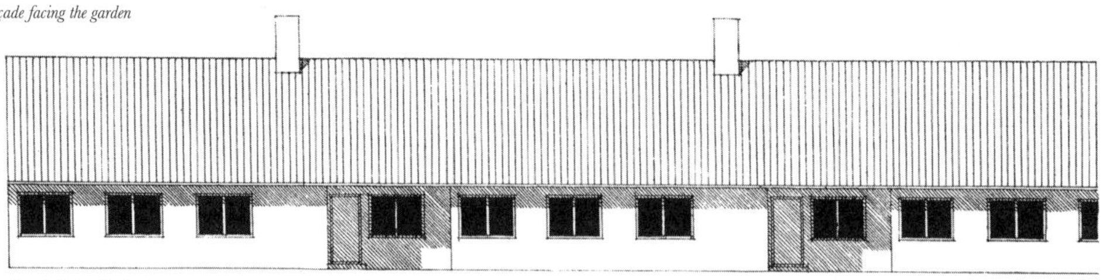

Façade facing the street

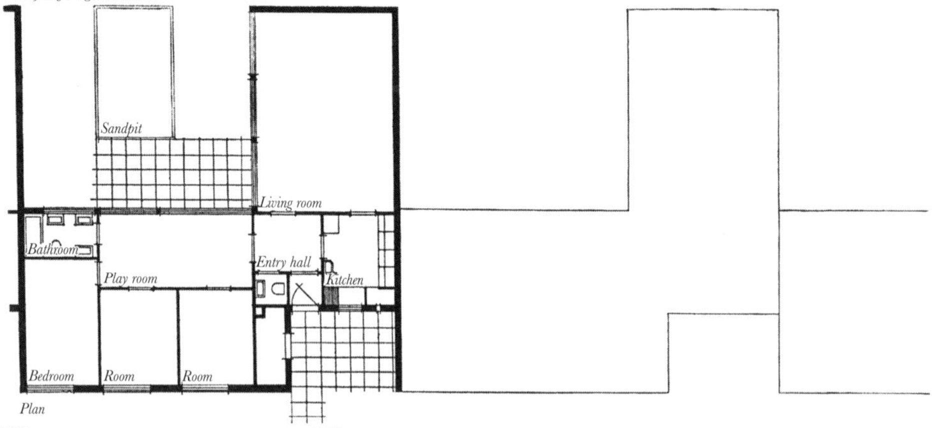

Plan

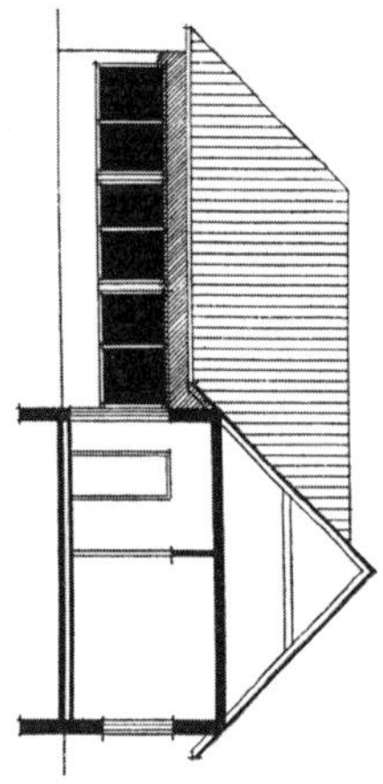

Location: *Project*
Client: *Student work carried out at the Academy of Arts on the basis of a German plan idea*
Year completed: *1932*
Road system: *one-sided road*
Built up area: *108 m²*
Plot area: *250 m²*
Floor area: *108 m²*
Volume: *324 m³*
Materials etc.: *The houses are planned to be built of reinforced concrete and the roof covered with pantiles.*

Elaborated by Ebbe Clemmens and Mogens Leth Redrawn from a slide of unknown origin

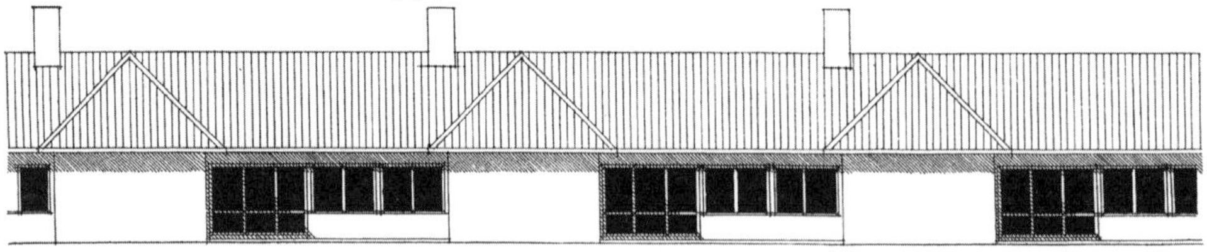

Façade facing the garden

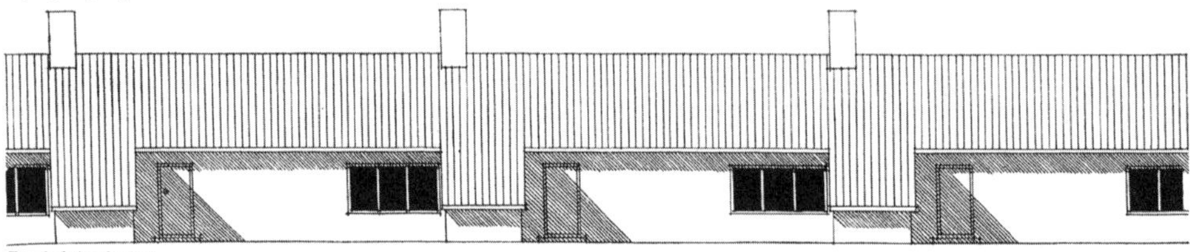

Façade facing the street

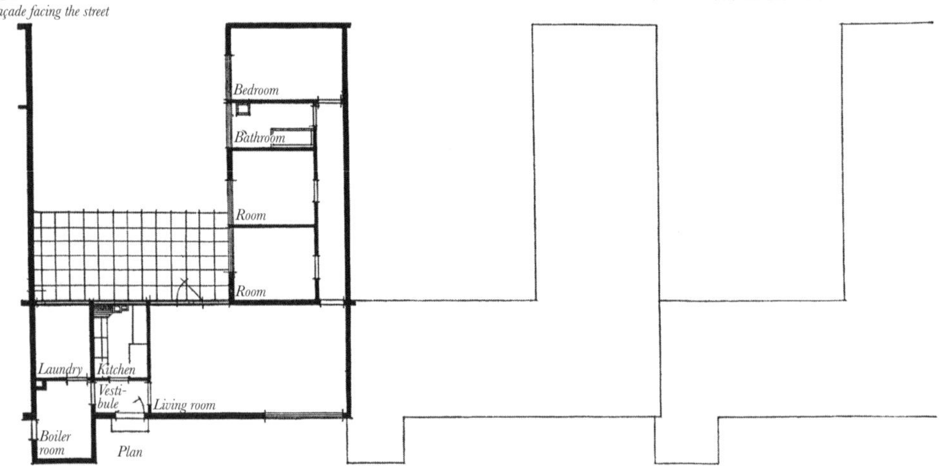

Plan

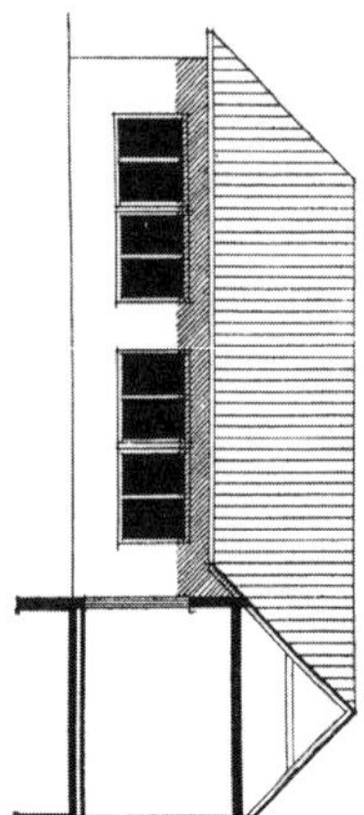

Location: *Project*
Client: *Student work carried out at the Academy of Arts on the basis of a German plan idea*
Year completed: *1932*
Road system: *one-sided road*
Built up area: *87 m²*
Plot area: *210 m²*
Floor area: *87 m²*
Volume: *261 m³*
Materials etc.: *The houses are planned to be built of reinforced concrete and the roof covered with pantiles.*

Elaborated by Ebbe Clemmens and Mogens Leth Redrawn from a slide

Comb row houses. *One-storey types without basement. 1:250.*

Façade facing the garden

Location: *Project. Hampstead, London*
Architect: *M. H. Baillie Scott, Bedford*
Year completed: *ca 1902*
Road system: *one-sided road, East-West walking street*
Built up area: *90 m²*
Plot area: *ca 350 m²*
Floor area: *176 m²*
Volume: *ca 620 m³*
Materials etc.: *Partial brick construction. The roof is covered with flat tiles.*

Elaborated by Hack Kampmann
Redrawn from M. H. Baillie Scott: "House and Garden", London 1910

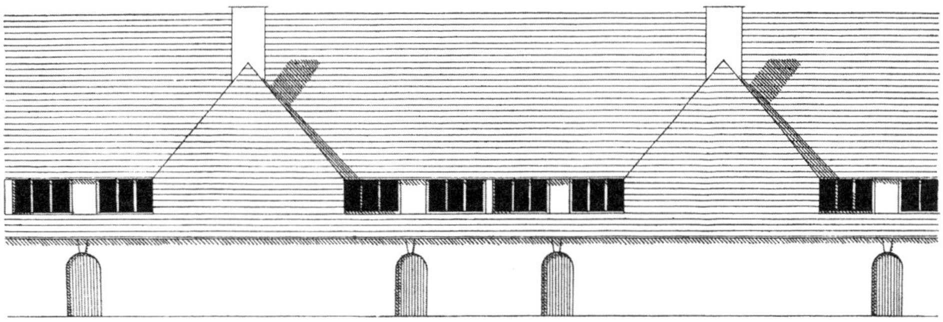

Façade facing the street

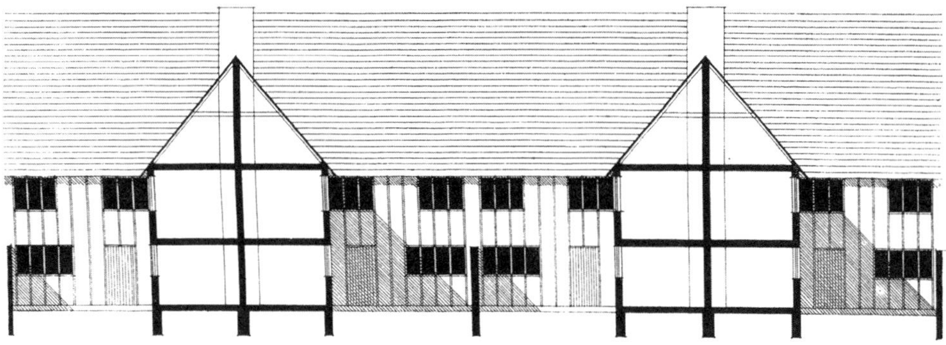

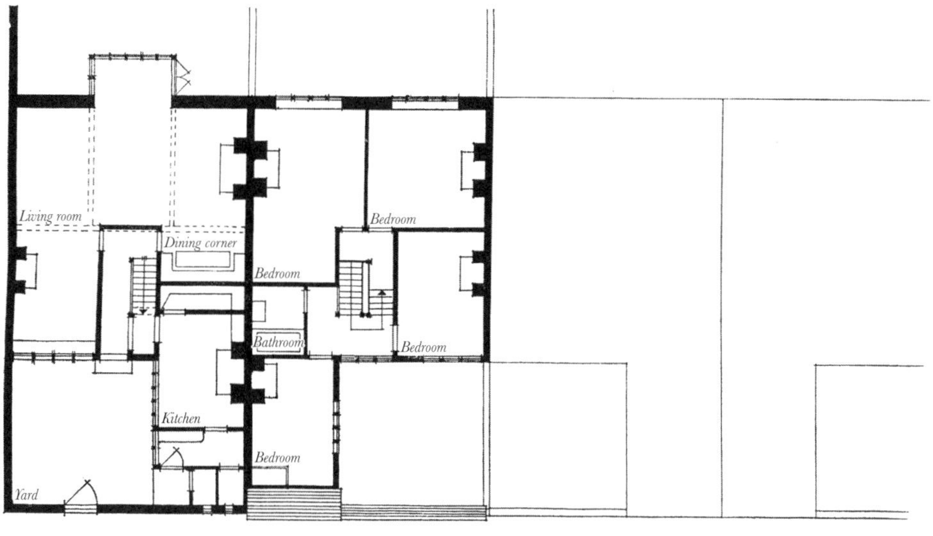

Ground floor *First floor*

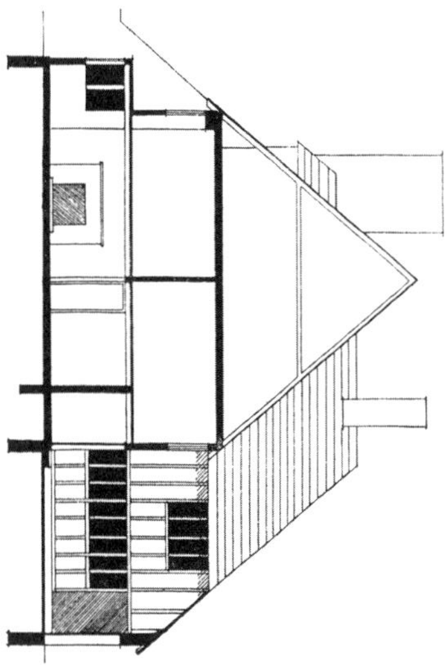

Comb row houses. *Two-storey types with attic but without basement. Houses are mirrored according to along transverse axis. 1:250. (See also perspective sketch p. 4)*

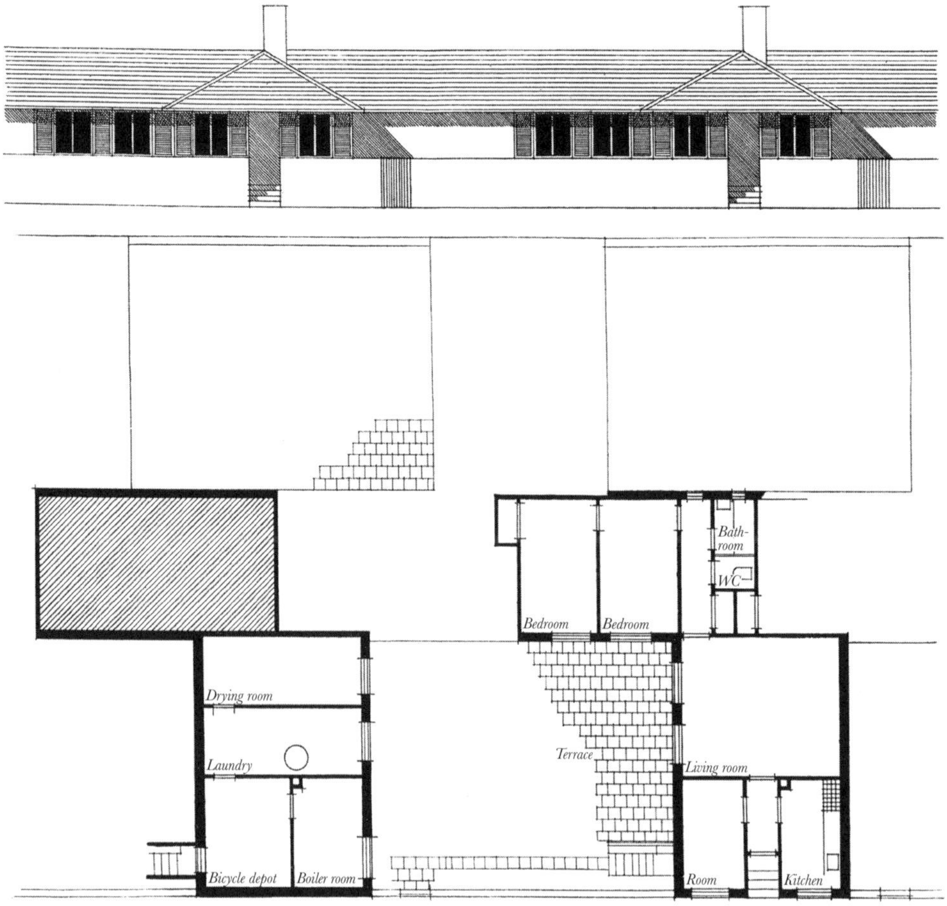

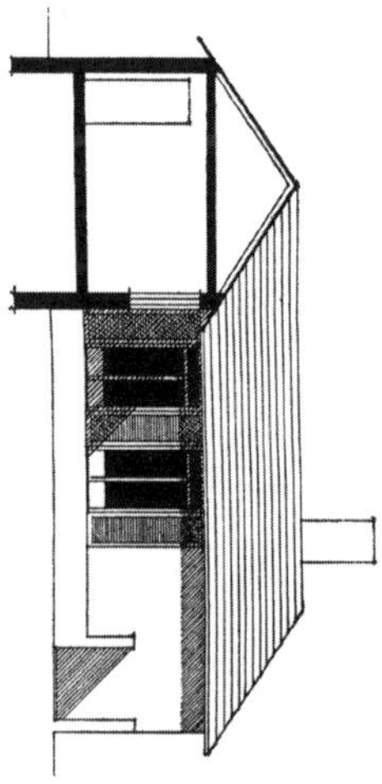

Location: *Project*
Architect: *Student work conducted at the Art Academy on the basis of an idea by Hilding Ekelund, Helsinki*
Road system: *two-sided road*
Built up area: *62 m²*
Plot area: *144 m²*
Floor area: *62 m²*
Volume: *310 m³*
Materials etc.: *The houses are planned to be built of brick and the roof covered with pantiles. The garden is very small, but it can not be seen from other houses.*

Elaborated by Mogens Leth
Redrawn from the report "Nordisk Byggnadsgad II", Helsingfors 1932

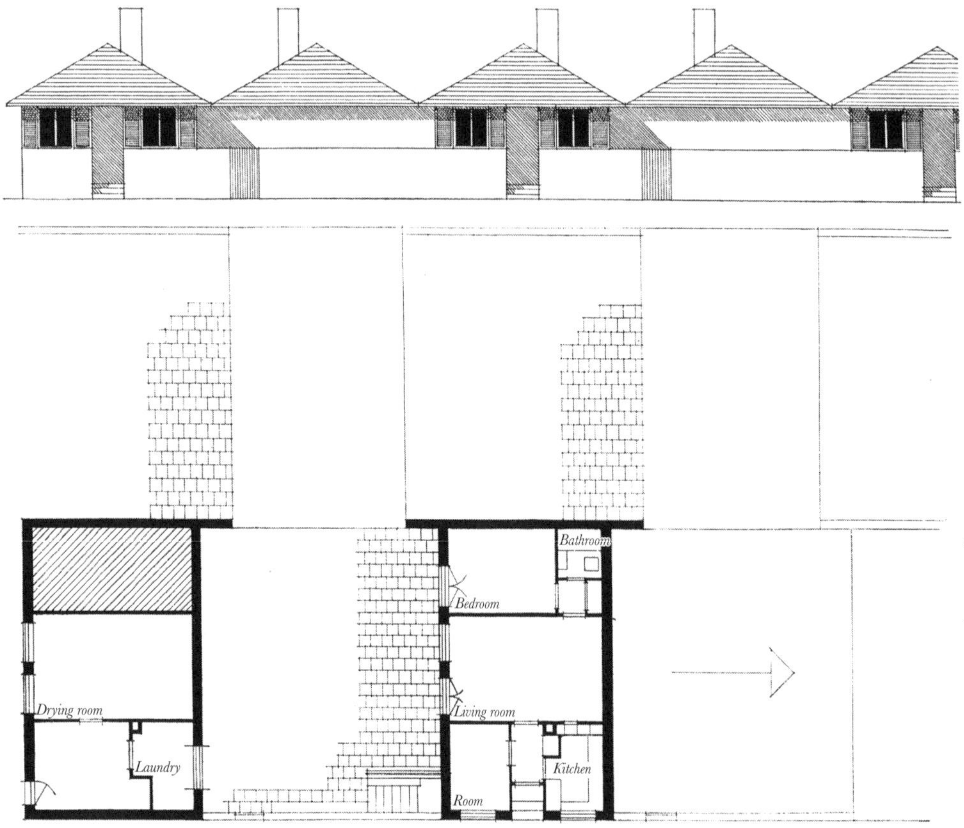

Location: *Project*
Architect: *Student work conducted at the Art Academy on the basis of a great idea by Ekelund, Helsinki*
Road system: *two-sided road*
Built up area: *61.50 m²*
Plot area: *145 m²*
Floor area: *103 m²*
Volume: *250 m³*
Materials etc.: *The houses are to be built of brick and the roof covered with pantiles.*

Elaborated by Mogens Leth
Redrawn from the report "Nordisk Byggnadsgad II", Helsingfors 1932

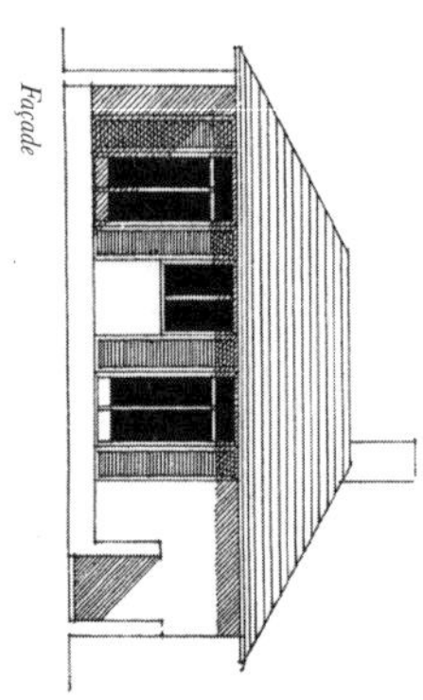

Comb row houses and Northern boundary row houses. *One-storey type with partial basement. At the top double comb row houses. At the bottom northern boundary row houses side-by-side in a double comb shape. 1:250*

Location: *Copenhagen, Akademisk Arkitekforening's Konkurrence om krisebyggeri*
Architect: *Jørgen Bo*
Road system: *one-sided road*
Built up area: *72 m²*
Floor area: *109 m²*
Plot area: *247 m²*
Volume: *310 m³*
Materials etc.: *The houses are planned to be built of brick, the south wall made as a post skeleton with Eternit corrugated sheets.*

Elaborated by H. Mygind
Redrawn from the project

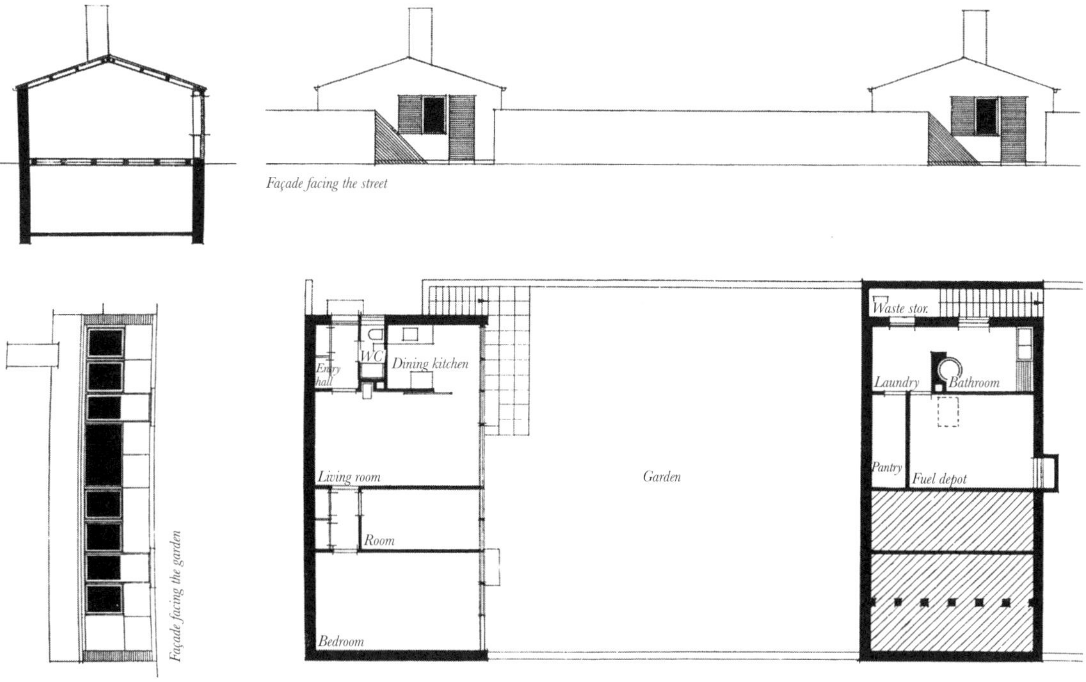

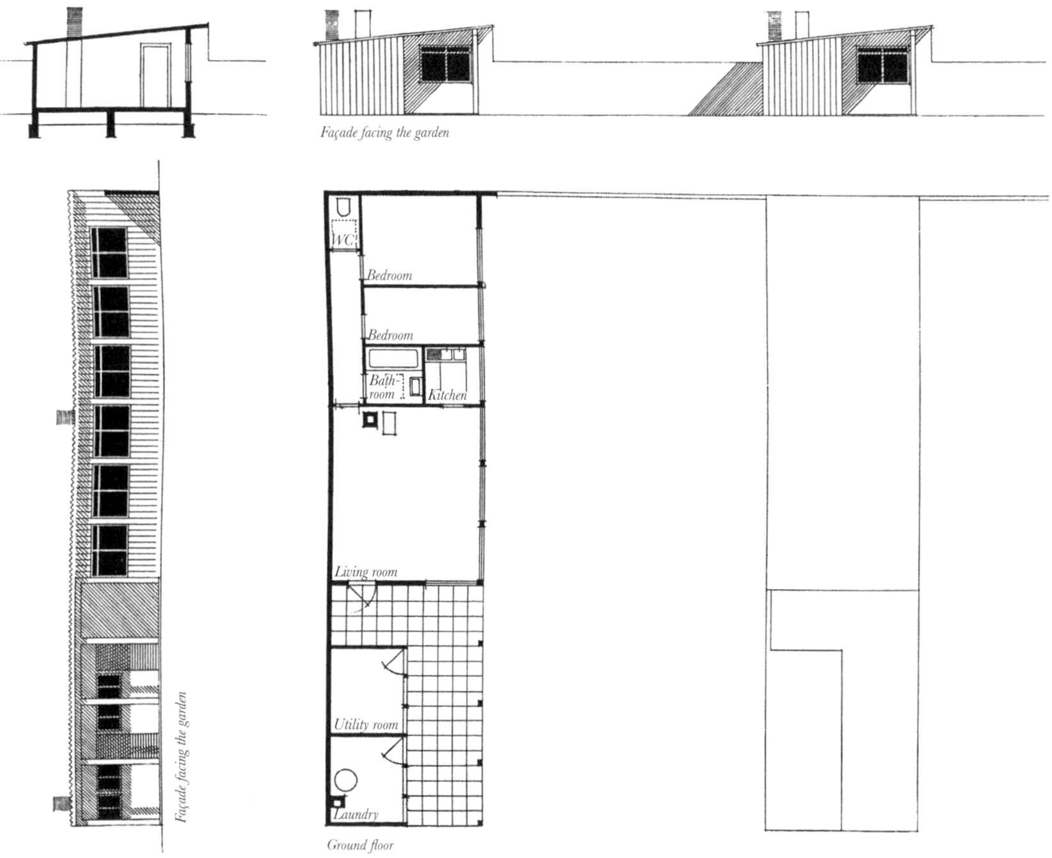

Location: *Model house, Schweizerische Landesausstellung, Zürich 1939*
Architect: *Paul Artaria*
Year completed: *1939*
Road system: *one-sided road*
Built up area: *110 m²*
Plot area: *320 m²*
Floor area: *110 m²*
Volume: *290 m³*
Materials etc.: *The house is built of vertical precast grooved concrete elements and clad with asbestos cement sheeting.*

Elaborated by Kai Børge Nielsen
Redrawn from Paul Artaria, "Vom Bauen und Wohnen", B. Wepp et Cie, Basel 1939

Northern boundary row houses. *One-storey type with and without basement. 1:250*

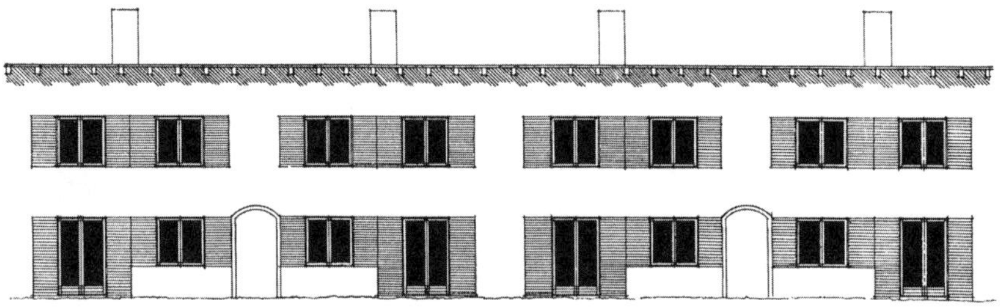

Façade

Location: *Munich*
Architect: *Unknown*
Year completed: *1934*
Road system: *two-sided road*
Built up area: *42.25 m²*
Floor area: *84.50 m²*
Volume: *235.50 m³*
Materials etc.: *The houses are built of brick and the roof is covered with slate. The house is built as a two-storey, quartered patio dwellings.*

Elaborated by W. Malling Petersen Redrawn from a slide of unknown origin

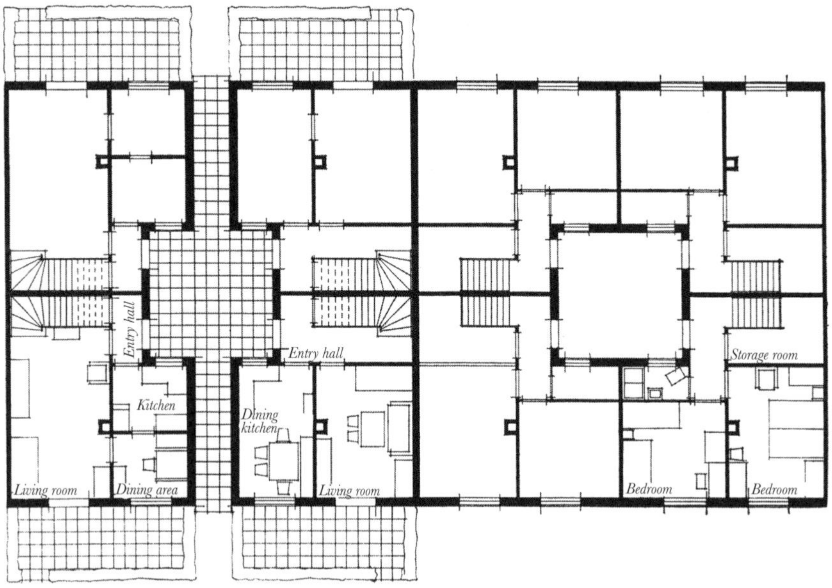

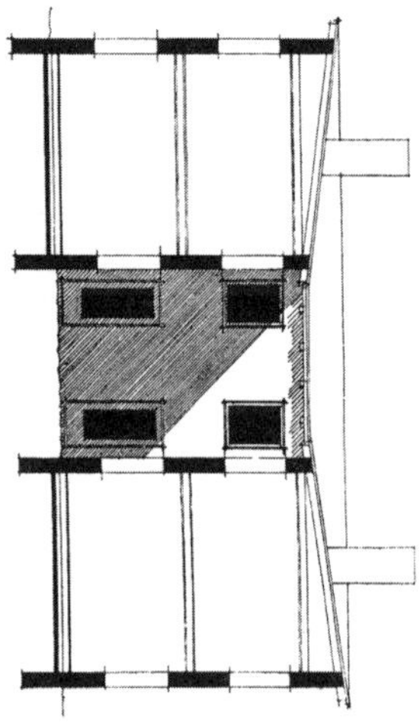

Location: *Munich- Bogenhausen.* **Architect:** *Uli Seeck.* **Year completed:** *1931.* **Road system:** *two-sided road.* **Built up area:** *215 m².* **Plot area:** *430 m².* **Floor area:** *215 m².* **Volume:** *635 m³.* **Materials etc.:** *The house is built of brick and the roof is covered with pantiles. The houses are built as one-storey, quartered patio dwellings. There is a basement under the kitchen.*

Elaborated by Niels Ole PoulsenRedrawn from Helmuth Richter, "Landhäuser, Gärten und Wochenendhäuser", in "Der Baumeister", XXX, p. 1

Patio houses. *The top two-storey type is without a basement. Quarter patio. Two different plan variants. The bottom one-storey type with partial basement. Four-part patio. (The façade corresponds to a variant of the reproduced plan, cf. photograph p. 18). 1:250*

Location: *Palm Beach, Florida U.S.A.*
Architect: *Major*
Road system: *two-sided road*
Built up area: *114 m^2*
Floor area: *114 m^2*
Volume: *536 m^3*
Materials etc.: *The houses are built of brick and plastered. Roof of slate. The houses are built as patio houses and are arranged 6 around each access path.*

Elaborated by Ole Kornerup Bang and Mogens Leth
Redrawn from the review "House and Garden", U.S.A., XXX

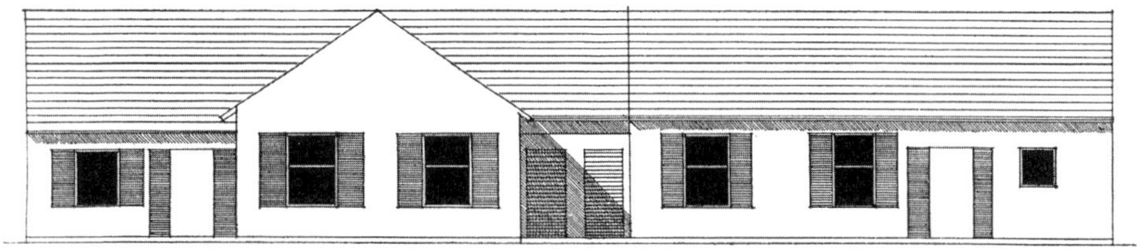

Façade facing the street

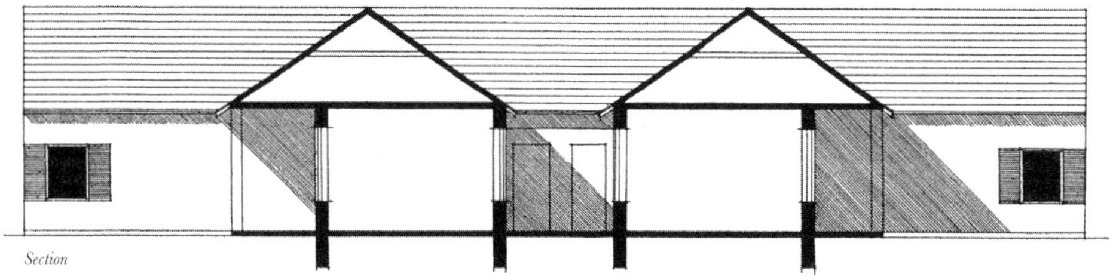

Section

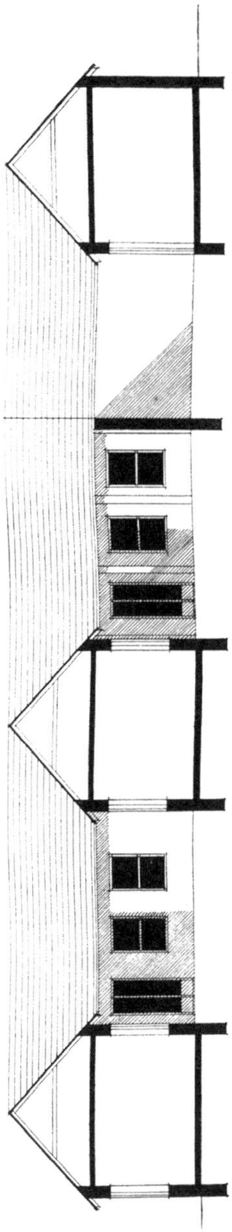

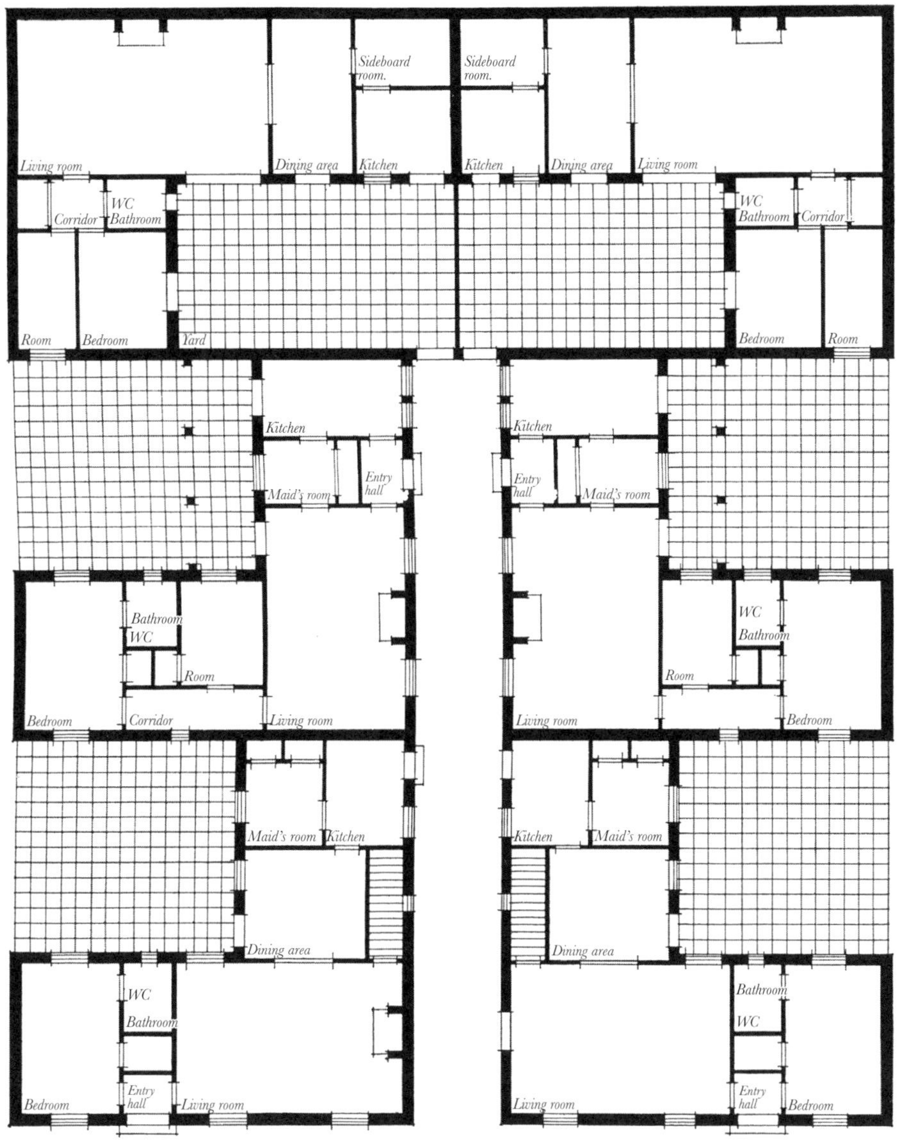

Patio houses. *Densely built around a narrow access path. L-shaped houses. Independent Patio.* *See also site layout plan p. 7 l.* *1:250*

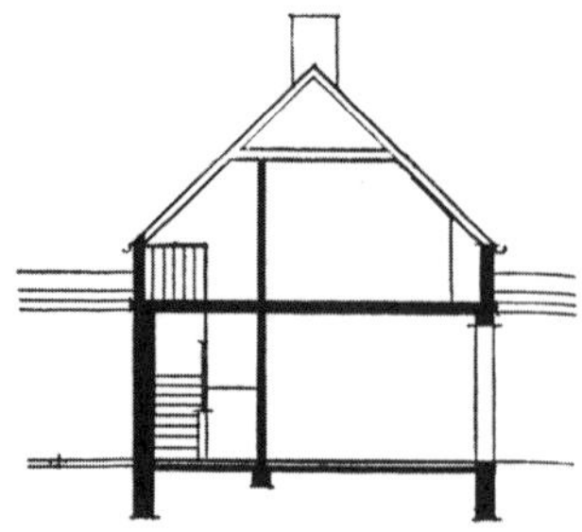

Location: *Copenhagen. Project for the Competition for New Housing Types, 1922*
Architect: *Tage Rue*
Road system: *two-sided road*
Built up area: *54 m²*
Plot area: *285 m²*
Floor area: *90 m²*
Volume: *450 m³*
Materials etc.: *The houses are planned to be built of brick and the roof covered with pantiles.*

Elaborated by Mogens Leth
Redrawn from the project, published in "Arkitekten", XXIV, p. 218
(see also the site plan, p. 12)

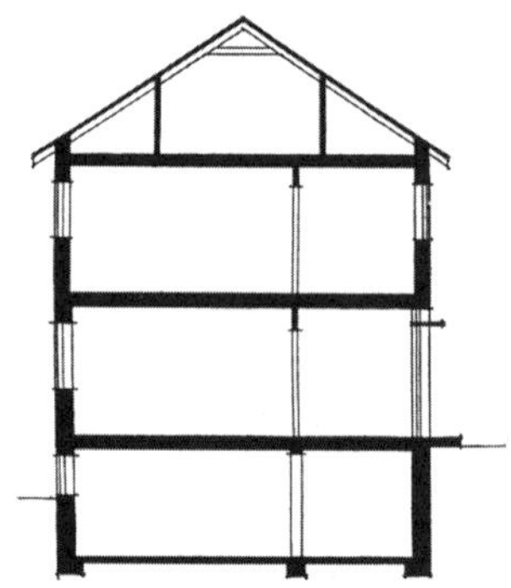

Location: *Im Vogelsang, Stuttgart*
Architect: *R. Arndts and S. Castens*
Year completed: *1935*
Road system: *two-sided road*
Built up area: *ca. 68 m²*
Plot area: *260 m²*
Floor area: *ca. 172 m²*
Volume: *520 m³*
Materials etc.: *The house is built of brick and the roof is covered with pantiles.*

Elaborated by Mogens Leth
Redrawn from "Baugilde", XVI, p. 284

Chain row houses. *At the top, one-storey, double semi-detached house type with three pitched roofs without basement. The types are mirrored along the longitudinal axis. At the bottom, two-storey type with utilised attic and full basement. 1:250*

Descriptions for the reproduced newer Danish row house buildings

Editors' notes

This descriptive appendix is only available in the separate version of the book and not in the papers published in the journal issue *Arkitekten Maanedshæfte*.

Row houses in Vigerslev

By Architect Professor Ivar Bentsen in co-operation with architects Ole Buhl and T. Miland Petersen

The row houses on the corner of Vigerslevvej-Vigerslev Allé-Lykkebovej were built by the municipality of Copenhagen. Construction on the row houses was initiated in March 1938 and completed in December 1939.

There are a total of 157 row houses, of which 112 have two large rooms and one small room and 45 have two large rooms and two small rooms. There is also a semi-detached house that includes two shops as well as dwellings. All of the residences are on a single floor with a basement under half of the building. On the ground floor is a living room with a bay window and a bedroom facing the garden (terrace) with the small rooms and the kitchen facing east. There is also a bathroom with a washbasin. In the basement there is a storage room, a fuel room and a bathroom-washroom with a bathtub. Heating is provided by a fireplace in the living room. The houses are built of red hand-moulded brick. The storey partitions consist of reinforced concrete with beech parquet on joists. The joists are placed on top of insulation made of dried sand and cork tiles.

The roof is a joist construction, insulated with Rockwool mats and covered with welded Icopal. Total construction costs were DKK 1,600,000 + plot at approximately DKK 300,000. The price per m^2 was DKK 147.66 and per m^3 DKK 119.75.

The project engineering was designed by Engineer Thiess at *Stadsarkitektens Ingeniørafdeling* (City Architect's Engineering Department), and the landscaping by municipal head gardener Bergmann.

Craftsmen and suppliers:

Masonry: Jens P. Arnung. *Carpentry*: N. and K. Fog. *Joinery*: Enoch Petersen. *Fireplaces*: Morsø. *Painting*: A. P. Olsson, *Gardener*: N. Nørgaard. *Glazing*: Edv. Storr.

Row houses at Bernstorffsvej

By Architect Harald G. Petersen

The row houses in Indelukket, which is a side road to Ammentorpsvej and parallel to Bernstorffsvej, were built by *Ejendomsselskabet af 20. Juni 1939*. Construction on the row houses began in late summer 1939 and was completed in 1941. They consist of 24 row houses on two floors. On the ground floor is an entrance hall, kitchen and living room with a dining area with a serving hatch to the kitchen. On the first floor there is a bedroom, a two large rooms and a spacious bathroom. Towards the garden, tiles have been laid across the entire width of the plot. There is no fence facing the road. The area between the pavement and the main staircase is paved with tiles, and grass beds have been laid between the access areas, so that the grass and tiles alternate and provide sufficient separation between the houses. The houses are built of red machine-made brick. The roof is covered with grey roofing felt. Equipment includes central heating, steel sink, tiles in the kitchen and bathroom, beechwood floor in the living room and electric kitchen. The latter was not entirely successful, however, as the majority of buyers wanted a gas kitchen, and it was therefore necessary to install both.

The built-up area is approx. 47 m^2 over two full storeys with a basement under the entire building, plus an extended window with flower box in the 2 m^2 living room.

Craftsmen and Suppliers:

Masonry: Aksel Juul. *Carpentry:* Chr. Engelbrecht Petersen and V. M. Brockhuus' Maskinsnedkeri. *Plumbing:* Th. Theisen. *Heating installations:* O. Skov Olesen. *Electrical installations:* K. Lindberg. *Painting:* Chr. Fuglsang. *Glazing:* H. A. Craner. *Ironwork:* Aksel Bredahl.

Emdrupvænge

By Kooperative Arkitekter

Emdrupvænge consists of 213 row houses located on sloping terrain south of Emdrupvej and was built by *Arbejdernes Andels-Boligforening* in 1938-40 as part of a larger overall development. The terrain and buildings are part of the future park belt from Lyngbyvej to Tagensvej, where there will also be permanent allotment gardens. Like Kantorparken, this development was built in accordance with the 1938 Act on Subsidies for Housing Construction and Housing Tax Reduction for Large Families, but the row houses are only partly used for large families.

The rent is normally DKK 91 per month. For families with 5 children it is DKK 45.50 per month. The row houses have façades facing south and north, i.e. with the garden located south of the house, which we believe is the correct orientation.

The location on the sloping terrain has given the house type its special shape with an entrance on the north side at a height midway between the living room and first floor. The living room faces south with

direct access to the garden on the same level. As can be seen from the sectional view, the rear (northernmost) part of the ground floor is thus a basement, while there is no excavated space under the living room.
The living room is quite large (the entire width of the house) and has poured flooring. A layer of Icopal with an aluminium surface is laid on top of the concrete and on top of that, battens and beech floorboards.
The storage room, which is quite spacious, also has a door that directly faces the road, and thus can be used to store a bicycle. In this way, there is no need for bicycle racks or sheds, an arrangement that the residents are happy with.
The gardens are separated from each other by 1.8-metre-high Eternit screens in front of the tiled seating areas and by a privet hedge in the remaining part. The layout of the individual gardens is partly left to the residents themselves, but various standard floor plans have been provided, which the residents must follow to a certain extent for the sake of the overall layout.
There is a common central heating system and common laundry rooms with laundry machines. A special playground has been set up outside the building containing the laundry room, where mothers doing laundry can keep an eye on their children. All main pipes run along the sides and into the houses.
In the bathroom on the first floor there is a special gas cock with a gas cooker for washing small items of clothing and heating food at night for small children. The houses are built of yellow bricks with wood floors and roofs of tongue-and-groove boards and Icopal, insulated with sea grass mats and a single-side roof slope. Construction costs are an average of DKK 10,760 per house. According to the final calculations, this amounts to DKK 121.06 per m^2 floor space or DKK 36.64 per m^3 and includes gardening and local roads. The project engineering was designed by civil engineer *Olaf Ellern*, and the landscaping by landscape architect *C. Th. Sørensen*.

Craftsmen and suppliers:

Masonry: Brunsøe & Vald. Nielsen. *Carpentry:* Kastrup Nielsen. *Joinery:* A/S "Silvan" and Bygningssnedkerne. *Roofing:* Villadsen og Frisenborg. *Glazing:* Craner. *Ironwork:* Roar Rossings Eftf. *Plumbing:* Th. Larsen & Co. *Electrical installations:* Ing. *Repsdorph. Painting:* A.A.B.s Malerafdeling. *Landscaping:* Wilh. Svenningsen. *Roads and sewerage: Jespersen* & Son. *Gas and water:* Th. Larsen & Co. *Central heating:* Storm Hansen & Co.

Row houses in Lyngby

By architects Knud Friderichsen and Arne Poulsen, among others

The row house development Æblevænget in Lyngby near Sorgenfri Station was built in 1937 by Master Bricklayer T. Marcussen, Lyngby, and Master Carpenter J. Schneidelbach, Hellerup.
Each house, with a floor area of 66 m^2 and a volume of 378 m^3 excluding the roof and basement, has a total lot size of 265 m^2.
The houses are built of yellow machine-made bricks, the roof is covered with roofing felt and there is a timber floor joist system.
The total craftsman costs per house total DKK 19,300.
The price per m^2 is therefore DKK 290 and DKK 51 per m^3.
Consulting Engineers: *Eigil Poulsen* and *R. Tylskjter*, Lyngby, for the heating system.

Craftsmen and suppliers:

Masonry: T. Marcussen, Lyngby. *Carpentry: J.* Schneidelbach, Hellerup.

Row houses in Vanløse

By A/S Dominias Tegnestue

The starting date for the construction of the *row houses at Hanstholmvej in Vanløse* is before the end of 1941. The houses will be built by the self-governing institution *Jyllandshuse*, a subsidiary of *Københavns Almindelige Boligselskab II A/S.* The two-storey row houses have a built-up area of 40.7 m^2, and a volume of 340 m^3. The houses are built of grouted brickwork. The floors above the basement and living room are slabs made of clinker concrete blocks (Sperle type). The roof is a lattice construction covered with corrugated Eternit. The houses are heated with tiled stoves. Beech parquet flooring is laid on the ground and first floors. The price per house is approximately DKK 13,983, yielding a price per m^2 of DKK 343.56 and DKK 42.30 per m^3.

Hasselvaenget

By Architects K. K. Søndergaard and Gunnar Milthers

Hasselvænget is named after its location on Hasselvej in Vanløse, between Damhussøen and Ålekistevej. The row houses frame an old park, the main part of which is now preserved as a common area. The building was constructed in 1939-40 by a limited liability company, represented by LRS. E. Høgsbro-Holm.
The development consists of 38 single-family homes, each with its own garden. The two types of houses are both approx. 55 m^2 in two full storeys, with a split living room, which has access to a terrace, and three bedrooms and a bathroom upstairs. In one of the types, the staircase ascends freely from the living room to the first floor, where the stairwell is extended with a small balcony, while a convenient connection to the heated room in the basement was created. Each house has its own heating system.
The houses are built of red and yellow hand-moulded brick with square recessed joints. Staircases and chimneys are enclosed in hard-burnt brick, the window ledges with cut roof tile pantiles. The roof is covered with red pantiles. The joists are of wood with beech parquet on the ground floor.
The project engineering was designed by civil engineer *P. Hirth.*
The site's previous proprietor, nursery owner Hastrup, who created the garden with its peculiar tree stock more than fifty years ago, has now helped us as a specialised expert to transform it for its new purpose.

Craftsmen and suppliers:

Masonry: N. Mikkelsen Sørensen. *Carpentry:* P. Jul. Hansen, Jesper Hansen and Jørgen Søndergaard. *Joinery:* A/S Silvan. *Plumbing, gas, water and sanitation:* Johan Haastrup og Søn. *Painting:* F. Friedmann. *Electrical installations:* A/S Alliance. *Central heating installation:* J. Bangs Ingeniørforretning

Præstehaven, Hasle, Aarhus

By Kooperative Arkitekter in conjunction with Architect N. Chr. Skjøtli

The row houses form part of the Præstehaven development, which was built by a subsidiary of *Socialt Boligbyggeri.* The development consists of 49 houses and is located by the road to Viborg, a few kilometres outside Aarhus, on a southern slope with a magnificent view of the city and the bay. The plot slope is so steep that there is a view from the upper houses over the lower rows.
In this case, the rows face east and west, but the west façade is fitted with bay windows, so that from the bay window in the living room one can look south.
The project has had to take into account a high-voltage system that cuts across the site.
The houses are built of yellow bricks and the storey partitions and roofs of slabs made of brick blocks (Bauma type). The roof is insulated on the upper side with 2.5 cm of cork and covered with roofing felt.
The cross partitions are load-bearing, and the entire west façade can therefore be divided into windows, door and bay windows facing the garden.
On average each house costs DKK 13,480 or DKK 134.80 per m^2 of floor area, or DKK 32.90 per m^3. The prices were calculated after the closing of accounts and include landscaping and road works. The project engineering was designed by civil engineer *I. O. Christensen*, Aarhus, and the landscaping by landscape architect *C. Th. Sørensen.*

Craftsmen and suppliers:

Masonry: Brdr. Knudsen, Murersvendenes Cooperative, Mougaard, Klostergaard and A. Mortensen. *Carpentry:* N. C. Christiansen, Børge Kirk Mikkelsen and H. L. Nielsen. *Joinery:* N. Bentsen and Grosen. *Roofing:* Ottesen. *Glazing:* Aarslev and Dinesen & Co. *Ironwork:* Aarhus Traadvarefabrik. *Plumbing:* Rasmus Hinge. *Electrical installations:* Svenstrup, P. E. Lauesen, A/S Frichs, S. Overgaard, N. Nielsen and Baltersen. *Painting:* Frode Mogensen. *Landscaping:* L. Kolding. *Road and sewerage work:* J. Bodilsen. *Gas and water, central heating:* Bernhard Olesen.

Row houses in Husum

By Architect Magnus Stephensen

The row houses shown here are to be built for the municipality of Copenhagen in Husum on a plot between Tersløsevej, Gislingevej, Grevingevej, and Stenmaglevej. The construction was put out to tender in mid-March and commenced immediately thereafter.
A total of 120 houses will be built, which are primarily intended for families with children. The built-up area per house is 40 m^2 and the volume is 316 m^3 including the basement. The houses are built with a cavity wall with red façade brick and parapets of autoclaved aerated concrete. Floors are made of wood and the roof is a wooden grid construction, covered with 1" boards and roofing felt.
The project engineering was designed by the City Architect's Engineering Department.

Brønsparken

By architects Kay Fisker, C. F. Møller and Erik Jensen

The row house development Brønsparken is being built by *Foreningen Socialt Boligbyggeri* with construction starting in January 1940. The development is located on Brønshøjvej on an old nursery lot surrounded on all four sides by tall thorn hedges, which are preserved. The two residential roads, Dønnerupvej and Saltovej, were projected to extend across the site, but by negotiating with the town planning department, it was possible to avoid having these roads built, thereby achieving a more suitable development.

As the development is intended for families with children, there in an emphasis in the design on allowing children to walk from the playground to their house without crossing any roads. From Brønshøjvej, two dead-end roads follow the northern and southern boundaries of the lot, where there is access to the individual houses and large playground, which is located along the centre between the blocks.

The individual houses are built without a basement, but with a common bicycle room, rubbish bin store and laundry facilities in the basement at the ends of the blocks.

Each house contains a living room on the ground floor, a large eat-in kitchen and an entry hall with a storm porch. On the first floor is a bedroom, two small rooms and a shower room. Facing the living room is an "open-air living room", a tiled terrace surrounded by a 1.4-metre-high wall.

The houses are built with a large building depth of 11.20 metres. This gives a minimal façade length (4.15 m) as the built-up area must be limited to 45-46 m^2. To prevent the seating areas from being too cramped, the houses are turned in relation to each other with the living room alternately facing east and west.

The timber floor joist system and roofing (longitudinal purlins) rest on the 16 cm cross partitions.

The houses are built with red machine-made bricks and the roof is covered with corrugated Eternit.

A common underground boiler house heats all of the blocks. The built-up area is 9,163 m^2 (excluding the boiler house), the volume of the blocks is 67,226 m^3 (including the heating centre). The lot size is 37,443 m^2.

The total price amounts to DKK 2,246,546. The price per m^2 of built-up area is DKK 245 and per m^3 is DKK 33.40. The project engineering was designed by civil engineer *Jørgen Glud*, and the landscaping by landscape architect *C. Th. Sørensen.*

Craftsmen and suppliers:

Masonry: Chr. Rassow. *Road and sewerage work:* Karl Nielsson. *Terrazzo:* A. Carnera. *Carpentry incl. Eternit roof:* Chr. Christensen. *Iron delivery:* Oluf Rønberg A/S. *Joinery:* Lützhøft Christiansen, Novus Maskinfabrik and Johs. Madsen & Son. *Glazing:* H. Storr. *Electrical installations:* Dansk Elektrisk Kompagni. *Plumbing:* Ib Roloff. *Ironwork:* H. P. Sørensen. *Painting:* Anton Hansen. *Central heating, sanitation etc.:* Christensen and Modler. *Radiators:* E. Mohr. *Boilers:* C. F. Reck's Opvarmnings Compagni A/S. *Electrolytic system:* I. Krüger. *Gardening work:* Vilh. Svenningsen.

Row houses at Ørholm

By Architect Frans Jastrau

The row houses at *Egegaardsvej in Ørholm* were built in 1937-39 by wholesaler Albert Svendsen of Copenhagen. The project comprised 100 houses, 75 of which have now been built. The small plan type contains two or three large rooms with two small rooms, a kitchen and a bathroom. The large plan type is identical, but with larger rooms.

The floor plans are designed in such a way that there are several possible variations in the position of the rooms. Some of the houses have only half a basement. The houses are built of yellow brick. The floors are made of wood with beech parquet in the living rooms. The roof is covered with roofing felt. Each house has its own independent central heating system, and some houses also have a fireplace in the living room. There is an electric cooker in the kitchen.

The price of the small plan type is approx. DKK 12,000 and the large plan type is approx. DKK 13,500. The unit prices will be DKK 150 per m^2 and DKK 35 per m^3 .

The procurement and delivery of materials is carried out by the client.

The Masonry was carried out by master masons Simonsen og Johansen of Lyngby.

Kantorparken Row Houses

By Kooperative Arkitekter, Architect Edvard Heiberg

Kantorparkens Rækkehuse, the 109 row houses built by *Foreningen Socialt Boligbyggeri* at Bispebjerg Parkallé in the years 1939-40, form part of the *Kantorparken* development.

As the development was carried out with public support in accordance with the Danish Act of 13 April 1938 on Loans for Housing Construction, it was decided to design some of the houses as row houses intended for families with children mentioned in the act. However, some of the families with three children were placed in flats with one large room and several small rooms, while those with four, and in most cases five, children or more were accommodated in the row houses. The row houses are therefore quite spacious. There are a total of two large rooms and two or three small rooms on two floors.

The rent is set as low as DKK 79 per month, but for families with five children, fifty per cent can be deducted according to the aforementioned law, so in reality most tenants pay no more than DKK 39.50 for a house with a garden. Admittedly, there is a deposit of DKK 500, but in certain cases this can be paid by the City of Copenhagen, which is paid back the money in small monthly instalments.

The row houses have façades facing south and north with access from the parallel roads either from the garden or street side. In order for the residents to maximise the space in front of the house, this is probably the right placement for row houses.

In some of the houses, the stairs ascend directly from the living room (like an open hall). It turns out that the residents are happy with this arrangement.

The basements are completely underground and contain an independent laundry room in each house. I think it is better to combine the laundries in common laundry rooms with machines. The central heating, on the other hand, is from a common boiler house, and all electrical wiring and main pipes, including drains, are located inside the houses along the row. This is one of the advantages of the combined row house buildings for rent. If we are to consider row houses as workers' dwellings, then the rental dwelling must be the only correct form. Only a few workers can afford to buy their own house, and especially those workers who have many children (in Kantorparken there are families with up to 15 children), do not have much money left over for housing charges and even less wealth to invest in their own house.

The houses are built of yellow bricks. All floors and storey partitions are made of hollow brick with beech wood flooring. The roof (the upper hollow block covering) is insulated on the upper side with a 5-cm-thickCorkoligno coupled panel and covered with a layer of paperboard. The cross partitions, which are 24 cm thick for sound insulation, support the floors, and the façade can therefore be lined with a 31 cm cavity wall with large windows and relatively small pillars. The load-bearing cross partitions appear in the façade as clinker pillars.

When you build two-storey row houses (which are 33 per cent cheaper than single-storey houses), there is a problem with the view from one house into the other's garden. In Kantorparken, we have therefore made the parapets on the first floor very high, so that you have to walk right up to the window to look out. This also has the advantage that there can be two beds in the small rooms, one right up against the wall with the window. In addition, a loggia of timber battens on angle iron has been built over the tiled forecourt south of the house, and a vine has been planted by each house, which in a few years will grow and form a roof over the forecourt. In winter, when the leaves have fallen off, there will be plenty of light in the rooms, and in summer the vine will provide shade.

The gardens are relatively small, but previous experience shows that the residents have a hard enough time maintaining them. On the other hand, a large common area has been laid out between the blocks, and is planted with pine trees, which in the course of ten years will create woods where the children can play. Consideration for the children (there are approx. 1,500 of them in Kantorparken) has thus taken precedence over the parents' passionate desire to be farmers.

The houses cost between DKK 8,900-10,500 to build. That is DKK 123 per m^2 of floor space or DKK 31 per metre (basement included). The prices include fencing, garden and road works. The project engineering was designed by civil engineer *Jørgen Glud*, and the landscaping by landscape architect *C. Th. Sørensen*.

Craftsmen and suppliers:

Masonry: Brdr. E. & V. Nielsen, V. Christoffersen, A. Jensen and Chr. Olsen. *Carpentry:* I. Chr. Thomsen, Chr. E. Christensen, Peter Johansen, Johs. Hansen and Jørn Krog. *Joinery:* A/S "Silvan", Lytzhøft Christiansen, Bygningssnedkernes A/S and Henrik Andersen. *Plumbing:* William Jensen & Son. *Electrical installations:* A/S Alliance and Carl Bjørnow. *Glazing:* Craner, Larsen & Henriksen and G. Jensen. *Ironwork:* K. & V. Hansen and Kaj Andersen. *Painting:* Anton Hansen. *Heating, gas, water, sanitation:* "Odin" and Christensen & Modler.

Row houses at Svejagervej

By Architects Professor Palle Suenson and Ib Martin Jensen

Svejgården's row houses are located on Svejagervej in Hellerup. The houses were built in 1935 by master mason Martin Jensen.

The main access to the houses is via a ten-metre-wide road that runs parallel to the façade. There is also a four-metre wide path behind the houses. There are two house types, 49 and 63 m^2, respectively. The houses are built of red, hand-moulded brick. The storey partitions consist of iron beams, insulated with moler in paper. The roof is made of crushed pumice concrete on iron beams with Icopal. Steel windows produced by Pedershåb A/S have been used. The price of the two types of houses including the plot is DKK 21,400 and DKK 27,000, respectively. The unit prices are thus DKK 365 and 375 per m^2 and 48 and 49 per m^3.

Row houses in Helsingør

By Aktieselskabet Dominia's Tegnestue

The row houses on Eiersvej in Helsingør were built by *Boligselskabet Christianshøj*. The houses are single-stories and have a built-up area of 65.66 m^2.

The row houses are built of grouted brickwork. The storey division above the basement is made of wood. The roof is a lattice construction covered with roof tiles. The houses are heated by a tiled stove.

The price per houses was DKK 9,573, yielding a price per m^2 of DKK 145.80 and a price per m^3 of DKK 29.30.

Row houses in Virum

By architects Helmer Remark and Svend Aage Petersen

Geelsdalens Haveby is located on the corner of Kongevejen and Nærumvejen. The plot was subdivided from the old Geelsgård; the corner plot itself was sold to a petrol company before the row house construction was started, but no petrol station was built. The roads between the blocks were determined by the municipality, as they would be connected to a later parcelling out of the surrounding areas. To avoid access to the houses through the gardens and to maintain a uniform house type, a four-metre wide path had to be built behind two of the blocks, so that each house has access to a road and a path. This also avoids the inconvenience of similar buildings where garden waste and the like must be transported through the houses.

The houses are built of red hand-moulded brick and grouted with a mortar made from a special type of sand found in Trørød. The roof is covered with white Icopal and all exterior woodwork is white.

Above the entrance door is a canopy made of 6-7 mm glass plate, from a special Belgian type of glass. The only support for this glass plate is where a joint in the brickwork above the door has been scratched out with the plate inserted 10 cm into it. The plate is almost invisible, and the price is not very high, approx. 40 DKK.

The houses are equipped with steel sinks in the kitchen and bathrooms, Expanko flooring in the two largest living rooms, and a separate central heating system for each house. The central heating system, which is ample in size, together with the associated hot water system, cost a total of DKK 800.

The houses were built in 1936-37, and the sale price was DKK 17,500. Construction costs were approximately DKK 140 per m^2 or DKK 35.50 per m^3.

The builders were wholesaler Steenfeldt-Hansen and Engineer L. Rathsach.

The contractor was master carpenter Lauritz M. Jensen, Bagsværd.

Row houses at Ordruphøj

By Architect Karl Almer Nielsen

The row house development Kollegievej 3-15 is located on land in Ordruphøj opposite Sct. Andreas Kollegiet in Charlottenlund. The properties were built in 1938, and each house has a built-up area of 88 m^2 and a lot size of 1,050 m^2 . By stepping down the fire parapets, the isolation rooms, entrance and hall have been better connected to each other and have been given a better shape. The kitchen and bathroom are placed in the centre of the house for reasons of acoustics. For the same reason, the curved staircase is not nailed to the firewall. No continuous beams are used in the properties, and all beam heads are laid on Icopal. The fire gables between the properties are constructed of hand-made rubble stone as a 28 cm hollow wall. The cavity is filled with sand. These measures have enabled the residents to live a relatively undisturbed life in their house.

Consulting Engineer: Civil Engineer *Svend Bruno Carlsen*. Garden architect: *Anka Rasmussen*.

Craftsmen and suppliers:
Masonry: Th. Hansen. *Carpentry:* C. Møller Thomsen. *Joinery:* C. P. J. Madsen. *Plumbing:* W. Jorgensen. *Painting:* Th. Lund. *Ironwork:* K. Olsen. *Glazing:* A. Guhle. *Heating installations:* E. Bendsen. *Steel washing and stainless steel installation. Electrical installations:* Viggo Dencker. *Steel windows:* Pedershåb, Maskinfabrik A/S. *Sanitary installations:* Hans Knudsen. *Parquet flooring:* A/S Juncker's Savværk.